UKRAINE UNDER KUCHMA

STUDIES IN RUSSIAN AND EAST EUROPEAN HISTORY AND
SOCIETY

*General Editors: R. W. Davies, Emeritus Professor of Soviet Economic
Studies, and E. A. Rees, Senior Lecturer in Soviet History, both at the Centre
for Russian and East European Studies, University of Birmingham*

Ukraine under Kuchma

Political Reform, Economic Transformation and Security Policy in Independent Ukraine

Taras Kuzio
Research Fellow
Centre for Russian and East European Studies
University of Birmingham

St. Martin's Press
New York

St. Martin's Press, Scholarly and Reference Division, 175 Fifth Avenue, New York, N.Y. 10010

First published in the United States of America in 1997

This book is printed on paper suitable for recycling and made from fully managed and sustained forest sources.

Printed in Great Britain

ISBN 0–312–17625–2

Library of Congress Cataloging-in-Publication Data
Kuzio, Taras.
Ukraine under Kuchma : political reform, economic transformation and security in independent Ukraine / Taras Kuzio.
p.   cm. — (Studies in Russian and East European history and society)
Includes bibliographical references and index.
ISBN 0–312–17625–2 (cloth)
1. Ukraine—Politics and government—1991–   2. Elections—Ukraine–
–History. 3. Ukraine—Economic policy—1991–   4. National security–
–Ukraine. I. Title. II. Series: Studies in Russian and East
European history and society series.
JN6630.K89 1997
324.9477'086—dc21   97–15184
                                                          CIP

Contents

List of Tables

List of Maps

KUZIO: *UKRAINE UNDER KUCHMA*

ERRATUM

Maps 2, 3, 4 and 5 are in fact the copyright of Dr Valerii Khmelko
and Dr Andrew Wilson, and accordingly should have been
acknowledged to them. The author and the publishers regret this
mistake.

Acknowledgements

The author is grateful to the Michael and Daria Kowalsky Endowment Fund, administered by the Canadian Institute of Ukrainian Studies of Edmonton, Alberta, for an award in 1993 which allowed him to undertake the initial research for this book.

The author is also grateful to the editors of *The Journal of Communist Studies and Transition Politics*,[1] *Jane's Intelligence Review*[2] and *Central Asian Survey*[3] for permission to publish materials which appeared in earlier and shorter versions in their publications.

I would like gratefully to acknowledge the Leverhulme Trust for supporting the research project on the 'Transition from Soviet to Independent Ukraine' from April 1995, at the Centre for Russian and East European Studies, The University of Birmingham, under its director, Professor Julian Cooper.

1. T. Kuzio, 'The 1994 Parliamentary Elections in Ukraine', *The Journal of Communist Studies and Transition Politics*, vol. 11, no. 4 (December 1995), pp. 335–61.
2. T. Kuzio, 'Ukraine and the Expansion of NATO', *Jane's Intelligence Review*, vol. 7, no. 9 (September 1995), 389–91.
3. T. Kuzio, 'The Chechen Crisis and the "Near Abroad"', *Central Asian Survey*, vol. 14, no. 4 (1995), pp. 553–72 published by Carfax Publishing Company, PO Box 25, Abingdon, Oxfordshire OX14 3UE.

Transliteration Note

L'viv (Lvov)
Uzhorod (Uzgorod)
Rivne (Rovno)
Kyiv (Kiev)
Luts'k
Zhitomir
Chernihiv (Chernigov)
Cherkasy (Cherkassy)
Ivano-Frankivsk (Ivano-Frankovsk)
Khmel'nyts'ky
Vinnytsya
Odesa (Odessa)
Mykolayiv (Nikolaiv)
Kherson
Poltava
Kirovohrad (Kirovograd)
Krivyi Rih (Krivyi Rog)
Zaporizhzhya (Zaporozhzhia)
Dnipropetrovs'k (Dnepropetrovsk)
Donets'k (Donetsk)
Kharkiv (Kharkov)
Chernivtsi (Chernovtsy)
Sumy
Luhans'k (Lugansk)
Simferopol
Sevastopol

1. Ukraine

Source: 'Russia and the Newly Independent Nations of the Former Soviet Union' map supplement to *National Geographic Magazine*, March 1993, and 'Note for Contributors', *Journal of Ukrainian Studies*, which uses the modified Library of Congress transliteration system.

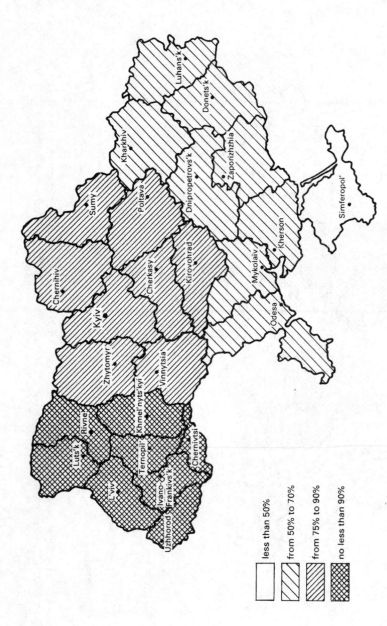

2. The variation of vote for independence of Ukraine (December 1991)

less than 50%

from 50% to 70%

from 75% to 90%

no less than 90%

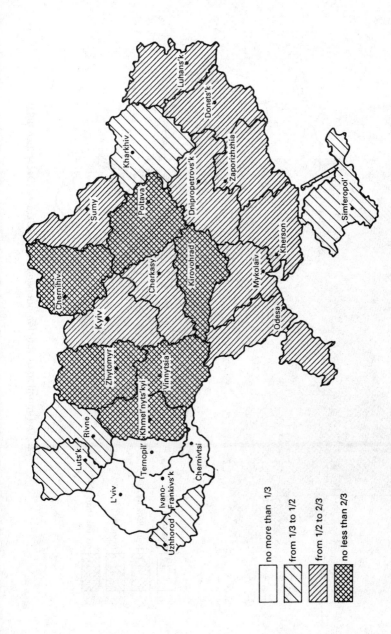

Luhans'k
Donets'k
Zaporizhzhia
Simferopol'
Kharkhiv
Dnipropetrovs'k
Sumy
Poltava
Kherson
Chernihiv
Cherkasy
Kirovohrad
Mykolaïv
Kyïv
Odesa
Zhytomyr
Vinnytsia
Khmel'nyts'kyi
Rivne
Luts'k
Ternopil'
Chernivtsi
L'viv
Ivano-Frankivs'k
Uzhhorod

no more than 1/3

from 1/3 to 1/2

from 1/2 to 2/3

no less than 2/3

3. The variation of Kravchuk's vote across the different regions (December 1991)

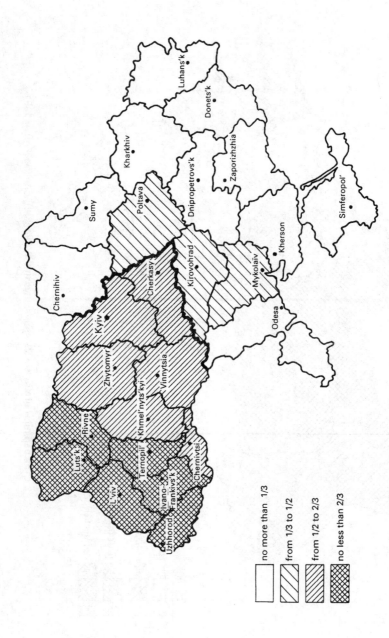

4. The variation of Kravchuk's vote across the different regions (July 1994)

no more than 1/3

from 1/3 to 1/2

from 1/2 to 2/3

no less than 2/3

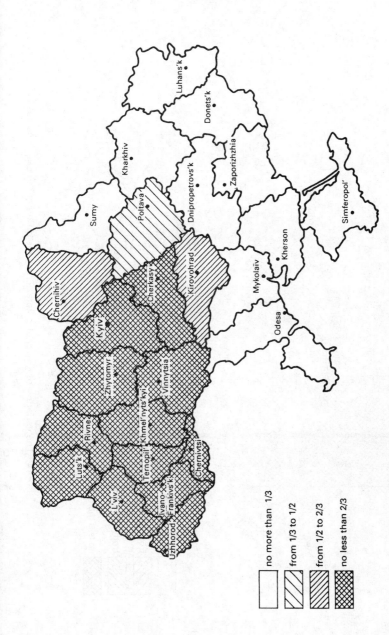

5. The share of the Ukrainian-speaking population of Ukraine

no more than 1/3

from 1/3 to 1/2

from 1/2 to 2/3

no less than 2/3

Contents

The situation is critical and if it is not changed, the country will face collapse, as is forecast by the American CIA. The situation in Ukraine is now more critical than it ever was in the entire history of our independence. With the unfavourable balance of trade standing at $5 billion, we have been drifting, doing nothing for the reform process.

(President Leonid Kuchma, 1994)

We have before us an historic decision. The question at hand is not about power. It is much broader and deeper – which path should Ukraine take.

(President Leonid Kuchma, 1995)

Introduction

Ukraine obtained its independence in December 1991 as a result of two main factors. First, the former Soviet centre imploded as the USSR, embodied by its president, Mikhail Gorbachev, fought for power with the Russian Federation, headed by its democratically elected president, Boris Yeltsin. This implosion of the centre after the failure of the communist hardliners' *coup d'état* in August 1991 gave the non-Russian republics, including the Ukraine, an opportunity to secede peacefully from the Soviet empire.[1]

The implosion of the Soviet centre ensured that the disintegration of the Soviet Union would be different from the situation in Yugoslavia, where Serbia had maintained the fiction of Yugoslavia's continued existence, even though it was obvious that Serbia was dominating the union. After the failure of the August *coup* Russia too called the shots and Yeltsin no longer supported the aspirations to sovereignty of the republics or autonomous republics, which he had done before August 1991. Between 1989 and August 1991, Yeltsin had relied on the non-Russian republics and autonomous republics as allies against the Soviet centre. With the defeat of the centre Russia could assert its right to be the real – and not the fictional, as in the Soviet era – leader of the pack. He then began to support the preservation of the USSR, albeit in a more confederal form as the Union of Sovereign Republics (SSR). Unlike the 14 non-Russian republics, therefore, Russia did not declare its independence from the USSR.[2]

Hence, it is no coincidence that Russia signed an SSR (Community Union of Sovereign Republics) Treaty in April 1996 with Belarus. With the exception of a brief flirtation with the liberal internationalism of Gorbachev's and Yegor Gaidar's 'common European home' during 1992, Russia had always opposed the disintegration of the USSR into 15 independent states going their separate ways. The former Ukrainian president, Leonid Kravchuk, reminiscing about the Belaya Pushcha meeting of 7–8 December 1991 which sealed the fate of the USSR, stated:

> Obviously, Yeltsin expected that the commonwealth [of independent states, CIS] would, in time, evolve into another union … he viewed the CIS as a temporary phenomenon. He didn't want the old union restored – here I give him credit. He didn't accept what Gorbachev had proposed. But he believed the CIS would become a new union, with a new president: Yeltsin. And the author of this whole process would be

1

Russia. The main goal was to end the Gorbachev era and begin a new one...[3]

It is little wonder then that Russian views on the geopolitical space of the former USSR differed markedly from the Ukraine's. Ukraine achieved independence as a consequence of a large nationalist lobby (although not quite as large as in the Trans-Caucasus or the Baltic states) in alliance with a large national-communist constituency, which historically had always been strong. The national-communists correctly understood that by jumping on the independence bandwagon they would distance themselves from the anti-communist Yeltsin who had ambitions to replace Gorbachev as Ukraine's elder brother. Yeltsin also had the audacity to introduce reforms to boot. The national-communists also rightly predicted that they would become the ruling elite in the political and economic spheres in an independent Ukraine.

Ukraine was helped by three factors. First, the Soviet and Russian leadership never believed that Ukrainians would vote for independence, especially in eastern Ukraine and the Crimea. Secondly, by late 1991, Ukraine had established its ethnic stability, and (unlike elsewhere in the former USSR) domestic relations between Russians and Ukrainians were not strained. By early 1991 the independent trade unions of eastern Ukraine had joined forces with the nationalists and democrats in an unstoppable anti-communist and pro-independence wave. Thirdly, the lack of ethnic conflict and the similarities between the Russian and Ukrainian languages and cultures enabled the Ukrainian leadership to nationalise the Soviet security forces quickly, thereby neutralising any potential domestic threat to independence. After the failure of the August coup the Soviet security forces outside Ukraine were in no condition to put down Ukrainian independence and, in any case, had deserted the sinking Soviet tanker in favour of the Russian ship.[4]

Ukrainian independence also proved to be peaceful and successful thanks to the election of Kravchuk as president. It was largely owing to him that a referendum on independence, held in the teeth of opposition from the democrats who were fearful of the outcome, was held on 1 December 1991. This gave a 90 per cent endorsement to the proposal – something it would be difficult to question both at the time and later.[5] Few other former Soviet republics held referendums on independence, including Belarus – something that has proved to be a major handicap in not giving its independence popular legitimacy.

In contrast to Russia, independent Ukraine under Kravchuk had to undertake not two (economic and political) but four difficult transitions from a command-administrative system to a market economy, from a totalitarian system to a democracy, from an incomplete and deformed national identity to a nation, and from a subject of empire to statehood. For *any* Ukrainian leader elected in December 1991 this task would have been daunting. Although with hindsight we can now speculate as to what would have happened if a nationalist or democrat had won the presidential election in December 1991, the fact is their record in other post-Soviet republics during the early 1990s was largely a failure. As 'outsiders' to the political system and former communist nepotistic clans, nationalists or democrats would probably have failed to promote reform, whilst at the same time provoking ethnic conflict and poor relations with Russia, which has exploited the former to advance its strategic interests in the 'Near Abroad'. Nationalist or democratic presidents were replaced by members of the Party of Power throughout the former USSR by 1993–4, either through the ballot box or by *coups d'état*.

Russia entered the post-Soviet era with an anti-communist president, who was committed to reform and who had defeated the *ancien régime* at home. In contrast, in Ukraine the *ancien régime* had remained in power after replacing their red and blue for blue and yellow colourings. This was confirmed by the election of Kravchuk as president.

Economic and political transition in Ukraine, therefore, had no choice but to be evolutionary. First, Kravchuk was indebted to the *ancien régime*, or Party of Power as the de-ideologised former national communists became known, and could not ride rough-shod over their interests. They preferred *rentier* capitalism and economic instability where their previous political power could be converted into economic and financial power. Secondly, any Ukrainian president would have inherited the Soviet era parliament, which had deep-seated vested interests and which supported evolutionary transition where it was to their personal benefit. Nationalists and democrats actually opposed Kravchuk's call in early 1992 for fresh elections to a new parliament, which would have brought in a large pro-reform lobby (the Communist Party was illegal between August 1991 and September 1993). Thirdly, Ukraine had to devote its energies to nation- and state-building which at times distracted, whilst at other times it simply contradicted, the economic and political transition. Fourthly, no post-Soviet state inherited the resources that could allow the use of shock-therapy measures. (Shock-therapy was not tried even in Russia.)

Evolutionary transition and transformation, therefore, were the order of the day for all the post-Soviet states. The countries which are generally regarded as most successful in transition are those such as Poland. But they have few national minorities (accounting for less than 2 per cent of the population), evolved from an authoritarian political culture (even under martial law in the 1980s), possessed a civil society of sorts (Church, media, political parties and civic groups), a well-developed national identity (united, pro-European with historical traditions), a private sector (agriculture and the service sector) with a population that had regularly travelled abroad and legally held hard currency. Ukraine inherited none of these factors.[6]

The Kravchuk era should not therefore be regarded as a failure in comparison to the Kuchma era that followed. Without Kravchuk there would have been no Kuchma. Without the nation- and state-building policies pursued during 1991–4 the policies adopted by Kuchma and elaborated in this study would not have been possible. Similarly, without even the modest, but certain, political and economic transition during the Kravchuk era the tremendous strides forward after mid-1994 would not have been possible. In many ways, therefore, Kuchma should be seen as continuing Kravchuk's policies; he learnt from his failures and built on his successes. They have more in common than that which separates them (see chapter 2).

This book surveys the transition from the era of Kravchuk (president of Ukraine from 1 December 1991 to 10 July 1994) to that of Kuchma. Chapters 1 and 2 deal with the parliamentary and presidential elections held throughout 1994 (and, in some cases, into 1995–6) which presaged one of the first – and certainly one of the most peaceful – transitions from the Soviet era to that of Ukraine's first elected post-Soviet parliament and president. Seen in the context of rising political violence and authoritarianism within the former USSR, this of itself was no mean feat.

Chapter 3 discusses the autonomous republic of the Crimea during the Kuchma era. Little attention is devoted to developments within the Crimea prior to the election of Kuchma as these are covered by this author and many others elsewhere (see the Bibliography of Selected Publications). The Crimea, it must be recalled, nearly went the way of many other 'hot spots' within the former USSR (Nagorno Karabakh, Abkhazia, the Trans-Dnister Republic, Tajikistan and Chechnya) on at least two occasions: May 1992 (when the Crimean parliament declared independence from Ukraine) and May 1994 (when the Crimean parliament reintroduced the May 1992 constitution). The May 1996 draft Crimean constitution, agreed with Kyiv, ended any further speculation about the peninsula's status as an integral part of Ukraine. Whoever was elected Russian president the following month could no longer play the Crimean card.

Political reform, the subject of chapter 4, was always a key concern of the new Kuchma administration; to President Kuchma political and economic reform were always the obverse of the same coin and neither could be accomplished without the other. This chapter deals with the development of the constitutional process in Ukraine and the dismantling of the Soviet system of government. A major break with the policies of the Kravchuk era were announced by President Kuchma in October 1994 in the field of economic reform; these are covered in chapter 5. Kuchma has successfully placed the economy at the centre of political debate and linked the survival of an independent Ukraine to resolving the economic crisis and building a market economy, all areas covered by this chapter.

Chapter 6 surveys the major changes that have occurred in the realm of foreign and defence policies. During the Kuchma era Western governments, international financial institutions, the academic world and even the media began treating Ukraine as a permanent feature and member of the international community of nations. There are now few – if any – conflicts over policy between Ukraine and the West. Relations with Russia (and, to a lesser degree, with Romania) have not made the full breakthrough that President Kuchma optimistically (and probably idealistically) expected when he was elected. Nevertheless, relations between Ukraine and Russia have improved and are no longer bedevilled by ideological and nationalistic tension.

1 A New Ukrainian Parliament[1]

'Of course I'll vote. I don't remember for whom. But whomever I'm supposed to vote for, that's whom I'll vote for.'[2]

(Kyiv pensioner)

Demands for new elections had been a recurrent feature of the Ukrainian political scene since the disintegration of the former USSR and establishment of an independent Ukrainian state in December 1991. Attempts by Rukh to collect signatures in 1992 to hold a referendum on dissolving parliament failed to collect the deliberately large number of 3 million signatures fixed to thwart such a referendum. Instead, widespread strikes by coalminers in June 1993[3] forced parliament to agree to hold referendums on itself and president Leonid Kravchuk in September of the same year. On 24 September 1993, a resolution of the Ukrainian parliament cancelled the referendum on confidence in the parliament and president in favour of early elections on 27 March (parliamentary) and 26 June 1994 (presidential and local).[4]

This chapter surveys the 1994 parliamentary elections which resulted in a peaceful transition of power from the Soviet era parliament and local councils which had been elected in March 1990. Chapter 3 deals with the elections in the Crimea to the Crimean and Ukrainian parliaments,[5] as well as the January 1994 Crimean presidential and local elections.[6] For convenience of analysis, this chapter is divided into three sections: Ukraine on the eve of Elections, The Election Campaign and The Aftermath. I shall show that most observers and analysts remained highly pessimistic about the outcome of the Ukrainian elections, a pessimism promoted by the election law, which was nevertheless adopted. But the new Ukrainian parliament has a pro-reform majority which has shown its willingness to co-operate with the president.

ON THE EVE OF THE ELECTIONS[7]

Independent Ukraine under Kravchuk

The 1990–4 parliament had long been discredited in the eyes of the Ukrainian public. A poll on confidence in the authorities on the eve of the

6

Table 1.1   Pre-election Poll of Public Confidence

Armed forces	20%
Militia	6%
President	4%
Viacheslav Chornovil (leader of Rukh)	4%
Cabinet of Ministers	2%
Local Councils	2%

elections found low levels of support for institutions in Ukraine (Table 1.1).[8]

Parliament decided against holding a referendum on confidence in itself in September 1993 because it knew it would lose. It was partly discredited by its inability to launch a reform programme or deal with the domestic crisis, as well as by much publicised evidence of corruption among deputies. Indeed, the mass circulation newspaper *Kyivskiye vedomosti* published an article during the election campaign entitled 'Vote for the current deputies – they have already managed to obtain apartments in the capital'. One poll summed up voter disillusionment with the Soviet era parliament (see Table 1.2).[9]

Another reason why voters were disillusioned with the 1990–4 parliament and, to a certain extent, with politics altogether, was its lack of accountability. Other polls showed that only 50 per cent of the electorate were fully committed to voting in the next elections; the remainder were either undecided or indifferent.

Opinion polls showed that three issues would dominate the elections: the economic crisis, relations with Russia and crime. The domestic crisis was severe and showed no sign of abating, while the government had no programme to overcome it. Only in Kyiv and western Ukraine did voters regard as election priorities the armed forces, cultural regeneration, maintaining territorial integrity and support for the Church. Support for

Table 1.2   Pre-election Poll of Voter Disillusionment

	Question A*	Question B*
Kyiv (no)	73%	71%
L'viv (no)	63%	69%

Notes:
Question A: Would you vote for the same candidate again as in March 1990?
Question B: Do you remember who you voted for in March 1990?

economic reform was also higher in western Ukraine and in southern Ukraine (where ports, such as Odesa, hoped to obtain free economic zone status). Crime prevention was high on the list of priorities of eastern and southern Ukrainian voters.

Another problem political parties found was their inability to put across their case to the voting public. Many opinion polls during 1992–4 testified to the fact that the bulk of the population were unaware of political party programmes. If anything, they identified with the personalities and leaders they knew. In a summer 1993 opinion poll undertaken by the Democratic Initiative organisation, the fictitious 'Party of Order and Justice' obtained more votes than many well-established parties, presumably due to its populistic-sounding name. This lack of public awareness was, in turn, a reflection of the narrow political space available to parties due to the absence or slow pace of reforms and weak civil society under Kravchuk. Voter participation, therefore, in the 27 March 1994 parliamentary elections was held against the background of a lack of confidence in institutions, lack of public self-confidence in the ability to marshal change, general socio-psychological depression, the amorphous and apathetic outlook of the 'man in the street', and a yearning for law and order.

Nevertheless, various opinion polls did show that political parties were popular in some regions and sections of the population. An RFE/RL Research Institute survey undertaken in mid-1993 found that half the respondents supported parties with a democratic orientation. Communist and socialist groups obtained 10 per cent in the poll, although the one third who remained undecided closely resembled the demographic profile of the communist and socialist electorate and were primarily based in eastern Ukraine. In the Polish and Lithuanian parliamentary elections this undecided electorate had also voted for communist and socialist parties.

The Multi-party System[10]

By the Kuchma era Ukraine had approaching 40 registered political parties. Although their number had grown since political parties had first appeared in Ukraine in 1990, their quality left a lot to be desired. Their membership had not grown significantly and their influence remained limited, a factor itself hindered by the majoritarian election law of November 1993.

Political parties in Ukraine could be divided into roughly four groups: the radical left, centre-left/liberals, national democrats and the radical right. The Communist Party (KPU) was registered in October 1993 as a new political structure with no claim to the title or property of its pre-August 1991 namesake. It has the largest number of members of any political party in Ukraine (120 000), but it is regionally based in the Donbas and other industrial eastern Ukrainian cities. The KPU is only the largest political party by default. It is still small by its pre-August 1991 standards, when it stood at 2.5 million, down from 3.5 million in 1985.

Its erstwhile allies are the Peasant Party of Ukraine (SelPU), representing the rural *nomenklatura* and the Agrarian faction in parliament, and the Socialist Party of Ukraine (SPU). The Agrarians are divided over economic reform and, during summer 1995, split into two, the group that broke away re-registering as the Agrarians for Reform faction. The SPU, with 30 000 members, was originally established to fill the political void created during the ban on the KPU (August 1991–September 1993). But, under its leader, parliamentary speaker Oleksandr Moroz, it has moved in two directions: towards a more 'national communist' and social democratic orientation. Its members are nearly all ethnic Ukrainians and the SPU, in contrast to the KPU, does not back the restoration of the former USSR.

The centre-left and liberals are probably the least developed section of Ukraine's embryonic multi-party system. Their main support base is in eastern and southern Ukraine, but here they face stiff competition from the radical left, the absence of a civil society and a highly atomised and lumpen proletariat.

During the 1994 elections Vladimir Grynev and Kuchma established the Inter-Regional Bloc of Reforms (MRBR) from a coalition of the New Ukraine bloc and the Union of Industrialists and Entrepreneurs of Ukraine. The MRBR fared far worse than they had expected though, and after the elections New Ukraine rejected calls for a merger of both blocs because of differences over the national question. (New Ukraine did not support MRBR's support for dual state languages and federalism.) The Social Democratic Party of Ukraine (SDPU), Green Party of Ukraine (ZPU) and the Labour Congress of Ukraine (TKU) are on the centre-left of New Ukraine, while the liberal wing is occupied by the Liberal Democratic Party of Ukraine (LDPU), Liberal Party of Ukraine (LPU) and the Party of Democratic Revival of Ukraine (PDVU). New Ukraine, together with the PDVU and the TKU, united to form the People's Democratic Party of Ukraine in February 1996.

In parliament there are three factions, Centre, Unity and the Independents, composed of unaffiliated candidates who do not belong to any political party. Many of these members are from the Party of Power, the Centre and Independents factions uniting deputies close to the former Kravchuk regime and Unity bringing together newly elected deputies from eastern Ukraine. The Social-Market Choice parliamentary faction was based on the Liberal Party.

The National Democrats propelled Ukraine into independence with the help of the national communists. Their main base is western and central Ukraine, including the capital city, Kyiv, where civil society is more sophisticated. Most of these regions of Ukraine were never part of the Tsarist Russian empire and were only incorporated within the former USSR in 1945. The more liberal nationalities policies of the Austrian and Polish authorities prior to 1939, compared to those endured by eastern and southern Ukrainians, had allowed the growth of a wide-embracing range of political parties and civic groups, as well as Ukrainian language societies and media. It is little wonder, therefore, that western-central Ukraine, the core Ukrainian ethnic territory, has the highest national consciousness and most developed civil society in Ukraine.

The national democrats included the Ukrainian Popular Movement (Rukh), the second largest political party after the KPU, and the Ukrainian Republican Party (URP), arguably one of the best organised and most prolific political parties in Ukraine in terms of their publishing activities. Other members of the national democratic camp are the Peasant Democratic Party of Ukraine (SelDPU), the Christian Democratic Party of Ukraine (KhDPU), the Democratic Party of Ukraine (DPU) and affiliated civic groups such as the Taras Shevchenko Ukrainian Language Society *Prosvita*, the Union of Ukrainian Officers, the Union of Ukrainian Students and the Ukrainian Cossacks. During the 1994 elections they united into the Democratic Coalition Ukraine electoral bloc. Within the newly elected parliament they are spread among the former Statehood, Rukh and Reform factions.

The radical right in Ukraine have failed to win a significant number of seats and thereby promote their causes within parliament, primarily due to the majoritarian election law used in the 1994 elections. The three main parties are divided amongst themselves and are unlikely to unite. Of these the two most important are the Ukrainian National Assembly (UNA) and the Congress of Ukrainian Nationalists (KUN).

The smaller Ukrainian State Independence (DSU), which won no seats in the 1994 elections, is on the extreme of the radical right and has a blatantly anti-Semitic and racist programme, an area it occupies with the even smaller Social-National party of Ukraine primarily based in L'viv. KUN is an offshoot of the émigré Organisation of Ukrainian Nationalists–Bandera faction, and therefore probably the best financed. Three of the four radical right groups have separate paramilitary formations (DSU, KUN and UNA). UNA was banned in August 1995.

THE ELECTION CAMPAIGN

Parliamentary Election Law[11]

On 18 November 1993 the election law was approved by parliament by 271:31 votes. The election law rejected the proposals made by democratic parties that at least 50 per cent of seats be elected on party lists.[12] Instead, all 450 deputies would be elected in single-seat constituencies on a majoritarian basis for a single-chamber legislative body by 50 per cent of those voting (which could not represent less than 25 per cent of the district's voters). The cost of the elections was initially estimated to be 1 billion *karbovanets* (approximately $10 million), but this figure was exceeded owing to the numerous by-elections held throughout the second half of 1994, and 1995 and 1996.[13] Twenty-eight political parties were registered to take part in the elections and 3574 candidates registered. Of these 2082 (58.25 per cent) were nominated by groups of electors, 1065 (29.80 per cent) by work collectives and 427 (11.95 per cent) by political parties and blocs. The largest number of competing candidates (15–20) were in six constituencies, notably Kyiv, Dnipropetrovs'k, Poltava, Sumy and elsewhere.

Citizens aged 25 or over who had resided in Ukraine for two years could be put forward as candidates by either 300 voters in an electoral district, political parties and blocs or labour collectives. There were three positive factors in the election law: parliamentary seats would be full-time paid posts (that is, deputies could not hold outside posts); deputies could not simultaneously hold posts in local councils (both problems had led to wide absenteeism in the 1990–4 parliament); in addition, presidential prefects, the armed forces, the judiciary and Ministry of Internal Affairs personnel were barred from putting themselves forward as candidates.

There are 450 single mandate districts in Ukraine and these comprise approximately equal numbers of voters.[14] These districts had to present the following conditions: average deviation in the number of voters in the district was not to exceed 12 per cent, the formation of electoral districts which included territories without mutual borders was not allowed and there should be a review of the district borders every eight years. Electoral districts were divided into polling divisions, normally of 20 000–30 000 voters.

Electoral commissions were divided into the Central, Regional and District Electoral Commissions. The Central Electoral Commission was approved by parliament on submission from the chairman where no less than one third of its members should have a legal background. All political parties and blocs registered to participate in the elections could appoint one representative to the Central Electoral Commission, which lasted four years (the same as the parliament).

The Central Electoral Commission has a large number of explicit duties. These include the organisation and conduct of elections, control of the implementation of the election law, direction of the regional and district election commissions, establishment of the order of use of funds for conducting elections, registered political parties and election blocs, organised re-elections and considered complaints.

Regional Electoral Commissions were appointed by the relevant praesidiums of local councils. Again, all parties and blocs registered in the district could appoint a representative to the Regional Electoral Commission. District Electoral Commissions were created by village, town or city councils, and the same rule applied to registered political parties and blocs.

Public funding for candidates was to be channelled through the Central Electoral Commission, while private funding was limited to 6 million *karbovanets* for each prospective deputy (at the time approximately US$200). Funding by foreign organisations was prohibited. But it was not explained how foreign funds (for example, from Russia or the Ukrainian diaspora) could be controlled or how the Central Electoral Commission proposed to ensure candidates did not overspend – $200 being a ridiculously small amount.

The nomination of candidates began 90 days and ended 60 days before the election date. The nomination of candidates by political parties or electoral blocs was undertaken in the following manner. The regional branch of the party/bloc held a meeting attended by two-thirds of its party membership or two-thirds of the delegates elected to participate in the meeting. The regional branch was required to have no fewer than 100 members of the overall party/bloc membership. The regional branch then applied to the local electoral commission with the nominee's personal details and certified minutes of the meeting.

No later than the third day after receipt of the application the local electoral commission would issue a certificate on the registration of the candidate. Alternatively, 300 voters in a given district could submit the candidate of a party/bloc no later than 45 days before polling day to the regional electoral commission.

From the moment of registration candidates had equal rights to media access. Candidates were not allowed to use their official position to promote their election campaign, whilst candidates were allowed free transport within the electoral district and were relieved of their normal employment for the duration of the campaign. During the election campaign registered candidates had immunity from arrest.

Candidates had the right to discuss their programmes in the press, radio and on television. Premises for meetings would also be authorised. Regional electoral commissions would print 2000 posters per candidate. Under article 32, 'Pre-election campaign publicity may be conducted in any form and through any means which do not violate the Constitution and the laws of Ukraine ...'

Candidates have the right to free use of the state mass media in 'equal measure'. Article 34 states that the 'concrete amount and time of radio and television programmes for pre-election publicity shall be established by the regional electoral commission in accordance with the manager of the appropriate agencies of mass media'. Publicity in the independent media should be charged at the same rate to all candidates.

An unorthodox voting procedure, a remnant of the Soviet era, made voting a daunting task. Voters were asked to cross out every candidate they did *not* want, leaving unmarked the single candidate of their choice. If a ballot was incorrectly filled out it was declared invalid. On the ballot each name was followed by the sponsoring group. If the candidate was an independent, the name would be followed by the number of citizens who endorsed him or her.

The election law stated that a valid election would have taken place when more than 50 per cent of those voting choose one candidate. This figure though must exceed 25 per cent of the total number of eligible voters in a district. Therefore, a quarter of registered voters must vote for a candidate. If the first round of elections did not produce a clear winner, the two candidates with the highest number of votes went into a second round two weeks later.

Criticism of the Election Law

The election law was criticised by a wide variety of observers. 'Ukraine has a very sophisticated election law. It is designed to prevent parliamentarians being elected,' one election monitor correctly predicted.[15] The election law was blamed for confusing the electorate with a large number of candidates and not filling all of the parliamentary seats.[16] In March 1996, parliament amended the election law giving the Central Electoral Commission the right not to set repeat elections in constituencies where elections have been deemed invalid twice in a row for a year from the date of the last vote.

The US Commission on Security and Co-operation in Europe pointed to a number of problems with the law:[17]

* Membership of the Central Electoral Commission was derived from the post-Soviet *nomenklatura* and included no democrats.
* It was far easier to submit nominations of candidates from labour collectives.
* More stringent and numerous criteria were placed on political parties in the nomination of candidates. Parties had to submit 30 items of information and descriptions dealing with the nomination of candidates while groups of voters and labour collectives only required eight and one document respectively.
* It favoured those candidates who already had a power base.
* It encouraged negative voting (electors had to cross out all the names they did not want instead of indicating positive support for a candidate) which increased the possibility of errors and abuse.

This criticism was echoed by democratic groups because it reduced the role of political parties to a minimum and ensured the domination of electoral commissions by the *nomenklatura*. Proportional representation would have been a

logical step towards helping to create a multi-party system since it encourages nascent political parties to take responsibility for policies advanced either by one dominant political force or by a coalition of forces. Proportional representation breaks down psychological barriers to political activism and to party affiliation on the part of a population largely used to avoid trouble by avoiding politics.[18]

As for electoral commissions, the power of nomination placed 'the same people who sat on them when the Soviet Union was in existence'.[19]

Opposition to the election law was led by Rukh and the New Ukraine bloc, who argued that the majoritarian system favoured the Party of Power,[20] and hindered political reform and democratisation in Ukraine.[21] Rukh accused the Party of Power of having 'placed parties on the same level as state enterprises and organisations in the pre-election campaign and thus factually left the old election laws intact'.[22] The election of a large number of independents would also prevent the creation of stable parliamentary factions. Democratic groups argued in favour of 50 per cent of seats elected on the majoritarian system, which would ensure representation of regional views, while the remainder elected on party lists would force political parties to adopt programmes geared towards all-Ukrainian questions.

Taras Stetskiv, a deputy in the 1990–4 parliament and later a member of the Party of Democratic Revival, argued that the law 'is a glaring reflection of the victory of post-communist forces in our parliament'. 'The communists, who dominate many regions, will have total control in their districts and in the media and will crush democratically oriented legislators,' he added.[23] Serhiy Holovatiy, a senior Rukh member, president of the Ukrainian Legal Foundation and subsequently minister of justice, believed the law would not ensure free elections and would delay Ukraine's entry into the Council of Europe. 'This system reduces political parties to nothing. This decision is a move towards totalitarianism,' Holovatiy believed.[24] Deputies who were elected would be accountable only to themselves, not to the discipline of political parties, the Christian Democratic Party of Ukraine argued.[25]

Rukh criticised the election law for helping the Party of Power to remain in power, claiming it was a throwback to the Soviet era when political parties were put on the same level as workers' collectives. 'Ukraine remains a stronghold of red autocracy in Europe. Under such conditions, Rukh will continue its struggle to turn Ukraine into a really democratic state,' their statement argued. The Green Party claimed that the new law 'serves nothing but corporate and regional interests'.[26]

New Election Law

Ukraine debated a new election law in 1996 at the same time as a new constitution was under consideration. The draft of the new election law had always been a compromise based on four proposals. Hence it still included the right of workers' collectives to nominate candidates in elections. But the new law would also facilitate the growth of political parties and the formation of political blocs. In order to register a candidate a party had to collect 200 000 signatures in no less than half of Ukraine's territory. 'Very few parties could accomplish this today in Ukraine' without uniting into some bloc, Oleksandr Lavrynovych, a Rukh member of the parliamentary committee on Legal Policy and Judicial Reform, stated.[27]

After the December 1995 by-elections Stetskiv, a member of the parliamentary Reform faction, commented: 'The by-elections have demonstrated the weakness of political parties and the strength of the *nomenklatura*. Democratic parties will be defeated in new by-elections if they fail to unite into one political bloc.[28] With the adoption of the new election law, Lavrynovych believed that the next Ukrainian parliament will in future be elected in a single day.[29]

Electoral Blocs[30]

In October 1993 Rukh called upon other national democratic parties to establish a 'centrist' electoral bloc entitled the Association of Democratic Forces Elections – 94.[31] In turn, national democratic parties and groups went on to form a Permanent Standing Commission of Democratic Parties and Organisations. Its composition is shown in Table 1.3.[32]

These parties wanted to prevent a repetition of the mistakes made during the December 1991 presidential elections when the democratic vote was divided between five candidates. In addition, they were all concerned at a victory by pro-communist and pro-Russian forces (which they viewed as synonymous). The parties and civic groups would refrain from conflict and only propose one candidate in each electoral district.[33] The Permanent Commission also aimed to ensure that parties and civic groups co-ordinated their election platforms and activities. The Small Council of Rukh then proposed the creation of a bloc entitled *Vybir–94* (Election–94)[34] from the Permanent Commission because 'the victory of centrist parties is possible only in case of their co-ordinated efforts'.[35]

Table 1.3   Election Blocs

Centre-Right	Centrist/Centre-Left
Rukh,	PDVU
DPU,	SDPU
URP,	ZPU
SelDPU,	Beer Lovers Party (PPL)
KhDU,	New Ukraine Bloc
KUN	Ukrainian Students Union
National Conservative Party	Social Democratic Youth
Memorial	
All Ukrainian Society of Former Political Prisoners and Repressed	
Union of Ukrainian Students	
Ukrainian Youth Association	
All-Ukrainian Union of Solidarity Toilers	
Crimea with Ukraine Committee	
Organisation of Soldier's Mothers	
Union of Ukrainian Writer's	
Union of Composers of Ukraine	
Union of Ukrainian Officers	
Ukrainian Cossacks	
Taras Shevchenko Ukrainian Language Society Prosvita	

All the national democratic members of the Permanent Commission went on to establish the Democratic Coalition Ukraine as an election bloc. Centrist and centre-left parties and civic groups left the Permanent Commission and joined two other electoral blocs (see later). Further national democratic political parties and civic groups which joined those from the Permanent Commission in the Democratic Coalition Ukraine election bloc are listed in Table 1.4.

The New Ukraine bloc, originally a member of the Permanent Commission, and the Union of Industrialists and Entrepreneurs of Ukraine (SPPU) formed the Inter-Regional Bloc of Reforms (MRBR) at its inaugural congress in Kharkiv on 21–22 January 1994.[36] From the launch of the Permanent Commission it was clear that centrist and centre-left political parties were ambivalent about co-operating with national democrats and created their own temporary Democratic Centre organisation which united New Ukraine, the PDVU, MRBR and the SDPU.[37] The joint chairmen of MRBR were Grynev and Kuchma, then joint chairmen of New Ukraine and the SPPU respectively. The MRBR mainly concentrated its election campaign in eastern and southern Ukraine where New Ukraine and the SPPU were strongest.[38] Nevertheless, commentators gave the MRBR a short lease of life following the elections because of the improbable alliance of the Slavophile Civic Congress, industrialists, the prowestern PDVU and others which 'made it seriously ill from the day it was born.'[39]

The MRBR was strongly disliked by the national democrats allied in the Democratic Coalition Ukraine because of its alleged pro-Russian orientation. Chornovil, leader of Rukh, warned that the MRBR could become the

Table 1.4 Democratic Coalition 'Ukraine' Election Bloc

Congress of National Democratic Forces (KNDS)
Organisation of Ukrainian Nationalists
Union of Chernobyl
Union of Ukrainian Women
Green World Association
Ukrainian Bible Society
Brotherhood of A. Pervozvanyi
League of Mothers and Sisters of Ukrainian Freedom Fighters
Union of Journalists of Ukraine
Union of Theatrical Women
Union of Artists
Organisation of Families with Many Children
Ukrainian All-World Co-ordinating Council

most powerful anti-Ukrainian group in parliament. Holovatiy dismissed
the MRBR as representing 'the thinking of only one region of Ukraine. It
doesn't have cross-country appeal and therefore can't unite', conveniently
forgetting that no election bloc or political party at that time had cross-
country appeal in Ukraine.[40] The feeling of hostility was mutual. Kuchma
threatened to resign as co-chairman of the MRBR if it proved true
that Grynev had indeed signed an agreement with 'national chauvinist
forces'.[41]

The national democrats were particularly concerned about the MRBR's
criticism of the 'cult of statehood', its support for a 'strategic partnership
with Russia', the removal of customs and border barriers with the CIS,
and its promotion of federalism and two state languages.[42] The election
slogan of Rukh, by contrast, emphasised 'Statehood–Democracy–Reform'
(a slogan which placed it close to western-style Conservative parties) and
united those in support of patriotism and a commitment to a market
economy. Federalism was perceived as a threat to Ukrainian statehood,
although Chornovil had supported it as chairman of L'viv *oblast* council
between 1990 and 1992. Rukh and the MRBR looked respectively towards
reintegration with Europe or Russia and the Commonwealth of
Independent States (CIS). But Rukh and the MRBR were united in their
anti-communism, support for reform and strong presidential power, areas
that have since allowed them to co-operate with President Kuchma against
the radical left in parliament.[43]

By mid-April 1994, after the second round of the parliamentary elections, the low number of elected democrats and the threat posed by the
election of a large number of communists forced Rukh and the MRBR at
least to begin negotiations on a tactical alliance. Kuchma, co-chairman of
the MRBR, called for 'unity among all centrist groups who hold Ukrainian
independence dear'.[44] Indeed, more united than divided Rukh and the
MRBR, especially with regard to reform (although the same could not be
said about the moderately nationalistic and centre-right KNDS). In reality,
'The Ukrainian President has a tendency always to exaggerate the "pro-
Moscow" sympathies of Grynev,'[45] one author noted. Kuchma never supported the revival of the former USSR nor the loss of Ukrainian
independence, but his comment that 'Ukraine cannot exist without Russia'
made the national democrats cool towards him.[46]

Other democratic parties, such as the Party of Justice, the Constitutional
Democrats, the Beer Lovers and the Party of Solidarity and Social Justice,
decided to contest seats in the election independent of blocs, although
some of these were also members of the New Ukraine bloc. The Labour
Congress of Ukraine created an election bloc entitled 'Solidarity in Favour

of Well-Being and Progress', which united the Union of Leased Enterprises and Union of Small Enterprises (as well as other smaller civic groups). The Liberal Party of Ukraine, which unites the representatives of new business and publishes a large number of party newspapers, attempted to compete against the Labour and Communist Parties in eastern Ukraine. The Liberals also opted not to forge an election alliance with any other parties. Instead, they became the kernel which created the Social-Market Choice faction in early 1992, the second largest faction after the communists (see Table 1.5).

The rural vote is important because 30–40 per cent of the electorate are based there, living in a highly conservative environment. 'The old mentality lives on here,' an inhabitant of a village 90 miles north-east of Kyiv said.[49] But the rural vote is divided between three parties: the Peasant Party, with links to the communists and largely based in central and southern Ukraine linking the interests of the rural *nomenklatura*, the Peasant Democratic Party of Ukraine, staunchly anti-communist with strong support only in western Ukraine, and the Free Peasant Party of Ukraine, which was established as an offshoot of the Association of Private Farmers of Ukraine.

The authoritarian left initially aimed to establish an election bloc entitled Labour Ukraine, but this did not come to fruition. The Labour Ukraine bloc would have united the KPU, registered on 5 October 1993, the SPU, the more moderate offshoot of the pre-August 1991 Communist Party,[50] the SelPU and possibly the Labour Party of Ukraine, with its links to state enterprise directors. It predicted that it would win 20 per cent of seats in the new parliament. The Civic Congress of Ukraine, an

Table 1.5   The Evolution of Election Blocs

National Democrats[47]
- Rukh and the Congress of National Democratic Forces
- Permanent Standing Commission of Political Parties & Organisations
- Election 94
- Democratic Coalition Ukraine
- Statehood, Rukh and Reform parliamentary factions

Liberal Democrats[48]
- New Ukraine bloc
- Democratic Centre
- Inter-Regional Bloc of Reforms
- Inter-Regional Bloc of Reforms (MRBR) Party
- MRBR parliamentary faction
- Social-Market Choice faction

Inter-Front-type organisation, also allies itself with the radical left on many questions (both are pro-Russian and anti-Western) and had the backing of the deputy mayor of Donets'k, Yury Boldyrev, who was quoted as saying after the elections, 'A new union of Russia, Belarus and Ukraine is inevitable.'[51] The Labour Party of Ukraine is an offshoot of the SPPU and represents that section of industry which relies on state credits and markets, as well as co-operation with Russia and the CIS. It has therefore been a strong proponent of Industrial-Financial Groups as a means of rescuing these moribund enterprises (see chapter 6).

The election platforms of the KPU, SPU and SelPU were comparable when concerning domestic political and economic affairs. The rhetoric of the KPU was often strikingly similar to that of the Soviet era when it proclaimed that it was against 'militant nationalism, anti-Orthodox clericalism, falsification of history, rehabilitation of the Organisation of Ukrainian nationalists and Ukrainian Insurgent Army, humiliation of the heroes who defended our Motherland'.[52] The KPU opposed any kind of privatisation, demanded state control of the economy, Russian and Ukrainian state languages as well as dual citizenship.

With regards to these questions there was little to differentiate the three radical left parties. The differences arose only with regard to foreign and military policy. Whereas the KPU called for the revival of the former USSR through a 'Union of Sovereign States' (similar to Mikhail Gorbachev's proposal before the disintegration of the Soviet Union and that of the Yeltsin Russian leadership), the SPU and SelPU were committed to an independent Ukraine. On foreign policy the SPU and SelPU, therefore, were closer to the MRBR, which championed a 'strategic partnership' with Russia primarily in the economic field but fell short of eroding Ukraine's independence through full political-military integration with Russia and the CIS. Hence during the presidential elections the left could readily transfer their support to Kuchma in the second round (in the first round they backed Moroz, leader of the SPU), although as the new parliament would show, the radical left and the MRBR were completely at odds over questions of economic and political reform (see chapters 4 and 5).[53] The KPU and SPU, although they contested the presidential elections, have remained hostile to the institution of the presidency as such. The revived Komsomol has allied itself with the KPU and has also put forward its election platform.[54]

The radical right was not united in any electoral bloc. KUN, an offshoot of the radical right *émigré* Organisation of Ukrainian Nationalists (Bandera faction), claimed to have 'democratised' itself during 1992–4 and espoused policies similar to the national democrats', hence its membership of the Democratic Coalition Ukraine.[55] But the election slogan of KUN reflected its radical right origins: 'Nationalistic Order – A Mighty State – Social Justice'.

The Conservative Republicans[56] (the radical right of the Republicans who were expelled or broke away to form their own party in summer 1992) proposed an electoral alliance with the most extreme of the radical right groups, the DSU, and the Organisation of Ukrainian Nationalists in Ukraine (OUNvU).[57] The Ministry of Nationalities and Migration condemned the election broadcast of the OUNvU for its claim that Russians and Jews ruled Ukraine. The Ministry believed that such statements promoted discord and inter-ethnic tension.[58]

The largest radical right party is the UNA, which ran by itself owing to the high public profile of the UNA and its paramilitary wing, the Ukrainian People's Self-Defence Forces (UNSO). The UNA championed the view: 'Vote for the UNA and you will never be asked to come to elections again' and its election slogan was 'Force–Order–Prosperity'. According to the head of UNA, Oleh Vitovych, 'Our main difference with democrats is in our way of thinking. It is like comparing people who wallow in the mud like pigs and others who stand up like Cossacks.'[59] The UNA election leaflets were highly populist: 'To each worker a country house, a car and apartment, to his wife the chance to raise children instead of working, to pensioners meat every day, to criminals a comfortable jail cell.'[60]

The election programme of the UNA called for an East Slavic empire centred on Kyiv, the annexation of neighbouring Ukrainian 'ethnic territories' in Moldova, Belarus and the Russian Federation, support for the Ukrainian diaspora in the former USSR, a military alliance with Belarus or its neutrality, opposition to the expansion of NATO and the maintenance of nuclear weapons and the military-industrial complex.[61] The UNA claimed that the publicity they had received during the elections had doubled their membership (a highly dubious claim), after they had won 2 of the 49 seats in the first round and 10 of their candidates had reached the second round, including in Kyiv.[62] The Social-National Party of Ukraine also ran independent of any blocs, but remained confined to L'viv *oblast*, where they failed to win any national seats. But their leader, Yuri Krivoruchko, warned, 'This is our first campaign and the idea is to publicise our name.'[63]

The Party of Power represented a fifth election force which could not be described as a 'bloc'. The Party of Power was represented by former high-ranking members of the Communist Party within the presidential administration, Cabinet of Ministers, security forces, enterprises and local councils. In the election campaign the Party of Power was not united and its members often competed against each other, depending on the region and loyalty to either parliamentary speaker or president. Because the Party of Power never represented a bloc, unlike the attempt to make two Party of Power blocs in the December 1995 Russian elections, they had no single election platform or election strategy.

Of the total number of candidates registered for the March 1994 parliamentary elections, the Party of Power was represented in the 300 presidential prefects, 250 collective farm chairmen, 28 former or current government ministers and 6 Security Service personnel.[64] Their main power base remained the largely rural, Ukrainian-speaking central Ukraine. The electoral strength of the Party of Power could be gauged from their influence in rural areas (approximately 30–40 per cent of the vote), enterprises and the state administration (approximately 20–30 per cent of the vote). The Party of Power is represented in the newly elected parliament within the Centre, Unity and the Independents factions.[65]

Regional Divisions

Ukraine can be readily divided into four regions and four significant political groups:

1. West: Ukrainian-speaking, nationally conscious peasantry;
2. East: Russian-speaking, highly urbanised;
3. Centre: Ukrainian-speaking, national consciousness eroded by the 1933 artificial famine;
4. South: Russian-speaking cities, inactive Ukrainian peasantry.

In the March 1990 parliamentary and local elections the Democratic Bloc won 122 out of 450 seats (27.1 per cent) concentrated in western Ukraine, Kyiv and the urban centres of central Ukraine. The countryside remained controlled by radical left groups except in western Ukraine. Independents and Centrists remained strongest in the urban centres of central and eastern Ukraine. This regional division of support for political tendencies was confirmed by the March 1991 referendum for a 'Renewed Federation' and the December 1991 presidential elections. The 1994 parliamentary elections showed that the national democrats had been unable to break through to Russian-speaking regions (Russian speakers account for 40 per cent of Ukraine's population according to the 1989 Soviet census), could not mobilise the peasantry outside western Ukraine and competed only in their traditional strongholds against the radical right.[66]

Table 1.6 Regional Election Blocs

Region	Name of Bloc	Members
L'viv[67]	New Wave	Liberals & Conservatives
Volyn[68]	Well-Being, Justice & Order	URP, DPU, KUN, KNDS
Donets'k[69]	People's Congress	KNDS
Donets'k	Democratic Donbas	Rukh and KUN
Zaporizhzhia[70]	We	PDVU
Dnipropetrovs'k[71]	Centre for Political Initiative	Liberals and Businessmen
Kharkiv[72]	Business Assembly	Liberals and Businessmen
Kharkiv	Inter-Party Electoral Association 'Justice'	National Democrats
Poltava[73]	Pre-Electoral Bloc of Officers	Union of Ukrainian Officers

Regional variations in the manner in which local branches of political parties allied themselves in the election campaign reflected the different local conditions and level of national consciousness (see Table 1.6).

In L'viv the *Nova Khvylia* (New Wave) electoral bloc united those centrist and centre-left political parties and civic groups which joined the MRBR in eastern and southern Ukraine, groups which had always been members of, or close to, the New Ukraine bloc. 'We established our movement as a bulwark against radicals (national democrats and the radical right). We bring together professionals and moderates,' Stetskiv explained.[74] Founded on 30 November 1993 as a centrist bloc by Victor Pynzenyk's Fund in Support of Reform, 'The New Wave is a general centrist association of national democratic forces. The association's economic programme is based on the principle of the need for urgent economic reforms, while its political principle is that of the middle class to power,' Ihor Koliushko, elected on a New Wave ticket, said.[75]

In contrast to the MRBR, which stressed its liberal democratic credentials and was accused by national democrats of 'cosmopolitanism', reformist blocs in western Ukraine had no choice but to adopt a patriotic image, which gave them a centre-right profile close to Western European and North American Conservative political parties. The New Wave bloc became the kernel that created the Reform parliamentary faction in the newly elected parliament (see later).

The growing power of the regions, particularly the Donbas of eastern Ukraine, was reflected in the 1994 elections in Ukraine.[76] In Dnipropetrovs'k a Centre for Political Initiative was established by 32-year-old businessman, Hennady Balashov, as a vehicle to unite reformist groups and entrepreneurs. In Kharkiv *Dilovi Zbory* (Business Assembly) was established by groups close to the MRBR and the New Ukraine bloc which agreed to co-operate with the Party of Labour, the political offshoot of the Union of Industrialists and Entrepreneurs of Ukraine, but rejected any *modus vivendi* with the radical left. National democratic groups (URP, DPU, KhDPU and SDPU) in Kharkiv created the much weaker Inter-Party Electoral Association 'Justice'. The Liberal Democratic Party resigned from this bloc after the removal from its election programme of a provision on a possible future federal territorial structure for Ukraine.[77] A major cleavage between national and liberal democratic groups continues to exist over their attitudes towards a federal structure for Ukraine.

Democratic groups in the Donbas though, despite their small numbers, failed to unite into one pre-electoral bloc. In October 1993 two nascent electoral blocs were established, entitled the People's Congress of the Donets'k Region (NKD) and Democratic Donbas (DD). The split occurred along fault-lines which had developed during 1992–3 between those who espoused a willingness to co-operate with national communists and the Party of Power in the interests of statehood (NKD) and those which had maintained an anti-communist profile (DD).

The former, therefore, included centre-right parties grouped within the KNDS, while the latter brought together Rukh and its allies, including the KUN. In November 1993, the NKD demanded that the government introduce a state of emergency in the economy, presidential rule in the Donbas, prohibit strikes and demonstrations, control the export of foodstuffs and struggle against profiteering and banditry. The NKD also adopted an election programme which called for Ukraine's withdrawal from the CIS, opposition to federalisation, support for national minority rights, priority for private enterprise and the creation of a social market economy, land reform, encouragement for the development of industry and defence of the national economy.

But the main battle in the parliamentary elections in the highly urbanised Donbas was between moderate and radical left groups (the KPU, SPU and the Labour Party of Ukraine), on the one hand, and the liberals (MRBR and the Liberal Party of Ukraine), on the other. The leadership of the NKD announced their intention to co-operate with the liberals, therefore, in an attempt to prevent the victory of the left and 'Red Directors', as the Labour Party of Ukraine is most commonly known. The Union of Donbas Community Organisations was also an ally of the radical left, which linked together separatist and pro-Russian movements, such as the Party of Slavic Unity and the Civic Congress of Ukraine.

THE AFTERMATH

Issues

The 1994 parliamentary elections were held at a time of deep economic crisis in Ukraine which would have tended to have led to the assumption that this issue would have dominated the election campaign. Unfortunately, this was not to be the case.

In a pre-election poll in Chernivtsi which asked whom the electorate would vote for, the highest figures were given for jurists (65.7 per cent) and economists (64.1 per cent).[78] Another poll asked a similar question: Who could rescue Ukraine from its crisis?[79] The results are shown in Table 1.7.

Those hankering for a strong hand or a nationalist saviour were in a minority, as reflected in the meagre electoral support granted to radical right parties in 1994 and their low ratings in opinion poll surveys. Another survey (see Table 1.8) also showed lack of support for a 'stronghand', or authoritarian or nationalist solutions to Ukraine's domestic crisis.

The economy was uppermost in the minds of electors, especially in eastern and southern Ukraine.[81] Yet, political parties and election blocs failed to reflect its concern. All political parties in the elections

> have one common weakness: they are burdened by unnecessary issues (e.g. the per cent of income taxes), while pivotal questions are articulated in general and vague terms. In particular, this weakness is most evident in the economic sections of party programmes, despite the fact that most of Ukraine's parties claim to put a premium on economic matters.[82]

Table 1.7   Pre-election Poll of Voter Confidence

Parties and organisations in favour of union with Russia	20%
The Inter-Regional Bloc of Reforms (MRBR)	12%
President Leonid Kravchuk	5%
Radical right nationalists	2%

Table 1.8   Negative Views within Ukrainian Society[80]

In favour of a strong hand	69%
Back the ideology of Ukrainian nationalism	67%
Introduction of an authoritarian state	66%

Even when election blocs discussed the causes of the economic crisis they blamed different factors:

1. Collapse of the former Soviet economic space and ties with Russia (MRBR).
2. Ukraine's continued colonial dependency economy (Democratic Coalition Ukraine).
3. Capitalisation of the economy and market reforms (radical left parties).

The MRBR and the Democratic Coalition Ukraine both agreed that the absence of reforms was a major factor in the economic crisis. But when the MRBR blamed the Party of Power for prioritising state- and nation-building at the expense of the economy the national democrats disagreed. The 'most comprehensive and candid' election platform was represented by the MRBR, but the bulk of the economic programmes only served to confuse voters.[83] In contrast, most of the political parties and civic groups which comprised the Democratic Coalition Ukraine lacked explicit socio-economic programmes. The call by the Democratic Coalition Ukraine for the strengthening of statehood 'will have little chance of success', one analyst believed.[84]

The Elections[85]

The importance of the elections to Ukraine's post-Soviet development were spelled out by President Kravchuk's presidential adviser on domestic questions, Mykola Mykhailchenko, who was concerned that insufficient voter participation in the elections would have made them 'invalid'. This would 'have been a direct threat to Ukrainian statehood'.[86]

President Kravchuk argued that if the elections did not take place or failed to elect a sufficient number of deputies for a constitutional quorum, then he would be forced to introduce presidential rule. 'This period could be very difficult. We face the threat of a power vacuum. We do not know how long the elections will last... . We do not know whom to elect for President.'[87] The prospect of presidential rule was sufficiently unpopular in itself to encourage voters to participate *en masse* in parliamentary elections.

Parliament appealed before the elections for a large voter turnout as a means to encourage the continued peaceful transformation of Ukraine as a European power. In reference to Russia, the appeal added that it was a positive sign that Ukraine 'has avoided the use of armed force to change political power'. Ukraine needed successful elections and rejected those that hoped for an invalid result, which would lead to a 'power vacuum'. If the elections were unsuccessful it would lead to 'political and economic instability and lead to a constitutional crisis in Ukraine'. Then the current unpopular parliament would be forced to continue until the end of its legal mandate (March 1995).[88]

In contrast to the apathy found in most electorates in the former Soviet states, 75 per cent of Ukrainian voters participated in the March 1994 election and 65 per cent in the first repeat April 1994 elections (20 per cent more than in the December 1993 Russian elections). The highest turnouts in the first round were in the three Galician *oblasts* of Ternopil (91.92 per cent), Ivano-Frankivsk (88.47 per cent) and L'viv (87.56 per cent). The areas with the lowest turnouts in the first rounds of the parliamentary election were the city of Kyiv and the Crimean Autonomous Republic. 'The pessimistic prediction that the turnout would be too low to be valid has been proved wrong. The Ukrainian people have demonstrated they want change for the better and are deciding their own future,' Ivan Yemets, chairman of the Central Electoral Commission, commented on the elections.[89] The turnouts were particularly encouraging because 47 per cent of respondents in one poll believed that the elections would change nothing.[90]

The first round of the elections in March–April 1994 elected 72 per cent of seats (324 out of 450).[91] The numerous run-offs to fill the vacant seats held between April and December 1994, 1995 and 1996 led to increasingly smaller turnouts. In the words of one voter, 'How many times can I go into vote? They're exhausting my democratic right.'[92]

Despite the severity of the economic crisis and strained relations with Russia the radical right failed to win a large number of seats (although they were also hampered by the majoritarian election law). They mainly competed with national democrats in western and central Ukraine. The KUN and UNA proved again that they were the only two radical right parties with influence and support. The remaining radical right groups – the SNPU, the OUNvU and the DSU – failed to win any seats.

The KPU won 90 seats, far fewer than the 239 they had obtained in March 1990 but nevertheless, represented the largest faction in the new parliament. They failed to obtain support throughout Ukraine and have become a regional party with their roots and base in the Donbas. In the newly elected parliament the communists joined forces with their radical left allies, the socialists and agrarians. But since the elections the agrarians had split into pro- and anti-reformist factions.

The democrats were divided along regional lines into two election blocs. The MRBR competed with the radical left in eastern and southern Ukraine, while in western and central Ukraine the Democratic Coalition

Ukraine largely competed against the radical right and independents in the 342 constituencies in which it put forward candidates.[93] The highly optimistic predictions of many leading democrats that they would win at least half the seats in the new parliament proved to be illusory; they barely increased their proportion won in the March 1990 elections.[94] The MRBR and Rukh claimed they would win at least 100 seats each; however, they succeeded in only obtaining some 25 per cent of this number.[95] Rukh qualified its statements in a press conference in Kyiv on 28 March 1994 when Chornovil claimed it would win 50 per cent of seats in the event of an electoral law similar to the one used in the December 1993 Russian elections. Rukh was forced to admit, though, that it had 'suffered a defeat' in the elections[96] and Chornovil said, 'This is no triumph for us. We have only work ahead.'[97] The socialists also admitted that they had been unsuccessful during the elections.[98]

The largest group of elected deputies had no party political allegiances. Those who stood as independents comprised a large body of academics, entrepreneurs, chairmen of collective farms, state officials and members of the presidential apparatus. These centrists and independents were mainly elected in 11 *oblasts* lying between radical left-dominated eastern Ukraine and the national democratic-dominated western Ukraine.[99]

By-elections

Further elections to fill the vacant 45 seats in the Ukrainian parliament were held on 10 December 1995.[100] Many democratic parties and groups had campaigned to hold these as 'new elections', not subject to the rigour of the old election law and therefore enabling candidates who had failed on previous occasions to try again.[101] But parliament voted on 13 September by 214:60 (with 11 abstentions) to describe them as 'repeat elections'. In the words of the chairman of the Central Electoral Commission, Yemets, 'it should not happen that deputies are elected to the same parliament according to different laws.'[102]

Of the registered candidates for the 10 December 1995 re-elections 30 had withdrawn, in many cases owing to outstanding legal cases against them, after they had initially hoped to obtain parliamentary immunity. Yemets noted that every fifth candidate was now a businessman, a new development in Ukraine. Of the nearly 360 candidates (or nearly nine candidates per district) the bulk of them had been nominated by voters' meetings (60 per cent) while the remainder were evenly divided between political parties and workers' collectives.[103]

Table 1.9   Candidates Registered According to Party Affiliation

(57)	*Radical Left* – KPU (34), SelPU (13), SPU (10)
(9)	*Affiliated to the Radical Left* – Party of Slavic Unity (5), Civic Congress of Ukraine (4)
(33)	*National Democrats* – KhDPU (13), Rukh (10), DPU (6), URP (4)
(15)	*Liberals/Social Democrats* – SDPU (5), MRBR (4), TKU (2), LPU (1), Party of Economic Revival of the Crimea (1), ZPU (1), Democratic Youth Union (1)
(2)	*Nationalists* – KUN (2)

The only political party publicly to call for a boycott of these repeat elections was the DSU (State Independence of Ukraine), a small radical right group that had failed to have any members elected in the 1994 parliamentary elections. The DSU had called for this boycott in order 'to prevent a communist-democrat victory'.[104] The Central Electoral Commission had also refused to register Volodymyr Bezymiannyi, a member of the Party of Slavic Unity, which was backed by Vladimir Zhirinovsky's Russian Liberal Democrats, who was simultaneously running in the Russian local elections in Belgrorod. Bezymiannyi had taken out Ukrainian and Russian citizenship even though Ukrainian law does not recognise dual citizenship.

The national democrats had established an electoral bloc ('Ukraina–Kyiv') in order to prevent duplication of candidates in the repeat elections in Ukraine's capital city.[105] The parliamentary faction Reform brought together a group of 21 candidates standing in the repeat elections, including the president of the *Ukrrichflot* river shipping company, Mykola Slavov, the editor of *Vechirnyi Kyiv*, Vitaliy Karpenko, and other prominent businessmen.[106] The radical left and their allies put forward the largest number of candidates and called on the electorate to vote for any of the members of their electoral bloc 'To Save the People of Ukraine' or independents with a 'socialist orientation'.[107]

With an average turnout of only 47 per cent, 27 districts could not hold a second round of elections on 24 December 1995 (the minimum was a 50 per cent turnout). Of the six newly elected deputies on 10 December, five were unaffiliated to any political group, with only one a member of the Sevastopol branch of the Communist Party (who had since died).[108] On the eve of the elections an assassination attempt was made on the L'viv candidate Ihor Pylypchuk, chief of the regional department of the main directorate for combating organised crime, who had been investigating the illegal export for adoptation of babies.[109] On 17 and 24 December 1995 a further seven deputies were elected, bringing parliament up to a total of 417 deputies (which was reduced to 416 after the death of another deputy from natural causes in January 1996).[110] Of these one was from Rukh, four from the KPU (including three from the Crimea) and the remainder were independents, leaving 33 seats in the Ukrainian parliament vacant.

Of these newly elected[111] deputies two, Anatoliy and Ihor Franchuk, were from the Crimea. Anatoliy Franchuk is President Kuchma's son-in-law and formerly the peninsula's prime minister until a vote of no confidence in him was passed by a vote of 73:8 on 8 December 1995. The high turnout in the Crimea had refuted claims that 'Crimean residents are separatists', Yemets argued, with all the Crimean seats to the Ukrainian parliament by then filled.[112] In Poltava then Prime Minister Yevhen Marchuk obtained a vote of 83.71 per cent, which he hoped would provide him with 'colossal support for further action', encourage greater support between parliament and government and 'also create a new model for solving old discord'. In Marchuk's view, his election clearly gave him a mandate to divide powers between the presidential administration and the government and gave him greater leverage *vis-à-vis* President Kuchma.[113]

The presidential administration had other ideas. Its head, Dmytro Tabachnyk, complained that holding the posts of deputy of parliament and prime minister was in breach of the Constitutional Agreement. Again, parliament disagreed. The chairman of the presidential commission on Regulations, Deputies' Ethics and Provisions for Deputies' Activities, Petro Sheyko, argued that the prime minister had the constitutional right to be elected a member of parliament. According to the 1978 constitution, which was still in operation, the prime minister was the only member of the executive with the right to hold a seat in parliament. Other members of parliament though, who still held government posts, such as the finance minister, Petro Hermanchuk,[114] were technically in breach of the constitution.[115]

In the words of one Kyiv analyst, 'This election is a demonstration of his ([Marchuk's] tremendous power. People at large and those in the corridors of power see him as a figure associated with reforms.' Marchuk, many believe, is placing himself in a position to challenge Kuchma (or any other contender) for the post of president at the next presidential elections.[116]

Further elections were scheduled for 7 April 1996 to fill 31 of the remaining 33 vacant seats in the Ukrainian parliament,[117] despite the fact that repeat balloting costs US$70 000 in each district.[118] Of those vacant seats 14 were in Kyiv, where the local newspaper accused the city's administration and mayor of not being interested in Kyiv's representation in parliament in order to have less public control over developments, such as privatisation, in the city.[119] Seven were in western and central Ukraine, or a total of 21 vacant seats (double the number in the remainder of Ukraine). One remained in the city of Sevastopol (where the elected deputy had died), whilst another nine were in eastern and southern Ukraine, making a total of ten vacant seats in that region.

In repeat elections on 7 April a further six deputies were elected at a cost of 400 billion *karbovantsi*, the parliamentary newspaper *Holos Ukrainy* (9 April 1996), complained. In 32 vacant seats, 153 candidates had stood – see Table 1.10 for the political breakdown.[120]

Together with the 13 deputies selected in December 1995, this meant that there were fewer than 20 seats remaining vacant in the 450-member parliament. Three communist members of parliament died of natural causes during April–May 1996 with constituencies in Kharkiv and Odesa *oblast*.

Violations[122]

The number of foreign observers for such a large country as Ukraine was small – only 470 for 34 000 polling stations. And of these three-quarters were not present for the second round of elections in April 1994. According to Jessica Douglas-Home, an observer from the British Helsinki Human Rights Group, multiple voting was widespread, as was greater use of pre-voting, whilst another concern of hers remained the lack of control over the mobile ballot boxes for the ill, disabled and prisoners.

This British observer described one particularly brutal incident in a Kyiv district where the former defence minister, Konstantin Morozov, was pitted against Viktor Medvedchuk, the chairman of the Union of Lawyers.

Table 1.10 Political Profile of Candidates in the 7 April 1996 Repeat Elections[121]

KPU – 21
Rukh – 10
URP – 10
KhDPU – 8
SPU – 7
KUN – 4
MRBR – 2
DPU – 1
GKU – 1
Constitutional Democratic Party of Ukraine – 1
ZPU – 1

The latter had allegedly distributed food parcels to the large number of elderly voters and promised them life insurance policies. Another accusation alleged that he had bribed the district electoral commission. As only 14 votes separated the candidates every vote counted:[123]

> Three British observers arrived just as the ballot boxes were being opened after eight pm. The electoral commission refused to admit the observers and a great deal of shouting and some pushing and shoving [of the observers] ensued. Eventually, they were admitted but every effort was made to prevent them scrutinising the count. The local observers had been obliged to sit along the wall farthest from the table where the count was taking place. It would have been impossible for them to see what was taking place. The British observers managed to situate themselves closer to the count and could see the proceedings despite the best efforts of the commission members to inhibit observation.
>
> The count in Kyiv (electoral district) 1/4 was haphazard in itself, but the key issue was the decision to invalidate successively more ballots as the counting and re-counting proceeded. It seems that the obdurate presence of the international observers led the commission to revise downwards the previous total of one candidate, Viktor Medvedechuk.

Douglas-Home found no systematic fraud but, at the same time, believed that the election law allowed an opportunity to influence the results by cheating or incompetence. She found widespread multiple voting, large-scale bribery and a lack of control over mobile ballot boxes.[124] According to the British observers, the election officials 'were looking for reasons to declare Morozov's vote invalid'.[125] Morozov stood unsuccessfully again in May 1996 in Borispil, Kyiv *oblast* in a seat made vacant by the death of a member of parliament (failed candidates could stand again in constituencies made vacant by deaths). His election campaign was backed by Rukh, the URP and the DPU.[126]

Numerous infringements were recorded by foreign observers during the Ukrainian elections. These included:

- threat of loss of employment;
- use of official cars;
- the Electoral Commission denied the registration of candidates without adequate reasons;
- local councils and electoral commissions favoured one candidate;
- some candidates were denied access to factories;
- physical assaults on democratic candidates;
- attempts to buy the loyalty of voters;

Table 1.11   Membership of Political Parties in the Ukrainian Parliament (as of 1 December 1994)[145]

Political Party	Number of Deputies
KPU	91
Rukh	22
SelPU	21
SPU	14
URP	11
KUN	5
Labour Party	5
PDVU	4
UNA	3
DPU	3
SDPU	2
Civic Congress	2
KhDPU	2
Ukrainian Conservative Republican Party	1
Party of Economic Revival of the Crimea	1
Total number of party affiliated deputies	187
Non-members of political parties	218
Total number of elected deputies	405

- pressure on businessmen who gave financial support to democratic candidates.[127]

UN and CSCE observers cited the pressuring of rural voters, a poorly functioning Central Election Commission and the denial of access to foreign observers into polling stations. The Parliamentary Assembly of the Council of Europe described the elections as successful within the law, 'carried out with great enthusiasm and a desire for accuracy'. The discrepancies which were found (physical force, spoilt ballots, withholding of information, voter manipulation and ballots with duplicate votes) 'could not be regarded as serious enough to invalidate either the individual polls or, more specifically, this first part of the election'.[128] The Non-Party Committee of Ukraine's Electors uniting 3880 members monitoring the elections in 150 districts of 20 *oblasts* compiled 265 reports of violations. Of these, 200 cases were filed at the Procurator's Office and another 85 at the Central Election Commission.[129]

Roman Zvarych, then head of the Elections 94 Press Centre, concluded that 'There has been systematic and widespread corruption'.[130] The former chairman of parliament, Ivan Pliushch, was alleged to have redirected

20 billion *karbovanets* (approximately $1 million) to his constituency in Chernihiv before the campaign.[131] In Dnipropetrovs'k[132] candidates handed out condoms to young voters with the slogan 'Make the safe choice',[133] whilst others pledged to promote a law making burials government-funded for elderly voters (who represented 76 per cent of eligible voters in that district).[134] Humanitarian aid was distributed in such a manner as to obtain signatures for registered candidates, whilst rural voters were often bribed with mineral fertiliser or construction materials.

Rukh complained of many instances of 'terror' against its candidates and supporting offices. 'Political pressure', 'pogroms' and 'physical violence' against members, candidates and local branches frequently occurred.[135] Rukh statements discussed threats made against businessmen who supported Rukh financially, which they characterised 'as nothing but an attempt to deprive our movement of any support during the election campaign'. Rukh offices in Chernivtsi, Ternopil and Kirovohrad were vandalised, the children of Rukh activists in Odesa were beaten; while an attempt to kidnap Les Taniuk, another prominent Rukh activist, failed. Rukh's candidate in Vynnytsia was also beaten. The Rukh leadership regarded the level of violence, intimidation and tension during the 1994 election campaign as worse than that encountered in the run-up to the March 1990 elections.

In mid-January 1994 Mykhailo Boychyshyn, then head of the Rukh secretariat in Kyiv and chairman of the Rukh Central Electoral Commission, was kidnapped by unknown assailants and has still not been found. It took the Ministry of Interior nearly two weeks before an operational investigation was established, which brought together the Ministry of Interior, the Procurator's Office and the Security Service.

After his abduction Rukh claimed that the disappearance was hushed up on state television and radio, which its members picketed. The co-ordinating committee for combating corruption and organised crime, which was chaired by President Kravchuk, ordered an investigation of Rukh's financial accounts in order 'to rake up as much dirt as possible on Rukh's finances'.[136] The reason for the disappearance of Boychyshyn, who would have played a key role in Rukh's election campaign, brought forth various theories. One was linked to the alleged receipt from unnamed US sources of $12 million for the parliamentary and presidential elections; others believed it was the work of organised crime afraid of the exposure by Rukh of their activities; and finally, elements of the security service afraid of a Rukh election victory. Other accusations centred on the Russian security services, because Boychyshyn was the secretary of the Baltic–Black Sea conference of Political Parties and was planning to hold an international conference of this organisation in Kyiv on 29–30 January 1994. The documents for this conference disappeared at the same time as he did.[137]

Other candidates of the People's Congress in the Donbas region complained that they were denied television and radio time, their campaign pamphlets were stolen and meetings with voters were disrupted.[138] Two deputies who were elected in Odesa and Kharkiv respectively – Grynev, co-chairman of MRBR, and Pavlo Kudiukhin, President of the Blasco Shipping Company – lost their mandates in a parliamentary vote by 205:49 on 12 May 1995. Their rivals had polled fewer votes in the first round and had withdrawn so Grynev and Kudiukhin had run unopposed in the second round. They were also accused of overspending on campaign funds, violating use of the media and extending the time open for the polls. Altogether ten violations of the electoral law were registered, including 18 types of campaign posters and introduction of food counters at polling stations.[139] The mandates of other deputies with similar infringements were registered by parliament and the refusal to register Grynev and Kudiukin could have been politically motivated. The MRBR was co-chaired by Kuchma as his presidential election bloc while Kudiukhin was later arrested on corruption charges.

CONCLUSIONS

The 1994 parliamentary elections in Ukraine led to the peaceful transfer of power from the Soviet era parliament to a newly elected Supreme Council. Yet, this occurred despite an election law that was deliberately biased against political parties, during an acute economic crisis, at a time of public apathy and widespread disillusionment. Participation rates remained high, although they understandably dropped as successive by-elections were held to fill vacant seats throughout the course of 1994–6. Although the election law used to elect the first, post-Soviet parliament had many shortcomings it has to be assessed in comparison to transition in other post-communist states.[140] 'All this was accomplished peacefully and without conflict, in contrast to some other regions. And we consider this the overriding accomplishment of the electoral "marathon" in Ukraine,' according to Yemets, the chairman of the Central Electoral Commission.[141]

The new parliament is not dominated by the radical left, as many initially feared, while the radical right fared poorly during the elections. Democratic parties did not improve on their March 1990 performance and remain regionally and urban-based. Despite the election of a large number of unaffiliated deputies, something designed to happen through the election law, by the beginning of 1995 parliament had settled into a number of structured factions (see Table 1.12).

Parliament had divided into two camps over the question of reform, but it remained committed to compromise over key questions which divided voters during the election campaign in order to overcome these divisions and secure a stable polity. The Law On State Power and Local Government, coupled with the Constitutional Agreement adopted in May and June 1995 respectively, also peacefully resolved constitutional conflicts between the legislature and executive which had plagued post-Soviet societies elsewhere (see chapter 4).

After the first two rounds of the elections in March–April 1994 most predictions concerning support for reform within the new parliament were negative. 'There will be no majority in parliament for reform,' Yuriy Yekhanurov, then deputy economics minister, complained.[142] Immediate prospects did not seem good for reform because the large number of radical left deputies were primarily elected in the first rounds, which enabled them to elect Moroz, leader of the SPU, as parliamentary chairman with both of his deputy speakers from the Agrarian faction and an independent allied to the left.

Table 1.12 The Ukrainian Parliament According to Membership of Factions

Parliamentary Faction	Number of Deputies
Communist	89
Reform	31
Social-Market Choice	30
Centre	29
Statehood	29
Rukh	29
Agrarians	26
Agrarians for Reform	25
Independents	25
Socialist	24
Unity	24
MRBR	21
Total number of deputies in factions	382
Unaffiliated deputies	34
Total	416

Source: *Chas*, 5 April 1996.

By the winter of 1994–5 the Ukrainian parliament had settled into stricter parliamentary factions and the number of unaffiliated deputies had dwindled to a fraction of their original number. Support by newly elected President Kuchma for a radical programme of political and economic reform proved crucial in forcing deputies to choose where they stood on the question of reform (a proposition that President Kravchuk had never posed to his parliament).

Although the majority of parliamentary factions had united in favour of reform and presidential power, they remained regionally divided. The overwhelming majority of members of the radical left, MRBR and Unity factions were from eastern and southern Ukraine. In contrast, Rukh and Statehood, who during the election campaign joined forces in the Democratic Coalition Ukraine, remained confined to western and central

Table 1.13 Division of Parliament According to Political Orientation and Affiliation to Political Parties

Faction	Membership	Political Party
Radical Left		
Communist	89	KPU
Agrarians	26	SelPU
Socialist	24	SPU
Total	139 (33.41%)	
Social Democratic/Centrist/Liberal		
Centre	31	None
Social-Market Choice	30	LPU
MRBR	29	MRBR
Independents	25	None
Agrarians for Reform	25	None
Unity	24	None
Total	164 (39.42%)	
Centre-Right/Nationalist		
Reform	31	People's Democratic Party of Ukraine & Rukh
Statehood	29	URP & DPU
Rukh	29	Rukh
Total	89 (21.53%)	

Source: *Chas*, 5 April 1996.

Ukraine. The Centre and Independents factions were based exclusively in central Ukraine. The newly created Reform faction primarily included former members of Rukh and New Ukraine, or post-nationalists who desire to create something resembling a western-style Conservative Party. Some of the members of the Reform faction joined the Liberal Party of Ukraine, which fared badly during the elections. Only the Reform and Social-Market Choice factions have country-wide support.

Centrists remained the largest group within parliament – an important development which singled out Ukraine from Russia and other post-Soviet states where left and right radical groups had grown in support. The large centre lobby would ensure stable – but gradual – political and economic transition as well as state-building in Ukraine.

Both the parliamentary and presidential elections in 1994 showed that *no* political force in Ukraine had country-wide appeal.[143] This reflected the twin legacies of external domination and totalitarianism which Ukraine inherited from the Tsarist empire and the former USSR.[144] Nation- and state-building would, presumably, eventually smooth out these regional differences creating the grounds for the election of presidents and parliamentarians on a national basis. This, though, required patience and time.[145]

2 Issues and Voters in the 1994 Ukrainian Presidential Elections

'Ukrainians are trying to decide not who would be the best president, but who would be the least bad.'

(*The Economist*, 18 June 1994)

'With Kravchuk I know there won't be war and with Kuchma I know I won't starve.'

(Kyiv voter)[1]

The 1994 presidential elections in Ukraine revealed many myths and legends, few of which are grounded in reality. Western media coverage was influenced by presidential elections held in neighbouring Belarus. The election of Alexander Lukashenko and Leonid Kuchma in Belarus and Ukraine respectively had the unfortunate result of being described as one and the same trend which looked set to reintegrate the former USSR with Russia. Regarding the 'legend of Kuchma as a friend of reform and the legend of Kravchuk as a hardened nationalist, if Kravchuk were a nationalist the national minorities would not have voted for him?' Myroslav Popovych, head of the Institute of Philosophy, National Academy of Sciences, pointed out.[2]

In reality, there was little to differentiate between the two leading candidates – Kravchuk and Kuchma. Only the implementation of these policies would differ as a consequence of their personal characters which, in turn, were formulated by their different career paths. In Ukraine the contest was between two Ukrainian patriots both from the Party of Power with different visions of state- and nation-building, while the electorate in both regions of Ukraine voted in accordance with how they 'view the past and the future'. As one Western analyst has rightly pointed out, 'being a Russian speaker in Ukraine does not denote a lack of patriotism or preference for rule from Russia, but only a different historical or political background'.[3] The myths of Kravchuk as 'father of the nation', 'state-builder', 'nation defender' and 'true patriot' were as confusing and misplaced as Kuchma's alleged 'pro-Russianism' or 'Little Russianism'.

This chapter on the 1994 presidential elections surveys the issues debated by the seven candidates and how different groups of voters within Ukrainian society responded to the debates. The chapter focuses in particular on the two leading candidates, Kravchuk and Kuchma. The chapter does not deal with the presidential election campaign, which the author has covered elsewhere.[4]

MYTHS AND LEGENDS OF THE 1994 PRESIDENTIAL ELECTIONS

The comparison of the Ukrainian presidential elections with Belarus was hollow. In Belarus the contest was between two frontrunners both of whom proposed different shades of pro-Russian policies. Belarusian voters were therefore given a choice between a pragmatic Viacheslav Kebich and a romantic, if rather eccentric, Lukashenko.

Nevertheless, Western analysis and media reports on the Ukrainian presidential elections adopted Kravchuk's language, a person they had on the whole been hostile towards during his term in office as president. Kuchma was therefore described as 'pro-Russian' like Lukashenko, and both were allegedly in favour of full reintegration with Russia. The fact that Kuchma on no occasion called for political-military integration with the CIS, which has been borne out by his policies since becoming president, was ignored. Various reports predicted that a Kuchma victory would inevitably lead to a Russian-dominated CIS by means of a new military-political bloc.[5] But, Kuchma's claims to be in favour of 'integration with Russia' would be as hollow and populist, and devoid of real content, as Kravchuk's preference for 'integration with Europe'.

Kuchma's 'pro-Russianism' was another myth widely accepted by many observers of the 1994 Ukrainian presidential elections. Kuchma admitted that he may have been partially to blame for helping Kravchuk to propagate this myth. 'I should have thought about something else, community or something like that. I suppose people are allergic to the word "Union".'[6] Kravchuk also complained during the election campaign: 'Now everyone is trying to prove their love for Russia. We must also turn to Russia and ask if it's proving its love for us,'[7] and he asked, 'When Boris Yeltsin defends his country, he's called a patriot: when I defend mine, I'm called a nationalist.'[8]

Kuchma never completely alienated these regions of Ukraine which were distrustful of him by calling into question Ukrainian independence. In contrast, in Belarus Lukashenko regularly pointed to himself as the only member of parliament to have voted against the dissolution of the former

USSR and creation of the CIS. Maintaining economic ties with Russia was never rejected by *any* Ukrainian presidential candidate. Kuchma's alleged 'pro-Russianism' did not ensure smooth bilateral relations with Russia during his tenure as prime minister and neither did he obtain any favourable benefits. 'On the contrary, during his term as prime minister one has the most tragic moments in Ukrainian–Russian relations,' one commentator has said.[9] As prime minister, Kuchma had openly complained about pressure being exerted on Ukraine, which was not motivated by economics but by the fact that 'Russia is trying to bring about a full paralysis of the Ukrainian economy'.[10]

Kuchma's emphasis on ensuring good relations with Russia was always stated in the same breath as good relations with the West, which was the only source for new technology (Kravchuk's argument).[11] Kuchma emphasised that Ukraine's 'strategic partnership' with Russia (a term he borrowed from Vladimir Grynev, his co-leader of the Inter-Regional Bloc of Reforms [MRBR]), the result of historical-cultural reasons and to overcome current economic problems, would not 'be allowed to be to the detriment of our relations with other states'. He would, therefore, 'keep the door open' to the West.[12] Russia, Kuchma may have reasoned, after watching Moscow's reluctance to bail out the Belarusian economy, would be unlikely to offer the credits and aid which the West had promised Ukraine in return for nuclear disarmament if it finally adopted a coherent reform programme.

In addition, unlike Lukashenko in Belarus who offered to rotate presidencies in a unified Belarusian–Russian state,[13] Kuchma never intended to share his power with anybody – whether at home or abroad.[14] Mark Urnov, a Yeltsin aide, agreed: 'I doubt Kuchma's actions will bear out his image as a totally pro-Russian politician.'[15] As for any new union with Russia, Kuchma told his Moscow interviewer, 'But you know I am not used to being a slave. I am used to being a master and I want to be a master in my country, without anyone above me.'[16]

Western reports also dismissed both leading Ukrainian candidates (Kravchuk and Kuchma) as unlikely to introduce reform if elected.[17] 'In Ukraine, voters were choosing between "coherent, but fair" reforms proposed by incumbent Leonid Kravchuk and a pledge to "restore order" by his challenger, former Prime Minister Leonid Kuchma.'[18] This was untrue. Although both candidates hold similar social-democratic and liberal socio-economic views, Kuchma's eastern Ukrainian industrialist background and his personal will would promote economic reform to the top of the Ukrainian political agenda (which it never had been under Kravchuk).

Other reports inevitably focused on the regional divide caused by the presidential elections: 'a great convenience for journalists, a great danger for Europe'.[19] Observers and analysts accepted Kravchuk's black-and-white depiction of himself as the man of 'peace' and his opponent's election as likely to lead to civil war (Kravchuk had used similar language to portray his main rival Viacheslav Chornovil in the December 1991 elections). Eastern and southern Ukraine, which largely but not exclusively voted for Kuchma, did not vote at the same time for separation from Ukraine. Apart from the Crimean peninsula, separatism has little, if any, support in these *oblasts*.

The regional divide during the second round of voting was not based on ethnic criteria, but on language. According to one study by the International Institute of Sociology, Kyiv Mohyla Academy, there were 1.5 times more Ukrainians in the Kravchuk electorate than for Kuchma, whereas this figure rose to three times more if Ukrainian-speakers only were taken into consideration. In contrast, there were five times more Russians in the Kuchma electorate than among his rivals.[20] One study claimed that the correlation between language and voting behaviour in the presidential elections was 0.92 and Kravchuk therefore lost because Russian-speaking Ukrainians voted for Kuchma.[21]

But this division along language lines reflects more the legacy of history and different perceptions of the myths, symbols and priorities of state-building in Ukraine than that portrayed in most analysis, namely something that was likely to lead to an ethnic conflict and civil war.[22] Yuriy Pestriakov, a Kuchma aide, pointed out that 'Russian-speaking Ukrainians are absolutely loyal to the Ukrainian state. But they were reduced to second-class citizens by Kravchuk'.[23] Both Ukrainian- and Russian-speaking Ukrainians are loyal to the Ukrainian independent state. Their division lies in the priorities they would demand of their elected leaders in terms of the policies which should be pursued by them when in office.

Borys Oliynyk, a communist and head of the parliamentary commission on foreign and CIS affairs, also cautioned that any portrayal of Kravchuk and Kuchma as 'pro-Western' and 'pro-Russian' respectively was mistaken. No leader of an independent Ukrainian state could follow an 'unbending line'. 'Turning the rudder full speed astern would be difficult now,' he believed.[24] Volodymyr Zolotariov, leader of the Constitutional Democratic Party of Ukraine, had called on voters to back Lanovyi in the first round and probably supported Kuchma in the second. He agreed that there was little difference between the programmes of Kravchuk and

Kuchma, while Kuchma's alleged 'pro-Russianism' was exaggerated. Zolotariov warned and correctly foresaw that:

> Kuchma's policy concerning Russia is doomed to failure. The logic of the post of president of an independent state will make Kuchma in the near future transform himself into a strong adherent of Ukrainian statehood and, as a result of which, will make him an idol of all the Ukrainian nationalists, as it happened to the communist Leonid Kravchuk.[25]

Indeed, to Ukrainian nationalists, such as the ideologist Hryhoriy Hrebeniuk of the State Independence of Ukraine (DSU) party, there was simply no difference between Kravchuk and Kuchma: 'Until recently they both were convinced enemies of the Ukrainian nation-state idea.'[26] Volodymyr Yavorivsky, critical of the national democrats for their support for Kravchuk, found that there was little original that Kuchma had proposed that Kravchuk had not already raised at an earlier date. In his view, they have more in common than that which divides them: 'They are both for independence, democracy, market reform and both are against building a state on the Ukrainian national idea, against the rejection of Russian elements out of Ukraine. And if we talk more generally, neither are independents (*samostijnykyamy*) in the true sense of that term.'[27]

ISSUES

Statehood

Although portrayed as an 'enemy' of Ukrainian statehood and a Ukrainian 'Lukashenko' waiting to 'sell Ukraine to the Russians', Kuchma in fact backed policies in favour of a strong, independent state. Nevertheless, nationally conscious Ukrainians feared that Kuchma's patriotism was only skin-deep. 'I don't particularly like Kravchuk, but to vote Kuchma into power means kissing independence good-bye,' a L'viv music composer believed.[28] A survey in Kyiv University found that 54 per cent believed that a candidate's attitude to statehood was crucial in determining their vote.[29]

Nevertheless, Kravchuk successfully diverted attention from his mismanagement of the economy to transform the presidential elections into a second referendum on independence. 'We face a historical choice in Ukraine. Which way is our state going?' Kravchuk emphasised.[30] 'The main thing is that people should vote for an independent Ukraine. People must elect someone whom they believe will safeguard this course. The nation is voting today on our future independence.'[31] In L'viv, Kravchuk warned a rally of 10 000: 'I feel there is a big threat to our young state. Some politicians want to turn back to the past.'[32]

This description of Kuchma as a threat to independence was a myth. Kuchma lamented that the lack of presidential power and weak economy, owing to the incumbent's 'romanticism', made Ukraine a weak state. His 'pragmatism', in contract, would deal with these two questions and 'build a real, sovereign, democratic state. For this we need to build a strong economy.'[33] This view was typical of eastern Ukrainians, who viewed independence not in a romantic manner like western Ukrainians, but requiring durable and pragmatic content. A Dnipropetrovs'k student pointed out that, 'With Kravchuk Ukrainian independence will die from hunger'.[34] In contrast, western Ukrainians looked at independence from a different angle: 'We are no longer a colony, and psychologically that means something to people here,' a L'viv resident said, even though, 'I have not got much from independence or Kravchuk.'[35] Independence, of itself, therefore was sufficient to western – but not eastern – Ukrainians.

Another key ingredient for nation- and state-building was 'unity', according to Kuchma, a theme that Kravchuk also repeatedly emphasised during his term in office. 'And those who undertake the opposite, they are enemies of our Ukraine and its statehood,' Kuchma added.[36] Kuchma pointed to the twin goals which should unite Ukrainians – the economy and, 'naturally, the construction of a sovereign, independent and democratic state'. In particular, 'The economy will put everything in its place and this confrontation will exist no more.'[37] Kuchma claimed that he had never rejected the 'national idea,' which voters associated with Kravchuk, but linked the building of a 'strong, sovereign and independent state' to a strong economy.[38]

After his election Kuchma promised to overcome the regional divisions brought out in the campaign and argued that 'Everything that happened during the campaign was criminal in terms of confrontation between east and west.'[39] As president of all Ukraine he would work 'in the interests of the entire Ukrainian nation and not just separate regions ... to the benefit of an independent, sovereign Ukraine.'[40]

Kravchuk campaigned strongly on a *derzhavnyk* (statesman) ticket, repeatedly stating that only he was capable of 'not permitting the violation of the territorial integrity and unity of the state'.[41] If Ukrainian independence was threatened by a Kuchma victory, as it was in Kravchuk's eyes, then this would lead to confrontation and even civil war.[42] Kravchuk told a gathering of Poltava voters that they value 'the fact that we have peace, tranquility and consensus – the basis for resolving all our social and economic problems.'[43] To have built an independent state within two and half years 'without a shot being fired, without war or cataclysm' was nothing short of miraculous and the main credit for this should, of course, go to Kravchuk.[44]

The Scientific Practical Centre for Political Psychology of the National Academy of Pedagogical Sciences backed this view and predicted disaster if Kuchma won – social conflict, economic decline, increased regional tension leading to its 'Yugoslavisation', loss of international gains and worsening relations with Russia.[45] Many voters undoubtedly accepted Kravchuk's argument that only he, and especially not Kuchma, represented 'stability'. In an appeal to Ukrainian voters on state television Kravchuk reminded them that they were electing a leader 'who will determine whether Ukraine remains a peaceful nation with constant policies or one that lurches down an unpredictable path'. This argument was especially appealing to pensioners, many of whom voted for Kravchuk 'because everyone says Kuchma could start a war here', one Kyivite feared.[46]

Kravchuk pointed to the differences which existed between Ukraine and other more established countries that would influence the outcome of the elections. 'In other countries, things are different. They may not like the country's leadership or economy but no one questions the state itself.' In Ukraine there were still 'anti-state forces' (within which he included Kuchma) who wished to destroy the Ukrainian state and resurrect the former USSR. Kravchuk warned that any attempt to do this would lead to bloodshed.[47] 'Ukraine for 340 years lived under Russia and had no state of its own. In two years people have not come to understand what statehood is,' Kravchuk argued.[48]

In addition, this argument also appealed to women voters, who tended to be more conservative and afraid that their menfolk would end up dying in conflicts either in Ukraine or abroad.[49] Halyna Katyuzhenko, a collective farm worker from Kyiv *oblast*, said, 'God forbid that anyone would vote for Kuchma. He would turn Ukraine into five Crimeas.'[50]

Political Reform

Moroz emphasised that he was the only presidential candidate who stood for a parliamentary republic. He never distanced himself from a resolution of a plenum of the central committee of the Communist Party of Ukraine that 'President Moroz alone is able to rid Ukraine of the president'.[51] Piotr

Symonenko, Communist Party leader, asked, 'What changed after we introduced the post of president? Everyone laughs that the emperor has no clothes, but the tragedy is that our nation is naked.'[52]

All other six candidates backed varying degrees of a presidential-parliamentary republic. Valeri Babych argued in favour of the fusion of the posts of president and prime minister, while Volodymyr Lanovyi believed that the president did not require additional powers – he already had sufficient to cope with the crisis.[53] Ivan Pliushch, former parliamentary speaker (1991–4), agreed with Moroz that parliament should be in a position to control the president, fearing that otherwise an authoritarian system could be created, as in the Russian Federation.[54]

Kuchma repeatedly emphasised during the election campaign his support for strong executive power, and this undoubtedly won him popularity (although his use of Yury Andropov as a role model may have aroused some suspicions).[55] 'I want to introduce dictatorship to this country – the dictatorship of law. No one is in charge,' he stated.[56] 'People want to have a master in their own house and they do not have that now,' Kuchma complained.[57] Ukrainian commentators pointed out that there was no mention of words such as 'liberty' in Kuchma's election platform – only collectivist slogans geared towards the more Sovietised eastern Ukrainian voters.[58]

In Kuchma's view, the functions of parliament and president are clear – to make laws and rule the country respectively. If this was not accepted by parliament, 'somebody will have to go. Presidential rule is inevitable,' he warned.[59] There were sufficient laws but only Kuchma, in contrast to Kravchuk, had the 'political will' to implement them. He would therefore amalgamate the posts of president and prime minister.[60]

Kravchuk also insisted that he was in favour of the president to be head of state and the executive. If he was re-elected, therefore, this would be interpreted as a referendum vote for a 'presidential-parliamentary republic'.[61] Kravchuk, unusually for him, threatened that 'If there is an attempt to limit my powers, matters will end as they have in some other countries. I don't want to use force or tanks.'[62] But Kravchuk also emphasised that he favoured 'a policy of harmony' between the Supreme Council and president and warned that Kuchma would be more confrontational when demanding additional powers.[63]

Under the influence of Kuchma no doubt, Kravchuk repeated his rival's view that whereas previously he had championed the notion that the individual should be for the state, now he believed that the state should serve the individual which would be best served by the adoption of a new post-Soviet constitution.[64] This transformation from a national democratic to liberal democratic position reflected Kuchma's success in convincing voters that preoccupation with state-building had led to neglect of other questions, such as the economy.

The Economic Crisis and Reform

Ukraine held the presidential elections during a time of acute economic crisis and after a period of severe hyperinflation. Yet, the economic crisis did not play as central a role in the elections as might have been expected. In the mistaken view of Mykola Mikhailchenko, domestic adviser to President Kravchuk, this was because 'The majority of Ukrainians are satisfied with the current path of reform.'[65]

Of the seven candidates, two (Lanovyi and Babych) had the most radical socio-economic programmes (although both included highly populist measures to distract voters from the unpopular measures in-evitable with shock therapy), while one candidate (Petro Talanchuk, former education minister) devoted little space to economic affairs, and another (Moroz) supported standard socialist and communist policies and criticised those who wished to 'experiment with one's own people'.[66] The remaining three candidates could be divided into two categories. Pliushch's policies were not very dissimilar to Kravchuk's, while Kuchma was one of the few candidates to emphasise the centrality of economics in his campaign platform and rhetoric.

Kuchma believed that other candidates had moved towards his pro-gramme of economic reform and that he was the first to call the economy 'catastrophic' and 'bankrupt' (describing Ukraine in this manner infuri-ated nationalists).[67] He described his difference with Kravchuk in simple terms – a vote for him meant a vote for 'change' whilst a vote for his main rival, Kravchuk, was a vote for 'more of the same'.[68]

Kuchma, like all of the other candidates apart from the two radicals (Babych and Lanovyi), supported a 'socially oriented economy', elements of which would even find favour with the socialist Moroz, whose policies were increasingly moving towards social democracy and in favour of a 'state-regulated market'.[69] But many of Kuchma's economic policies re-mained as hazy as did Kravchuk's and he, like Kravchuk, always insisted he remained in favour of evolutionary – not revolutionary – reform.[70] This could have been deliberate in order not to make him too unattractive for left-wing voters in the second round.

Although Kuchma's 'social market economy' may be similar to Kravchuk's, the difference between them was twofold. First, Kuchma would not shy away from increasing and normalising economic relations within the CIS and bilaterally with its member-states, especially Russia. Kuchma was unafraid, therefore, of stating that Ukraine could not extricate itself from its economic crisis without 're-establishing ties with Russia'[71] because Ukraine's economy could not function in the outside world.[72] Secondly, Kuchma, in contrast to Kravchuk, claimed to possess the 'political will' to implement economic reform and, again in contrast to Kravchuk, was unafraid of treading on people's toes in promoting his vision. In this manner he was closer to Yeltsin and, unlike Kravchuk, whose attempt to be all things to all men had led to stagnation.[73]

Kuchma's approach to the economy was different from the national democrats' (Kravchuk, Talanchuk or Pliushch) by placing it at the centre of his programme. Kuchma's description of himself as a pragmatist meant that politics would never take precedence over the economy.[74] 'Ukraine will be a real state only when the economy starts working, when production starts to increase, when we create a powerful economic system,' Kuchma emphasised, while complaining that Kravchuk's alliance with the national democrats had served to prioritise national symbols and statehood at the expense of the economy and individual rights.[75]

Kuchma, therefore, promised to conduct thorough market reforms in view of his belief that there was no turning back to the command administrative economy, just as there was no going back to the former USSR.[76] This would include reform and liberalisation of the tax system with only profits – not income – taxed, equal conditions for all forms of ownership, land would belong to all those who farmed it and could be sold if it were under buildings and factories, unproductive or for dachas.[77] But collective farms could not be allowed to disintegrate because 'we will all die.'[78]

The inability to appreciate that re-establishing economic ties with a Russia that was far ahead of Ukraine in terms of reform with a geopolitical agenda that regarded economic union as the prelude to political-military integration was also described as 'romantic' and 'populist' by the Kravchuk camp.[79] Kravchuk repeatedly pointed to Kuchma's performance as prime minister to argue that his policies and the legislation he had introduced had failed (and not, as Kuchma claimed, because the then president had blocked their implementation), a view that Viktor Pynzenyk, then deputy prime minister under Kuchma, also shared.[80] Kravchuk advised his rival: 'It's time to stop whining and stop exhibiting such shameful behaviour before the entire world. Be a man. You have to uphold your honour, not merely wag your tail.'[81]

Kravchuk insisted that Kuchma's emphasis on economic reform was 'populist' because a *rapid* transformation of the economy and improvement in living standards was impossible. Two and half years in office as president was insufficient time for this purpose.[82] Reforms were taking place, Kravchuk insisted, although he admitted they were going slowly. But he predicted that it would take at least 10–15 years to 'achieve the desired level'.[83] The experience accumulated in Kravchuk's term in office would enable him to improve the reforms if re-elected, Kravchuk claimed. Consequently, if he were re-elected Kravchuk would regard the result as a vote of confidence in his cautious, evolutionary policies which would merely require 'enrichment of the course according to the situation that has developed'.[84]

Kravchuk insisted he was in favour of reform: 'I would like to say that, both in my previous term [in office] and if I am elected this time, I did and shall take the position of reforms.'[85] But Kravchuk blamed the crisis on the fact that 'concepts' had still not been elaborated: 'We have not agreed on a single understanding of this issue.'[86] This statement reflected Kravchuk's penchant for consensus politics and his firm belief that revolutionary or radical reforms would lead to political and ethnic instability, as in the Russian Federation (the violence in Moscow in October 1993 between Yeltsin and the State Duma was pointed to as evidence of the folly of going down this path).[87] If re-elected, therefore, Kravchuk would 'consolidate the state and speed up reforms with the help of civic accord'.[88] But the drawing up of a programme satisfactory to everybody, from communists to radical free marketers, had proved impossible and led to stagnation under Kravchuk.

Organised Crime and Corruption

All the candidates backed populist calls for a struggle against organised crime and corruption. Pliushch promised to 'stop criminals profiting through impoverishing the overwhelming majority'.[89] But the greatest criticism came from Kuchma, who repeatedly said, 'What our leaders call reforms are nothing other than the utter plundering of an altogether wealthy country.'[90] Kravchuk retorted that he would, if re-elected, step up the struggle against organised crime and corruption. 'We must not make Kuchma into a hero – a fighter against corruption and the mafia. He never was and never will be,' Kravchuk added.[91] The truth of the matter was that all candidates included populist slogans in their election manifestos against organised crime and corruption, which, if they had been elected, would have been difficult to implement.

National Symbols and Language

Kuchma never raised the question of national symbols during the election campaign, a highly contentious issue in Ukraine which would have immediately added to the general mistrust about his patriotic credentials. On one occasion Kuchma did suggest adding crimson, the traditional colour of Ukrainian Cossack symbols, to the sky blue and yellow flag, but it was never pursued with any determination and was later quietly dropped.[92]

The communists, with nearly a quarter of deputies in the newly elected Ukrainian parliament, did raise the question for debate in the Supreme Council in autumn 1994 hoping that President Kuchma would back them as they had voted for him in the second round. But, unlike President Lukashenko in neighbouring Belarus, the communists did not find an ally in the newly elected president.

Kuchma, a Russian-speaking Ukrainian, began learning the Ukrainian language prior to the presidential elections for two reasons. First, both President Kravchuk and parliamentary speaker Moroz, like his predecessor Pliushch, spoke Ukrainian. Secondly, the law on presidential elections specified that candidates had to know the state language.

In Kuchma's view, the fact that a large proportion of ethnic Ukrainians' mother tongue was Russian did not signify that they were disloyal 'Little Russians', as Kravchuk, Pliushch and many national democrats argued.[93] A voter asked Kuchma why he wasn't fluent in Ukrainian, to which he replied, 'It is my problem, but it is a problem I share with a great number of Ukrainians who do not speak fluent Ukrainian.'[94]

But many Ukrainian-speakers remained suspicious of Kuchma.[95] Slava Kravchenko, a journalist specialising in women's issues, said, 'I oppose any reunification, cultural or otherwise, with Russia. If Kuchma becomes president, Ukraine will end up speaking Russian. We cannot have a man who speaks a language other than ours.'[96]

In fact, there were few differences between Kuchma and Kravchuk on this emotive question. *Both* Kravchuk and Kuchma supported the retention of Ukrainian as the sole state language, while favouring Russian as the second official language. During the election campaign in eastern and southern Ukraine, Kravchuk often talked in Russian.[97]

In the words of Kravchuk, 'If Ukrainian is to have a second official language, Ukraine will not turn for the worse. It will not stop being an independent state.'[98] The only difference was that, 'The national democrats forgive Kravchuk's promise to make Russian an official language, explain this as necessary at this political moment in time.'[99] The Writer's Union of

Ukraine associated the demand for Russian to be granted the status of an official language with Kuchma. This, they feared, 'could lead not to consolidation of the people, but even to quarrels and divisions of Ukraine. Official status of Russian language in Ukraine means the continuation of the process of deukrainianisation.'[100]

In other words, nationally conscious Ukrainians believed Kravchuk's warnings not to 'trust' Kuchma. 'What I fear most about Kuchma is that he would be on the phone to Moscow every five minutes,' Marta Okhmok, a resident of Donets'k, feared.[101]

Foreign and Defence Policy

The most contentious issue during the presidential elections proved to be foreign and defence policies. Which orientation should Ukraine follow – Europe or Eurasia? This was the highly simplistic manner in which the Kravchuk:Kuchma contest was portrayed.[102] Yet, undoubtedly, the manner in which candidates described Russia, in particular whether they viewed it as 'The Other' or as a 'Strategic Partner', influenced voters' attitudes.

Babych and Talanchuk devoted little attention to foreign and defence policies, but only Lanovyi of the seven candidates completely rejected any economic union with the CIS. Pliushch saw less need than most candidates to single out Russia for close relations. 'The fact that my mother-in-law lives in the Russian city of Rostov does not mean that we should form a single state with Russia,' he told residents of Dnipropetrovs'k.[103]

Moroz's election platform, despite his left-wing support, did not outline any policies in favour of political-military integration with Russia and the CIS. His Socialist Party stood for an independent, socialist Ukraine and its attitude towards the recent past was best encapsulated by Moroz: 'Anyone who does not miss the days of the Soviet Union does not have a heart; and anyone who thinks it can be brought back does not have a head.'[104]

Kuchma was heavily criticised for offering to transfer the entire Black Sea Fleet and lease Sevastopol as a base for the Fleet to Russia in return for energy supplies. Kravchuk asked, 'Where in the world will you find a presidential candidate already giving away national territory who says it is up to the people to decide what will happen?'[105] 'Imagine another country where a presidential candidate says Silesia, for instance, is not of key importance. It would cause a scandal of huge proportions. Here he gets applause,' Kravchuk added.[106]

Kuchma admitted that the Black Sea Fleet and Sevastopol questions were complex problems and 'there were no ready answers to these issues'.[107] He remained in favour, like Moroz, of transferring the Fleet to

Russia and leasing Sevastopol as a base. Both candidates, though, viewed this as a short-term lease, during which Russia would remove its Fleet to Russian or CIS naval bases. Kuchma claimed that his views on how to solve the Black Sea Fleet and Sevastopol questions had been proposed while he was prime minister in spring 1993 and were based on world experience of leasing foreign bases, that Ukraine could not finance the fleet and did not require it militarily.[108] All these arguments had been accepted by Kravchuk himself when he attended the Massandra summit in September 1993 with the prime minister, Kuchma. During the election campaign, though, the national democrats had conveniently forgotten Kravchuk's Cassandra [i.e. disaster] at Massandra and associated these policies only with Kuchma.[109]

Nevertheless, Kuchma repeatedly emphasised that 'There is no going back to the Soviet Union',[110] an argument he has repeated since his election as president, 'because a return to the past is impossible'[111] and, 'I have never proposed that Ukraine return to the Russian empire'.[112] On no occasion did Kuchma campaign for a political or military union with Russia or the CIS; indeed, these were even absent from his election programme. Kuchma, exasperated, stated in one interview: 'I have never, not even in my sleep, ever said anywhere to anyone anything about a political union with Russia.'[113]

But Kuchma did back Ukraine's full (in contrast to associate) membership in the CIS Economic Union because 'Losing the Russian market is tantamount to death for Ukraine'. Both Kuchma and Kravchuk backed Ukraine's membership of the CIS Economic Union, although Kuchma accused Kravchuk of not backing his words with deeds. Kuchma believed that this lack of action in the CIS Economic Union had harmed Ukraine's economic interests. Kuchma proposed instead that Ukraine should take an active role in the process of Eurasian economic integration rather than playing the role of a passive associate member romantically believing that integration with the West was likely.[114] But it was precisely such sentiments that caused doubt to emerge about Kuchma's patriotic credentials. One Kyiv voter asked him at a rally: 'Are you running for president of Ukraine or governor of Little Russia?'[115]

Kuchma's championing of the necessity of an economic union to alleviate its economic crisis proved popular as a populist alternative to radical reform. Viktoria Miroshnichenko, an employee of a turbine factory in Donets'k, typified this faith placed in the 'renewal of economic ties' as the quick-fix panacea for Ukraine's economic ills: 'We rely on Russian raw materials, energy and spare parts to keep our enterprises working. It doesn't take a genius to see we need a common currency with Russia and the removal of trade barriers.'[116] Kravchuk cautioned though, that whilst Russian domestic energy prices were still subsidised (in contrast to the world prices charged Ukraine since 1993), customs barriers had to remain between Ukraine and Russia.[117]

After all, it had been on Kravchuk's instructions that then prime minister, Kuchma, had drawn up proposals to establish such an Economic Union with Belarus and Russia in mid-1993. But under Kravchuk Ukraine had remained only an associate member (as it still has under President Kuchma. Kuchma has also refused to rejoin the rouble zone for the same reasons – threat to sovereignty).[118] During the election campaign Kuchma had argued that one of the policies to extricate Ukraine from its economic crisis was by joining the CIS Economic Union as a full member. But even Kuchma cautioned that 'Economic Union [with Russia] is not merely something fanciful that Kuchma has dreamed up. It's reality. My dream – and it is still a dream – is to build a sovereign, democratic state without any federation of any sort.'[119] Kuchma pointed to economic integration as in accord with world trends in the Baltic republics, North America and western Europe.

Nevertheless, Kuchma's rejection of 'self-isolation', his descriptions of the economic ties inherited from the former USSR as 'a complex network of blood and veins' and his support for the restoration of 'economic, spiritual and cultural links' with Russia made his patriotic credentials highly suspect in the eyes of certain Ukrainian regions and political groups.[120] After all, many of them preferred these veins to be cut open and the blood drained out in order to forestall the revival of these links and Ukraine's 'return to Europe'.

Kravchuk also never called for secession from the CIS, although he, unlike Kuchma, had fewer illusions about its effectiveness. Kravchuk even rejected any accusations of 'isolationism', pointing to the signing by Ukraine of 300 documents in the CIS and 73 with Russia. Kravchuk's policies towards Russia would remain the same as before, that is a readiness for co-operation and the search for normal, equal and friendly relations of partnership. Policies towards Russia had only two options – to develop either good or very good relations. No third option existed, Kravchuk believed. But – and this is where he differed more from Kuchma, who seemed to prefer to ignore the problems he encountered during his term as prime minister (see earlier) – Kravchuk's experiences as president had meant he had been unable to establish successfully either of the two options, 'when Russia is constantly trying to bring us to our knees'.[121]

Kuchma's preference during the presidential elections to ignore the Russian great power policies and pressures even he had spoken out against as prime minister may have been a deliberate policy to woo Russian-speaking voters. He therefore rejected calls by Kravchuk–Pliushch for Ukraine to become a 'counter-balance' to Russia and opposed building an independent state, 'on the basis of anti-Russian feeling'.[122] Kuchma's rejection of 'self-isolation' and anti-Russian policies, support for retaining historical, cultural and spiritual links with Russia were not policies that Kravchuk openly expressed an interest in. Kuchma accused Kravchuk of blaming the economic crisis solely on external factors while neglecting his own mismanagement of the economy.[123] Kravchuk should have admitted the economic problems and talked not only of sovereign statehood but also of a sovereign economy.[124]

These policies nevertheless proved crucial in winning votes for Kuchma from Russian-speaking Ukrainians and Russians as well as ensuring Moscow's support in the elections.[125] 'He understands that we do not see Russia as enemy number one, as do many politicians in Kyiv', an employee of his former *Pivdenmash* plant said.[126]

Kravchuk and Kuchma both stressed their desire for equal relations with Russia. Kuchma was portrayed though as Ukraine's 'Lukashenko', somebody who wanted 'to unite [with Russia] and become unequal'. Kravchuk agreed with Kuchma that 'Ukraine cannot live and develop without equal and friendly relations with Russia.'[127] But he criticised those who servilely expressed their love for Russia and the need to restore ties (a clear reference to Kuchma) because of the belief that this would win votes. But, nobody bothered to ask, 'if Russia declared its love for us', Kravchuk complained.[128] 'I want everyone to live in his own flat and drink tea with his neighbours and friends. Others want three to share the kitchen, five to share the bath and six to share the toilet,' Kravchuk complained about some of his fellow candidates.[129]

Kuchma's problems in establishing equal relations with Russia since his election clearly showed Moscow's preference for a leader such as Lukashenko, who openly looked to Russia as the leader of the pack in the CIS. Kuchma had noted, though relatively early, 'I am categorically against what Belarus is doing because it is not partnership with Russia but subordination.'[130]

In choosing between Kravchuk and Kuchma Russia clearly preferred the latter, although there are indications that Moscow also wrongly perceived of Kuchma as a Ukrainian 'Lukashenko'.[131] Kuchma's failure as president to normalise relations completely with Russia has led to a preference to persevere in these attempts without raising the political temperature between both countries, preferring to ignore them rather than publicly air Ukraine's grievances (unlike Kravchuk).

Clearly, though, Kravchuk preferred to regard Ukraine as a 'European' country even though he contradicted himself on occasion by stressing that 'Our greatest priority is co-operation with the CIS'.[132] His election broadcasts on television portrayed his international image, meeting Western leaders and signing the Partnership and Co-operation agreement with the European Union. Some voters argued in favour of the need to concentrate on 'traditional friends', whilst others looked to Kravchuk's record in establishing Ukraine's presence on the international stage, contacts which would be lost if he was replaced.[133]

Kuchma's patriotic credentials were further marred by his criticism of the lack of Western aid and support which forced Ukraine to look to Eurasia and, especially, Russia. Kuchma repeated a theme he had often raised as prime minister, namely that Ukraine's geo-political options were limited because it had been abandoned by the West.[134] Kuchma was highly sceptical about Western promises of aid: 'Where are they, those businessmen in the West and other countries who you say are eager to invest in our economy? These are illusions.'[135] To large areas of Ukraine, including the capital city, and certain political groups it was precisely the West and 'Europe' that were attractive, the criticism of which made them suspicious that Kuchma backed 'pro-Russian' (Eurasian) policies.

VOTERS

Political Parties

Radical right Nationalists, such as the DSU, who had always been critical of Kravchuk's nationalist credentials, saw only two Ukrainian patriotic candidates – Talanchuk and Pliushch.[136] But Dmytro Pavlychko, chairman of the Democratic Coalition 'Ukraine' election bloc, the body that united the more mainstream national democrats, typified the view of this section of voters: 'This is a second referendum on independence. That is why it is so crucial for Kravchuk to win.'[137] Pavlychko called on all patriotic forces to rally in defence of independence and prevent the victory of anti-Ukrainian forces because only Kravchuk was the 'guarantor of our statehood'.[138] They, therefore, unconditionally backed Kravchuk in the second round. The Congress of National Democratic Forces, with a similar composition to Pavlychko's electoral bloc, was even more forthright: 'Today he [Kuchma] wants to be president to realise his idea of an alliance with Russia.'[139]

Rukh, the largest of the national democratic parties, did not feel it was ready to co-operate with Kuchma after the elections. Rukh had preferred Lanovyi in the first round, but in the second it reluctantly backed Kravchuk as the lesser of two evils. Kuchma, in Rukh's eyes, had to be stopped because he was 'the henchman of [Russian] imperialist forces',[140] somebody 'who will lead Ukraine into the Russian swamp'.[141] A vote against Kuchma and Moroz was a vote for statehood, Rukh attempted to convince itself. Chornovil himself, who had had poor relations with Kravchuk since the December 1991 presidential elections, admitted: 'Who would have ever thought I would one day support Kravchuk.'[142]

It regarded the results not as a victory for Kuchma but as a defeat for Kravchuk, who had proclaimed his adherence to the ideals of statehood, political and economic reform, but had not backed up these words with action. But the inability of the national democrats to promote their own candidate in the 1994 presidential elections, in contrast to December 1991, showed the weakness of political parties to influence the outcome of the elections.[143] After the victory of Kuchma, national democrats looked to his policies in the hope of ensuring that he would continue policies of state-building and would not turn out to be a 'Ukrainian Lukashenko' after all. The Democratic Coalition 'Ukraine' stated: 'In the new president we would like to see a guarantee of sovereignty, territorial integrity and non-infringement of Ukraine's borders.'[144] They attempted to play down the significance of Kuchma's victory, which 'was not desirable', but was 'not a tragedy', according to the Ukrainian Republican Party.[145] An editorial in Kyiv's evening newspaper *Vechirnyi Kyiv* (15 July 1994), which had backed Pliushch in the first round and Kravchuk in the second, also believed it should not be regarded as a 'tragedy', but a new chapter in Ukraine's history because the choice had always been between two people, 'who had failed to fulfil the people's hopes'.[146]

The small Constitutional Democratic Party of Ukraine backed Lanovyi in the first round and instructed all their candidates for posts on local councils to back him.[147] They were in agreement with Kravchuk's initial decision not to run in the elections which was 'no doubt for Ukraine's good'.[148] After the elections, Zolotaryov, the leader of the Constitutional Democrats, did not welcome Kuchma's victory: 'We had a west Ukrainian nationalist and got an east Ukrainian nationalist. There will be no considerable changes in the near future.'[149] They regretted the fact that Kuchma's idea of reform was limited when Ukraine required 'a politician with liberal views who can introduce tough economic reforms...'

The Liberal Democratic Party of Ukraine was highly concerned at the possibility that the socialist presidential candidate, Moroz, might win, which would lead to the collapse of Ukraine as an independent state. In their view, only one candidate was capable of introducing reform – Lanovyi.[150] In both rounds, the MRBR wholeheartedly backed Kuchma, who was also co-chairman of this election bloc with Grynev.

In contrast, the Liberal Party of Ukraine took a different line – it backed Kravchuk in both rounds. They credited Kravchuk with having developed Ukraine's parliamentary-presidential system so that power and responsibilities were clearly separated and domestic and international issues were dealt with competently. They supported Kravchuk's programme of state-building, which would be capable of 'building a law-based state on the basis of common sense, a market economy, democracy and ensure progress.'[151] Kravchuk had ensured peace, and 'Society knows his liberal state activities and has the right to be entrusted with Ukraine's fate. We Liberals are for Leonid Kravchuk because his name is also tied to the course of contemporary Ukraine, independence and for his maintenance of wise relations with all close and far away countries.'

In L'viv the *Nova Khvylia* (New Wave)[152] election bloc campaigned not for Kravchuk 'but the idea he stood for' – Ukraine's integration with Europe. In their eyes, Kuchma's campaign was dominated by calls for Ukraine's domination by Russia and therefore he would 'not be our president'. Originally, they had intended to back Pliushch (not Lanovyi, the usual Liberal choice) for the first round, but clearly saw early in the campaign that Kuchma and Kravchuk were the only serious candidates. 'Although we have certain reservations about him, and we are particularly dissatisfied with his indecisive attitude to economic reform and his personnel policy, *Nova Khvylia* sees no alternative to Kravchuk.'[153] In the event of Kuchma's victory and Ukraine's forcible entry into the CIS, *Nova Khvylia* would be ready to undertake radical civil disobedience: 'Then would be the time to raise people in defence of statehood with all available, bloodless methods.'[154]

The Citizens' Forum of Odesa, like many liberal groups, also backed Lanovyi in the first round. They feared that the results of the second round might have led to bloodshed and a split in the Ukrainian state. Kuchma won owing to the larger demographic weight of eastern and southern Ukraine, his 'pro-Russianism' and Kravchuk's 'inertia'. The Professionals Fund of Kharkiv, a civic group uniting Russian-language intellectuals, likewise did not give Kuchma their full backing. Like their Odesa counterparts, they feared civil war and a split in the country if Kuchma came to power. Many of these liberal parties and civic groups based their attitudes towards Kuchma on his weak programme of reform and support for statehood. They may have backed Russian as a second official language in local areas, but not federalism.

Initially, both the communists and socialists proposed their respective leaders as presidential candidates – Symonenko (who later withdrew) and Moroz.[155] The fourth extraordinary congress of the Socialist Party of Ukraine proposed Moroz as a candidate not from an 'extreme left-wing force' but a 'party of the centre left'.[156] After Symonenko withdrew, the Communist Party of Ukraine, Socialist Party of Ukraine, Peasant Party of Ukraine, Agricultural Trade Unions and Association of War Veterans issued a joint statement backing Moroz as the only candidate who could change things for the better.[157] This new alliance of the radical left was backed by 123 newly elected members of parliament who backed Moroz as the only candidate who would renew broken ties with the former USSR, eliminate conflict between the executive and legislative branches and support social welfare.[158]

The Communist Party of the Crimea preferred Kuchma, but this was dependent on three conditions – his rejection of nationalism, declaration in favour of unity into one state of the former USSR beginning in the economic field, and a socialist orientation. As for the Communist Party of Ukraine (KPU), they remained critical of Kuchma 'because his stand on certain issues is incomprehensible'. The communists liked Kuchma's idea of closer relations with Russia and tougher policies against organised crime. But they rejected any privatisation of land and state industry.[159]

At a plenum of the central committee of the KPU on 2 July 1994, they instructed their members not to vote for Kravchuk in the second round. Although no clear instructions were given to communists to vote for Kuchma, Symonenko believed that 'in all probability most communists will cast their votes for Leonid Kuchma.'[160]

The KPU was banned for allegedly supporting the *coup d'état* in August 1991. A new Communist Party was registered in October 1993 with no legal claims to the property and assets of its predecessor. It was hostile to Kravchuk whom it regards as a 'nationalist traitor'. Kravchuk accused the then newly elected left-wing majority in parliament of attempting to discredit him by levying corruption charges against him. 'Who gave the communists the right to go to parliament's tribune and practically call for the annihilation of the head of state?' Kravchuk asked.[161] Kravchuk linked the attack by the communists against him as an attempt to remove those who dissolved the former USSR, then denounce the CIS and revive the USSR.[162]

Civic and Social Groups

Women voters account for 55 per cent of the electorate and are therefore an important constituency. Kravchuk was clearly a favourite with them and he assiduously courted women's civic groups. Kravchuk's patriarchal looks and his emphasis on his ability to steer Ukraine away from conflicts made him popular with women. In the words of one woman voter, 'Leonid Kravchuk is our guardian angel. We like him as a man. He looks like a president. Kuchma doesn't.' Maria Oliynyk, head of the Union of Ukrainian Women, did not emphasise Kravchuk's 'good looks' (in contrast to Kuchma's 'dowdiness') but his experience in affairs of state and the fact that 'Kravchuk is the guarantor of stability in our society'.[163]

Pensioners, like women, are also conservative voters in Ukraine. Again, they are a large voter constituency (10 million) who need to be wooed by prospective presidential candidates. Few, if any, pensioners have experienced any benefits from Ukrainian independence or the transition to a market economy. 'It is simply difficult to trust our leaders because they have promised much but have done little.' 'When we got independence, everything went downhill,' one pensioner complained.[164] But Kravchuk remained popular with pensioners for two reasons. First, as with women voters, he emphasised continuity. Secondly, pensioners looked to his ability to maintain stability. Some pensioners, though, were also attracted by the idea of closer ties to Russia as proposed by Kuchma.[165]

Young people are notorious for their voting apathy. In voting behaviour they are similar to pensioners, believing that Kuchma would take Ukraine further backwards than Kravchuk. Taras Pastushenko, leader of the Union of Ukrainian Students, reflected student opinion when he complained that in independent Ukraine young people's views were ignored (in contrast to 1990–1). Many were therefore indifferent or cynical: 'The romance and illusions of democracy have melted away in the economic chaos of everyday life,' Oles Doniy, a student activist bemoaned.[166] Lanovyi was a favourite candidate with many students in the first round. In the second round, some may have voted for Kravchuk, although they were angered by his appointment of Vitalii Masol as prime minister in May 1994 in a vain attempt to win left-wing support.[167]

Religion

Orthodox believers remain the largest religious denomination in Ukraine, but they are divided into three camps. The Ukrainian Orthodox Church has the largest number of parishes and is under the jurisdiction of the Russian patriarchate. The Ukrainian Orthodox Church–Kyiv Patriarch (UPTs-KP) separated from the Ukrainian Orthodox Church in 1991–2 and was slated by then President Kravchuk to become the nucleus of a state Orthodox Church. The Ukrainian Autocephalous Orthodox Church (UAPTs) inherited the traditions of the UAPTs from the 1920s which had been kept alive in the Ukrainian diaspora. For a brief period between 1992 and 1993 the UAPTs and the UPTs-KP united into one body.

Understandably, therefore, religious leaders also had their favourite candidates. The UPTs-KP believed that voters should back Kravchuk because 'He is experienced and a guarantor of Ukraine's independence.' The UPTs, on the other hand, tended to back Kuchma because it felt hostility from the Kravchuk leadership, which had supported the UPTs-KP as the 'State Church'. Kravchuk's offer to transfer the Pecherska-Lavra Monastery to its control failed to win the allegiance of the UPTs. The hierarchy of the Ukrainian Greek Catholic Church (or Uniate Church), based mainly in the three Galician *oblasts* and Trans-Carpathia, had to tell its priests to stop openly campaigning for Kravchuk. Likewise, the Jews (0.9 per cent of the Ukrainian population) and Muslims (who are mainly Crimean Tartars [0.3 per cent of the Ukrainian population]) backed Kravchuk.[168]

The Armed Forces and Civil–Military Relations

Military civic groups, such as the Ukrainian Cossacks and Union of Ukrainian Officers (SOU),[169] are firmly based in the national democratic camp. The commander of the Cossacks, Major-General Volodymyr Muliava,[170] and the sixth congress of the SOU therefore backed Kravchuk in the presidential elections.[171]

Both Kravchuk and Kuchma courted the armed forces. Kravchuk, as commander-in-chief, appealed to the fact that he was associated in the eyes of the public with building the Ukrainian armed forces as the guarantor of Ukrainian statehood. Kravchuk also accused Kuchma of wanting to give away the Black Sea Fleet and Sevastopol. Kravchuk admitted to military officers that 'There is insufficient money in the budget to finance the army in its current form. The question is quite simple – do we look after the harvest or maintain the army? The choice must be clear even to those sitting here.'[172] During the elections the Ministry of Defence had increased salaries twofold, but Kravchuk had refused to sign the order, believing that if he had, he would have been accused of trying to buy military votes.

Kravchuk was often shown on state television alongside the military at public ceremonies. On one occasion, he was seen presenting a ceremonial flag to a paratroop regiment in Bolgrad, near Odesa and then dining with troops. He told those present that Ukraine's armed forces were defensive, but that they were also 'prepared to defend their land and sovereignty and the inviolability of state borders'.[173] Kravchuk, therefore, linked his fate to those of the armed forces, both institutions and personages, who could only be trusted to fulfil these functions.

In contrast, Kuchma appealed to the military as one of 'theirs' from the Military-Industrial Complex. He also appealed to their frustration over socio-economic problems facing officers whose faith in Kravchuk's ability to fulfil his December 1991 election promises (for example, providing apartments for officers) had evaporated. 'I would like once again to see respect for people in uniform as was the case after World War Two,' Kuchma argued.[174]

Industrialists

Industrialists were divided during the elections between those whose main export markets were the West, who supported Kravchuk, and those who relied on the CIS, who backed Kuchma. The metallurgical sector, in particular, strongly backed Kravchuk with whom was associated the signing of a Partnership and Co-operation Agreement with the EU. The metallurgical sector earns 70 per cent of Ukraine's hard currency, has modernised its equipment and exports largely to hard currency-earning countries. Donets'k steelmakers nominated Kravchuk for president and established supporter's clubs to re-elect him.[175]

The directors of plants such as *Krivorizhstal*, the main steel mill in Krivyi Rih, had little interest in Kuchma's election platform of 'reviving economic ties to Russia'. 'Last year we sent three billion roubles worth of production to Russia but we never got paid. Can Kuchma tell me just who broke our links, Russia or Ukraine? I know of no country more shameless than Russia,' the director, Mykola Omes, said.[176] Alexander Bulianda, general director of *Azovstal*, backed Kravchuk because they argued that Kuchma's background in the Military-Industrial Complex made him 'see the old system through rose-coloured glasses'. If Kravchuk was re-elected, he believed that he would allow the Cabinet of Ministers to run the economy while Kravchuk concerned himself with politics.[177]

The nuclear power industry was also a strong backer of Kravchuk because of Ukraine's increasing reliance upon this sector to limit its dependence on imported oil and gas. Other sectors which backed

Kravchuk included trade and chemicals. The coal industry, though, was hostile to Kravchuk and he, when touring eastern Ukraine, largely ignored them in favour of the steel mills. Few coalminers or directors of mines had any faith in his programme to put new life into the industry. Some directors also backed Kravchuk's calls to postpone the presidential elections if he agreed to revise his policies. Two of the areas singled out by Kravchuk were the payments crisis and foreign trade,[178] while Kravchuk agreed to support a policy of radical reforms if he was re-elected.[179]

The Military-Industrial Complex, in contrast, backed Kuchma, who had been director of *Pivdenmash*, the world's former largest nuclear missile plant in Dnipropetrovs'k which employs 50 000 people. In the view of Kuchma, 'No one is waiting for us in the West. No one needs our ageing technology. Eighty per cent of production depends on raw materials from Russia.'[180] *Pivdenmash* was on a four-day week and had no orders from the West – only from Russia – for satellites and rocket launchers. The deputy director of *Pivdenmash*, Mykola Mezhuyev, was convinced that 'You can be sure 50 000 people who work here are going to vote for Kuchma and integration with Russia.'[181]

Kuchma was also perceived in a populist manner as someone who could provide 'a shock-free and painless transition towards a civilised economy, towards a democratic, socially-oriented society'.[182] But new businessmen in eastern Ukraine, such as those who supported the Liberal Party, were alienated by Kuchma's 'pro-Russianism' and lack of a clear-cut reform programme.

In Zaporizhzhia these divisions were also present in two 'clans' within the industrialist lobby *vis-à-vis* Kravchuk:Kuchma.[183] One 'clan' had little interest in the CIS market and felt confidant of operating within a market economy. The second 'clan' included many enterprises which were loss-making or likely to be in the transition to a market economy and felt a reliance on the CIS and Russian markets.

The directors of these plants had direct political (as well as economic) influence over their large number of employees. Many of these employees will vote 'as the director tells them to'. During 1992–3 many members of this first 'clan' were brought to Kyiv to work within the Kravchuk administration.

Within the first 'clan' one could include the metallurgical enterprises (such as *Zaporizhstal* and *Dniprospetstal*) as well as the Zaporizhzhian Transformer Plant. Both of these groups had managed to reorient their exports quickly to Latin America, the Middle East, China and East Asia in a move to lessen their reliance on Russia and the CIS.[184] Sixty per cent of *Zaporizhstal's* production now goes for export outside the former

USSR with the proportion represented by raw materials declining in favour of semi-finished and finished products. *Zaporizhstal* has also managed to increase its exports to Germany, Switzerland and the Far East.

Since 1985, these enterprises had been transformed from being merely industrial units into 'mini-princedoms', which included production, agriculture (called 'kibbutzim' by the locals), banks (e.g. *Slovianskyi* and *Metalurg*), intermediary services, trading and commercial firms. These enterprises were, therefore, more adaptable to face the economic crisis which engulfed the former USSR from the late 1980s and the 'breakdown of ties' with Russia and the CIS from 1992.

The second 'clan' were more closely tied to the Kuchma camp, that is enterprises belonging to the Military-Industrial Complex such as *Motor-Sich*, which specialised in the production of helicopters and military transport aeroplanes.[185] For Russia, the loss of the *Motor-Sich* plant was a major blow. Other's plants which remain crucial to the Russian aerospace industry include aluminium and titanium–magnesium plants. Most of these plants rely exclusively on state credits and would be declared bankrupt in a market economy. They, therefore, see little way out of their predicament except through the 'renewal of ties' with Russia, a major policy plank of Kuchma's presidential election programme.

It is not surprising, therefore, that Kuchma has repaid his debt to them for backing him in the 1994 presidential elections by supporting Industrial-Financial Groups which are geared to helping the second 'clan' of enterprises from escaping both the economic crisis and easing their transition towards a market economy. The directors of the second 'clan' are grouped together in the Inter-Regional Association of Enterprises, which included the most 'pro-Russian' plants of left-bank Ukraine, especially within the Military-Industrial Complex, and the Party of Labour, the political offshoot of the Union of Industrialists and Entrepreneurs of Ukraine, which Kuchma headed between 1993 and 1994. This large directors' lobby by April 1995 had been largely successful in halting the radical (monetarist) economic reform programme launched by President Kuchma in October 1994.

On 27 March 1994, outside Kyiv, a conference was held of the directors of the former USSR's largest (largely loss-making) plants on the initiative of the Union of Industrialists and Entrepreneurs of Ukraine, the chairman of which was Kuchma. The mood of the meeting very much reflected the programme later promoted by Kuchma during the presidential elections. The conference heard calls against 'separatism' and 'capitalism' and in favour of less reform and greater attention and credits to the state sector.

In the words of one director who attended the conference, the period until then 'was a temporary period of victory by those forces who don't want to see the economic force of one geo-political complex.'[186] The conference established an Inter-State Association of Directors, and may have been a valuable source of funds for the Kuchma presidential campaign (Kuchma is alleged to have spent the most of any of the candidates). One newspaper commented that the 'revival of the former Union can begin from the reintegration of the industrial *nomenklatura*'.[187]

CONCLUSION

The panic among many parties, officials and voters after Kuchma's election victory proved to be without foundation. Kuchma immediately set out to heal regional divisions and promised to work in the interests of Ukraine as a whole. He faced the same problems as Kravchuk had done after his election in December 1991; namely, if he ruled on the basis of his electorate only he would not be in a position to unite Ukraine and rule the whole country, and would merely be 'a *gubernator* of a Little Russian province of a socialist superstate'.[188] Kuchma would be unlikely to ignore the wishes of 12 million voters or 45 per cent of the electorate who had voted for Kravchuk, an editorial in the newspaper *Vechimyi Kyiv* (15 July 1994) believed.

In reality, whoever won the elections would have had to make concessions: Kravchuk towards the east (he had already attempted this by promoting the conservative Masol to the post of prime minister in May 1994) and Kuchma towards the west (greater emphasis upon state-building and defence of Ukraine's territorial integrity).[189] 'The involvement of areas such as the Crimea, Donets'k and Luhans'k in the electoral process not only secured Kuchma's victory but also legitimised Ukrainian statehood where it had been least popular,' one author has pointed out.[190]

To describe Kravchuk as a 'nationalist' is as mistaken as claiming that Kuchma is 'pro-Russian'. Kravchuk never called himself a nationalist and his support for multi-culturalism, pluralism and liberalism in his domestic policies support this view. His speeches do not mention traditional nationalist appeals to the 'national struggle', 'national goals', 'national sacrifice' and 'national mission'. This lack of nationalistic slogans was matched by his lack of nationalistic policies,[191] such as his alleged support for 'Ukrainianisation'.[192]

Both Kravchuk and Kuchma were representatives of the Party of Power. The only 'outsider' to the Party of Power was Lanovyi, the one presidential candidate who backed radical reform. The differences between Kravchuk and Kuchma lay more in their personalities, which evolved as a consequence of their respective different career paths respectively within the Communist Party and the Military-Industrial Complex.[193] In addition, Kravchuk's and Kuchma's different policy priorities reflected those of the regions where they were born and later worked (western and eastern Ukraine respectively). It would be mistaken to believe that Russian-speaking Ukrainians, many of whom voted for Kuchma, are disloyal to the idea of an independent Ukrainian state.

There were indeed more policies that united than divided Kravchuk and Kuchma. If one were to characterise their political views, then they were both centrists. But whereas Kravchuk was always closer to the centre-right, Kuchma has centre-left views. Hence Kravchuk had close co-operative re-lations as president (which he has maintained since his defeat) with the national democrats, whose main base of support is western and central Ukraine and the capital city Kyiv (where he won a majority of votes in the summer 1994 presidential elections) as well as among the majority of the Ukrainian diaspora (the bulk of whom are from western Ukraine). Kuchma, in contrast, came to power as a result of an alliance of social-democrats and some liberals and the industrial directors' foremost lobby, the Union of Industrialists and Entrepreneurs of Ukraine, in the form of the Inter-Regional Bloc of Reforms. Both of these structures, as well as these political tendencies, are dominant in eastern and southern Ukraine, where Kuchma won the majority of votes in the summer 1994 presidential elections.

Those who voted for Kravchuk have no argument with Kuchma's state-building policies, his defence of national interests and territorial integrity and his support for economic and political reform. The similarity in poli-cies between Kravchuk and Kuchma is even true in the socio-economic field. Radical monetarist reform was dropped in April 1995 after just eight months, in favour of a specific 'Ukrainian path' to a social market economy under state guidance.

The main debate within Ukraine and the arguments made against Kuchma rest on his lack of attention to the national question, particularly after he said that the 'national idea had not worked'. Kuchma's policies and views, as a Russian-speaking Ukrainian from the highly denation-alised eastern Ukraine, reflect the lack of prioritisation that the national idea has among the electorate that voted for him. It is this question that may be Kuchma's undoing – it is not disputed that Kuchma is a *derzavh-nyk* but will he build a *derzhava* or a *gosudartsvo*?[194] This was the main theme which dominated discussions during the Congress of the Ukrainian Intelligentsia held in Kyiv on 11 November 1995.[195]

It is only by analysing the large number of issues that were raised in the political, economic and security spheres during the 1994 presidential elections that we can see how viewing Kuchma as 'unpatriotic' and 'pro-Russian' does not allow us to understand his policies since his election, for example *vis-à-vis* the Crimea, which have at times shown him to be more of a *derzhavnyk* than his predecessor.

3 The Crimea Returns to Ukraine

'It's like a game of roulette. We don't know who they are or what they stand for.'

(Crimean voter)[1]

'... we again appear to be better interests of the Ukrainian state than the Ukrainians themselves.'

(Crimean Tartars)[2]

The Crimea has on at least two occasions nearly become another 'hot spot' among the many that have engulfed the former USSR since its disintegration in December 1991.[3] The two peaks of crisis in relations between Ukraine and the Crimea occurred in May 1992, when the peninsula declared its independence, and during the first half of 1994, when the Russia bloc came to power in the Crimea.

The Ukrainian leadership can be credited, though, with possessing the political skills to refrain from adopting a violent solution to the Crimean problem, in stark contrast to that employed by Boris Yeltsin in Chechnya in December 1994. Violent policies to suppress separatism have not been successful in the former USSR, and the most glaring example of the failure of this use of force has been witnessed in Chechnya.

The use of a variety of non-violent methods by the Ukrainian leadership to restore the Crimea to its sovereignty were successful. Within the space of only one year – between spring 1994 and spring 1995 – support for pro-Russian separatism in the Crimea collapsed, and the leadership of the autonomous region was replaced by pro-Ukrainian local leaders. The credit for this change in political climate in the Crimea should also be given to the incompetence of the nationalistic Russia bloc, which came to power in early 1994 with a 'ragbag of promises' that they could not but fail to implement.[4]

Earlier events in the Crimea and its relations with Kyiv are not covered in this chapter.[5] Rather this chapter surveys the three crucial years from 1994 to 1996 when the Crimea evolved from open confrontation with Kyiv to the stabilisation of its relations with Ukraine, as reflected by the adoption of the Ukrainian law enacting the new draft Crimean constitution in May 1996.

ELECTIONS IN THE CRIMEA

Presidential Elections

During the first round of the January 1994 Crimean presidential elections six candidates competed for the post, of which only one, Nikolai Bagrov, was 'pro-Ukrainian'. Of the other candidates only one – Vladimir Verkoshansky, a local businessman – focused on economic affairs. Other businessmen backed Bagrov, who portrayed himself (in a manner similar to Leonid Kravchuk) as the candidate of 'stability'.[6] 'We support Bagrov only because we see him as a peaceful way to economic self-determination. If Crimea declared itself independent it will definitely end in war. Kravchuk, as President, would be obliged to guarantee the territorial integrity of Ukraine', local businessmen feared.[7]

Yet Bagrov, like his fellow Party of Power colleagues in Ukraine (either individually or through similar groups such as the Labour Party of Ukraine, the Party of Power in the Donbas), did not back privatisation or radical economic reform. In Bagrov's view, foreign investment could not be allowed in the Crimea because 'Morgans, Rockefellers and other big capitalists from the West will buy up the whole of the Crimea'.[8] Bagrov was also cautious about private property, especially on land, because 'We are unsure yet just how much Crimean land is worth'.[9]

One of Bagrov's main backers was the Party of Economic Revival of the Crimea (PEVK), the party of the 'fat cats',[10] which linked together the clannish interests of the post-communist Crimean *nomenklatura* (or the Party of Power). It therefore was firmly opposed to both the Russia bloc and the communists. Ironically, the backing that Bagrov received as presidential candidate from the December 1993 PEVK congress (after a proposal to back Ivan Yermakov was supported by only a minority of delegates) transformed him into a 'great Ukrainian patriot'[11] – the very same individual who, as Crimean parliamentary speaker, had orchestrated the May 1992 declaration of independence. Other groups which backed Bagrov were allied to the PEVK, such as the Party of Social Guarantees of the Crimea, the National Concord Party of the Crimea and the Agrarian Party of the Crimea.

Viktor Mezhak, leader of the People's Party of the Crimea, was refused registration as a presidential candidate as his party had registered on

25 November 1993 four days after the deadline for registration of candidates.[12] He therefore gave his support to Meshkov and joined the Russia bloc. Vladimir Shuvaynikov was expelled from his own Russian Party of the Crimea on the eve of the presidential elections for 'betrayal of the Crimea's and Russia's interests' – the result of his refusal to join the Russia bloc, thereby splitting the pro-Russian vote (Meshkov accused him of preventing his victory in the first round).[13] 'We have a common Russian history. Imperial perhaps, but this empire united us,' Shuvaynikov argued, placing less emphasis on his 'Crimeanness' than on his ethnic Russian identity.[14]

Other pro-Russian candidates from the Russian Society, Movement of Voters for the Crimean Republic, led by Nikolai Tiuriyev, and other constituent members of the Russia bloc had dropped their candidacy in favour of Meshkov (unlike Shuvaynikov). A close ally of Meshkov's was the Movement of Voters for the Crimean Republic whose inaugural congress in December 1993 was marred by an 'anti-Ukrainian character'. The Movement was the prime organiser of the Russia bloc; in late 1995 it was threatened with disbandment by the Sevastopol prosecutor for inciting ethnic tension and threatening Ukraine's territorial integrity.[15]

Meshkov, presidential candidate from the Russia bloc, was also leader of the Republican Movement of the Crimea (RDK), the main body which had campaigned for Crimean separatism in 1991–3. His view of the Russia bloc was to unite all patriotic forces into one 'great anti-Bagrov bloc', who 'stand for Crimea within Russia and for the independent development of the Crimean Republic ...'. He was especially critical of Bagrov for having used the RDK to exert pressure on Kyiv to extract a large degree of autonomy only to be ditched by him after he had obtained what he sought from Kyiv. The RDK, therefore, backed calls for a return to the May 1992 proposal to hold a referendum on 'independence' (*nezalezhnist*) and a return to the 6 May 1992 constitution, both of which had been 'suspended' by Bagrov as parliamentary speaker in return for concessions by Kyiv.[16]

Meshkov's policies combined a mixture of local Crimean nationalism coupled with pro-Russian separatism, backing the Crimea's 'orientation towards union with Russia' and a relationship to Ukraine only on the basis of a federal treaty. On the whole his policies remained vague, which ultimately led to his downfall a year after he was elected. Meshkov admitted he favoured Crimean independence, 'but not in the sense of independence like Ukraine, but rather an independent republic that has the right to return to that single economic, political and cultural space from which it was forcibly torn.'[17] Meshkov, therefore, backed calls for the Crimea to join the Commonwealth of Independent States (CIS) as a separate member, a demand shared by other separatist leaders in Moldova and Georgia. Meshkov argued that 'the republic itself should have the rights of an independent state and act as a subject of inter-state relations.'[18]

In contrast to Meshkov the Russian-speaking Ukrainian from Kherson, Bagrov stood for 'real independence for the Crimea', but not 'from the established state-territorial arrangement and long years of ties [to Ukraine].' In other words, he backed the continuation of the status quo and believed that the president 'should be neither pro-Ukrainian nor pro-Russia, but pro-Crimean.'[19] Meshkov retorted:

> To remain a part of Ukraine, which supposedly gives us a share of its rights, is a myth. Ukraine will never give us anything. It is more advantageous for Crimea to resolve many issues, including economic and defence ones, not with Ukraine, but with the Russian Federation.[20]

All candidates called for the 'demilitarisation' of the Crimea and all, except Bagrov, supported the Black Sea Fleet being placed under exclusive Russian control, based in Sevastopol.[21]

Other candidates such as Leonid Grach, leader of the Crimean communists, openly called for the revival of the former USSR and the criminal prosecution of Boris Yeltsin and Leonid Kravchuk for dissolving the former USSR. Others who were in favour of a confederal CIS included Yermakov, former presidential prefect in Sevastopol; whilst those who backed the unification of the Crimea with Russia, the situation before 1954, included Shuvaynikov, leader of the Zhirinovsky-backed Russian Party of the Crimea. Bagrov's more sober view, that 'We live in the Ukrainian state and one has to understand this', did not go down well at that time when the Crimea was at the height of its nationalistic mood.[22]

The Crimean communists, although opposed to the anti-communism of Meshkov and his overt Russian nationalism, nevertheless shared many views with the Russia bloc: the Crimea was threatened by Tartar Islamic fundamentalism, they argued; the region should join the CIS as a separate entity to Ukraine; and its economic problems would be solved by large Russian credits through a long-term 'free loan', in a similar manner to Meshkov's Russia bloc. The Crimean communists also backed calls by the Russia bloc to rejoin the rouble zone. But where they differed was in their unreformed adherence to Soviet-style communism by supporting a return to state subsidies, full employment, free medical care, lower food prices and no privatisation.[23] A more extreme alternative to the 'revisionist' Communist Party, the Communist Party of Working People of the Crimea led by Viktor Zarechnyi, could not nominate any candidates because it was not officially registered.[24]

Yermakov had been the presidential prefect in Sevastopol but had increasingly taken a pro-Russian line and was consequently dismissed by a presidential decree on 17 January 1994, which came rather late in the Crimean presidential elections. He also supported Crimea's re-entry into the rouble zone, criticised Ukrainian national symbols, backed dual state languages and dual citizenship, and supported Russia's retention of the entire Black Sea Fleet, 'because the Fleet cannot serve two presidents.'[25]

Bagrov lost the elections, like Kravchuk in Ukraine seven months later, owing to the Crimean voters associating him with the Party of Power and blaming him for the economic crisis.[26] 'Discontent is the only answer in this election. People don't vote for a programme and this is our tragedy. They want to live better but I can't make promises. They will be disappointed very soon,' Bagrov correctly predicted.[27] After losing the elections, which he (like Kravchuk in Ukraine in the summer of that year) had expected to win, Bagrov declared his intention of going into retirement.[28]

The elections in the Crimea were marred by widespread violence, but the degree to which this was politically inspired or linked to organised crime is impossible to ascertain because the two are closely intertwined in the peninsula.[29] In his previous occupation as a border guard Meshkov had won competitions in marksmanship organised by the KGB, which then ran these units. As he warned, 'I have not been practising a lot, but I think this is a skill that could be regained quickly.'[30] A number of political leaders became victims of violence, including Iskander Memetov, the Tartar adviser to Bagrov, who was assassinated. Various political party headquarters were bombed or came under fire. Meshkov himself was attacked at a bus stop by an assailant wielding a metal rod, only to be saved by his fur hat[31] after himself warning: 'There is operative information that they [Kyiv?] will try to influence the election outcome through physical liquidation.'[32] The Tartars warned that if Meshkov launched anti-Tartar policies, 'we in turn shall respond appropriately.'[33]

The Tartars had backed Bagrov as the 'lesser of two evils' (the greater evil being Meshkov). They refused to recognise Meshkov as president of the Crimean Tartar people[34] and were highly disappointed by Kyiv's muted response to Meshkov's victory.[35] Kyiv had failed, in the view of the Tartars, to protect their national interests in the Crimea. During 1991–3 Kyiv had taken 'an indulgent attitude towards separatists', hoping to 'cool separatist sentiment in the Crimea. Time has proven, however, that this only encourages them.'[36] They blamed economic collapse, political instability and an insecure society for the Crimean electorate's 'inclination to believe the most adventurist aims and programmes'.[37] In the view of the

Tartar leadership, Meshkov was to the Crimea what Zhirinovsky was to
Russia – a destabilising factor.[38]

The Ukrainian Civic Congress of the Crimea (UHKK), which held its
inaugural congress on 28 November 1993 and was officially registered on
8 February 1994,[39] called for a boycott of the presidential elections,
believing that the post of Crimean presidency should be abolished.
Launched three days after the deadline, the UHKK could not put forward
an overtly pro-Ukrainian presidential candidate. Although many
Ukrainians voted for Grach and Bagrov, some must have also voted for
Meshkov.

The main contest was always between Meshkov and Bagrov, with the
latter backed by Kyiv (Bagrov is a close friend of former President
Kravchuk), the Tartars and Ukrainians. In the first round on 16 January
1994 (Table 3.1), Meshkov and Bagrov obtained 38.49 and 17.55 per cent
respectively of the vote. The other candidates obtained less than 15 per
cent each, with Shuvainikov and Grach, leaders of the Crimean branch of
the Communist Party of Ukraine and Russian Party of the Crimea respectively, obtaining a respectable 13.65 and 12.18 per cent. These votes undoubtedly went to Meshkov in the second round (held two weeks later, on
30 January; see Table 3.2) when Meshkov and Bagrov obtained 72.9 and
23 per cent respectively:[40]

Table 3.1   Round 1 of the Presidential Elections in the Crimea (16 January
1994)[41]

Candidate	Vote	Per cent
Yury Meshkov	557 226	38.5
Nikolai Bagrov	245 042	16.9
Sergei Shuvaynikov	196 342	13.6
Leonid Grach	176 330	12.2
Ivan Yermakov	90 347	6.2
Vladimir Verkoshansky	14 205	0.1

Table 3.2   Round 2 of the Presidential Elections in the Crimea (30 January 1994)

Candidate	Vote	Per cent
Yury Meshkov	1 040 888	72.9
Nikolai Bagrov	333 243	23.4

Ukrainian Reactions to the Presidential Elections

The election of President Meshkov was portrayed as the victory of the 'Crimean–Russian idea', an idea that had gathered force as the economic and political crisis escalated in Ukraine, a claim that was unlikely to go down well in Kyiv.[42] The entire presidential campaign was conducted in an atmosphere of allegations of the 'threat' of Ukrainian nationalism to the Crimea. 'All of Ukraine's and the Crimea's woes are in west Ukrainian nationalism,' the leader of the People's Party of the Crimea claimed.[43]

Predictably, national democratic and nationalist parties and civic organisations in Kyiv protested loudly at Meshkov's election. Meshkov's election was an infringement of the (Soviet era) constitution, represented another step in the revival of the Russian empire and Crimean independence, which will lead to 'severe discrimination against Ukrainians and Crimean Tartars'.[44] 'They [the elections] were held in an atmosphere of blatant Ukrainophobia, with overt financial support from benefactors from the rouble zone,' the Congress of National Democratic Forces (KNDS) complained.[45] Meshkov's election represented the victory of 'pro-fascist, pro-imperial chauvinistic forces who are attempting to tear the Crimea from Ukraine' which will lead, they warned, to a 'new Karabakh'.[46]

The Democratic Coalition Ukraine electoral bloc demanded the establishment of law and order by bringing the Crimea to heel in a more forceful manner.[47] Their colleagues in the KNDS complained that former President Kravchuk 'keeps resorting to defensive statements as he watches it happen'.[48] Rukh, strongly critical of Kravchuk on many issues unlike the KNDS, condemned his inertia in the Crimea, supported calls for the post of Crimean presidency to be abolished, demanded that a presidential prefect be appointed to the Crimea and called for a ban on the activities of 'separatist [groups] financed from abroad'.[49]

The radical right protested in even stronger terms. The State Independence of Ukraine (DSU) organisation, which has been the official representative of the Tartars in Kyiv since late 1995, called the Ukrainian leadership 'powerless and inefficient. It is incapable of fighting for Ukrainian interests being accustomed to submitting to foreign will and carrying out decisions taken in Moscow'. Kravchuk ought to be impeached, the DSU demanded.[50] The Ukrainian National Assembly threatened that 'Crimea will be Ukrainian or depopulated!' The victory of Meshkov resembled that 'of a mafia baron in the criminal world', which will lead to the 'Crimea steadily marching towards the victory of a civil war'.[51]

Oleksandr Moroz, although a socialist, was as critical as his nationalist colleagues of Kravchuk for his ineptitude in handling the Crimean question. On 20 January 1994, after the first round had shown that Kyiv's 'favourite' was unlikely to win the Crimean presidential elections, parliament had granted President Kravchuk the right to annul any acts that infringed the Ukrainian constitution,[52] although even at this stage Kravchuk said, 'We must heed the will of the [Crimean] people.'[53] The results of the first round had, though, 'brought panic not only to the top power echelons but to the Central Electoral Commission too ...'[54] It seemed rather strange, and indeed inept, as Moroz had claimed, that the domestic presidential adviser, Mykola Mikhailchenko, only saw fit to call the elections illegal *after* they had begun, because 'there is no post of Crimean president in the Ukrainian constitution.'[55] After all, one has to assume that the elections were funded by the Ukrainian government and could have been prevented from being held *before* they began.

A parliamentary resolution four days later, entitled 'The Status of the Autonomous Republic of the Crimea in Conformity with the Existing Constitution and Legislation of Ukraine', outlined the following demands:[56]

- the Crimea has no state sovereignty;
- the Crimea cannot conduct foreign policy;
- the Crimean constitution cannot infringe the Ukrainian constitution;
- the Crimea is an integral component of Ukraine whose borders cannot be altered;
- the Crimea does not possess separate citizenship, security forces or monetary-financial system;
- the Crimea was given one month to bring its constitution and legislation into conformity with Ukraine's.

President Meshkov

Meshkov far outstripped his rivals in terms of funds spent on the elections, as seen in the huge number of leaflets produced and distributed in Simferopol.[57] There were few pro-Bagrov leaflets.[58] Meshkov refused to answer questions about the source of his financial backing, but the leader of the People's Party of the Crimea admitted it had come from commercial structures established by his Afghan veteran allies and from political parties in Russia. The officially declared sum of 200 million roubles was a gross underestimate, the People's Party leader believed.

Meshkov came to power in the Crimea as its first and arguably last president on a rabidly anti-Ukrainian platform. One of his first acts – a symbolic one – was to change Crimea to Russian time, putting it one hour behind Ukraine. His demands that the security forces in the Crimea be subordinated to the Crimean republic and that Crimean conscripts serve in the peninsula only were highly inflammatory in Kyiv's eyes, which had a national consensus across the political spectrum in adopting a tough – though non violent – approach to the Crimean crisis during 1994–5.

Meshkov and then President Kravchuk could not see eye to eye; a wide personality clash and ideological gulf separated them. After returning from a visit to Moscow immediately after he was elected, Meshkov un-diplomatically said, 'I do not report back to the Ukrainian president'. Yaroslav Mendus, political presidential adviser to Kravchuk, put comments such as this down to the fact that 'Meshkov is going through growing pains.'[59] When Kravchuk and Meshkov finally met the meeting was described as having been undertaken in an 'open and constructive atmosphere', diplomatic jargon for not very cordially. This was because 'they openly dislike each other'.[60]

Prior to being elected Meshkov had frequently called Kravchuk a 'Nazi' or 'fascist.' 'What filthy epithets he used when speaking about Ukrainian President Leonid Kravchuk, but now he calls him an outspoken politician of our time,' the *Mejlis* leader, Mustafa Dzhemilev, commented wryly.[61] In Meshkov's eyes, 'The situation is that we are trying to rescue ourselves from a nationalistic Ukraine with the help of a democratic Russia.'[62] By seceding from Ukraine, the Crimea could become a 'showcase' for economic reform. 'We have one goal: to split from Kyiv's silly economic and political policies,' Meshkov declared.[63]

Meshkov came to power with such 'a ragbag of promises'[64] (rejoining the rouble zone, peace, unity, stable incomes, independence, union with Russia, etc.) they would have been impossible for any politician to implement. This was compounded by the fact that his priorities were constantly changing and the manner in which he would implement policies always remained very vague – hence his fear of televised debates with the more articulate and professional politician, Bagrov. Meshkov never answered questions directly, had no real policy to solve the economic crisis and no professional team to implement his policies.[65] As one commentator pointed out, 'Meshkov, for his part, is now faced with the unenviable task of fulfilling his campaign promises.'[66]

One such example related to his firm belief that re-entry to the rouble zone would be easy and would immediately solve the Crimea's economic crisis. This contradicted the views of experts who pointed to inflation in Russia and its severe financial stabilisation policies.[67] Meshkov claimed that the rouble and *karbovanets* would initially circulate simultaneously and that the 'Kyiv administration and a top official' had agreed to these plans. Meshkov rejected accusations that he was dependent on the Russian Central Bank providing rouble notes for the Crimea, because in Moscow he had not met officials but 'specialists'. According to Meshkov, 'only God Almighty could be higher' than the meetings he had held in Moscow, which had solved the problem of the Crimea rejoining the rouble zone.[68]

After failing to obtain rouble notes from the Russian Central Bank Meshkov began to sing a different tune. The Crimea would instead obtain roubles from trade and tourists, a view characterised by experts (other than the 'specialists' that Meshkov had allegedly met in Moscow) as 'idealistic'. The implementation of this 'ragbag of promises' was entrusted to Yevgenii Saburov, Soviet economics minister from June 1990 to September 1991, who was born in the Crimea and where his relatives resided. Saburov's Russian citizenship prevented him from holding Ukrainian state posts which gave him access to 'state secrets', Kravchuk's presidential advisers complained.[69]

Meshkov's election demand for separation changed after his election to one of living under *both* Ukraine *and* Russia. The Crimea would undertake this by becoming a separate member of the CIS as 'a subject of the union treaty'[70] (a curious choice of phrase; the former USSR – not the CIS – was bound together by a union treaty). The Crimea formed part of the Russian people, Meshkov believed, therefore, 'The restoration of unity is, I hope, a question of the very near future'.[71]

During the election campaign Meshkov brazenly lied when he claimed, 'No one is talking about separation from Ukraine. The main task if I become president, is to decide on economic ties with Russia and an agreement on co-operation with Ukraine. No one is talking about changing borders'.[72] This is flatly contradicted by his comment made at the same time that 'I have made the choice made long ago by many in the Crimea – unity with Russia. It is impossible to build Crimea with Kyiv's policy of a split with Russia.'[73] Meshkov, therefore, viewed the establishment of Crimean statehood in the same manner as his Ukrainian nationalist critics accused him of – namely, as a stepping-stone to the renewal of unity with Russia.[74]

Some of Meshkov's election statements resembled Leonid Kuchma's during the Ukrainian presidential elections held in June–July of the same year. Hence the Crimea's preference for Kuchma over Kravchuk. Calls by Meshkov for reviving economic ties to Russia and condemnation of Kravchuk's 'isolationist' policies *vis-à-vis* Russia and the CIS could all have come from Kuchma's phrase book.[75] Where Meshkov was mistaken was in believing that Kuchma would back calls for Ukraine's transformation along federal lines, a view supported by Kuchma's co-leader in the

Inter-Regional Bloc of Reforms, Vladimir Grynev,[76] which would lead to the Crimea and Ukraine signing a federal treaty.

Some of Meshkov's more inflammatory language concerned security questions, potentially the most sensitive for the Ukrainian authorities. Meshkov backed the following policies in this field:[77]

- retention of the Black Sea Fleet in Sevastopol under sole Russian control as a 'long-term guarantee of stability and peace in the Crimea';
- military service in the Crimea;
- conclusion of a military-political pact between the Crimea and Russia;
- subordination of the Power Ministries in the Crimea to Crimean control;
- withdrawal of Ukrainian security forces from the Crimea;
- the right to conduct independent foreign policy;[78]
- appointment of Dmitriy Kuznetsov as presidential military adviser;
- appointment of Colonel Valeriy Grishankov as his chief of staff (his previous post had been former head of the 32nd Crimean Corps Special Department).

Parliamentary Elections

The elections to the Crimean parliament were held at the same time as those to the Ukrainian parliament on 27 March 1994. There were a bewildering number of over 1000 candidates competing for just 98 seats to the Crimean parliament from an assortment of four political parties and one electoral bloc registered for the elections.[79] Of the 98 seats, 66 would be elected on a majoritarian basis, 14 by proportional voting and 14 were allocated to national electoral districts. Voters were required to vote twice, once for the 66 territorial single member constituencies and again for the ethnic and party lists.

The 1.9 million Crimean voters expressed bewilderment and irritation at the large number of candidates, as well as at the large number of independents with no distinct programme. 'It's like a game of roulette. We don't know who they are or what they stand for,' one voter complained.[80] The parliament ended up with 54 Russia bloc deputies, 15 communists, 14 Tartars and the remainder centrists.[81]

The Russia bloc fielded the largest number of its candidates in Sevastopol and Yalta.[82] It was precisely in these regions along the southern Crimean coast that it also received the highest number of votes[83] and where the lowest turnouts were recorded. This is an area cut off from the more rural northern Crimea and teeming with former soviet retirees (pensioners represent a third of the Crimean electorate),[84] dachas, sanatoria and former military personnel. The victory of the Russia bloc enabled it to dominate the Crimean parliament by ensuring that the speaker and his deputies came from within their ranks. The Tartar candidates complained vociferously that this had become a 'puppet' parliament.[85]

The programmatic sentiments of the Russia bloc were echoed in the then widely held views of a large swathe of Crimeans: 'We don't need Ukraine! They are trying to suppress us! We have our roots in Russia, in Russian culture. Crimea will be Russian again!' a Simferopol pensioner stated.[86] The Russia bloc consisted of the Republican Party of the Crimea (successor to the Republic Movement of the Crimea), the People's Party of the Crimea, the Russian Language Movement of the Crimea, the Afghan Veterans Union, the Russian Society of the Crimea, the Bloc of Leftist and Patriotic Forces (formerly the Sevastopol branch of the National Salvation Front) and the Union of Officers of the Crimea. Within the less radical and more pro-reform People's Party of the Crimea were many Russian-speaking Ukrainians. It demanded a confederal East Slavic Union in contrast to unification of the Crimea with Russia.[87]

The challenge to the Russia bloc came from the Russian Party of the Crimea backed by Zhirinovsky, the leader of the inappropriately named Russian Liberal Democratic Party. The Russian Party was more overtly ethnic Russian, stood for outright unification of the Crimea with Russia and placed less emphasis on separate Crimean sovereignty. In this it was in agreement with Zhirinovsky, who devoted an entire chapter of his recently published book to this programme: 'Strategically, the Crimea is part of Russia, as is the Donbas, as well as Kyiv. All of them are part of the Russian Empire.' Zhirinovsky continued: 'we won't only take the Crimea, but the entire Black Sea coast ... I can imagine how a Russian's heart is breaking when he hears that the Crimea is foreign territory.'[88]

A factor which undoubtedly contributed to a rapid decline in former President Meshkov's popularity and that of his Russia bloc was the Crimeans' view that his extreme nationalism had caused a precipitous decline in relations with Kyiv. The new ruling Russia bloc lacked political experience and sophistication. Its appointment of outsiders, such as former Crimean Prime Minister Saburov from Moscow, led to resentment from local officials who had expected a greater share of the 'spoils'.[89]

Ukrainians living in the Crimea, therefore, did not heed calls by their nationalist parties to boycott the Crimean presidential elections or vote against the Russia bloc, a view propounded by the Ukrainian Civic Congress of the Crimea[90] through its newspaper *Krymska Svitlytsia*. Many Ukrainians, therefore, must have voted for either the Russia bloc or the communists in rural areas. Nearly half (47.4 per cent) of Ukrainians gave Russian as their 'mother language' in the 1989 Soviet census and nearly all of them are Orthodox (the majority of the parishes in the Crimea come under the jurisdiction of the Moscow Patriarchate through the Ukrainian Orthodox Church).

In contrast, the *Kurultai* (Tartar Assembly)[91] won all 14 Tartar seats. As the leaders of the Tartars pointed out, 'we again appear to be better interests of the Ukrainian state than the Ukrainians themselves'.[92] The pro-Russian National Movement of Crimean Tartars won only 5.5 per cent of the vote (and hence no seats) after it decided to go into the elections in alliance with the Russia bloc.

Opinion Polls[93]

Three legally non-binding opinion polls were held simultaneously with the Crimean and Ukrainian parliamentary elections on 27 March 1994. After threats from Kyiv, Meshkov's aides admitted they were not legally binding, only 'consultations', and therefore no threat to Ukraine's territorial integrity.[94] As merely 'consultative opinion polls' their results were quickly forgotten and ignored.

With a 67.2 per cent average turnout the support given to the four questions included in the opinion poll held simultaneously with the elections is shown in Table 3.3.[95]

Decline of the Russia Bloc

The Russia bloc was always an artificial, hastily cobbled together entity, and soon after the elections began to disintegrate. With just five seats clear of a majority (54 out of 98) in the Crimean parliament any splits within their ranks proved to be disastrous in pushing their agenda against the remainder of the deputies (communists, centrists, pro-Ukrainian and Tartars), who had no sympathy for the extreme nationalism of the Russia

Table 3.3 Election Opinion Poll

Question	Crimea %	Sevastopol %
Restoration of the		
May 1992 constitution	78.4	83.3
Dual citizenship	82.8	87.8
Presidential power	77.9	82.3

bloc. 'There is no longer such an entity as the Russia bloc. It has disappeared... There will be two factions. The Crimean parliament will never be whole,' Vadim Mordashov, leader of the People's Party of the Crimea, said soon after the elections.[96] It had always been a compromise of two tendencies. One of these stood for a 'sovereign democratic [Crimean] state' in union with Ukraine, Belarus and Russia within the CIS, whilst the other called for unification of the Crimea with Russia.[97] Conflicts within the Russia bloc 'bankrupted the Crimean–Russia idea'.[98]

Support for the Russia bloc had petered out by the end of 1994 owing to squabbling between parliament and president (despite both being led by leaders from the same Russia bloc), their inability to deal with the economic crisis or attract foreign investment and tourists, and Russia's preoccupation with Chechnya. Support also collapsed because the election promises made by the Russia bloc were the usual romantic promises ungrounded in real socioeconomic factors, propounded by nationalistic groups in the former USSR. The entire presidential campaign in the Crimea had been dominated 'by illusions of the republic's economic potential with Russia's patronage'. In fact, the Crimea is heavily subsidised by Kyiv. Yet Meshkov and his entourage told their fellow Crimeans that, 'With Russia we'll have a real currency and oil. They'll take care of us.'[99]

An opinion poll held in May 1995 by the Crimean Centre for Humanitarian Studies asked those polled: 'Which institutions do you trust most of all?' The results (see Table 3.4) reflected the extent of the decline in popularity of the former president and parliament.[100]

The rapid decline in the fortunes of the Russia bloc can be seen in the June 1995 local elections, when not a single council chairman was elected from the Russia bloc. The local councils had been in the forefront in backing the re-subordination of the Crimea under Kyiv's control during 1994–5. The majority of these new council chairmen had been elected

Table 3.4 Poll of Public Confidence in Crimean Institutions

Nobody	27 per cent
Media	21 per cent
Others	16 per cent
Religious organisations	12 per cent
Armed forces	8 per cent
Trade unions	4 per cent
Law enforcement bodies	4 per cent
Government	4 per cent

from centrist parties as representatives of the Party of Power.[101] 'The fact that people loyal to Kyiv have retained their positions enables the central government to control the situation on the peninsula,' one Ukrainian newspaper pointed out.[102] Kyiv had deliberately provided support to the heads of local executive committees (as the councils had become under the June 1995 Constitutional Agreement), who supported pro-Ukrainian positions and the new pro-Ukrainian Crimean government.[103]

NEW CONSTITUTION

The 'Separatist' Constitution

On 20 May 1994, the Crimean parliament, whose leadership was at that time under the control of the Russia bloc and backed by then President Meshkov, reintroduced the 6 May 1992 constitution. The May 1992 constitution had been adopted only days after the Crimean parliament had declared independence from Ukraine. The vote in favour of the re-adoption of the May 1992 constitution was 69 in favour (out of 98 deputies). Grach, the leader of the Crimean communists, came out against the adoption of the May 1992 constitution, fearing it would lead to conflict with Kyiv.

The re-adoption of the May 1992 constitution was accompanied by an appeal by the Crimean parliament to the UN, CSCE, Russian President and Federal Assembly, as well as to the Ukrainian people.[104] It claimed that the then Ukrainian leadership was 'aiming to destroy the statehood of the Republic of Crimea. It threatens to use force, including military force'.[105] It rejected claims that the May 1992 constitution, 'the foundation of the statehood of the Republic of Crimea', infringed Ukraine's territorial integrity.[106]

The main points of the May 1992 constitution included:[107]

- 'The Crimean Republic forms part of the Ukrainian state and determines its relations with that state on the basis of a treaty and agreement' (chapter 3, article 9);
- relations between Ukraine and the Republic of the Crimea were those between two sovereign states and based on a federal treaty;
- the Crimea held supreme right over the disposition of natural resources found on its territory;
- the only source of power in the Crimea were Crimean citizens;
- Crimeans had the right to dual citizenship;
- the Crimean Republic had the right to its own security forces.

Ukraine threatened direct presidential rule if the Crimean parliament did not rescind its decision to re-adopt the May 1992 constitution, but this threat was never utilised because it would have had to have been backed up by force. Tsekov admitted that, originally, they had intended also to declare independence, in the same manner as in May 1992, but ruled this out as being too provocative to Kyiv.

The Crimean leadership backed down after numerous threats from Kyiv. A referendum in support of the re-adoption of the May 1992 constitution was dropped, after the Crimean Central Electoral Commission admitted that it did not have sufficient funds.[108] 'We agreed to this unpopular but necessary decision in the present situation only for the sake of the preservation of peace and civic accord on our land,' Tsekov admitted.[109] An opinion poll, which would have been held at the same time as the constitutional referendum on the day of the local Crimean elections on 15 June 1995, was also cancelled. The opinion poll would have called for a new East Slavic Union, an aim of the then Crimean leadership which had been given inspiration by the Belarusian referendum on union with Russia held only a month earlier.

The New Crimean Constitution[110]

A new Crimean constitution could only be adopted after the institution of Crimean presidency was abolished in March 1995 and the leadership of the Crimean parliament was changed in June of the same year. Although there were initially threats made to prosecute Meshkov for exceeding his powers while in office under Part 2 of Article 166 of the Ukrainian criminal code, these charges were later suspended in February 1996. The new Crimean parliamentary and government leadership was more amenable to negotiating a compromise constitution with Kyiv through the mediation of the OSCE.

On 31 May 1995, the Crimean parliament adopted in its first reading the draft of the new constitution. In contrast to the May 1992 constitution, which described the Crimean Republic and Ukraine as two separate states, the new draft described the Crimea as a component part of Ukraine. Its powers would be fixed according to both the Ukrainian and 25 September 1992 Crimean constitutions, the laws 'On the Crimean Autonomous Republic' and 'On the Division of Power Between the Ukrainian State Organs of Power and the Crimean Republic'. It failed to mention the institution of a Crimean presidency.[111]

Between May and October 1995 the Ukrainian and Crimean authorities discussed various contentious issues within the first draft of the new constitution. There were numerous complaints that Kyiv was unwilling to give the Crimea full powers.[112] Ukrainian objections focused upon its claim to 'statehood', separate citizenship, ownership over all natural resources in the Crimea,[113] appointments within the Power Ministries and the institution of presidency (which the Russian Unity Crimean parliamentary faction continued to support).[114] The new draft, in contrast to the May 1992 constitution, did not mention the 'statehood of the Crimea' or the 'people of the Crimea'. In the words of Crimean Deputy Speaker Anushevan Danelian they 'had to make political concessions to receive economic concessions', reflecting the Crimea's dependency upon Kyiv for subsidies.[115]

On 1 November 1995, the Crimean parliament approved its draft constitution by a vote of 74:1, which then awaited approval by Kyiv (although most of the major points had been agreed in advance with the Ukrainian leadership). The final draft included the following important provisions:[116]

- the Republic of Crimea was an autonomous component of Ukraine (article 100);
- Crimeans possessed internal Crimean citizenship within Ukraine;
- Sevastopol was a part of the Crimea, whose status was determined by Ukrainian legislation;
- Ukrainian, Russian and Tartar were the state languages, whilst Russian was the official language of government and business;
- the head of the Security Service main directorate was appointed by the chairman of the Security Service of Ukraine in co-ordination with the praesidium of the Crimean parliament;
- the head of the Ministry of Internal Affairs main directorate was appointed by the head of the Ukrainian Ministry of Internal Affairs in co-ordination with the Crimean parliament;
- the Crimean parliament retained the right to appoint its own Prime Minister.

Ukrainian Reactions

The speaker of the Crimean parliament, Yevhen Supryniuk, complained that the adoption of the Crimean constitution 'is being dragged out in every way and is becoming dependent on the adoption of the Ukrainian constitution'.[117] Moroz, Ukrainian parliamentary speaker, did not hide his support for the adoption of the Crimean constitution by a simple parliamentary majority as a new law or resolution – but only after Ukraine had adopted its own new constitution.

Ukraine did not want to see the new Crimean constitution adopted by referendum as this may have led to additional questions being added. In addition, the new Crimean constitution created a parliamentary autonomous republic which, if it had been adopted before the Ukrainian constitution, might have given support to the radical left within the Ukrainian parliament, who were also opposed to the institution of a presidency. The Ukrainian authorities also remained concerned about state symbols, property rights and citizenship in the final draft of the new Crimean constitution. If the Crimea was not described as a state, but a territorial-administrative autonomous unit, then why did it need its own state symbols? Volodymyr Stretovych, head of the Ukrainian parliamentary commission on Legal Policy and Judicial Reforms, wondered.[118]

The Crimean constitution was discussed in the Ukrainian parliament on 1 February 1996, although there were still differences that needed to be resolved at that stage. Deputy speaker of the Ukrainian parliament Oleksandr Tkachenko told the OSCE High Commissioner for National Minorities, Max van der Stoel, that a new Crimean constitution would be welcomed because it would bring regional stability. He warned, though, that the Crimean constitution had to conform with Ukrainian legislation.

By March 1996, the Crimean parliament had appealed to the Council of Europe, the OSCE, the presidents of Russia and Ukraine as well as the Russian and Ukrainian parliaments in protest at the draft Ukrainian constitution, which was approved overwhelmingly by the 39 member commission and submitted for approval to the Ukrainian parliament.[119] The draft deleted references to the Crimea as a 'republic', replaced its constitution with a 'charter' and barred the Crimean Supreme Soviet from legislative initiative. Justice Minister Holovatiy, a strong supporter of these moves to curb the powers of the Crimea, said, 'There cannot be two republics or two constitutions in one country.'[120] This view, long that of the nationalist spectrum in Ukraine, argued that in a unitary state the existence of more than one constitution would lead to its federalisation. In addition, many Ukrainian members of parliament argued against the Crimea possessing its own citizenship and state symbols.[121]

Although the Ukrainian Ministry of Justice dismissed Crimean accusations as 'groundless and provocative', nevertheless, the draft Ukrainian constitution's new provisions had clearly stirred up a hornets' nest in the Crimea. In many ways the tables had been turned. In May 1992 the weakness of the Ukrainian state and the strength of the Crimean separatists had allowed the latter to wrest many concessions from Kyiv. By spring 1996, Kyiv was in a far stronger position and was attempting to claw back some of the concessions it had granted four years earlier. Clearly, a compromise had to be found between the maximalist desires on both sides between those who wanted to reduce autonomy to a regional status and those who desired the creation of a *de facto* separate Crimean state in a confederal treaty arrangement with Kyiv (similar to the treaty relationships between the centre and the republics in the Russian Federation). In the words of Pavlo Movchan, head of the Taras Shevchenko Ukrainian Language Society *Prosvita*, 'We must make clear once and for all the difference between a region and a country.'[122]

The Crimean parliament narrowly voted against relaunching a referendum drive on independence and the adoption of the 6 May 1992 constitution in reaction to the latest draft of the Ukrainian constitution, something which would have led to unpredictable consequences. In addition, President Kuchma was sympathetic to calls to act as a mediator between the maximalist demands of the Ukrainian and Crimean parliaments. It was also in the interests of Ukraine, everyone understood, to have the Crimean constitution in place and approved by both the Ukrainian and Crimean parliaments which legally established the Crimea as a component part of Ukrainian territory *before* the Russian presidential elections in June 1996.

An Honourable Solution is Found

The draft Crimean constitution submitted to the Ukrainian parliament in late March included the same troublesome provisions included in the draft Ukrainian constitution submitted earlier that month. On 4 April 1996, the Ukrainian parliament adopted a law 'On the Autonomous Republic of Crimea' approving 116 of the 136 articles of the Crimean constitution, but without the 'separatist' clauses that had referred to separate citizenship, state symbols, the 'Crimean people' and proclamation of Russian as the state language.[123] It had also refused to allow the Crimean Supreme Soviet to enact legislation, removed any references to the head of executive authority in the Crimea and on the Crimean status of Sevastopol. 'The main thing we achieved is recognition of Crimea as an autonomous republic and not some sort of region,' the Crimean parliamentary deputy chairman, Anushevan Danelyan, said.[124]

Although Ukraine refused to support approximately 20 of the 136 articles in the Crimean constitution the compromise reached by both sides was thought sufficiently important to lay the question to rest – for the time being at least. Neither side had wanted the failure to resolve the constitutional question to lead to a situation developing, 'as in the Dnistr or Gagauz regions [of Moldova],' Crimean parliamentary chairman, Supryniuk, said.

The constitution approved by both sides would be built on by the Crimea, which would attempt to increase the peninsula's powers, the subordination of its internal affairs and the judicial authorities.[125]

On 15 May, the Ukrainian parliament enacted a new law putting into effect the Crimean constitution which enshrined the peninsula as Ukrainian territory. This came just over four years after the Crimean parliamentary declaration of independence had nearly led to violent conflict with Kyiv. The adoption of a new constitution, which enshrined the Crimea as Ukrainian territory, weakened Russia's position at the same time, coming as it did one month before the Russian presidential elections. The adoption of the Crimean constitution would not be long coming, it was now believed.

UKRAINIAN ELECTIONS

Parliamentary Elections

The Crimea sends 23 deputies to the Ukrainian parliament. Despite a widespread indirect call by the Russia bloc to boycott the Ukrainian elections (the Crimean President Meshkov told Crimeans on local television his recommendations for a boycott: 'I will take away the ballot paper containing the names, first names and patronymics of candidates for the Supreme Council of Ukraine'[126]) all the seats were taken up, the remainder being taken in the December 1995 by-elections (see chapter 1).

As Grach, leader of the Crimean branch of the Communist Party of Ukraine, pointed out, Crimeans ignored the call for a boycott and voted in the Ukrainian elections.[127] The communists saw it as their duty to vote in large numbers and thereby add additional weight in Kyiv to their Ukrainian colleagues who were calling for the restoration of the former USSR. There were no candidates from the Black Sea Fleet owing to Ukraine's refusal to grant dual citizenship. The only military candidates came from the Ukrainian security forces in the Crimea and Sevastopol. Other political parties, besides the communists, who ignored the call for a boycott included the PEVK, Union in Support of the Crimean Republic (SPK), Ukrainian parties and civic groups.

The communists stood in opposition to the centrists in the PEVK, who were termed the local 'Party of Power' as they had supported the former Crimean speaker Bagrov, Meshkov's main challenger for presidency. The communists opposed calls for free economic zones, claiming the only way out of the economic crisis was to revive the former USSR as a voluntary union through republic-wide referendums.

That the boycott of the Ukrainian parliamentary elections failed can be seen by the turnout – 62.4 and 64.7 per cent in the first and second rounds respectively, a turnout similar to that for the Crimean parliamentary elections. But the call for a boycott by the Russian bloc, then the most popular political group in the Crimea, which had won 54 out of 98 seats in the Crimean parliament, opened the way for its only other strong rival – the communists – to gain the majority of the Crimean seats allocated to the Ukrainian parliament. In rejecting the call for a boycott the Crimean electorate initially ignored centrist and Ukrainian candidates in favour of the communists. This was probably because the electorate for the Russia bloc and the communists overlapped.

In the first and second rounds in March–April 1994, 12 of the 23 seats were filled, of which 11 were won by communists. A number of Ukrainian candidates came through to the second round with an average vote of 28 per cent (compared to the Ukrainian 23.6 per cent share of the Crimean population). The remaining 12 seats were filled during the course of repeat elections between May 1994 and December 1995. Only two of the newly elected members of parliament were deputies elected in March 1990 to the previous Ukrainian parliament, including the pro-Russian writer Volodymyr Terekhov, who declared: 'We are all Russians, Ukrainians, Belarusians – one nation and people.'[128]

Presidential Elections

The Crimea voted overwhelmingly for Kuchma in the Ukrainian presidential elections. Meshkov backed Kuchma in the presidential elections on numerous occasions and congratulated him on his victory. During the first round of voting in the Ukrainian presidential elections the Crimea and Sevastopol voted for Kuchma, by a high margin, despite the popularity of the local communist party. The total number of votes for the seven candidates are shown in Table 3.5.[129]

During the second round of the Ukrainian presidential elections Kuchma's and Kravchuk's support in the Crimea and the city of Sevastopol were similar to their level of support in the first round of voting[130] (see Table 3.6).

Clearly Kuchma's very popular mandate in the Crimea was a rejection of Kravchuk's policies within Ukraine since 1992 as well as those towards Russia and the Crimea. Kuchma used his popular mandate to reimpose 'order', an important plank of his election campaign. This included suppressing, by non-violent methods, separatism as a threat to Ukraine's

Table 3.5   Crimean Votes for Ukrainian Presidential Candidates (Round 1)

	Leonid Kravchuk		Leonid Kuchma
Crimea	7.43%		82.58%
Sevastopol	5.55%		82.11%
	Volodymyr Lanovyi		Oleksandr Moroz
Crimea	3.36%		1.26%
Sevastopol	3.97%		2.42%
	Valerii Babych	Petro Talanchuk	Vasyl Pliushch
Crimea	1.93%	0.22%	0.30%
Sevastopol	1.05%	0.30%	0.44%

Table 3.6   Crimean Votes for Ukrainian Presidential Candidates (Round 2)

	Kravchuk	Kuchma
Crimea	8.88%	89.70%
Sevastopol	6.54%	91.98%

territorial integrity, which he, as president, is sworn to uphold. This was largely accomplished with the help of Yevhen Marchuk, head of the Security Service of Ukraine under Kravchuk and appointed deputy prime minister with responsibility for security and the Crimea between 1994 and 1995. Kuchma's popular mandate also allowed him, through Marchuk, who led negotiations with Russia over the Black Sea Fleet during 1994–95 before he became prime minister in June 1995, to adopt a tough line on the withdrawal of Russian military personnel and the lease of Sevastopol (see chapter 6).

The rapid shift in popular mood in the Crimea was reflected in an opinion poll conducted in autumn 1995 in which Prime Minister Anatoliy Franchuk (Kuchma's son-in-law) was voted the most popular politician in the Crimea. Refat Chubarov, leader of the *Kurultai* Tartar faction in the Crimean parliament, and Dhemiliev, leader of the Tartar *Medzhilis* outside parliament, came second and fourth respectively. Volodymyr Sheviov, leader of the (pro-Bagrov) PEVK, came third. Grach and Tsekov, leader of the Crimean branch of the Communist Party of Ukraine and former Crimean parliamentary speaker from the Russia bloc respectively, came fifth and sixth.[131]

The factors outlined earlier in this chapter enabled President Kuchma to deal more rigorously with Crimean separatism than his predecessor had done, abolishing the post of president in March 1995 and temporarily placing its government directly under Kyiv's control. By the second half of 1995 and first half of 1996, the Crimea was firmly back under Kyiv's control, with a pro-Ukrainian parliamentary leadership,[132] pro-Ukrainian government,[133] no troublesome president and a draft constitution which the Crimean parliament recognised required prior approval from Kyiv, as well as recognising Ukrainian sovereignty over the peninsula.

CONCLUSIONS

During the period 1994–6 a remarkable U-turn took place within the Crimea and its relations with Ukraine. Disillusionment with the 'ragbag of promises' made by the Russia bloc that could not be implemented, internal squabbling within the Russia bloc, heightened confrontation between the Crimea and Kyiv, a worsening economic crisis, dependency upon Kyiv for subsidies and lack of overt support from the Russian leadership embroiled in a civil war in Chechnya all worked in favour of a peaceful resolution of the Crimean question in Ukraine's favour.

The adoption of the Crimean constitution in May 1996 and resolution of the division of the Black Sea Fleet between Russia and Ukraine at the November 1995 Sochi meeting of both countries defence ministers made the Crimean situation more stable and less likely to become a European flashpoint, as it had looked like becoming in May 1992 and May 1994. Foreign Minister Hennadiy Udovenko's confidence in stability within the Crimea and in its relations with Kyiv were so high after the adoption of the draft Crimean constitution in May 1996 that he suggested that Ukraine would no longer be requiring the services of the OSCE as a body which had helped Simferopol–Kyiv reach a compromise during 1994–6.

The draft May 1996 Crimean constitution legally enshrined Ukrainian sovereignty over the Crimea and Sevastopol, making Ukraine's case the strongest it ever had been since it achieved independence in December 1991. Nevertheless, its sovereignty was still not accepted by the majority of Russian public opinion and political parties – a factor that could still trigger a future crisis.[134]

4 Political Reform and an End to the Soviet System

'I would love to take our deputies in parliament and send them into orbit aboard one of our rockets. We would welcome them back, say, in two years, with open arms.'

(President Leonid Kuchma[1])

The parliamentary elections held primarily in March–April and the presidential elections held in June–July 1994 were a watershed in the development of post-Soviet Ukraine. The era launched by the 24 August 1991 declaration of independence and 1 December 1991 referendum under former President Leonid Kravchuk ended. That period can best be described as one of 'romanticism' in comparison to the 'pragmatism' espoused by his successor, Leonid Kuchma. Dmytro Tabachnyk, the head of the Kuchma presidential administration, has said,

> If I were asked, what is the main difference between the new leadership and the one before it? I would say that the period of romanticism is over. The new government will be approaching solutions to all problems from the pragmatic position of common sense and the economic value of the decision which is made.[2]

The Kravchuk era was also a period when domestic reform was largely postponed in favour of nation- and state-building after the collapse of the former USSR and an attempt to distance Ukraine as far as possible from the Soviet and Russian legacy (creation of security forces, diplomatic representation abroad, institutionalisation of national myths and symbols, establishment of state structures and administration, etc.). The debate between nationalists and communists during the Kravchuk era had rested over statehood; now the debate would concentrate on political and economic reform.[3]

This chapter surveys the changes in policies of the newly elected presidential and parliamentary leadership, and focuses on political reform and the adoption of Ukraine's first post-Soviet constitution.

COMPROMISE AND THE SEARCH FOR NEW ALLIES

Victory by a Small Margin

President Kuchma did not expect to win the presidential elections, especially after the defeated incumbent obtained 7 per cent more votes than he did in the first round. Of the other presidential candidates only the communists, who had backed parliamentary speaker Oleksandr Moroz, chairman of the Socialist Party and the second most powerful figure in Ukraine, openly declared their allegiance in the second round for Kuchma. It was clear that Kuchma's victory was clinched by the support he received from the sizeable left-wing Communist, Socialist and Peasant Parties, whose support base lies in southern and eastern Ukraine, where Kuchma won an overwhelming victory.

Kuchma's second source of support came from central and eastern Ukrainian reformers based in the social democratic/liberal bloc whose electoral machine *de facto* became the Inter-Regional Bloc of Reforms. They, like their New Ukraine bloc allies at the time, had always strongly supported economic integration within the commonwealth of Independent States (CIS).

The second group of reformers, primarily grouped in the Reform parliamentary faction, are 'post-nationalists' who originally started their political careers in the late Gorbachev era in the Ukrainian Popular Movement (Rukh) and other nationalist groups, but have since distanced themselves from them. Many members of this reform lobby, with strong support in Kyiv (where Kuchma lost to Kravchuk) and western and central Ukraine, such as Volodymyr Lanovyi, also voted for Kuchma in the second round because of their disillusionment with Kravchuk's lack of commitment to reform during 1991–4. Lanovyi himself came fourth in the first round of the presidential elections, trailing just behind Moroz, who came third.[4] The bulk of the vote for Kuchma in the second round, particularly those from the three left-wing parties, were votes *against* Kravchuk rather than votes in favour of Kuchma. During the presidential elections the economic programmes of both main contenders were vague (see chapter 2).

From Romanticism to Pragmatism

The twin realities of the regional bias of the presidential elections coupled with the small Kuchma majority of only 7 per cent served to reinforce the newly elected president's 'pragmatism' and 'realism' when formulating his new policies. To win the backing of reformers outside eastern Ukraine he needed to be both radical and anti-communist, much to the consternation of his left-wing supporters who had ensured his victory in the second round. To win the backing of nationalists and become an all-Ukrainian president, thereby overcoming the regional divisions brought about in the presidential elections, he needed to be resolute in defending Ukrainian territorial integrity and the Crimea, as well as limiting Ukrainian participation in the CIS to economic issues: 'The chief duty of the president is to maintain and consolidate peace and calm in Ukraine as the main prerequisite of consistently reforming society,' President Kuchma told an audience on the 50th anniversary of the liberation of Kyiv.[5]

President Kuchma is also aware that his 7 per cent majority over the defeated incumbent may rapidly dwindle after economic reform was implemented. Higher standards of living and visible improvements would not occur in the immediate short term and therefore his popularity might fall before it rose, especially because unemployment was likely to increase.

The importance of the West and its financial institutions are crucial to the success of Ukraine's new zeal for reform, including the creation of a social safety net, as Russia has neither the resources nor the inclination to bail out Ukraine (monetary union between Belarus, a country a fifth of Ukraine's size, and Russia was postponed by Moscow in 1994). President Kuchma had therefore to balance his personal support for enhanced economic co-operation within the CIS to maintaining open channels and ties to the West (which would appease the 'post-nationalist' reformist camp who look to the West, not Russia or the CIS, for inspiration). Under Kuchma, Ukraine immediately pushed for membership of GATT, the EU and the Council of Europe (which it was successful in achieving in November 1995), three institutions that would aid its integration with the West.

President Kuchma's first official visit abroad was to Canada (not to Russia) between 23–27 October 1994. This was important symbolically, where the one million expatriate Ukrainian community (which at that stage was still distrustful of his patriotic credentials) has considerable influence and where he attended a G7 meeting devoted to aid to Ukraine. The American Ukrainian community also successfully applied pressure on the Clinton administration to upgrade Kuchma's visit to a state visit (initially its status was 'official'). The Ukrainian diaspora, which has largely funded and provided property for Ukraine's diplomatic representation in the West, have to be courted by President Kuchma (as seen during President Kuchma's visit to the United Kingdom in December 1995).

Compromises

A year into Kuchma's presidency the radical left had openly declared their opposition to his policies – the very same groups that had backed him in the second round of the presidential elections in July 1994 (see chapter 2). The national democrats, on the other hand, who had firmly backed Kravchuk believing that Kuchma would 'sell out' Ukraine, moved hesitatingly into Kuchma's camp. His support for economic reform, dismantling the Soviet system (see later) and tough line on Ukraine's territorial integrity in the Crimea all changed his image in the eyes of national democrats.

Kuchma, a social democratic centrist at heart, has been increasingly squeezed between the left and right. Two centrist blocs could be useful allies – but they were divided over what both regarded as questions of principle. Whereas New Ukraine had supported a unitary state and one state language, the Inter-Regional Bloc of Reforms (MRBR, which Kuchma headed jointly with Vladimir Grynev in the 1994 elections) advocated a federal system and two state languages. (The policies of another centrist parliamentary faction – Unity – were very vague.) New Ukraine does not have a faction in parliament, but its policies were similar to those espoused by the Reform and Social-Market Choice factions, whose influence has grown (as seen by the appointment of its members into new posts). New Ukraine, the Party of Democratic Revival of Ukraine and the Labour Congress of Ukraine united into the People's Democratic Party of Ukraine at a congress held in February 1996, thereby further distancing themselves from the MRBR.

'Balancing between the positions of the two will let the president enter into agreements with the "right" and "left" and hence ensure the flexibility of their strategic line,' one commentator wrote.[6] After the 18 July 1995 attack by *Berkut* riot police at the funeral of Patriarch Volodymyr (Romaniv) of the Ukrainian Orthodox Church–Kyiv Patriarchate some national democratic groups had also cooled towards Kuchma and had transferred their allegiance to the former prime minister, Yevhen Marchuk, one of the most serious candidates in the next presidential elections. Henceforth the national democrats would not back Kuchma automatically but on a case-by-case basis.[7]

Three policy planks with which President Kuchma was wrongly associated during the 1994 elections were support for federalism, dual state languages and dual citizenship, all areas popular within eastern and southern Ukraine and the Crimea (and part of the policy arsenal of Russian security policy towards its 'Near abroad'). All three areas were probably the main factor in the inability of the reformist camp previously to unite in Ukraine. Hence President Kuchma understood that to obtain solid domestic backing for his political and economic reforms, as well as not to accentuate the regional divisions opened up in the presidential elections, he had to compromise by not raising them and ensuring that supporters of these policies, such as Grynev, his adviser on regional affairs, only propagated them in his capacity as chairman of the MRBR, and not as a member of the presidential administration.

Federalism, which had the potential to lead to Ukraine's disintegration (before the nation- and state-building process had been launched) and work against the strong executive power that Kuchma favours, has been declared to be 'premature' for Ukraine. Dual citizenship, which could theoretically be extended to 11 million Russians (20 per cent of the population), has also been rejected outright, and President Boris Yeltsin announced at the October 1994 CIS summit that Russia would no longer be demanding its inclusion within the draft inter-state treaty then being negotiated with Ukraine – a demand that was until recently one of the factors holding up its completion. Not only Ukraine, but even more pliant pro-Russian members of the CIS such as Kazakhstan and Uzbekistan, have also opposed dual citizenship. (The only CIS member state which has agreed to dual citizenship is Turkmenistan.)[8]

The question of dual state languages has been more difficult to compromise over. President Kuchma himself only recently learnt the Ukrainian language, having been born in Chernihiv and worked in Dnipropetrovs'k, both Russian-speaking regions. The 20 per cent Russian population, together with the approximately additional 20 per cent of the population who are Russian-speaking Ukrainians (according to the 1989 census), are a sizeable proportion of the population, representing the majority of the population in eastern and southern Ukraine where Kuchma won the presidential election. President Kuchma's compromise is to maintain Ukrainian as the 'state language', but to have more than one 'official language', such as Russian, which could be used in areas where it predominates, for example, the Donbas.[9] All citizens are nevertheless required to learn Ukrainian and government officials will be required to show a good command of it.[10]

Debate over this question and hostility towards even this compromise filled the Ukrainian press after Kuchma's election and became the subject of countless conferences.[11] The Union of Ukrainian Officers,[12] together with many other military commentators, argued forcibly that the armed forces needed a unified purpose and traditions which only one language, Ukrainian, could provide. The educational system, therefore, together with the armed forces, would be the incubators out of which patriotic, Ukrainian-speaking citizens would eventually emerge. Support by the Communist Party of Ukraine (KPU) for the Russian language as a second state language had also tarnished the arguments of those in favour of dual state languages, branding them as allies of the communists and 'mortal' enemies of Ukrainian independence.[13] Many commentators had even gone so far as to link the survival of the Ukrainian language to that of the state. 'If there is no state, then why was there still a need for a president?' one commentator asked.[14].

A NEW ADMINISTRATION[15]

'I will have a young team,' President Kuchma said at one of his first press conferences, immediately after the elections. The president abided by his promise and in the presidential administration a young team took over. The majority of them had an academic background and declared themselves to be pragmatic politicians. In contrast to the team which surrounded former President Kravchuk the new team looked more Western, informal, better dressed and more approachable.

Initially, President Kuchma surrounded himself with people he could trust from his home base of Dnipropetrovs'k; this was also an attempt to reduce what had been thought to be the disproportionate influence of western Ukrainians in the previous administration. These included individuals such as Vladimir Horbulin, Valerie Pustovoitenko, Volodymyr Yatsuba, Viktor Bohatyr, Vitaliy Boiko, Leonid Derkach, Volodymyr Kuznetsov, Valeri Shmarov and Leonid Borodych.

The later dismissal of Petro Lelyk, the strategic planner of Kuchma's election campaign, Oleksandr Novikov and others reflected a need to enlarge the president's support base beyond the Dnipropetrovs'k base. Hence the appointment of Serhiy Teleshun, Ivan Saliy (previously Kravchuk's presidential prefect in the city of Kyiv) and Volodymyr Syvokin to the presidential administration. Nevertheless, the influence of the Dnipropetrovs'k base remained with the appointment of Pavlo Lazarenko to the post of first deputy prime minister in autumn 1995 (formerly he held the posts of Dnipropetrov'sk *oblast* presidential prefect and head of the state administration).

It would not be true to say that only personnel from Dnipropetrovs'k were promoted, as seen by the appointment of Serhiy Osyka, Hennadiy Udovenko, Vasyl Durdynets, Viktor Pynzenyk, Yury Yekhanurov and others. Udovenko is Ukraine's most experienced diplomat and therefore was the best candidate for the post of foreign minister. Pynzenyk kept his post, despite the 'corrections' in economic reform from April 1995, because of his west Ukrainian origins and his popularity with international financial institutions.[16]

The appointment between 1994 and 1995 of Durdynets to Marchuk's post of deputy prime minister with responsibility for security questions reflected another phase in President Kuchma's hope of expanding his support base to those who had been Kravchuk loyalists or initially lukewarm towards Kuchma. Two further examples of this were the promotion of Anton Buteiko and Serhiy Holovatiy to the posts of deputy foreign minister and minister of justice respectively (both the Centre and Reform factions, from where they came respectively, are critical of non-economic integration within the CIS or with Russia). In May 1996 Volodymyr Lanovyi, briefly deputy prime minister in 1992 and author of the May 1992 programme of economic reform submitted to the IMF, was appointed as presidential economic adviser. Lanovyi stood as a presidential candidate in opposition to Kuchma in June 1994, coming fourth in the first round.

The major difference between Kravchuk and Kuchma rested in their intellectual and personal capabilities as well as their approach. Kravchuk surrounded himself with the older generation of the former *nomenklatura*, whose main interest seemed often to be solely to grab a 'slice of the action' before they retired, and whose advice he never listened to, partly out of vanity and his self-confidence as a skilled politician. Kuchma, on the other hand, with fewer political skills and a more limited intellect, listens attentively to his advisers and staff, and follows their proposals. They are younger, less prone to corruption, more idealistic, ambitious and have a vision of the way ahead, which Kravchuk always lacked.

The youngest member of the new presidential team when Kuchma came to power was 30-year-old Tabachnyk, his closest confidant. Tabachnyk graduated from the History Faculty of Kyiv State University, after which he worked in the Communist Youth League (*Komsomol*) and was then elected a member of the Kyiv city council. Tabachnyk's articles on historical and political themes were frequently published in newspapers and journals and, on the basis of these primarily historical themes, he was awarded a doctorate.

When Kuchma was appointed prime minister in October 1992 Tabachnyk became his press secretary and confidant. In September 1993 Kuchma resigned, and Tabachnyk refused a diplomatic posting offered him by President Kravchuk. Tabachnyk remained a close adviser of Kuchma's, going on to lead the presidential campaign on his behalf and then being awarded the post of head of the presidential staff.

Tabachnyk does not have a clear political orientation and one will not hear a clear strategic line from him. He is a tactician, organiser and adviser who was never independently minded and therefore lacked the experience of leadership. With his help the new presidential administration was filled with many of his Kyiv colleagues who, in part, sidelined those new faces from Dnipropetrovs'k. The head of the presidential apparatus all but single-handedly decided personnel questions, acting as a filter between the establishment and president. In the early days of the Kuchma administration this led to complaints from the administration.

Many have found it difficult to accept the orders and decisions of a man in his thirties and he has been constantly criticised in the Ukrainian media as someone 'With an arrogance that compensates for other qualities that a statesman ... should possess'. He 'lay[s] claim to a special role in our state', has '"little Napolean" pretensions', and is 'a politician of a rather low calibre' whose hobby is to be 'always in the public eye'.[17] Tabachnyk was dismissed in December 1996.

Fifty-year-old Horbulin is an old associate of President Kuchma.[18] A former professor, he was appointed secretary to the National Security Council. Horbulin is the nerve centre of the new presidential team and President Kuchma always asks him for his opinion. Horbulin takes over Tabachnyk's functions when the latter is unavailable. Horbulin was previously employed with Kuchma at the *Pivdenmash* nuclear missile plant in Dnipropetrovs'k. He is therefore a strong supporter of the Military-Industrial Complex and of maintaining bilateral ties with Russia.

Thirty-four year old Oleksander Rozumkov was a leading member of the presidential administration, an old colleague of Tabachnyk from his *Komsomol* days. With four years' organisational experience, when he was secretary of one of the former parliamentary commissions, those that knew him recalled that he was good at executing decisions but was not independently minded. Rozumkov has close ties with the Labour Congress of Ukraine (TKU), a social-democratic party with strong ties to the former *Komsomol* which united with the Party of Democratic Revival of Ukraine and New Ukraine to form the People's Democratic Party in February 1996. The TKU had a stable relationship with former President Kravchuk and these have continued (the TKU was the initiator of the Foundation in Support of the Arts, the head of which is Kravchuk).

Within the presidential administration foreign policy was initially dealt with by Volodymyr Furkalo (who was replaced by Volodymyr Ohryzko in early 1996). Furkalo was previously employed in the Ministry of Foreign Affairs as deputy head of the Department on International Organisations; prior to this he was employed in the Academy of Sciences. Diplomats regardeded him as an 'outsider' because he was not a career diplomat, whilst academics claimed him as 'their own'.

The new foreign minister, Udovenko, is one of a handful of the most experienced diplomats in Ukraine. The question now was, who would forge Ukraine's foreign policy? Would this be the presidential administration, the parliamentary commission on Foreign Affairs and CIS Ties, or the Ministry of Foreign Affairs, or perhaps a combination of them? Udovenko is a strong-willed, independent character, who will not accept competition from other quarters. His first move was to dismiss Ukraine's ambassadors to the United States and the Russian Federation because 'Complaints against our ambassadors in both countries were not uncommon'. Udovenko has called for the 'normalisation of relations' with Russia, but this should not be undertaken 'at the expense of relations with other states' (see chapter 6).

Shmarov, then newly appointed defence minister, was the first civilian to hold this post in the CIS. He was well known as strongly in favour of Ukraine's nuclear disarmament. Although in favour of close bilateral ties with Russia, particularly in the field of co-operation over military technology, he upholds Ukraine's military doctrine which proposed a non-bloc and neutral status for Ukraine.

The appointment of a civilian defence minister signalled President Kuchma's intention of asserting political control over the armed forces as well as re-establishing close co-operation between the Russian and Ukrainian Military-Industrial Complexes. His dismissal on 11 July 1996 signalled the failure of attempting to assert civilian control over the armed forces at such an early stage in Ukraine's post-Soviet transition. His successor was Lieutenant-General Oleksandr Kuzmuk, previously Commander of the National Guard. Shmarov had long been criticised by national democrats as being too 'pro-Russian' and the newspaper *Vechirnyi Kyiv* had contested this with him in court (Shmarov had sued the newspaper in a libel action.) His plans for military reform were condemned by the national democrats and the former Chief of the General Staff, Colonel-General Anatoly Lopata, was dismissed in February 1996 after serious disagreements with Shmarov. 'Unfortunately, he could not carry out the role assigned to him,' President Kuchma said of Shmarov after his dismissal.[19]

Former Defence Minister Shmarov ruled out joining any military blocs and rejected the Russian proposal to include in the draft inter-state treaty an article dealing with 'joint repulsion' of attacks against one another's territory (an issue first raised by Russia in August 1992). But improved bilateral ties with Russia could lead to co-operation in arms exports and President Kuchma made Ukraine an associate member of the CIS Joint Air Defence Agreement in February 1995. Ukraine is planning to increase its arms exports from its 1993 figure of $100 million to $10 billion, notably by sales of the T-84 'Super Tank' produced in Kharkiv, according to Shmarov.

Volodymyr Kuznetsov dealt with the question of foreign economic ties in the presidential apparatus. A 34-year-old academic from Dnipropetrovs'k who studied under the well-known economist Stanislav Shatalin in Moscow, he is a career academic with little practical experience of governmental work until appointed to this post. Kuznetsov claims that he is an admirer of former Russian Prime Minister Yegor Gaidar, leader of the Russia's Choice Party and former Russian prime minister. One of his main aims is to ensure a working relationship with the IMF.

Serhiy Osyka was the new minister for foreign economic ties and the principal lobbyist for Ukraine to join GATT. He is in favour of free trade with both the West and the CIS. Completely oriented towards the West, he claims to know English better than Ukrainian. He regards Russia, ironically, as the raw material appendage of Ukraine, which Kyiv should use to the maximum of its ability.

The head of the newly created department within the presidential administration entitled Control was 33-year-old Oleksander Novikov. This department would have the function of controlling the utilisation of foreign credits, state property and privatisation, ensuring implementation of presidential decrees and investigating corruption in higher official circles. Novikov is a parliamentarian from Kyiv *oblast* and his deputy is Derkach, whose father is a high-ranking member of the Security Service.

The main problems confronting the new presidential team were personal clashes between ambitious individuals, and between those from Kyiv and Dnipropetrovs'k, their youth and their lack of experience. Another serious problem was the question of the duplication of responsibility between different advisers, ministers and parliament, which could only be solved by the adoption of a new constitution. A problem in the past has not been the lack of reformers in Ukraine, but their inability to find common ground.

By the end of 1995 visible strains and divisions had appeared in the presidential administration.[20]

POLITICAL REFORM

Executive Power

President Kuchma had campaigned during the 1994 elections for the creation of a vertical executive structure, headed by the president. In August 1994, less than a month into his presidency, he issued a decree to strengthen the leadership of executive bodies and placed the government directly under his control through which he would 'determine the basic directions of its activity and priority issues that need to be resolved as a matter of urgency'. Another decree on the same question subordinated local councils to the president, thereby filling an executive power vacuum after presidential prefects were abolished in June 1994.[21] Kuchma's rationale for issuing these decrees has remained consistent throughout his term as president; namely, that economic reform cannot be implemented without political reform and a clear division of powers.

The president also established a Council of the Regions on 20 September 1994 which would meet regularly under his leadership.[22] The Council of the Regions has proved to be an important source of support in Kuchma's campaign for political and economic reform at the local level where it was often blocked,[23] as well as subordinating Kyiv's control over developments in the Crimea.[24] It is also perceived as providing strong support for a bicameral parliament, something backed by Kuchma in the November 1995 draft constitution.

The presidential administration also began discussing proposals for a draft law 'On State Power and Local Self Government' (hereafter called the 'Law on Power'). 'We shall not make a single step of progress towards reform without reorganising every branch of power,' Grynev, presidential adviser on regional questions and head of the Inter-Regional Bloc of Reforms Party, stated.[25] He favoured a presidential republic along the lines adopted in the Russian Federation when a new constitution was approved by a referendum in December 1993. The 'Law on Power' 'practically puts an end to the history of the existence of Soviet power in Ukraine', according to Grynev, because it gives parliament exclusive legislative powers and enhances the presidential executive vertical structure.[26]

The parliament must concentrate on the legislative process while the president and government perform executive and administrative functions, according to Kuchma. In a press conference held on 31 October 1994 after returning from Canada Kuchma stressed that he was ready for compromise with parliament except in two areas – radical reforms and the reorganisation of the executive power branch. If parliament blocked the 'Law on Power', he would call a referendum, he warned.[27]

Kuchma claimed that he had achieved full understanding with the regional state power structures, and the Council of the Regions was functioning smoothly. The role of the regions in the implementation of the new economic reform programme was decisive as it was precisely there that some of the most radical changes in economic and social life were now to take place, according to Grynev. Although the new presidential administration was in favour of expanding the economic powers of the regions, it was categorically against granting them political autonomy and has backed down from any territorial reorganisation of Ukraine along federal lines.

The draft 'Law on Power' was put before parliament on 2 December 1994.[28] Kuchma criticised parliament for acting more like a 'political club' than a legislature. He believed that if he conceded on this question, presidential power would become irrelevant and Ukraine would not be able to implement the necessary reforms to resolve the economic crisis.[29] The lack of political and economic reform, Kuchma warned, would lead to the collapse of the Ukrainian state.[30] After much pressure from all sides and heated debate, the 'Law on Power' was finally adopted at its first reading on 28 December 1994.

The second reading of the 'Law on Power' did not take place until April 1995, much to the annoyance of Kuchma. During the debate on 12 April, Kuchma stormed out of parliament after it was severely criticised. Left-wing deputies blocked discussion of the draft law the following day by refusing to register their attendance in parliament. The draft law was 'unacceptable', 'anti-democratic' and 'authoritarian', Oleksandr Steshenko, chairman of the Commission on State Building, Council Activities and Self Government, told parliament.[31] Relations between Moroz and Kuchma had deteriorated alarmingly and Kuchma accused the parliamentary speaker of seeing himself as head of state and of attempting to subordinate the president to the Supreme Council.[32] The battle-lines had already been drawn between the left wing, which opposed the law, and the centrists and national democrats, who backed it, the majority of whom eventually signed the Constitutional Agreement in June 1995.[33]

The 'Law on Power' was finally approved on 18 May 1995 by a vote of 219:104. Its implementation was delayed because it required constitutional amendments, which, in turn, required a two-thirds vote in parliament (that is, 300+ votes). Hence President Kuchma's support for a referendum to allow the law to be implemented. The implementation of the law required the suspension of 60 of the 170 articles of the 1978 constitution as well as two further laws to bring it into force and interpret articles in the Ukrainian constitution where contradictions would inevitably occur.[34] The newly adopted 'Law on Power' removed both contentious clauses: the right of parliament to impeach the president and the president to dissolve parliament.

Areas which the 'Law on Power' divided between the executive and legislature included:

The Executive
- independently forms a government;
- appoints a prime minister;
- is commander-in-chief of the armed forces;
- appoints and removes military commanders;
- recognises foreign countries;
- is head of state;
- is head of the National Security Council.

The Legislature
- adopts a constitution;
- passes legislation;
- establishes a Defence Council;
- can pass a vote of no confidence in governments;
- vetoes presidential decrees (if they are 'anti-constitutional');
- affirms the national budget;
- establishes foreign policy guidelines;
- ratifies government programmes.

In the words of Ihor Yukhnovsky, leader of the Statehood parliamentary faction: 'Society is going through its biggest crisis right now, and it is critical to give the president the chance to take responsibility for the country and implement economic reform.' Horbulin, presidential national security adviser, agrees: 'This law gives President Leonid Kuchma legal grounds for carrying out resolute economic reforms.'[36]

The radical left in parliament, who are either ambivalent (the Socialists and Agrarians) or hostile to economic reforms (the Communists) obviously disagreed, because they were opposed to any mechanism that destroyed the Soviet system in Ukraine which would allow the implementation of reform that was anathema to them. 'This law strips the Ukrainian people of their social guarantees and rights as citizens. It is a state *coup*,' Piotr Symonenko, leader of the KPU and the Communist parliamentary faction, believed.[37] The Constitutional Agreement, Symonenko told a plenum of the KPU, gave the president the green light to abolish Soviet power in Ukraine, 'which remains the last obstacle in the way of Ukraine's total capitalisation'.[38]

The Agrarian faction, as well as many industrialists in parliament, dissented from their radical left colleagues and many backed the president, some of them seduced by the promise of personal enrichment associated with economic reform. As a result, during summer 1995 half the Agrarian faction split away and temporarily created a new Agrarians for Reform faction within the Ukrainian parliament.[39]

The Threat of a Referendum

The inability to obtain a parliamentary constitutional two-thirds majority to implement the 'Law on Power' forced Kuchma to look to the option of a referendum to decide the issue, which was stalling the implementation of his October 1994 economic reform programme. The 'Law on Power' had been torn to shreds in parliament since December 1994 with 900 amendments to its 56 articles.

But, according to parliamentary Reform faction leader Serhiy Soboliev, the president was prevented from undertaking a referendum on any question other than those dealing with constitutional questions. The problem, though, was that there was no legal mechanism to hold such a referendum. The president held the right only to call a sociological opinion poll, not a referendum, Volodymyr Stretovych, chairman of the Commission on Legal Policy and Judicial Reforms, said.

This was not taken into consideration. 'The presidential team will adopt such a mechanism if need be,' Mykhailo Doroshenko, Kuchma's press secretary, insisted.[40] 'A political crisis has virtually paralysed Ukraine. Further co-existence of the president and parliament is impossible,' Kuchma warned.[41] 'Attempts by each branch of power to remove the other entail the risk of losing civil accord and peace,' he added.[42]

On 1 June 1995, President Kuchma issued a decree on holding a referendum on confidence in president or parliament (similar to the referendum which was to have been held in September 1993 but was then dropped in favour of elections the following year). Kuchma also regarded the holding of a referendum as the only non-violent method of resolving the question of the 'Law on Power'. Parliament vetoed the decree calling for a referendum, but this in turn was annulled by the president. Kuchma said that this was 'the natural right of the head of state to seek his people's advice in a situation when a political crisis in the state assumes extremely dangerous proportions'.[43] If parliament implemented the 'Law on Power', there would be no need for a referendum. 'I have nothing against sitting down at the negotiating table. But there must be one master of the house. When there are many, the house is a mess,' Kuchma said on a visit to Cherkasy.[44]

In an appeal to the Ukrainian people Kuchma pointed out that economic reforms would be impossible without political reforms (as was seen under his predecessor, Kravchuk).[45] The president was not attempting to take over the functions of parliament, he claimed. Rejecting accusations of 'authoritarianism', Kuchma accused parliament of blocking the 'Law on Power' and the work of the new government. In addition, the president was stripped of his authority over local state administrations. Kuchma told his Ukrainian citizens, 'The experience of almost four years of an independent Ukraine shows that the current deformed state system is one of the main obstacles on the path to halting the ruinous processes; it is a tangible break on the path towards the implementation of anti-crisis measures.'[46]

Parliament had other views. As one newspaper wrote, the referendum is 'a weapon that may turn against Kuchma. I do not think that parliament will surrender without any resistance.'[47] On 1 June 1995, parliament vetoed the presidential decree to hold a referendum on 28 June by a vote of 259:9 (with 20 abstentions), a very high majority. It forbade the government from financing the referendum which would have cost \$23 million (3.5 trillion *karbovanets*).

The leader of the communists, Symonenko, understandably believed that Kuchma's policies were merely 'another step to dictatorship in Ukraine. The main aim of all this is to draw attention away from Ukraine's economic catastrophe.' But even Volodymyr Yavorivsky, leader of the Democratic Party and a member of the Centre parliamentary faction, complained that 'Our president has issued the most illiterate decree which could have been issued – it provides no answers to the political crisis and just pushes it deeper into a dead end.'[48] Most parliamentary factions opposed the call for a referendum, even those from MRBR, which Kuchma had co-chaired during the 1994 elections.[49]

The fear of holding a referendum was twofold. First, parliament was more unpopular than the president and would lose (the same fear that had been expressed in September 1993). Secondly, it could lead to certain Russian-speaking regions, such as the Donbas and the Crimea, adding additional questions that could threaten Ukraine's sovereignty and territorial integrity. 'A referendum ... will murder the country. We will ruin our society ... That could very well destroy our statehood,' even the chairman of the Socialist Party and Parliamentary Speaker, Moroz warned.[50] 'This decision opens the door to civil war and will push away Kuchma's closest allies in parliament,' Taras Stetskiv, a member of the Reform parliamentary faction, added.[51]

The Constitutional Agreement

The impasse of a referendum, in the aftermath of the Belarusian referendum in May 1995 which turned it from an independent state into a Russian dominion, was extremely worrying to many shades of Ukrainian political opinion. Therefore, a number of leading members of parliament, including Oleksandr Lavrynovych of the Rukh faction and Valeriy Cherep of the Centre faction, proposed the idea of a Constitutional Agreement between the president and those parliamentarians who supported the implementation of the 'Law on Power'.[52] Those that had voted for the 'Law on Power' were 'constructive forces' which rose above party interests and demonstrated their readiness to compromise 'in the name of an all-national idea', Kuchma said.[53]

Parliament voted in favour of a Constitutional Agreement on 7 June 1995 which was signed by president and parliamentary speaker a day later, together with those deputies that supported it.[54] Parliamentary speaker Moroz called on his fellow members of parliament to vote for the Constitutional Agreement in order to get out of the impasse and remove the need for a referendum. 'And let every deputy's conscience be his guide,' Moroz said. 'It will lead us out of the political crisis.'[55]

The Constitutional Agreement was signed by 240 deputies in favour, (21 more than had voted for the 'Law on Power' three weeks earlier but still 61 votes, short of the constitutional two-thirds majority). The Constitutional Agreement was proclaimed by *Uriadovyi Kurier*, the newspaper of the Cabinet of Ministers, as a triumph 'When *Zlahoda* (Concord) Wins Out'. President Kuchma proclaimed it as a triumph for 'reason and restraint', while Moroz, whose socialist parliamentary faction on the whole (but not unanimously) opposed the Constitutional Agreement, said that 'parliament had made the right decision'. Looking back at the violent conflict in Moscow in September–October 1993 between president and parliament, Ukrainian leaders, such as Kuchma, could congratulate everybody for having 'given a conscious and meaningful form to our determination to guarantee civil peace, stability and accord in society' (see Tables 4.1 and 4.2).[56]

The most strongly opposed to the Constitutional Agreement were the communists and their Civic Congress allies. The socialists split in two over the question after Moroz, their leader, called on parliamentarians to vote in favour of the agreement, thereby placing the interests of the state above those of his political party (which one would expect him to do in his position as parliamentary speaker). But the leadership of the Kyiv branch

Table 4.1 Voting by Parliamentary Faction for the Constitutional Agreement[57]

Faction	For:Against	Political Orientation
Communists	14:64	radical left
Agrarians	36:1	radical left
Reform	28:2	liberal
Rukh	27:1	centre-right
Unity	26:0	centrist
Statehood	26:1	centre-right
Centre	25:0	centrist
MRBR	24:0	liberal
Independents	24:1	centrist
Socialists	7:8:3	centre-left/radical left

Table 4.2 Opposition to the Constitutional Agreement by Parliamentary Faction

Communists	64
Socialists	8
Non aligned	3
Reform	2
Rukh	1
Statehood	1
Independents	1
Agrarian	1

of the Socialist Party disagreed. It demanded the expulsion from their party of those socialists who had voted in favour of the Constitutional Agreement, which would have left them without the minimum number to form a parliamentary faction, and the holding of an Extraordinary Congress, which would raise the question of collecting 3 million signatures to call a referendum on abolishing the presidency.[58]

In the Crimea, Ukrainian civic groups and political parties backed the Constitutional Agreement; the same organisations which had backed the abolition of the institution of Crimean presidency only three months earlier, in March 1995. As for the radical left in parliament, 'they have again proved that their activities are aimed against Ukraine as an independent state, that they are trying to destroy society and provoke Moscow-type slaughter and bloodshed'.[59]

The Constitutional Agreement, Moroz believed, was a compromise document, which would allow the implementation of the 'Law on Power' without a constitutional majority. 'The president is very pleased with the parliamentary decision. This is a civilised, legal means of escaping the political crisis,' Razumkov, at the time an adviser to President Kuchma, said.[60] Undoubtedly, this was the case, but optimism about the worthiness of the Constitutional Agreement soon arose.

The Constitutional Agreement was also described as a 'mini-constitution', which would spur the adoption of Ukraine's long-delayed post-Soviet constitution as well as ensure its membership application of 1992 to join the Council of Europe. (This proved successful in November of the same year.) Moroz argued in favour of the Constitutional Agreement being based on the July 1990 Declaration of Sovereignty, the August 1991 Declaration of Independence and the December 1991 referendum on independence (as should the new post-Soviet constitution). The Constitutional Agreement should also seek to undertake to:[61]

- co-ordinate the reform process;
- help form a new government (Vitaliy Masol had resigned as Prime Minister in March 1995 and Marchuk was only acting Prime Minster at the time);
- ensure parliamentary approval of the government's programme;
- consolidate society based upon reform, law and order, social guarantees and human rights.

Conflicting Interpretations

The Constitutional Agreement came into dispute very quickly. On 21 June, only 13 days after the Agreement was signed, a parliamentary resolution dismissed the general prosecutor, Vladislav Datsiuk. This contravened article 44 of the separation of powers between the executive and legislature where parliament had the right to dismiss the procurator only on the president's recommendation. The parliamentary resolution accused Datsiuk of having failed to halt the growth of crime, whereas Datsiuk retorted that it was revenge, because of his exposure of corruption in high places. 'The ink has not yet dried on the Constitutional Agreement but the Supreme Council has already violated it,' Tabachnyk, head of the presidential administration, lamented.[62]

Rukh, one of the largest parliamentary factions, backed the president because parliament had 'grossly violated the treaty literally one week after its signature'. They called for fresh parliamentary elections if Moroz continued to flout the Constitutional Agreement.[63] The president was also backed by an appeal signed by prominent organisations – the Association of Lawyers, the Union of Advocates, the Union of Jurists and the Ukrainian Legal Foundation.[64]

The parliamentary resolution was inconsistent as it had first assessed the procurator general's work as unsatisfactory and only then formed a commission to investigate him. The commission accused him not only of heading an ineffective campaign against organised crime but also of corruption (links to the director of Blasco [the Black Sea Shipping Company], who had been arrested on corruption charges), giving apartments to his family when employed in the provinces, and lack of reform of the procuracy, whilst unnecessarily inflating the size of its management and the number of employees with the rank of general.[65]

Another problem that raised its head was the question of the subordination of local councils. Between April 1992 and June 1994 presidential prefects as representatives of the executive power had clashed with local soviets subordinated to the *Verkhovna Rada* (Supreme Soviet); hence they were largely ineffective and could not implement presidential policy at the local level (although economic reform was largely absent during this period under former President Kravchuk). The legislation on elections to local councils in June 1994 had abolished these presidential prefects (see chapter 1).

According to the 'Law on Power' (18 May 1995) as well as the Constitutional Agreement (8 June 1995) local councils (soviets) would be abolished and converted into state administrations directly subordinated to the presidential executive. Local state administrations would have responsibility for social security, budgets and culture. The chairmen of the state administrations would answer directly to the president, who had the power to dismiss them if they violated the constitution or did not implement his decrees. Therefore, a presidential decree on 9 August 1995 entitled 'On the Basic Organisation and Functioning of State Power and Local Self Government in Ukraine in the Period Until the Adoption of a New Ukrainian Constitution', which was based on the Constitutional Agreement, placed local councils under the president.[66]

Not surprisingly, owing to the fear among the left wing in parliament that this would destroy the Soviet system of power in Ukraine, the presidential decree was vetoed by parliament on 31 October 1995. Kuchma had never hidden the fact that he believed that 'We have before us an historic decision. The question at hand is not about power. It is much broader and deeper – which path should Ukraine take.'[67]

A further presidential decree on 21 August 1995 entitled 'The Status of *Oblast*, Kyiv, Sevastopol city State Administrations and the Status of *Rayon, Rayons* in the City of Kyiv and Sevastopol State Administrations' was also vetoed by parliament. But President Kuchma backed his decree with a further one on 18 November as 'the guarantor of the constitution'.[68]

In view of the absence of a constitutional court the vetoing of presidential decrees by parliament did not comply with the Constitutional Agreement, Viktor Musiyaka, presidential permanent representative in parliament, told President Kuchma.[69] In a speech to the National Law Academy, Kuchma remained highly critical of parliament for blocking his decrees and dragging its feet over the enacting of laws. In his view, conflict between the executive and legislature had actually *increased* since the adoption of the Constitutional Agreement.

After the signing of the Constitutional Agreement, Oleh Taranov, head of the parliamentary commission on Economic Reform, became confident that radical reforms could now be implemented with parliament no longer blocking them.[70] This did not prove to be the case. Parliament continued to debate issues outside its competence – taxation, customs and other areas of government policy (one third of issues considered by parliament during 1995 were within the competence of the government). By the end of 1995 it had failed to examine over 100 draft laws submitted to it by the presidential administration. 'We shall not allow our anti-crisis activities in the economy to be blocked. We shall find ways of limiting the destructive influence of these forces while operating strictly within the law,' Kuchma said.[71] Parliament was 'underperforming' and had still not at that stage begun to examine the new draft constitution.[72]

Parliament retorted that Tabachnyk, head of the presidential administration, or any civil servant, had no legal training to give advice on the legislative process in parliament. A parliamentary resolution pointed out that Tabachnyk previously had been employed as a copier and restorer in the State Archives, then a junior researcher in the Institute of History, Academy of Sciences and finally Kuchma's press officer when he was prime minister (October 1992–September 1993).[73] Tabachnyk, therefore, was not qualified to offer legal advice: 'Past experience does not indicate that he is the kind of competent specialist who has knowledge about all the things he talks about', whilst 'the stridency of the recent archive copier and junior scientific associate' was out of place in his post as head of the state administration. His post 'is not legalised by any state act and is not co-equal with either the office of the chairman of the Supreme Council, or that of the prime minister, or even the principal ministers and deputy prime ministers ...' Tabachnyk's 'often simply absurd attempts to rank himself as their equal or even above them, is based solely on his inordinate ambition'.[74]

A NEW CONSTITUTION

The Soviet Ukrainian Constitution

The new Ukrainian constitution began to be discussed in parliament in the early part of 1991, but the *coup d'etat* later that August and the declaration of independence prevented its adoption. The discussion was undertaken within the context of Soviet power and the communist majority within the Ukrainian parliament (although the 'Group of 239', as they were then called, had divided into national and orthodox factions by that time).

In October 1990 a resolution of parliament created a 59-member constitutional commission, which would decide the state structure, name, political and economic system, electoral regime, citizens' legal status, state and national symbols and the administrative-territorial structure. They aimed to complete the first draft by 1 April 1991.[75]

The major areas of agreement of the Constitutional Commission included

- that the constitution should be based upon the Declaration of Sovereignty;
- that there should be a clear division of powers between the executive and legislature;
- opposition to a federal territorial arrangement.

The Areas of Disagreement

- the name of the state ('Ukrainian Republic',[76] 'Ukrainian SSR, 'Ukrainian People's Republic' or 'Ukrainian Democratic Republic');[77]
- whether it should have an ideological accent, such as a 'socialist choice';[78]
- a bicameral parliament (the majority view), made up of a House of Peoples (elected for 3–4 years) and a House of Representatives or Senate (elected for 6 years), which would represent the regions;
- presidential–parliamentary republic (the majority view);[79]
- which authority local councils would be subordinated to;
- right to private property;
- the role of the Prosecutor's Office.

A referendum held in May 1991 was mooted over whether the new constitution should be 'socialist', which state symbols should be adopted and Ukraine's administrative system. The Supreme Council voted in June of that year to maintain a unicameral parliament (316 in favour), rejected federalism (with the exception of the autonomous Crimea)[80] and the proposal that local soviets remain with elected chairmen.[81] The majority of parliamentarians remained in favour of maintaining in the preamble to the new constitution a 'socialist choice'. With regard to the presidency, orthodox communists opposed it as a new form of dictatorship (they have therefore remained consistent to this day), whilst democrats opposed the introduction of a presidency until statehood had been achieved.[82]

Orthodox communists, of whom Moroz was then a leading light (and parliamentary speaker from May 1994), remained vehemently opposed to the 'de-ideologisation' of the constitution as the prelude to the destruction of the Soviet system and introduction of a bourgeois society. They remained strongly committed to the alleged 'people's power' of the soviets.[83]

The politburo of the Communist Party of Ukraine (KPU) proposed its draft on 23 January 1991, which insisted on it being guided by the 'socialist choice' and that the Ukrainian people had allegedly chosen Soviet rule. This draft was based on the 1918 and 1919 constitutions of the Russian Federated Socialist Republic and the Ukrainian SSR respectively. They also criticised other drafts for their emphasis on presidential power and the 'core Ukrainian nation'.[84]

On 19 June 1991 the draft constitution was approved by parliament. But of the 61 articles, only 29 were supported. There was majority support in favour of a unicameral parliament. The August 1991 coup and declaration of independence, which led to the banning of the KPU, prevented the adoption of this draft and a new one was submitted in the summer of 1992.

The Kravchuk Constitutions

A correspondent of the parliamentary daily newspaper *Holos Ukrainy* predicted in mid-1992 that the 'adoption of the constitution of Ukraine is a far-off perspective'. He was correct.[85] The constitutional process between 1990 and 1996 often revolved around the same sticking points and questions. The only degree of consensus was to reject the socialist orientation clauses in the pre-1991 drafts and not to include clauses in future draft constitutions supporting an ideological direction or monopoly. The 1992 draft constitution 'at last destroys the totalitarian order of the past', Petro Martinenko, a member of the Constitutional Commission and the chief consultant to the parliamentary secretariat, argued.[86]

The main stumbling block was always the left wing in parliament, which has remained opposed throughout the Kravchuk and Kuchma eras to the following areas of principle:

- a bicameral parliament;
- destruction of the system of local soviets;
- de-ideologisation of the constitution;
- removal of socio-economic safeguards.

In contrast, the democrats and centre-right within parliament always complained about the following:

- no rights outlined for the Ukrainian people;
- no regulation of the state language;
- no clear description of the state's national symbols;
- political parties were placed on the same level as civic groups.

Another factor which was often repeated was that 'The most important thing is not that it will be an American or a German constitution – but a Ukrainian one'.[87] The post-1991 drafts, therefore, should take into account Ukraine's historical experience whilst conforming to international standards.[88]

In 1992 and 1993 draft constitutions were proposed for discussion in parliament but were not adopted before the 1994 parliamentary and presidential elections.[89] After the presentation of the draft 1992 constitution President Kravchuk argued in its favour to the Supreme Council as a document that would help to consolidate Ukraine because 'the constitution is a state's calling card'. Areas of contention remained Ukraine's territorial state management and its cultural identity.[90] The 1992 constitution was still defined as a 'democratic-social state' which would ensure the development of democracy, legality and social justice to appease the left-wing members of parliament.

There was little debate against the introduction of the right to private property and entrepreneurship within the Ukrainian constitutional process, especially as no Communist Party was legally registered from August 1991 until October 1993.[91] The problem was less with these 'rights' than with the socio-economic 'positive rights' which were 'not rights in the proper sense of this concept, in so far as they cannot be guaranteed fully, in part by means of legal protection,' Kravchuk said.[92] There were, therefore, demands for their exclusion from the constitution as they could not be guaranteed and were merely 'social intentions'.

Kravchuk told the Ukrainian parliament:

Let us be realists. Such rights as the right to work, to housing, to education, to participation in cultural life, to surroundings that are environmentally safe for life and health, safe food and articles in everyday use, and certain others would not today always be easy to defend in legal form. But this does not mean that these rights should not be protected by the constitution. Their inclusion in the constitution, even in the form of social intentions, would stimulate the state to safeguard and protect them.[93]

The 1992 draft constitution was described, as have all drafts since, as creating a 'presidential–parliamentary republic', the 'so-called French model', in Kravchuk's view. Nevertheless, there was less intention on Kravchuk's part than on Kuchma's to restrict the powers of parliament.

The National Assembly within a bicameral parliament (which Kravchuk and Kuchma had both always backed) would still, under the 1992 draft constitution, have a wide range of powers. The House of Deputies (roughly similar to the US House of Representatives) would be composed of 350 deputies, whilst the House of Ambassadors (roughly equivalent to the US Senate) would include five representatives from each *oblast*, city or autonomous republic (regardless of size). The 1993 draft constitution reverted back to a unicameral parliament.

The 1992 draft constitution could not decide an issue which had still not gone away by 1995–6 – should the Cabinet of Ministers be under the president in a single executive line of authority? It did describe the president as the head of both the executive and the state. There would be no vice-president; this would be the prime minister if the government were placed under the president. A second contentious issue, again one that was prevalent even as late as 1995–6, was the status of local soviets. Should they be released of their state duties (which would be passed to local representatives of the executive power, the presidential prefects created in April 1992), and would presidential prefects become the chairman of local soviets?[94]

The 1992 draft constitution, like all its future variants, stood for a unitary, inviolable and indivisible, territorially integral Ukrainian state. This was always described as a cross between unitary and federal structures; in other words, a 'unitary, decentralised state'. Some outside observers thought there could be a problem with unitarianism, 'but I can understand why they chose it. Ukraine would do better with a federal state if it were not for the threat of separation,' Justice Walter Tarnopolsky, a Canadian-Ukrainian, said after attending a conference on the 1992 draft constitution.[95]

International criticism of the 1992 draft constitution was unanimous in its verdicts:

- too long (258 articles);
- excessive in detail;

- the implications of many provisions were not analysed (especially guarantees of socio-economic rights);
- it included duplication and inconsistency (for example, 'a strong president controlled by parliament');
- it was insufficiently strong with no independent judiciary;
- it was weak on local democracy if local authorities were controlled through executives.

The absence of a Ukrainian constitution led to Ukraine's first serious conflict between the different branches of power in May–June 1993 (which preceded the same struggle exactly two years later). On 18 November 1992, parliament voted to suspend constitutional articles which gave parliament and president the right to adopt laws and decrees on socio-economic questions. These powers were transferred to the prime minister at the time, Kuchma, for a six-month trial period. When they came up for renewal on 21 May 1993 parliament voted by 354:6 not to extend them. But it also refused to let Kuchma resign in a vote of 223:90, as he had demanded after parliament had refused to extend his extra powers. There was stinging criticism of Kuchma's government, which was accused of being 'conservative' and not pro-reform.[96]

Kravchuk proposed a compromise whereby a single source of executive power would be created with a vice-president who would be, in effect, prime minister too. Kravchuk insisted that if parliament backed this compromise, his choice for prime minister – Kuchma – would have to adopt 'tough policies', policies which he claimed he had supported during the November 1992–May 1993 Kuchma government.[97] Kuchma would be placed in charge of an 'emergency committee' to run the economy, whilst Kravchuk oversaw government policy.

Fearing either a powerful prime minister and/or president, parliament rejected Kravchuk's compromise. It was so opposed across the political spectrum that, in the end, it was not even put to a vote (although it had been backed by Rukh and New Ukraine, the only two pro-reform factions in parliament). At the same time, parliament refused to take responsibility for the economy itself and Ukraine's economy nose-dived during that year resulting in hyperinflation.

The causes of this crisis between different branches of power and its impact upon Ukraine's economic transition must have been strongly brought home to Kuchma in May–June 1993. The impact of these events must have served to reinforce his belief that political and economic reform were interlinked, something he put into practice a year later when he introduced programmes of economic and political reform in October and December 1994 respectively.

In the same year – 1993 – another draft constitution was put before the Ukrainian parliament. At a symposium organised by the Ukrainian Legal Foundation and the Advisory Council to parliament to discuss the draft President Kravchuk outlined his vision of the significance of this draft constitution: 'It is the new constitution that must become the founding document asserting the philosophy of nation building. It must give the answer to the questions which are most acute today: what kind of state are we building and which path are we going to take?'

Kravchuk favoured a 'strong authoritative – but not authoritarian – power'. The 1993 draft included clauses guaranteeing individual democracy, a socially oriented state, a law-based state, priority of human over state rights, division of powers between the executive and legislature, a compromise state administration ('unitary, decentralised, territorial structure with broad local self government') and measures to promote nation- and state-building.[98] The 1993 draft constitution, in contrast to the 1992 draft, also showed the ascendancy of parliament (and its then chairman, Ivan Pliushch) *vis-à-vis* the president; who was no longer described as chief executive, but only a state figurehead.

The 1993 draft, in Kravchuk's view, was still far from being 'ideal'. Although it was de-ideologised, like its 1992 variant, the draft again failed to define the social, ideological and moral foundation of the society being built in independent, post-Soviet Ukraine. The sharpest discussion surrounded the division of powers, the territorial system to be adopted, the constitutional mechanism for exercising individual rights and the method of adoption of the new constitution, as has been the case throughout Ukraine's constitutional process. Kravchuk admitted that the discussion surrounding the territorial question 'was particularly sharp' after they had agreed on a formula of 'uniting the state, regional and local interests within the unitary decentralised construction of a single system for Ukraine's territorial organisation'.[99]

By January 1994, on the eve of parliamentary elections, Kravchuk felt satisfied with the revised draft of the constitution. In his view, it had resolved the question of the division of powers, would not create social tensions and had resolved the division of authority between the centre and regions. To avoid centrifugal and separatist forces, local councils would be placed under the authority of the Cabinet of Ministers, which in turn would be placed under the executive (not dissimilar to Kuchma's December 1994 'Law on Power').

Another contentious issue, which had not gone away under Kuchma, were state symbols and language policies. Kravchuk admitted that 'there is no uniform perception of them today in various regions of Ukraine.'[100] If they were put to a referendum, as in Belarus in May 1995, it would lead to sharp regional conflicts and divisions of society and therefore Kravchuk was opposed to holding a referendum on these questions. He proposed instead that the basic draft of the new constitution be put to a referendum on election day (27 March 1994) without the clauses on languages, symbols and citizenship. This proposal was turned down by the Constitutional Commission.

An international symposium in Kyiv held at the end of 1993 also examined the July 1993 draft constitution. Some of the criticisms of the draft voiced by the symposium's participants were similar to those expressed a year before:[101]

- there was tension between an attempt to forget the past whilst maintaining socialist ideals;
- there was legitimate fear of a return of the Soviet regime;
- fear of, and a lack of confidence in, capitalism;
- too long and descriptive;
- it attempted to be all-encompassing (which would make it very difficult to enforce. How could the courts enforce socio-economic rights and the government, short of funds, implement them?);
- there were limits on local self-government;
- most authority was given to the National Council (parliament) while the executive was left with little power;
- there was no equality between the legislature and executive while there was too much interference of the former in the latter.

International advisers therefore proposed six recommendations:

1. shorten the text;
2. limit its aspirations and purposes;
3. strengthen the section on judicial review;
4. guarantee an independent judiciary;
5. define the sphere of activities of the separated powers;
6. protect individual rights.

The Kuchma Constitution

The Constitutional Commission created under Kuchma was composed of new members of parliament and the presidency elected in 1994 (the

Commission created in October 1990 had operated throughout the Soviet, 1992 and 1993 draft constitutions). The new Constitutional Commission included most parliamentary factions and many well-known members of parliament. Of the 38-member Constitutional Commission 15 were from parliament and 15 from the presidential administration with the remainder from the Crimea, the Constitutional Court, the Higher Court, the Higher Arbitration Court and the General Procuracy.[102]

The new Constitutional Commission had received four draft proposals by December 1994 from the presidential administration, the Institute of State and Law, the Congress of Ukrainian Nationalists and the Christian Democratic Party of Ukraine.[103] Although optimistic that they would put forward their own compromise version by spring 1995, the first draft of the new constitution was not put before parliament until 15 November 1995. This came after the Constitutional Commission had voted 17:9 to adopt it 'as the basis for further editing'. Kuchma voted with the majority, whilst Moroz's supporters had voted only to 'take note' of the draft.[104]

Of the 159 articles of the draft constitution 111 were not contentious between the Kuchma and Moroz camps. But they still debated, as they had under Kravchuk, whether to write in the constitution's preamble 'the Ukrainian people' or 'people of Ukraine,' the result of the Soviet legacy of not wanting to be seen to propagate nationalism.[105] The majority of the Constitutional Commission supported the priority of human rights, a bicameral parliament, one state language (as there was only one 'core people – Ukrainians'), a division of powers and clauses on national security. There were no variations on the national flag, but some members of the Commission were concerned about the national anthem which 'does not really apply' after Ukraine had obtained its independence (the anthem's refrain repeatedly states that 'Ukraine had not yet perished').[106]

Moroz's concerns with the new draft constitution were that it concentrated too much power in the executive's hands and there was an absence of clearly defined presidential functions. In addition, he did not favour a bicameral parliament (which would lead to an ineffective legislature and threat of separatism), whilst there were provisions in the draft constitution which were even worse than those in the Constitutional Agreement, he believed.

Kuchma, in contrast, supported a bicameral parliament because it would give the regions economic decentralisation and unite Ukraine's different regions within the overall national process of state-building. He openly admitted that both the Constitutional Agreement and the new draft constitution would end Soviet rule in Ukraine. In Moroz's view this was wrong and only stored up problems for the future. 'The constitution should reflect the specific features of the present day, so that it would not mark a victory of one political force over another, but rather their accord.'[107]

It was vital, in Moroz's view, to prevent mistakes creeping into the new draft constitution in the early stages of the debate. But Moroz was also critical of the new draft constitution in more forthright terms:[108]

- a bicameral parliament was merely copied from Russia;
- there was no section on civil society;
- presidential decrees should not have the force of law;
- a strengthened judiciary was necessary;
- individual rights and freedoms should be expanded;
- it still failed to resolve the division of powers;
- it deprived parliament of any control functions;
- it was 'based on abstract ideas and does not reflect the country's social development and public standards'.

Holovatiy, the minister of justice, also remained critically disposed to the clauses on the Crimea which should not provide it with the rights of statehood (a demand which Kyiv officials had argued *vis-à-vis* the adoption of a Crimean constitution which should be called instead a 'statute' – see chapter 3). In addition, the new draft was contradictory: it created five (not three) levels of power.[109]

Kuchma would not remain as patient as his predecessor over the adoption of a new constitution. It was required for the implementation of political reforms and was a condition of Ukraine's acceptance into the Council of Europe (the deadline was 9 November 1996, one year after joining). The Constitutional Agreement was valid until the adoption of a new constitution, according to Lavrynovych, deputy head of the parliamentary commission on Legal Policy and Legislation.[110] Kuchma therefore threatened that, 'If parliament doesn't agree to holding a referendum, then I will call one' in order to speed up the adoption of the constitution. He refused to sit back and wait seven months for parliament to debate the draft constitution – as it had with the draft 'Law on Power'.

National democratic organisations also remained critical of the new draft constitution.[111] In 1992–3 they had welcomed the draft's support for a unitary state, national symbols and human rights, but were critical of the weakness of sections devoted to civil society, elections and voters' rights.[112] Their objections to the draft constitution presented in late 1995 rested on a number of contentious areas:[113]

- use of the phrase 'people of Ukraine'. The constitution should reflect the fact that the new state is a product of the self-determination of the Ukrainian nation;

- remove the clause 'the Ukrainian people are composed of citizens of all nationalities';
- national should be higher than individual rights;
- the concept of local self-government was vague;
- remove the conflict between state and official languages (it should read that the 'state (official) language is Ukrainian');
- there should be no mention of historical-territorial cleavages which could be used at a later stage for the backdoor introduction of federalism;
- it should include a statement banning any acts against Ukrainian statehood and its territorial integrity;
- it should include a clause that the rights and liberties of individuals could only be curtailed if they undertook 'anti-constitutional' actions;
- include the right to propagate religious views;
- a bicameral parliament – the upper house should be elected by equal numbers of representatives from all regions, regardless of their size;
- remove the clause on the responsibility of the government before parliament;
- add that all state officials should know the state language;
- the procurator should be under the minister of justice.

Viacheslav Chornovil, leader of Rukh, echoed some of these criticisms. Ukrainians are the 'core nation', a fact that should be reflected within the new constitution. The constitution should fix Ukraine's state and national symbols – and not leave this question to future legislation. Although the draft mentions the rights of national minorities, Chornovil, like other national democrats, asked about the rights of the 'core nationality' (Ukrainians). The draft was also too anti-parliamentarian and anti-political party.[114] The Ukrainian Republican Party expressed its fear that a bicameral parliament could be a stepping-stone on the path to federalism (although the URP had included support for a bicameral parliament within its programme).[115] Holovatiy, minister of justice and a member of the parliamentary Reform faction, also opposed a bicameral parliament.[116]

The left wing in parliament had strong reservations about certain aspects of the new draft constitution which, for them, were also matters of principle:[117]

- abolish the post of presidency (the draft gave 'unlimited authoritarian power' to the president);
- a bicameral parliament made one branch of the state too powerful (that is, the executive over the legislature and judiciary);

- a bicameral parliament would weaken parliament and promote separatism (Russia, which had a bicameral parliament, was a federal state. Ukraine is an integral, unitary state);
- the new constitution ended Soviet power in Ukraine;[118]
- they remained opposed to the dominance of private ownership;
- the constitution should enshrine the 'socialist course of development' and the 'core social achievements made during the years of soviet rule' (something removed from all drafts since 1992);
- it should include guarantees about the 'people's ownership of the means of production';
- it should include Russian as a second state language;
- it should describe what society was being built;
- state symbols should be those of the Soviet era.

The Central Electoral Commission (CEC) and Holovatiy denied the right of the KPU and the Socialist Party of Ukraine (SPU) to collect signatures to hold a referendum on their objections in the draft constitution. The CEC pointed out that referendums could only be held on the adoption of new constitutions and public confidence in parliament or president.[119] But the KPU agitated for a referendum to solicit public opinion on these fundamental questions before the new constitution was adopted[120] and collected an alleged 2.5 million signatures for its demand to hold a referendum on provisions in the draft constitution (such as national symbols). The CEC had not registered these initiative groups and therefore refused to accept the validity of the signatures.[121] The presidential administration accused the KPU of wanting to destabilise Ukrainian society through its demands for a change in national symbols and a revival of the former USSR.

The SPU had similar reservations to their KPU allies. They proposed that a Declaration on Human Rights be adopted by parliament whose main points would then be incorporated within the new constitution (a similar Declaration on the Rights of Nationalities was adopted in November 1991 and used as the basis for the law on national minorities in the following year).[122] The SPU, like their communist colleagues, preferred a parliamentary to a presidential–parliamentary republic and they opposed the use of the Constitutional Agreement as the basis for Ukraine's new constitution.

A three-day conference on the draft constitution was held in Ivano-Frankivs'k in early January 1996 and was attended by a wide variety of domestic and foreign experts. The conference was sponsored by the World Congress of Ukrainian Lawyers, the International Foundation for Electoral Systems, the local *oblast* state administration, the United States Agency for International Development, the Rule of Law Consortium, the Canadian Agency for International Development and the German Foundation for International Legal Co-operation. The conference recommended the following *vis-à-vis* the new constitution:[123]

- the president should head both the state and executive;
- the president should appoint the cabinet of ministers who are nominated by the prime minister;
- the president should be able to sign three legal documents – decrees, orders regulating the work of his administration and universals to regulate activity;
- the president should appoint chairmen of *oblast* state administrations after they were nominated by the prime minister.

'There was no more important task in the state today than the adoption of a new constitution', Kuchma repeatedly stressed.[124] Public opinion backed Kuchma. An opinion poll conducted throughout Ukraine in March 1996 found 67 per cent of respondents supporting the speedy adoption of a new constitution with only 7 per cent calling for the Soviet era one to be maintained; 64 per cent were ready to take part in a constitutional referendum.[125] Since the submission of the 23 November 1995 draft constitution the Ukrainian media had intensely debated the constitutional process in a way that it had never done before.[126]

A number of 'deadlines' approached before which many Ukrainian commentators argued it was imperative that Ukraine should have adopted a new constitution:

- the 8 June Constitutional Agreement (different members of parliament argued whether this was valid for only one year or until a new constitution was approved, see earlier);
- the 16 June Russian presidential elections (national democrats accused Moroz of dragging the process out in the hope that Gennadiy Zyuganov, Russian Communist Party leader, would be Russia's next president);[127]
- the 10 November first anniversary of Ukraine's membership of the Council of Europe.

On 24 February 1996 a further draft constitution was approved by the Constitutional Commission on the basis of the text approved and submitted in November 1995 (see earlier).[128] After less than a month of debate within the parliamentary commissions the Constitutional Commission resolved to put it before parliament on 11 March with additional remarks and proposals, although this view was by no means unanimous.[129] Of the 40-member Constitutional Commission only 26 of the 33 present voted to submit it to parliament for consideration. Moroz abstained from voting. Only then, for the first time since the October 1993 draft, was it subsequently made public by the Ukrainian media.[130] A commission was then drawn up of 17 members with the purpose of publicising the new draft and ensuring widespread debate in the media and in conferences, seminars and other meetings. The commission included such notables as Holovatiy, Artur Bilous, editor of *Nova Polityka* and head of the Association of Young Political Scientists, Serhiy Pirozhkov, director of the National Institute of Strategic Studies (attached to the National Security Council), and Oleksandr Yemets, deputy prime minister with responsibility for political-legal questions and others.[131] Yemets was also instructed to ensure regular broadcasts on state television and radio about the constitutional debate.

In a speech outlining the draft constitution to parliament, President Kuchma pointed out that it was the result of a 'joint, painstaking and lengthy effort' by many people. It had taken note of all draft constitutions which had been submitted by political parties, proposals from the Constitutional Commission, Ukrainian and foreign experts. Its articles were in accordance with international conventions and treaties[132] dealing with human rights, national minority rights, labour rights and charters of local self government.[133]

As with all previous drafts submitted since 1991, the fiercest debates rested over a bicameral/unicameral parliament, the right mix of checks and balances and the division of authority between the judiciary/ parliament/president and whether the new constitution signalled the final nail in the coffin for the Soviet system of power in Ukraine. The majority of deputies finally reached a consensus over their opposition to a bicameral parliament. Yury Orobets, deputy head of the Reform parliamentary faction, went even further in his criticism arguing that the November 1995 and February 1996 draft constitutions were too closely based on the December 1993 Russian (something even Moroz had condemned),[134] that a bicameral parliament would only lead to the backdoor introduction of federalism but also weaken parliament in the face of a strong presidency. Strong presidents could not be trusted, Orobets believed, no doubt looking to neighbouring Belarus where an authoritarian president had turned his country into a Russian dominion.[135]

The Ukrainian Perspectives think-tank in Kyiv also argued that the 23 November 1995 draft constitution was too closely modelled on Russia's.[136] In comparison, they believed, the 23 February draft had many positive changes, which had been carried over into the March reworked draft submitted to parliament:[137]

- it included reference to national symbols;
- it codified Ukraine as a unitary state;
- it pointed to the right of Ukrainians to national self-expression in their independent state;
- the president and parliament would be requested to take an oath of loyalty to Ukraine (in addition to that already requested of the president).

But the Ukrainian Perspectives Fund also remained critical of it, notably in the following areas:

- it was more authoritarian and had fewer parliamentary powers;
- the presidential range of powers, in effect, eradicated the idea of a division of powers;
- it liquidated local self-government.

Many of these areas which were criticised by the Ukrainian Perspectives think-tank were the subject of intense debate during March–May 1996 when parliament successfully clawed back some of its powers and reduced the authoritarian tendencies in the draft constitution evidently to the approval of Kuchma and his entourage. Always an ardent supporter of a bicameral parliament, Kuchma was also forced to compromise on this question. Ukraine would have a unicameral parliament for a five-year transition period, after which it could become bicameral. Moroz summed up the Ukrainian reservation that in principle there was nothing wrong with federalism and a bicameral parliament. Nevertheless, 'there was a time for everything' and clearly this was not it. Federalism and a bicameral parliament would, he believed, 'put an end to all democratic transformations in Ukraine'.[138]

The KPU claimed that it had collected 3 million signatures by March 1996 in support of its proposals to hold a referendum on the contentious issues of the constitution (national symbols, restoration of the former USSR, Russian as a second state language, a bicameral parliament, institution of presidency and soviet local power). In view of the fact that the initiative groups were not officially registered by the Central Electoral Commission the petition had no legal force. The Ministry of Justice pointed to article 61 of the Constitutional Agreement which forbade anybody from agitating for any referendum until a new constitution was adopted.[139]

The KPU then proceeded to introduce its own version of a draft constitution of 'The Fundamental Law of the Ukrainian Soviet Socialist

Republic' on 23 March 1996.[140] The draft, supported by 125 members of the radical left in parliament, did not include an article on the presidency, whilst the Supreme Soviet was described as the highest organ of state power. The highest organ of executive power would be the Council of Ministers. The draft also included articles making Russian the second state language and reintroducing the Soviet era symbols.[141] The draft fell short of calling for the restoration of the former USSR, but described Ukraine as a 'socialist state'.[142] Rukh, with the backing of other national democratic parties, went on to launch a petition drive of its own to ban the KPU.[143]

By May, the three radical left parties and factions (communists, socialists and agrarians) were using any tactic available to slow down or block the constitutional process, including not registering in parliament (thereby failing to ensure a quorum) and walking out of the Constitutional Commission.[144] The KPU leader, Piotr Symonenko, told local KPU branch leaders that 'Communists must counter the government's attempts to push forward an anti-popular draft constitution with mass protest actions'.[145] Kuchma accused the communists of deliberately dragging out the process in the hope of a Zyuganov victory in Russia. Moroz believed the problem was more complicated. The constitutional process had dragged on because of 'The lack of trust in political relations between the branches of power, between political forces in parliament on the one hand, and the people and the authorities on the other, and their ability to find a compromise.'[146]

In contrast to the radical left, seven national and liberal democratic-oriented parties – the Congress of Ukrainian Nationalists, Rukh, the Ukrainian Republican Party, the Christian Democratic Party of Ukraine, the People's Democratic Party of Ukraine, the Liberal Party of Ukraine and the Democratic Party of Ukraine all voiced their readiness in principle to support the draft constitution submitted to parliament in March 1996 for consideration.[147] The parties emphasised that their support depended on inclusion within the constitution of provisions guaranteeing Ukrainian independence, a unitary state, a democratic system, civil rights and national symbols. In a separate appeal to President Kuchma, the Liberals, MRBR Party, Ukrainian Party of Justice, the Labour Congress of Ukraine and the Party of Democratic Revival of Ukraine (the latter two had since united in the People's Democratic Party) outlined their views on why a new constitution was urgently needed to ensure the spiritual, socio-political and economic revival of Ukraine.[148]

On 5 May 1996, a compromise final draft of the constitution was submitted to parliament which had been agreed on the basis of the draft submitted two months earlier between the executive and legislature.[149]

Despite President Kuchma agreeing to numerous compromises, which were enshrined within the 5 May 1996 draft constitution, its adoption continued to drag along in parliament. This forced Kuchma, with backing from the National Security Council, to issue a decree on 26 June 1996 to hold a referendum on 25 September of that year on the adoption of the earlier 11 March draft constitution. This approach was similar to that used a year earlier to jolt parliament into accepting the constitutional agreement.

This move spread panic among left-wing deputies. Not only would it have been likely that President Kuchma would have won the referendum, which would have reduced the significance of parliament, but it also would have voted in the March 1996 draft constitution, which included a bicameral parliament and more extensive presidential powers. After a marathon, all-night session, parliament voted in favour of the compromise May draft constitution by a vote of 316:36 (with 12 abstentions, while 26 did not vote) on 28 June.[150] 'This is an historic event, one of the key moments in Ukraine's modern history ... You showed the world in dignified fashion that our parliament is a healthy one,' President Kuchma said in an address to parliament after the vote.[151] Parliamentary speaker Moroz added: 'The strength of this constitution is the fact that it created a precedent of unity in the Supreme Council, which I hope will be a lasting factor in the work of the legislature. We are now one united family, a feeling that has for so long evaded us.'[152]

What is clear from Table 4.3 is that two of the three left-wing factions – communists and socialists – divided over the vote on the constitution. Seventeen socialists and 20 communists voted in favour of the draft constitution, whilst only six of the former faction and 29 of the latter voted against it. The Peasant Party faction (formerly the Agrarians) voted heavily in favour of the draft constitution by a margin of 21:2. But 60 members of parliament (a figure larger than the number which voted against the constitution) nevertheless refused to swear the oath of loyalty to the Ukrainian state, an act which is demanded in the adopted constitution. In view of the fact that they were elected prior to the constitution's adoption they were allowed to retain their seats.

Clearly, therefore, the large vote in favour of the constitution even by left-wing deputies ensured that it would be difficult to argue that the adopted draft constitution, voted in by a two-thirds majority, is not the product of a healthy compromise between the executive and the legislature on the one hand, and within parliament itself among the politically and regionally divided factions on the other. Both these factors are likely to be of great use in nation- and state-building as well as to reform within Ukraine (see Table 4.3).

Table 4.3 Vote by Faction for the Constitution (28 June 1996)[153]

	Yes	No	Abstain	No Vote
Communist	20	29	10	20
Socialist	17	6	2	-
Peasant	21	-	-	2
Rukh	27	-	-	-
Reform	29	-	-	1
Statehood	25	-	-	-
Centre	26	-	-	1
Unity	24	-	-	1
Inter-regional bloc reforms	23	-	-	1
Independent	22	-	-	-
Agrarians Reform	25	-	-	-
Social-Market Choice	23	-	-	3
No faction	34	1	-	-
Total	316	36	12	26

Comparisons of Draft Constitutions

The 1995 draft constitution,[154] in contrast to the 1992 version,[155] was 'very much shorter and less loaded with various demagogy'. It had evolved into accepting that with a clear division of powers parliament should only be responsible for legislation.[156] In contrast to the pre-1991 constitutions all draft constitutions since 1992 have no sections dealing with the political and economic foundations of society. Another new departure was the right to private property and entrepreneurship, reflecting at least the Ukrainian leadership's lip-service adherence to economic reform under Kravchuk.

The main differences between pre- and post-1991 constitutions were their emphasis on individual as opposed to state rights and interests. International treaties which Ukraine had signed since becoming an independent state would be reflected in the new constitution. In the words of former President Kravchuk: 'This distinguishes itself from the draft of all previous constitutions, in which preference was shown to all-state interests and the state stood above man and was counterpoised to society.'[157]

In the 1993 draft constitution[158] there had been some improvements, but Kravchuk's unwillingness to commit himself to a particular course of development for post-Soviet Ukraine (that is, is Ukraine-building a market economy?), unlike Kuchma, failed to provide the guidelines and parameters within which the constitution could be adopted. The debate had though moved on. 'In particular, we gave up the stereotypes formed throughout the decades in the shape of a narrow class approach to the constitution and laying down natural, all-human values in the draft,' something Kravchuk welcomed.[159]

In addition, by 1995, it was clear that Ukraine desperately needed a new constitution. The 1978 Soviet Ukrainian constitution had been amended 140 times, several articles had been invalidated and 5 had been removed.[160] In comparison to the July 1993 draft the November 1995[161] draft constitution was an improvement.[162] It was shorter, with only 159 articles divided into 12 sections and a product of compromise reflecting the current balance of political forces in Ukraine. It was described as a constitution of the 'transition period' only.

Many areas of the 1993 and 1995 draft constitutions were similar:

- both derive their legitimacy from the 24 August and 1 December 1991 declaration and referendum on independence;
- 'Ukraine is a democratic, social legal state';
- Ukrainian territory is unified, inviolable and integral;
- it is de-ideologised;
- champions the supremacy of law;
- the state language is Ukrainian;
- guarantees national minority rights;
- has a single citizenship (that is, no dual citizenship is foreseen);
- international law is higher than Ukrainian legislation and is to be incorporated (except in certain cases, such as the rights of national minorities, citizenship, state symbols, national security and the status of languages);
- includes guarantees of democratic rights (privacy of correspondence and communication, freedom of conscience, the right to strike, freedom of thought, right to conscientious objection, right to demonstrate, the right to foreign travel, etc.);
- the right to form political parties and civic groups, except those that espouse violence, threaten Ukraine's territorial integrity and sovereignty or propagate racism is provided for;
- supports the right to private property;
- backs the right to undertake entrepreneurial activity;
- socio-economic rights are upheld (health care, social security, housing, an ecologically safe environment, satisfactory living standards, education, etc.) are still included;
- argues that the duty of citizens is defence of the Motherland, its independence and territorial integrity.

The 1993 and 1995 draft constitutions differed over the question of a unicameral or bicameral parliament. The 1992 and 1995 draft constitutions backed bicameral parliaments, with the latter composed of a National Assembly consisting of a House of Deputies (220 deputies elected over four years) and a Senate (three senators were to be elected from each *oblast*, the Crimea and the city of Kyiv plus two from the city of Sevastopol for a four-year term). Members of the National Assembly could not be senators and deputies simultaneously, whereas the 1991 and 1993 draft constitutions supported unicameral parliaments, reflecting the power of the communists in the Soviet era, on the one hand, and Kravchuk's limited power as president *vis-à-vis* parliament in the latter.

Kuchma had strongly backed a bicameral parliament, thereby clashing with the chairman of parliament. In Kuchma's view, 'as of now the world has not invented anything better than a necessary counterbalance in legislative power itself'. The Council of the Regions, which Kuchma established in autumn 1994 and which had continued to back him, 'is the prototype of an upper chamber which outlines a state position based on regional interests'. Ukraine's regions would only be allowed economic – not political – autonomy. 'I think that we should limit ourselves to the autonomy of the Crimea and derive experience from this. I imply negative experience here. We see what can be triggered by extraordinary regionalisation that results in the emergence of political problems,' Kuchma argued.[163]

The 1995 draft (in contrast to the 1993 version) also reflected President Kuchma's insistence on a tight executive structure and the subordination of the Cabinet of Ministers under the president (see Table 4.4).[164]

The 1995 draft constitution also contained a greater amount of detail on Ukraine's territorial arrangement, described as an 'optimal combination of centralisation and decentralisation in exercising state power' (article 135) as well as greater clarity with regard to Kyiv's relationship to the Crimea. The Crimean constitution could not contradict the Ukrainian and was only valid once it had been ratified by the National Assembly. The Crimea possessed its own executive and legislative bodies (but no presidential institution, the executive here referred to the government). The president, who had a permanent representative in the Crimea, could suspend Crimean laws if they infringed the Ukrainian constitution. The adoption of the May 1996 Ukrainian draft constitution enabled the Crimea and Ukraine to work out a division of powers between Kyiv and the autonomous republic. The communists had agreed to compromise over national symbols in the May 1996 Ukrainian draft constitution in return for the national democrats dropping their demand

Table 4.4   The Cabinet of Ministers According to the Draft Constitutions

---

The 1993 Draft
- 'Guided by the presidential programme...'
- 'Accountable and responsible to the Supreme Soviet...'
- 'The prime minister submits the programme of activity of the government to the President and the Supreme Soviet for review'.
- *Oblast* soviets and *oblast* executive committees, which operate according to the principle of the separation of powers, are created in the *oblasts* in order to resolve issues relegated by the Constitution and constitutional laws of Ukraine to their authority'.

The 1995 Draft
- 'The government is responsible to the President of Ukraine and is under the control of the National Assembly...'
- 'The government follows the constitution and laws of Ukraine in its activities as well as decrees and directives by the President of Ukraine'.
- 'The legislative powers in *oblasts*, in the cities of Kyiv and Sevastopol, are exercised by heads of state administrations respectively who are to be appointed and dismissed by the President of Ukraine on application to the government.'

---

for the Crimea to be granted only a statute or charter, not a constitution (as enshrined within the March 1996 draft constitution). Nevertheless, the Crimean constitution cannot contradict the Ukrainian and enshrines the peninsula as 'an inseparable integral part of Ukraine and resolves issues attributed to its authority within the limits established by this constitution' (chapter 10, article 134).

Nevertheless, a step backwards had occurred with regard to national symbols and the national anthem which were no longer included, but left to future legislation (which could theoretically leave the door open for them to be changed). 'State symbols of Ukraine are State Colours, State Coat of Arms and State Anthem. Their description and the order of usage are provided by law', according to article 15 in section 1 ('General Clauses') of the 1995 edition. In the 1992 and 1993 draft constitutions state symbols had separate sections where they (the trident and flag) and the anthem were fully described (articles 250–3, section 9 and articles 203–5, section 11 of the 1992 and 1993 draft constitutions respectively).

The 1995 draft edition, in contrast to its 1993 predecessor, included the clause, 'None of the religions may be recognised obligatorily by the state' (article 30). This was an attempt to reject the policy under former President Kravchuk that one 'pro-Ukrainian' branch of the Orthodox Church should be favoured as the State Church. President Kuchma had supported a policy of strict neutrality, whilst supporting the unification of the three Orthodox Churches in Ukraine.

Moroz, the parliamentary chairman, continued to insist that parliament should be the sole source of law-making because enforceable presidential decrees were a 'permanent source of tensions'. In the new constitution, therefore, there should be a provision which stipulated that parliament had exclusive right to legislation, Moroz believed.[165] 'Parliament, and only parliament, should write the laws. Legislation cannot be changed by edicts, decrees or orders,' he added.[166] Moroz also continued to insist that the Constitutional Agreement could not be the basis for a new constitution because it is 'a legal convention of a temporary nature. The agreement is imperfect, and the practical results of its implementation have confirmed this.'[167]

The constitution adopted on 28 June 1996 included the following salient points which were the product of extensive compromises:[168]

- one third of the articles deal with human rights and citizens' duties and are similar to rights guaranteed in various international conventions;
- while the blue and yellow flag is defined in the constitution, the trident is not mentioned but is referred to as the 'Royal State Seal of Volodymyr the Great'. The national anthem is not mentioned as its words are to be changed;
- Russian was added to the section on minority languages. Ukrainian is the state language and the state 'guarantees the comprehensive development and use of the Ukrainian language in all spheres of society throughout the entire territory of Ukraine' (article 10);
- deputies elected to the next parliament will not be allowed to take their seats unless they swear the oath of allegiance;
- the right of legislative initiative now belongs to the president, deputies, the Cabinet of Ministers and the National Bank (but not to the parliamentary committees);
- the president is now the head of state with the cabinet of ministers subordinated under him as the highest executive body. The president appoints a prime minister following his approval by parliament;
- the president appoints members of the cabinet of ministers and chairmen of local state administrations;
- legislative authority remains with the unicameral parliament but the president has the right to issue economic decrees approved by his prime minister for a three-year period;

- parliament can override a presidential veto by a two-thirds majority and can hold a vote of no confidence in the cabinet of ministers by a simple majority;
- the right to private property and business activities are enshrined, but private land ownership is more circumspect;
- Ukraine will remain a unitary state with elected councils and appointed state administrations;
- foreign military bases are prohibited on Ukrainian territory except for a transitional period through lease agreements.

How Should the Constitution be Adopted?

There were only a limited number of ways in which to adopt a new constitution in Ukraine. Judge Bohdan A. Futey, an American-Ukrainian expert, divided the procedure of adoption into three stages:[169]

- a Constitutional Assembly would write it;
- the draft would be submitted to a referendum;
- the Constitutional Assembly would be disbanded.

Kravchuk initially announced to the Ukrainian media on 30 December 1993 that he would submit a draft 'Law on Power' to a referendum on the same day as parliamentary elections on 27 March 1994. This would define the nature of the political system and the division of powers at the centre. But no such referendum was held (although Kuchma threatened to hold the same referendum on 28 May 1995). To circumvent the problem of obtaining a constitutional majority Kravchuk had originally proposed to adopt only two or three laws in parliament as the foundation for the constitutional process. Then Ukraine would hold elections, after which parliament would return to the constitution. But this proposal was rejected by the Constitutional Commission.

As seen earlier, Kuchma had always been inclined to put the 'Law on Power' or a new constitution to a referendum, a fact probably reflected by how quickly the issue had been resolved by this method in the Russian Federation in December 1993. In his previous post of prime minister, Kuchma had been backed by the trade unions in his calls for what sort of society Ukraine was building also to be put to a referendum.[170] On the eve of presidential elections in summer 1994, he outlined the questions that he believed should be decided by a plebiscite:[171]

- a presidential or parliamentary republic?
- a unitary or federal state?

- which socio-economic system?
- orientation on socialist values?

Moroz always remained resolutely opposed to referendums[172] or Constitutional Assemblies[173] to decide such questions. Parliament would, he believed, be more than likely to adopt a new constitution if it incorporated universal documents (he later backtracked from this view and admitted the difficulties associated with this procedure). He felt that if it had gone to a referendum, then it should have first been approved by at least a simple majority in parliament. The referendum in Russia on the adoption of a new constitution in December 1993 was not a good example to follow in Ukraine, as it had merely shown how the public would vote for anything, 'from monarchy to anarchy'.[174]

Moroz was backed in the rejection of the use of a referendum by Holovatiy, an anti-communist member of the Reform parliamentary faction and then newly appointed minister of justice. The adoption of a new constitution, he believed, could not be adopted by a simple 'yes' or 'no' vote in a referendum. Ukraine should not repeat the mistakes of Russia or Uzbekistan on this question, Holovatiy argued. The draft constitution should be adopted through a mixture of debate within the Constitutional Commission, discussion in parliament, public hearings and include recommendations from the Council of Europe.[175] The constitution should ensure that the division of powers were strictly enforced, unlike that which existed in the Constitutional Agreement, which had led to unlawful presidential decrees.

A Consultative Council was created by Moroz to discuss the draft constitution which would ensure that the ideals of the Declaration of State Sovereignty were incorporated, decide the type of state system and government, ensure the division of functions between different branches of authority and decide the procedure adoption. But the Consultative Council was described as superfluous because the Constitutional Commission had already prepared the draft constitution, Lavrynovych, deputy head of the commission on Legal Policy and Legislation, argued.[176] This body was merely an attempt by Moroz to create a pressure group to espouse his proposals in the constitutional debate.

Debate surrounding the procedure for the adoption of the new constitution continued to go round in circles during the first half of 1996. There was an earnest desire for parliament to attempt to obtain a two-thirds majority vote to adopt the new constitution. But how this was possible in view of the fact that over a quarter of deputies (125) had backed the

Table 4.5 Attitude of Political Groups to the Constitutional Process

	Human and National Rights	State Structure	Power Structure
President			
Approach	In line with international norms. Striving to protect social policies (not social rights)	Unitary, decentralised.	Presidential–parliamentary.
Interests	Rapid integration into Europe.	Control over regions and regional self-government.	Control over policies and cadres.
Left			
Approach	Social guarantees.	Unitary, decentralised.	Supreme Soviet.
Interests	Soviet system.	System of Soviet government.	Liquidation of presidency
Centrist			
Approach	Striving to protect social policies (not social rights).	Unitary, decentralised or federal system.	Parliamentary–presidential.
Interests	Support new middle class and entrepreneurs.	Support regional elites.	Status quo.
Right			
Approach	Removal of social guarantees, priority national rights.	Unitary, decentralised.	Presidential republic.
Interests	Support for national feelings.	Strong vertical structure, elements of authoritarianism.	Increase executive power.

Source: *Chas*, 5 April 1996.

KPU draft constitution was never really discussed. A second alternative was proposed; namely that parliament adopt the constitution by a simple majority, then return it to the president who would call a nation-wide referendum. In one opinion poll in Odesa, 73 per cent backed this method.[177]

The radical left remained opposed to a referendum, especially the parliamentary speaker, Moroz.[178] This was surprising as many national democrats, whilst backing a referendum, were nevertheless concerned that certain Russian-speaking regions would add their own additional questions, as in the March 1994 parliamentary elections in the Donbas and the Crimea. There was also tremendous caution about holding referendums because of what they had led to in neighbouring Belarus.[179] Moroz also claimed that a referendum was undesirable because it would cost 10 trillion *karbovantsi* ($52 million). Nevertheless, the Christian Democrats and Rukh both backed a referendum, with the former even going so far as to argue that it should be classified as valid whether or not there was a 50 per cent turnout.[180]

In the final analysis, on 28 June parliament voted by a 316 majority in favour of a new constitution after President Kuchma threatened to hold a referendum on this question in September of that year. The threat of a referendum forced the left-wing factions to compromise and a large majority of them voted in favour of the constitution (see earlier).

CONCLUSIONS

President Kuchma came to power in July 1994 determined to initiate a radical programme of political reform which he regarded as inseparable from economic reform and democratic change. Without political reform Ukraine could not escape from the economic crisis that threatened Ukraine's statehood, Kuchma argued. Undoubtedly he was convinced of the correctness of this line after his experiences as prime minister during 1992–3, when he found his best efforts at implementing policies frustrated at every level, as well as the legal and administrative chaos which prevailed under his predecessor, Kravchuk. Key elements of this programme of political reform included the adoption of a 'mini-constitution' (the 'Law on Power') and Ukraine's first post-Soviet constitution, adopted in June 1995 and June 1996 respectively. This, in turn, helped to ensure the adoption of the first draft Crimean constitution which fully conformed with Ukrainian legislation and recognised Ukrainian sovereignty in May 1996 (see chapter 3). The adoption of

Table 4.6 Members of the Ukrainian Parliament Who Refused to Take the Ukrainian Oath of Loyalty (as Demanded by the Ukrainian Constitution)

Oblast/Region	Faction	Number of Refusals	Total Number of Electoral Districts
Donbas			
Donets'k	Communist	15	47
Luhans'k	Communist	13	25
Eastern Ukraine			
Kharkiv	Communist/Inter-Regional Group	3/1 (4)	28
Zaporizhzhia	Communist	2	18
North-Eastern Ukraine			
Sumy	Communist/Progressive Socialist	2/2 (4)	13
Chernihiv	Communist/Peasant Party	2/1 (3)	12
Poltava	Communist	1	16
Central Ukraine			
Vinnytsia	Communist	1	17
Cherkasy	Communist	1	13
Kirovohrad	Communist	2	11
Southern Ukraine			
Mykolaiv	Communist	4	11
Kherson	Communist	2	11
Odesa	Communist/Independents	2/2 (4)	23
Crimean Autonomous Republic			
Crimea	Communist	5	19
Sevastopol	Communist	3	4

Source: Vechirnyi Kyiv, 25 September 1996.

Ukraine's first post-Soviet constitution on 28 June 1996, therefore, signalled a break with its Soviet legacy, a victory for Ukraine's nation- and state-building programme and a boost to political and economic transformation of Ukrainian society.

5 Economic Transformation and Structural Change[1]

'Ukraine cannot randomly and unquestioningly follow someone else's course, the more so in that our own history is extraordinarily rich.'
(Former Prime Minister Yevhen Marchuk)[2]

'Privatisation will occur in Ukraine! I guarantee it. Because I am the terminator who has been hired to make sure that it happens and it will.'
(Yury Yekhanurov, Chairman, State Property Fund)[3]

Kuchma inherited an economic disaster from his predecessor. Official GDP had collapsed further than that recorded in the United States during the Great Depression (not taking into account the large and vibrant black economy). At the UN summit on social development the 'Ukraine Human Development Report 1995' outlined how Ukrainian living standards had declined by 80 per cent since independence.[4] The real unemployment rate was upwards of 40 per cent if one included those on unpaid leave.[5]

Alexander Pashkaver, economic adviser to President Kuchma, commented: 'There is a very big difference between Kuchma as a prime minister and Kuchma as a president. He has shown a very great capacity to learn. A very important element of his economic policy is that all the decrees he issues are consistent with an integral programme of economic reform.'[6] Between holding the posts of prime minister and president Kuchma had led the Union of Industrialists and Entrepreneurs of Ukraine between 1993 and 1994, which had been labelled disparagingly as an association of 'Red Directors'. His chairmanship of that influential body had successfully brought over the majority of industrial directors to the cause of reform. Kuchma is also persuading the Agrarian Party (primarily agricultural directors) that reform is in their self-interest. Nevertheless, Kuchma's election programme was not consistent on economic reform (see chapter 2), but after October 1994 there was no question that he had rejected any calls to return Ukraine to a command-administrative system.

ECONOMIC AND SOCIAL REFORM

A New Programme

On 11 October 1994, President Kuchma outlined his reform programme in a 30-page document to parliament.[7] 'It's time to stop talking about reforms. We are about to embark on something big,' the socialist parliamentary speaker, Oleksandr Moroz, said.[8] Serhiy Holovatiy, a leading member of the Reform faction and president of the Ukrainian Legal Foundation and Minister of Justice, said, 'I regard this as an historic address, the first such report by a head of the Ukrainian state. Finally, we have a real leader of the independent Ukrainian state, somebody who will take responsibility and who has shown his intentions to do everything possible to integrate Ukraine into the world economy.'[9]

The programme was met by support across the non-left-wing parliamentary factions, who saw it as a break with the Soviet and command-administrative system when Kuchma argued that 'Private ownership is the basis for the radical rebirth of our economy.' This would be guaranteed by radical economic reform, especially in the realm of privatisation, and political reform (see chapter 4). Kuchma has continued to insist that 'In today's conditions there are no alternatives' to 'The Path of Radical Economic Reforms' programme.[10]

The speech to parliament was careful to utilise patriotic arguments to bolster his parliamentary and public support for the reform programme. In Kuchma's view, 'Ukraine has not yet achieved real independence. In 1991 it achieved only the attributes of a sovereign state but over the last three years it was unable to fill it with real content.' Ukraine would pursue relations with the West as well as with Russia and the Commonwealth of Independent States (CIS). Although Kuchma supported greater economic co-operation with the CIS he cautioned that 'at the same time the issue of Ukraine's sovereignty and territorial integrity is not even subject for discussion'. Kuchma also warned the radical left to 'abandon hopes for the restoration of the Soviet Union. If Ukraine is deprived of its statehood, this means civil war.'

The major points outlined in President Kuchma's economic reform programme can be divided into ten policy areas. These included financial stabilisation, dealing with the payments crisis, reform of the banking and monetary sectors as well as institutional reform, supporting the newly emerging private sector, strengthening law and order, restructuring the economy, reform of the agricultural sector, liberalising foreign trade and methods towards implementation of market economic reforms.[11]

Reform Speeded Up

President Kuchma has not wavered from the general policy outlines of his economic reform programme. Prices were largely freed in early November 1994 after a meeting of the Council of the Regions which decided to allow each region to set its own prices for food products. On 11 November, parliament adopted a compromise resolution which agreed to go along with the liberalisation of prices, despite overwhelming opposition from the three radical left parliamentary factions. At the November 1994 meeting of the Council of the Regions the majority of Ukraine's regions endorsed the presidential economic reform programme, asking parliament to take its views into account.

Interviewed in the parliamentary newspaper *Holos Ukrainy* President Kuchma stated: 'In my opinion, the choice of an economic strategy is not a matter for discussion now. I have never had any doubts about the correctness of the reform course, aimed at a market-oriented transformation of the national economy.'[2] The reform programme is backed by the majority of the population and political parties, according to President Kuchma, and he would not contemplate any U-turns. A collegium of advisers to prepare macroeconomic and reform proposals was created which included leading bankers, academics, reformist politicians and entrepreneurs committed to the reform programme.[13]

A presidential decree entitled 'On Measures to Implement Decisions Relating to Economic Reforms in Ukraine' showed Kuchma's determination to ensure that reforms did not merely end up as words – but were acted upon and implemented. 'Proceeding from the fact that certain state executive bodies block the Cabinet of Ministers' actions on economic reforms, fix monopolistically high prices that should be formed exclusively between producers and consumers which leads to opposition by the population to radical reforms' the decree outlined measures to ensure compliance with Kuchma's reform programme. These included making heads of ministries, other central state executive bodies, the Crimean government and heads of local councils personally responsible for the non-fulfilment of the Cabinet's decisions on economic reforms and for fixing monopolistically high prices and tariffs. The persons found guilty would be made responsible for such actions pursuant to the law, including dismissals from their posts. The Anti-Monopoly Committee and the Ministry of Economics were to submit proposals on limiting monopolies in certain sectors, whilst the Ministry of Economics, other ministries and local authorities were ordered to submit proposals on the formation of prices for basic products manufactured in Ukraine.[14]

Foreign trade was a key area which received immediate attention from Kuchma's reformist team. A government decree on the liberalisation of export operations drastically reduced the list of goods which still were subject to quotas or export licences. Export licences on grain, coal, scrap metals, pig iron and scrap ferrous metals were still in place. But the export of precious metals and articles made from these raw materials would be henceforth permitted by the Finance Ministry.

A presidential decree also liberalised import rules by creating an Inter-Departmental Commission on Import Regulations headed by the first deputy premier of Ukraine. The main aims of the new body were to reduce the balance of trade deficit and balance the balance of payments, protect the interest of domestic and foreign business entities from unfair competition, reduce the volume of non-essential imports, ensure the rational utilisation of hard currency funds, prevent the import of poor quality goods and halt economically unjustifiable inflation of prices of imported goods.

The new body would also 'develop and ensure the implementation of a mechanism for applying unilateral restrictions on imports in compliance with the norms and principles of GATT'. This would include the compilation of a list of products that could be produced in Ukraine to replace imports, the producers of which would obtain tax and credit benefits. A list of states whose imports into Ukraine should be granted preferential rates under the unified customs rate of Ukraine would be drawn up. A number of measures to implement these proposals were to be introduced which included differential excise duty rates on non-essential imports depending on their quality and country of origin, establishment of the legal principles governing the servicing of foreign goods and the establishment of state registration of barter transactions that would include the timely delivery of imports from barter and imposing duties on barter transactions,

From 2 November 1994 commercial banks and *bureaux de change* were no longer required to follow official exchange rates for the *karbovanets* established by the Ukrainian Inter-Bank Currency Exchange. Henceforth, exchange offices and banks 'could re-establish free exchange rates of the *karbovanets* against foreign currency,' Pynzenyk said. Commercial banks are allowed to issue their *bureaux de change* with sufficient *karbovanets* and hard currency to meet daily demand. amounts of hard currency issued in this manner must not exceed 20 per cent of the previous day's volume of sales. An improvement in currency regulation was greatly aided by the introduction of a single rate for the *karbovanets*, renewal of the Inter-Bank Currency Exchange on 7 October 1994 and reform of the currency committee to aid regulation. The aims of the reforms were to develop foreign trade, stimulate exports and increase the flow of convertible currency to Ukraine.

Other planks of the Kuchma reform programme included a halt to financial credits to state industries unless they provided a business plan or restructuring programme and the introduction of a system of promissory notes that would allow for a system of bankruptcy. VAT was reduced from 28 to 20 per cent and maximum income tax was set at 50 per cent (down from 90 per cent).

On 4 April 1995, President Kuchma delivered a report to the Ukrainian Parliament on 'Ukraine's Economy in 1994' intended to shock members of parliament into continuing to follow the tough prescriptions he has continuously proposed since coming to office. According to President Kuchma, national income and GDP decreased by 24.9 and 23 per cent respectively in 1994, the largest declines since 1989. The budget deficit in 1994 had totalled 9.6 per cent. In President Kuchma's view, the financial system remains the weakest component of the national economy. The only positive indicator in 1994 remained inflation which slowed considerably compared to the hyperinflation of 1993.

Kuchma told his parliament:

> The first results from the implementation of this policy have been received. Essentially, the formation of global stabilising factors in the life of society has begun: the creation of an efficient economic system, a strong state, developed institutions of democracy and citizenship of society, the raising of Ukraine's authority and influence in the international arena. The key link in the stabilisation is the implementation of radical economic reform and the building of a qualitatively new economic system in Ukraine. (*Holos Ukrainy*, 6 April 1995)

Kuchma outlined ten priority areas where reform would be focused. These included a substantial speeding up of the privatisation process, stimulation of the most productive agricultural sectors, especially private land, switch to world energy prices in industry, agriculture and for domestic consumers, additional liberalisation of the taxation system, an end to subsidies to loss-making industries which would be declared bankrupt, lower priority for centralised capital investment and an increase in investment funds from the privatisation of state property, personal savings and the capital market. In addition, Kuchma called for an improvement in the manageability of the economy through the reduction in the number of ministries, accountability of ministers and stronger executive power, creation of an effective budget policy, including full independence for the National Bank, formulation of a state programme for the development of Ukraine's export potential and the establishment of free economic zones.

The Rise of Yevhen Marchuk

President Kuchma's job of cajoling parliament into accepting his reform programme was greatly aided by the resignation of the Vitaliy Masol government on the same day as he gave his report after parliament voted a motion of no confidence in it. Parliament also voted by 224:62 to accept the retirement of Prime Minister Masol, who had resigned on 1 March 1995.[15] First Deputy Prime Minister Marchuk became acting head of the government. Masol was forced to resign by hunger-striking students in October 1990, but was brought back by Leonid Kravchuk in June 1994 in a vain attempt to woo the communist vote in the summer 1994 presidential elections. Masol had long opposed the reduction of the budget deficit and other IMF conditions.

The vote of no confidence was supported by the communists on the one hand, who were hostile to economic reform which they termed a 'failure', and supporters of the president on the other, who believed it would lead to the domination by reformers of the new Cabinet. The resignation of the Masol government enabled President Kuchma to draw up a new government of his own. 'The political situation in Ukraine is not an easy one, but it is stable. The president has his own views on how to run the country and on that basis he will form his government,' Vladimir Horbulin, secretary of the National Security Council, confidently asserted.[16]

Contrary to Western press reports at the time, the vote of no confidence strengthened Kuchma's reformist hand as the conservative government had been inherited from his predecessor. As Kuchma warned, 'I'll accelerate radical economic reform irrespective of the political opposition. Without unpopular measures our economy won't survive.'

The vote of no confidence in the government was followed two days later by parliamentary approval at its second reading of the 1995 budget. Negotiations over an IMF Stabilisation Fund began in December 1994. The IMF insisted that their agreement to provide these credits would only come after parliamentary approval of the 1995 budget and concrete measures by the government. Then Deputy Prime Minister Ihor Mitiukov was appointed by President Kuchma as special co-ordinator for foreign assistance. Deputy Economics Minister Viktor Kalnyk admitted, 'We desperately need international financial assistance, particularly in this phase of economic reforms.'

Opposition to the IMF conditions in the 1995 budget were heard loudest from communist members of parliament. 'We categorically reject the dictates of the IMF. We are being forced to open the way to a decline in all our social programmes,' Communist Party of Ukraine and faction leader Pyotr Symonenko said. The chairman of the parliamentary commission on banking and financial questions, Viktor Suslov, also questioned the IMF conditions which threatened Ukrainian sovereignty. Most of the criticism rested on the cuts in agricultural subsidies and social expenditure. President Kuchma replied though that, 'Either we achieve consensus and create conditions for reform, or our economy will again fall victim to hyperinflation.'[17]

The number of amendments to the 1995 budget were kept to a minimum and expenditure was cut by 4 per cent in all areas, except social welfare. The largest budget cuts were for the military (hence the urgency of the need for the 'normalisation' of relations with Russia). The budget deficit was to be no more than 3.3 per cent (in Ukrainian calculations 7.3 per cent). Besides the reduction of monthly inflation of between 1 and 2 per cent the budget also abolished agricultural and industrial credits, imposed a strict incomes policy, increased household utility prices, normalised financial relations with Ukraine's creditors and increased its exports potential. Subsidies to the coal industry were replaced by inter-industry transfers.

The passage of the budget was praised by the IMF. 'The programme that the Ukrainian authorities have launched represents a clear break with the past, both in its commitment to rigorous financial discipline and in the implementation of substantial structural reforms,' the IMF believed.[18] Parliamentary speaker Moroz also gave his approval to the budget, which he claimed allowed for an increase in expenditure on funding production, the economy and social welfare. The 1995 state budget was brought into legal effect by a parliamentary vote of 256:5.

Speaking at the April 1995 London annual meeting of the EBRD, Roman Shpek, then Ukraine's economics minister, said, 'It is very early to start anticipating success for the reform programme but we are now a long way down a path from which there is no return.' But Shpek warned: 'If Western European institutions will not embrace Ukraine we can easily look to other centres of economic capital, such as Japan and the United States.'[19]

On 10 April 1995, President Kuchma established a commission headed by Shpek to elaborate state industrial policy guidelines for the period 1996–2000. President Kuchma also ordered the winding down of the state committee in support of small enterprises and its functions assumed by a new department within the Ministry of the Economy. The allocation of state credits to enterprises in 1995 was pegged to the restructuring of enterprises in which the state holding was 50 per cent or more. The National Bank was advised to allocate up to 20 per cent of primary credit emission to enterprises which met these requirements and possessed a business plan. The loans would be secured on enterprise assets or promissory notes received from customers. Sixteen unprofitable enterprises in the Donbas area were closed in 1995 after their accumulated losses amounted to 2000 billion *karbovanets*.

In further measures to speed up reforms and achieve fiscal stabilisation a presidential decree offered shares in restructured joint stock companies on the stock exchange. Up to 30 per cent of these shares would be for sale to individual and corporate investors, the proceeds of which would finance the establishment of new voucher auction centres as well as a national electronic stock exchange. The State Property Fund was instructed to compile a list of 100 joint stock firms whose value exceeded 45 billion *karbovanets* and those valued at between 0.7 and 45 billion *karbovanets* (C and D categories) which would be made available on the stock exchange.

Ukraine also planned to issue 17 trillion *karbovanets* in bonds to help reduce the budget deficit by 8 per cent in 1995. In early April 1995 the second issue of Treasury Bills proved to be an overwhelming success when all were sold at higher than their face value (the first auction was held on 10 March and raised 267.8 billion *karbovanets*). The Treasury Bills, each with 100 million *karbovanets* ($757) face value, were sold to 35 participating banks at a price of 108 million *karbovanets* ($818). The second issue raised a total of $1.83 million and 'showed that state bonds were increasingly attractive to investors', according to Vitaliy Mihashko, head of the certificates department of the National Bank. A third auction was held on 18 April where 5000 Treasury Bills valued at 100 million *karbovanets* each were sold.[20]

Correction of Economic Reform[21]

The programme of radical economic reform outlined in October 1994 by President Kuchma largely followed the prescriptions of international financial institutions. By spring 1995 these prescriptions were not only being ignored, but openly denounced by the Ukrainian leadership in favour of a Ukrainian 'state-regulated transition to a social-market economy'. 'But this does not mean we are going to revert to state planning,' Marchuk told an investment forum in London in late May 1995.[22] The need to reduce the 'shock' of economic reform was also probably geared to widening Kuchma's support in parliament and with the general public, which he needed to win support for a new constitution, the political reform that he regarded as essential for the success of economic transformation.

In Kuchma's annual address to parliament on 4 April 1995, he criticised those who backed a 'blind monetarist policy'. Economic reform, he said, should be state-regulated and provide a social safety net.[23] An immediate casualty of this 'correction' to Ukraine's economic reform programme was the radical Pynzenyk, deputy prime minister for economic reform. Kuchma initially did not include Pynzenyk in his new government created after the June 1995 Constitutional Agreement. But during a visit by the IMF to negotiate the next instalment of the $1.5 billion loan, Pynzenyk was brought back into the government as a sop to international financial institutions which often link personalities with the continuation of reform in the former Soviet bloc.[24] This is probably one reason why Volodymyr Lanovyi, author of the May 1992 programme of economic reform presented to the IMF when he was then deputy prime minister, was appointed presidential economic adviser in May 1996.

In June 1995, President Kuchma outlined a fundamental policy correction. The IMF target of 1 or 2 per cent monthly inflation was dropped in favour of 4 or 5 per cent by the end of the year. Then economic adviser to President Kuchma, Anatoliy Halchynsky, the author of the October 1994 economic reform programme, said the different targets were the result of different aims. This second stage of economic reform, Halchynsky believed, involved adjustments to the reform process. Whereas the first stage had aimed at financial stabilisation, the second sought to combine monetarist methods with raising production (during the 1990–4 period the Ukrainian government seemed uninterested in macro-stabilisation).[25] Deputy Prime Minister Pynzenyk pointed to the urgent need for the state to protect domestic producers and the domestic market.[26]

Despite announcing the 'correction' of Ukraine's economic reform in April and June 1995, the wrangling with parliament over the 'Law on Power' also effectively prevented any focus on the economy until June. President Kuchma pointed to a number of problem areas that still remained in Ukraine's economy:

- economic stabilisation was still unsteady;
- stabilisation of the *karbovanets* exchange rate resulted in a severe non-payments crisis;[27]

• using purely monetarist methods to ensure low inflation could not ensure stabilisation of the productive process.

The new government would henceforth focus on the structural reorganisation of the economy, provide substantial support for domestic producers and attempt to improve standards of living and social welfare. If Ukraine overcame its decline in production in 1995, it could enter a phase of sustained economic recovery in 1996, Kuchma believed. Support for domestic producers

> will ensure Ukraine's integration into the world market in its capacity as a highly developed country, rather than as a banana republic. Certain sectors would be earmarked for priority development – the agro-industrial complex, aircraft manufacturing, nuclear power engineering, shipbuilding, gold production, the aerospace industry and others – to which foreign investment would be directed.[28]

A State Credit and Investment company was established in August 1995 to attract foreign investment into these key areas, ensure the implementation of government policy and to facilitate the settlement of Ukraine's foreign debt.

Kuchma continued to insist, though, that these 'corrections' did not mean that Ukraine had again abandoned economic reform, 'which was the republic's last chance to survive'.[29] These 'corrections' would merely shift emphasis towards production, Marchuk said, including more 'radical' privatisation and finding a solution to the payments crisis. The new government plan, proposed in July 1995, 'will implement deep corrections in economic reforms, increasing stimulation of production and its social orientation'. This required an easing of monetary policy, which would entail slightly higher inflation targets.

Why, only seven months into the radical reform programme, did President Kuchma feel there was a need for a 'correction'? Three possible reasons may have accounted for this:[30]

1. The government failed to create the conditions for success (privatisation targets were not met, the *hryvna* was not introduced and a market in government securities was not created).
2. There was little public support for a programme of radical economic reform. There was public support though, for slow economic reform that was 'regulated' and included preservation of the social safety net.
3. It reflected a change in the political landscape of Ukraine. The October 1994 programme reflected post-election euphoria by Kuchma's team eager to distance themselves from the Krachuk era and to gain accep-

tance by international financial institutions and Western governments. The rise of the more conservative former prime minister, Marchuk, lobbying by pro-industrialist lobbies (one of which Kuchma had himself headed between 1993-1994) and the need to reach compromise over constitutional questions all necessitated a 'correction'.[31]

Speaking at an all-Ukrainian Conference of Economists on 14 and 15 September 1995, Kuchma and Marchuk reiterated their support for the Ukrainian 'corrected' model of economic reform. The need for the correction was in order that 'it would be accepted by public opinion and the majority of the population', Kuchma admitted. Adjustments were only natural; maintaining 'a dogmatic attitude towards what was proclaimed earlier would be inadmissible'.

Ukraine could not 'blindly copy the West's economic model' and other states in the process of rebuilding their economies because states did not follow 'a course of blindly copying others' experiences ... ' 'Our people will never agree to the role of a secondary state lagging behind and reproducing others' experiments, because we paid dearly for our statehood,' Kuchma added. Ukraine 'will not be able, and does not need, to repeat, much less duplicate, the course once pursued by the now economically-developed nations,' Marchuk told the economists gathered at the meeting. 'From this point of view, the so-called market blitzkrieg, intended to generate and accelerate self-regulating economic processes by using and demonstrating the laws of a classic market economy, turned out to be premature,' Marchuk added. Therefore, Ukraine 'cannot randomly and unquestioningly follow someone else's course, the more so in that our own history is extraordinarily rich'.

The successful transformations, Kuchma believes, were where countries, 'based themselves as much as possible not only on their economic individuality, but also on their historic traditions, genetic roots, national identity and their people's culture'.[32] One of the lessons that Ukraine should learn from world experience is that 'every country without exception acted on the basis of their own strength, historical traditions and the mentality of their own people'. In other words, 'where large-scale reforms were a success, their implementation rested upon the foundation of traditional fundamentals in the life of the public at large,' Marchuk told the conference.[33]

Despite these 'corrections' President Kuchma was always at pains to point out to both domestic and international observers that economic reform was still a high priority for him. Addressing the National Press Club for Market Reform on 18 November 1995, he stated that one of his main policy aims was to ensure that economic reform was irreversible and extricating the economy out of its crisis through financial stabilisation. 'There is no alternative to our economic reform course, and the transformation of our economy is irreversible,' he added.[34] Western diplomats based in Kyiv were not surprised at the 'corrections' to Ukraine's economic reforms; in their eyes, the IMF targets were always unrealistic.[35]

The Ukrainian model and the lessons that Ukraine would learn from world experience have the following attributes:

- rejection of Western economic models in favour of a 'state-regulated transition to a socially oriented market'. The transition to a market economy would come about through state regulation. Both absolutes would be rejected – the reimposition of total state control or the complete withering away of the state;
- social support of the population during the transition to a market economy;
- protection of the domestic market and producers, especially foodstuffs and light industries;[36]
- establishment of a mixed economy allowing the conditions for all types of ownership;
- the division of the state sector into government and joint stock enterprises through corporatisation where the state would retain 51 per cent of stock;
- the preservation of the monopoly status of certain key enterprises that could help Ukraine enter the world market;
- state control through economic levers of prices;
- the need for a rigid vertical structure of government and the strengthening of the executive and administrative authorities.

After the summer recess parliament did not return to the draft economic programme until mid-October 1995. On 11 October, by a vote of 234:61 (with 17 abstentions), parliament voted to accept the government programme of evolutionary economic reform, the ninth such programme since August 1991.[37] The 116-page programme covered every conceivable topic, ranging from financial and budgetary policy to foreign economic activity, taxation[38] and social policy. Former Prime Minister Marchuk, who addressed parliament, warned, though, that 'the crisis which our society is now undergoing is prolonged and deep, but to hope for an easy and simple way out would be a naive illusion'.[39] But Marchuk did point to a number of positive developments in the budget: taxation, growth in exports and Ukraine's fulfilment of foreign payment obligations. The vote gave the government *carte blanche* for one year to implement economic and political reforms in Ukraine without any threat from the legislature. 'Kuchma is winning – but it's inch by inch,' a Western diplomat in Kyiv said. The general consensus was that Ukraine *was* moving forward but *slowly*.[40]

Although the vote gave the government and president the authority to continue pursuing their policy of gradual market reform, the left wing in parliament nevertheless remain determined to block all moves to create a capitalist economy and non-Soviet presidential–parliamentary republic. During the debate on 11 October 1995, a socialist member of parliament attempted to introduce voting on her faction's alternative programme – something contrary to the Constitutional Agreement. In addition, on the following day, parliament voted in a minimum wage which 'has actually cancelled the government programme of action adopted yesterday'.[41] 'What we had before was a satanic blitzkrieg. We are now being presented with genocide against our own people,' Symonenko, leader of the communists, said after the vote.[42] In contrast, two members from the eight parliamentary factions which backed the government programme were rewarded with new government posts (Anton Buteiko and Holovatiy as deputy foreign minister and minister of justice from the Centre and Reform factions respectively).

Critics of the Marchuk programme pointed to its perilous political balancing act between economic reform and left-wing and industrialist lobbies. Its mixture of free market and command administrative methods may make it unworkable. Anders Aslund, a Western adviser to the Ukrainian government, remained very critical of its industrial policy: 'What "industrial policy" really means is that directors of state enterprises want to sit on their hands and think that the state should pay them for that.'[43] One Kyiv commentator and president of the Ukrainian Media Club pointed to contradictions in five areas in the programme – foreign trade liberalisation, social welfare, taxation policy, lack of budgetary funds[44] and promotion of both privatisation and the maintenance of state monopolies.[45]

Fiscal and Monetary Reform

The introduction of the new *hryvna* currency, ready since 1992, had been long predicted and new printing equipment was moved into the Kyiv mint in early 1995. The entire issue of the *hryvna* had been printed locally by the end of 1994, apart from a small order placed abroad for 1, 5, 10, 50 and 100 *hryvnas*. 'How important is the *hryvna*? How important is fresh air to people's health?' National Bank chairman, Viktor Yushchenko, said.[46] It was initially claimed that Ukrainian citizens who lost their savings in 1992 from inflation were to be granted privileges when the *hryvna* was eventually introduced.[47]

In May 1995, Yushchenko pointed to stabilisation of the *karbovanets*, a sharp fall in inflation, control of the budget deficit and money supply as well as large international credits as providing the ideal opportunity to introduce the *hryvna*. Inflation was less than 5 per cent per month in May 1995 and the National Bank had slashed its annual interest rate from 150 to 96 per cent (down from its high of 252 per cent in December 1994). But as late as May of that year, Pynzenyk, then deputy prime minister, argued that the new currency could be introduced only when inflation had dropped to less than 1 per cent per month.[48]

In late May 1995, the National Bank had slashed the number of firms entitled to licences to conduct trade in foreign currency, part of a delayed plan to make the *karbovanets* the sole legal means of payment in Ukraine. The National Bank had issued licences to just 150 companies, down from 1300, granting them only to companies with a monthly turnover of $70 000 or more. 'This is another step to strengthen our national currency, boost its authority and to boost the authority of the future currency, the *hryvna*. Every self-respecting country has its national currency. Our actions intend to limit foreign currency as a means of payment. No one is banning or planning to ban the holding of currency or depositing in accounts,' Serhiy Brahin, head of the National Bank's foreign currency control section, said.[49]

From 1 August 1995, Ukraine banned the use of foreign currency from cash retail and service transactions (something originally intended to take place in February 1995). The National Bank instructed commercial banks and those businesses formerly licensed to trade in hard currency to turn over all available foreign currency to the central bank. Commercial banks were not allowed to take hard currency for deposit. Businesses retained the right to have hard currency accounts to clear settlements, whilst hard currency deposits in personal accounts would be preserved.

At a meeting of Kyiv local administrations on 26 July 1995, President Kuchma said that Ukraine would introduce the new national currency – the *hryvna* – no later than October of that year. After its introduction, Ukraine 'would pursue a tough budget and monetary policy which is meant to contribute to stability of the new currency unit'.[50] One *hryvna* would be exchanged for 10 000 or 100 000 *karbovanets* and would not be pegged to a hard currency, like the Estonian kroon was to the Deutschmark, as this would require a stabilisation fund of $5 billion. The National Bank had already accumulated $2 billion in reserves to support the new currency (the target had been $1.5 billion). On 2 August 1995, Kuchma repeated his pledge to introduce a 'strong currency' during a visit to the Ukrainian Commodity Exchange.

These announcements led to a dramatic devaluation of the *karbovanets* from 152 000 to over 170 000:$1 on the National Bank's Interbank Currency Exchange in August 1995. Officials blamed the devaluation on panic-buying of US dollars after the announcement of the impending introduction of the *hryvna* as a permanent legal tender. Officials said that this was a voluntary way to mop up excess *karbovanets*. 'People will be notified of it well in advance and no confiscatory measures will be taken,' Deputy Prime Minister Mitiukov said. The National Bank stated that they could take out a large volume of money within 10–15 days.

But the *hryvna* was not introduced in October 1995, as President Kuchma said it would be, and its introduction was postponed until 1996. For the new currency to function properly other factors had to be taken into account: the level of output, the rate of inflation (its introduction required a monthly rate of no more than 1–2 per cent), the dollar exchange rate against the *karbovanets*, the foreign and domestic debt. The higher than average monthly inflation rate in the second half of 1995 (inflation stood at 14.2 and 9.1 per cent in September and October respectively), lower than expected budget revenues from privatisation and insufficiently large stabilisation fund all prevented the *hryvna* from being introduced. Kuchma also blamed the lack of a 1996 budget. 'It is impossible to approve the budget first and then recalculate it in another currency,' he said.[51]

The following year conditions had sufficiently improved with inflation falling to very low levels that a presidential decree on 25 August, the day following Ukraine's fifth anniversary of independence, announced the introduction of the *hryvna* on 2 September 1996.[52] A combination of accumlated hard currency reserves in the National Bank and IMF support for a stabilisation fund also ensured the *hryvnia's* introduction. Between 2 and 16 September the *karbovanets* was exchanged for the *hryvna* at a rate of k100 000:h1 and to the Russian rouble for r3000:h1.

The introduction of the long-awaited *hryvna* had more than economic value. It symbolised the new self-confidence of the Ukrainian elites that there was no going back and represented the final element of the state-building process. Ukraine's elites believed that an independent country required its own currency which ruled out any return to the rouble zone. The introduction of the *hryvna* also had powerful symbolic value because it linked the post-1991 Ukrainian independent state to its medieval Kyiv Rus' and Central Rada predecessors, thereby giving it an added 1000-year-old legitimacy.

The Black Economy

No discussion of Ukraine's post-Soviet economic transition would be complete without reference to the black economy. Although official figures showed large falls in GDP, these revealed only part of the story. The decline in the command-administrative system and Ukraine's economy in general had forced the majority of people by 1994 to need more than one salary. Salaries in the state sector were either too low to provide a decent standard of living or they were not paid for months on end, or both.[53] Seventy-five per cent of these other jobs were in the black economy.

The problem, of course, is the fact that by its very nature it was a covert part of the economy about which precise details were difficult to obtain. Everybody knew it existed and many people supplemented their official state salaries with other sources of income. In the words of Dmytriy Levin, commercial director of SC Johnson, a US company with a large presence in Ukraine, 'It is a curious situation of a crisis country with booming residential construction and increasing car purchases.'[54]

In January 1995, the black economy was officially acknowledged in Ukraine and a special group headed by Halchynsky was formed to study it. There were growing calls to legalise the black economy (apart from certain areas, such as narcotics, traditionally the preserve of organised crime).[55] A high-level meeting held in spring 1996 devoted to the influence of the black economy and organised crime in Ukraine set up by the Centre for Economic and Political Research was attended by members of the Security Service, presidential administration, government and academic institutions. The meeting produced some of the first details about the size and scope of the black economy in Ukraine.[56]

Whereas the black economy accounted for 40 per cent of Ukraine's GDP in 1994, by 1995 this had grown to nearly 50 per cent; it was therefore nearly as large as the official economy (the latter figure was backed by World Bank studies). In 1993 and 1994, when hyperinflation allowed many high-ranking individuals to earn large sums from currency speculation, the black economy accounted for 24.1 and 36.1 per cent respectively.

Those attending the meeting, organised by former presidential adviser Oleksandr Rozumkov, alleged that organised criminal groups had taken control of a large number of private enterprises and state enterprises. Owing to the black economy's unofficial status as something outside the law, untaxed and involved in corruption, predictably it had been penetrated by organised crime.

Each year $3 billion were siphoned off to the West, an amount which in 1993 amounted to 50 per cent of legal exports. The illegal export of capital from Ukraine was put at:

1991 – $3.9 billion
1992 – $3 billion
1993 – $2.9 billion
1994 – $2.5 billion
1995 – $2.6 billion (20 per cent of the total value of Ukrainian exports)

Within Ukraine there was a large volume of cash unaccounted for, which fuelled the black economy and other illegal activities, to the tune of $8–10 billion. According to the Main Directorate for Combating Organised Crime within the Ministry of Internal Affairs, 223 000 billion *karbovantsi* were circulating in the black economy, representing a third of the entire volume of money supply within Ukraine.[57] The capital flight from Ukraine, which had reached $15–20 billion during 1991–5, had only enriched a small number of those who were involved in these illegal activities.

The worst aspect of these developments, the meeting heard, was the interconnection of high-level state structures with corruption and organised criminal groups. Those high-ranking officials who attended the meeting expressed their concern that the growing size of the black economy prevented the state from exerting any leverage over it or collecting taxes from up to half of the economy. In addition, those involved in the black economy were not interested in capital investment but the stripping of assets. The continued existence of the black economy also promoted a negative attitude on the part of the population towards paying taxes, obeying the law and the benefits of a market economy.

PRIVATISATION[58]

Preconditions and Contradictions[59]

In October 1991, the Ukrainian government adopted a programme entitled. 'The Principal Directions of the Economic Policies in the Conditions of Independence'. The core of the proposed transformation would cover the privatisation of state enterprises, transformation of totally state-owned enterprises and a move to a market economy with mixed forms of ownership. Before the launch of privatisation in Ukraine, only 2.9 per cent of employees worked in the private sector, whilst state enterprises (at the central and municipal level) absorbed 94 per cent of Ukraine's workforce.[60]

Legislative preconditions for privatisation were mostly outlined during the following year. These included the key laws 'On Privatisation Certificates', 'On the Privatisation of Small Enterprises' and the 'State Privatisation Programme'. A positive aspect of this new legislation was that it defined the objects and means of privatisation. According to the quality indexes and balance value of assets all enterprises belonged to one of six groups to be privatised. The categories of state properties included small, medium and large enterprises, their level of state subordination, monopoly enterprises, unfinished construction projects, the Military-Industrial Complex and areas suitable for foreign investment.

The legislation outlined different methods of privatisation – buy-out of small privatisation objects by associations of buyers, the lease of state property with the option of a future buy-out, sales through commercial or non-commercial tenders, the sale of state properties by auction, creation of joint stock companies and sales of its shares (corporatisation of enterprises). This legislation envisaged that each citizen had the right to a share of the privatised property with 40 per cent of certificates (vouchers) going to them.

Hyperinflation, causing the recalculation of the assets balance of enterprises, delayed the privatisation programme and the 1992 legislation therefore failed to ensure the implementation of the privatisation programme. The political, social and economical environment remained unattractive to economic reforms. Divisions arose between the executive and legislatures, different political parties and within parliament between the 'Red Directors' of state enterprises, the Party of Power (the former top *nomenklatura* within the disbanded Communist Party of Ukraine) and the pro-reform national democrats. With the introduction of presidential prefects in spring 1992 reform was also held up by conflict between local representatives of the executive and legislature. In addition, reform was blocked by the absence of an organisational system to implement privatisation, with no establishment of State Property Fund regional branches and insufficient staff. Investment banks and the securities market were also largely underdeveloped.

Trust companies, set up ostensibly to help investment into privatised objects, allegedly cheated depositors out of $160 million (28 200 billion *karbovanets*), after an inspection of over 2000 companies by a newly appointed state commission, established under President Kuchma, to trace lost property and assets and return them to their original owners.[61] Ninety-three criminal cases had already been launched against Trust companies by December 1995. Gaps in legislation and the lack of state control triggered a fraud boom with many of the Trust companies operating as pyramids.[62] In December 1995 parliament suspended registration of new Trust companies and imposed a ban on cash transactions with any institutions other than banks and insurance companies. A new law on Trust companies was adopted in the first quarter of 1996 to ensure state regulation of this process.[63]

Some 'Red Directors' quickly realised that enterprise buy-outs by employees on preferential terms or transitions to leases with further buy-outs provided them with practically unlimited possibilities of enterprise management. Privatisation of state property, therefore, coincided with the narrow pragmatic interests of these directors. There remained a noticeable difference in the approach to privatisation by members of parliament from western Ukraine. They consistently backed the programme of mass privatisation and publicised this among the population. A priority was given to land privatisation owing to western Ukraine's largely agricultural economic base (although the region lagged behind in privatisation of industry and the service sectors, see later). In contrast, in eastern Ukraine privatisation was more often than not *prykvatizatsia* (*nomenklatura* privatisation).[64] In western Ukraine privatisation was reportedly a more open process with less emphasis on insider trading by those with the right connections. *Prykvatizatsia* existed in both western and eastern Ukraine though; it was more a question of degree rather than being something totally absent from one area of the country.

The Pace of Privatisation[65]

The state privatisation programme envisaged that the share of state enterprises would drop to 93 per cent in 1993, 81 per cent the following year and reach 60 per cent by 1995. In reality, in 1992–4 under President Kravchuk the pace of privatisation was very slow, primarily owing to insufficient managerial and organisational preconditions and lack of political support by the then Ukrainian leadership for economic reform.[66] According to Ukrainian sources, at the 1992–4 pace of privatisation it would have taken Ukraine more than ten years to restructure the ownership system radically.[67] According to the IMF, if the 1992–4 privatisation pace had been maintained, it would have taken 15–17 years to complete the process.[68] Yet the majority of Ukrainian public opinion had constantly backed privatisation.[69] Another problem was that 'In technical terms it is hard to proceed with privatisation. The laws are not up to scratch,' Yuriy Yekhanurov, head of the State Property Fund, admitted.[70]

The slow pace of privatisation during 1992–4 can be gauged from the following figures:

- only 23 per cent of state-owned apartments were privatised (approximately 1.6 million), especially in Luhans'k, Kherson and Trans-Carpathian *oblasts*;
- 60 per cent of all industries remained state-owned, 20 per cent had mixed ownership and 20 per cent were collectively owned;
- only 5 per cent of all production originated in the private sector.

The Ukrainian government reported that 7967 enterprises were privatised in 1994. This was in comparison to 3585 in 1993 and 30 in 1992. The 1994 figures, broken down, are shown in Table 5.1.[71]

The areas with the highest degree of privatisation were not western Ukraine, which one might have expected, but areas in the traditional industrial regions of eastern Ukraine where President Kuchma won solid backing in the July 1994 elections. Donets'k and Kharkiv held first and second place respectively in the rate of privatisation with the majority of objects found in the trade and light industrial sectors. In contrast, in L'viv

Table 5.1   Privatisation in Ukraine (as of 1994)

Sector	Number Privatised
Industry	1331
Agriculture	218
Transport & communications	165
Construction	680
Incomplete Construction Projects	31
Retail & catering	3264
Supply and sales of machinery	130
Agricultural trade	7
Other production facilities	19
Housing & utilities	85
Public amenities & services	1885
Health care	12
Culture & arts	11
Scientific	45
Educational	8
Other sectors	48
Not specified	28

oblast, the rate of privatisation was far slower and closer to the bottom of the list of Ukrainian regions.

Two reasons accounted for this. First, western Ukraine, as has already been pointed out, was largely agricultural and therefore there was less to privatise. The only exception was L'viv *oblast*, which had a sizeable industrial base. Secondly, a large majority of privatisation in eastern Ukraine was *prykhvatizatsia* by local political and economic elites. Eighty per cent of privatisations during 1992–4 was undertaken through lease-to-buy and in the majority of them there were violations of the law, according to the chairman of the State Property Fund, Yekhanurov.

The law 'On Leasing the Property of State Enterprises and Organisations' allowed local elites to buy out state-owned property that hindered privatisation. State-owned property was purchased at very low prices not adjusted to inflation which, in turn, contributed to the poor perception of privatisation as a whole as 'fraud'. The lease of enterprises was performed on a non-tender basis which made their employees the only candidates for ownership. The lease payment was established for the entire length of the lease and could not exceed 5 per cent of enterprise income. Employees could buy out the enterprise within three years for the price agreed at the beginning of the lease. Eighty per cent of these buy-outs of state property were undertaken by the workers' collectives which have failed to lead to higher productivity, efficiency or improved financial health and liquidity, according to then First Deputy Prime Minister Pavlo Lazarenko.[72] Privatised enterprises, in contrast, were lauded as working more efficiently than when they had been state firms.[73]

Under President Kuchma amendments to the lease law halted the right of lessors to a buy-out. The lease of state property may be denied in the event of the corporatisation of an enterprise or interest by foreign investors. The profits of leased enterprises would not be used for a buy-out of state property but for the development and purchase of new equipment.

Parliament Suspends Privatisation

Besides amending the lease law, the Ukrainian parliament adopted a resolution 'On Perfecting the Privatisation Mechanism in Ukraine and Reinforcing Control Over its Course' on 29 July 1994.[74] The resolution was widely condemned, coming as it did on the eve of a G7 summit in Naples, but it included a number of positive points:

• income earned from the sale of privatised objects should be reinvested in the production process (not lost in the government budget);

- efforts were made to reconcile contradictions in previously enacted privatisation and lease laws;
- the resolution did not apply to small scale (communal) property privatisation.

Further government resolutions also outlined plans to:

- improve the mechanism of informing Ukrainian citizens through the mass media of privatisation in order to increase their participation in the process;
- create a single system of privatisation structures by incorporating under the State Property Fund several departments that would safeguard the operation of regional branches and development of a legal basis of co-operation between the central and local powers;
- call for foreign investment in enterprises undergoing privatisation.

The moratorium on privatisation was lifted on 7 December 1994. But this was only undertaken after the demand contained in the parliamentary resolution for the government to draw up a list of enterprises excluded from privatisation was accepted. A total of 5414 enterprises in the energy, transportation and communications sphere were initially excluded from privatisation. 'We can consider this issue is resolved. We have confirmed a list of enterprises which are exempt from privatisation,' Moroz said.[75]

On 23 February 1995, the government finally approved a list of 5600 state enterprises which could not be privatised, but a parliamentary resolution (of 3 March 1995) increased this to 6102 enterprises in different branches of the economy, and they were all removed from the list of state objects to be privatised. On the same day, the Ukrainian parliament approved another list of enterprises exempt from privatisation which listed 90 companies in the defence, oil refining and baking industries (although communist deputies had demanded that all 'strategic' industries be exempted and not only the 1 per cent of those enterprises in these sectors included in the additional list).[76]

In September 1995, two presidential decrees allowed the state to retain control over enterprises deemed to be strategically important and to maintain a government monopoly in transportation, communications, energy, ports, pipelines, postal services and the manufacture of spirits. The second decree gave the state 51 per cent of shares in enterprises to be transformed into joint stock companies but barred from total privatisation by parliament (see 'Correction of Economic Reform' above).

Of particular concern was Russian interest in Ukraine's oil and gas industries. The State Property Fund suspended privatisation of the gas company *Ukrhazprom* and the oil company *Ukrnafta* in December 1995 in line with a parliamentary resolution the previous month. The state maintained a 60 per cent share in *Ukrnafta* while *Ukrhazprom* had not yet been privatised.

The battle which was waged between parliament and president concerned the degree to which the figure of 6004 enterprises could be reduced. President Kuchma, who spent the majority of his working life in the Military-Industrial Complex, believed that this sector should be one of the first to be privatised. Many in parliament, both communists and nationalists, disagreed and had demanded that the Military-Industrial Complex be added to the list of exempt enterprises.

Many nationalists back the moratorium on privatisation of 'strategic objects' in the energy sector because of the fear of Russian capital purchasing a majority share in Ukraine's oil and gas industries which included the pipelines that transported Russian fuel to Europe. But President Kuchma is strongly in favour of allowing Russian investment into Ukraine's privatised energy sector and believes that denationalisation of the Military-Industrial Complex is the only way to keep it afloat because the state can no longer afford to subsidise it with cheap inflationary credits. Formally, there are no conditions or limits on Russian investment in Ukraine and legally this process is regulated by the same stipulations covering investments of foreign capital. There do exist large possibilities for Russian companies to invest in corporatised Ukrainian firms, especially where the technological process requires Russian–Ukrainian co-operation, for example, through Industrial-Financial Groups (see chapter 6).

Privatisation Takes Off

The draft State Privatisation Programme for 1995 looked impressive.[77] The total number of enterprises to be privatised was estimated at 31 650, including 22 450 small firms, 8000 middle and large companies and 1200 uncompleted construction sites. But during discussion of the programme in parliament these figures proved to be unrealistic. In the end the figures which it settled for were 10 000 and 2660 small and large enterprises respectively slated for privatisation. But, it was doubtful whether these figures would be implemented on the basis of the slow pace of privatisation during 1992–4. In 1994, for example, only 28.4 per cent of the State Programme of Privatisation was completed.

The subdivision of all privatisations into small, medium and large within six groups of state facilities subjected to privatisation were incorporated within the bias of economic reform methodology and legislation. The principal differences between these enterprises lay in their volume of accumulated productive assets, their number of employees, the sources of the buy-out assets and the types of privatisation to be carried out. The size of the enterprise being privatised defined the potential investor – individuals, firms or foreign.

The small privatisation list was mainly compiled within the trade, public catering, public services, light and foodstuffs industry. The balance value of their capital assets did not exceed 1.5 million *karbovantsi* in 1992 prices. The main manner in which they were privatised was through auctions, tenders or buy-outs by employees. For medium and large enterprises privatisation was undertaken through corporatisation and their transformation into joint stock companies.

On 11 April 1995 a presidential decree attempted to deal with the question of improving media coverage and *hlasnist* (glasnost) in the privatisation process.[78] The decree set out to ensure openness in the privatisation process, instructing state television and radio to air information daily about it and for the authorities to ensure adequate and timely information in the media programmes on privatisation and the reform process. Another concern of the authorities remained the prevention of abuses. A new Anti-Monopoly Committee was established to monitor individual violations of Ukraine's anti-monopoly legislation which would examine instances in which monopolies could be disbanded.

A noticeable qualitative change occurred in the privatisation mechanism after the change in the leadership of the State Property Fund. Yekhanurov, unlike his predecessor at the State Property Fund, had political backing from President Kuchma to push privatisation. 'The political will is here, with President Leonid Kuchma's radical programme of reforms approved by parliament,' he pointed out.[79] 'Collective ownership is an absolute anachronism. Ownership should be personified, while all the collective enterprises should be transformed into open stock companies,' he believed. 'Privatisation will occur in Ukraine! I guarantee it. Because I am the terminator who has been hired to make sure that it happens and it will,' he stated.[80] Western consultants working in Kyiv praised Yekhanurov, in comparison with his predecessor, whose aggressive, pro-market policies had transformed the State Property Fund.[81]

These new qualitative changes in the leadership of the State Property Fund resulted in the creation of a single state privatisation organ. The State Property Fund, as the main methodological, managerial and control centre, increasingly relied on the activities of regional and representatives offices. In addition, a network of centres for certificate auctions was created, the main task of which was to ensure public participation in the privatisation process through the issuing of certificates (until December 1994 they had existed as privatisation deposit accounts). Citizens could exchange their certificates through the purchase of state property in these regional auction centres. This had the effect of increasing the pace of privatisation. If in January–February 1995 demand for shares was only 715 000 per month, by April this had risen to 1 750 000. By May 1995, the number of issued shares had grown to 5 354 247.[82] By the end of 1996, it was estimated that upwards of three-quarters of Ukrainian adults would have taken their privatisation shares.[83]

On 11 April 1995 the left-wing lobby in parliament returned for adjustment the 1995 privatisation programme presented by Yekhanurov, head of the State Property Fund. But Yekhanurov pledged to proceed with privatisation, 'no matter what points of view parliament has', whilst criticising the West for failing to provide sufficient technical and financial assistance to accomplish privatisation.[84]

On 23 June 1995, President Kuchma signed a decree 'On Means to Ensure Privatisation in 1995' in the absence of a parliamentary privatisation programme.[85] Under the decree foreign investors would be granted the 'national regime in the privatisation process'; that is, foreigners would be able to take part in privatisation on the same terms as Ukrainian citizens. The decree set state and communal privatisation targets during 1995, which included a total of 8000 medium-sized and large enterprises and another 1200 enterprises, the construction of which were not completed.

On 5 July, parliament adopted a resolution 'On the Ukrainian State Property Fund's Report' which called on it to:

- step up its work on supervising the efficient use of state property;
- ensure that privatisation is implemented in Ukraine in accordance with current legislation;
- conduct preparatory work on establishing a register of the state's share in the assets of enterprises;
- the Cabinet of Ministers was to undertake an inventory of property by 1 October 1995;
- the parliamentary commission for Economic Policy and Management of the National Economy, together with the Cabinet of Ministers, were to speed up the adoption of laws on changing the form of ownership and the draft law 'On Nationalising Property in Ukraine';
- the supervisory commission for privatisation issues were instructed to continuously analyse the privatisation process;

- the Cabinet of Ministers was to draw up measures to improve the system of statistical reporting of the socio-economic consequences of privatisation;
- the supervisory commission and the Cabinet of Ministers were told to analyse the results of the experimental privatisation of the *Motor Sich* plant in Zaporizhzhia and prepare proposals on making amendments to the law on the privatisation of facilities of special importance to the economy and national security;
- the Cabinet of Ministers was to ensure better publicity on privatisation;
- the Cabinet of Ministers was to ensure the timely submission of the 1996 privatisation programme.

In October 1995, President Leonid Kuchma announced plans to speed up privatisation by temporarily maintaining the state sector in a large number of companies. The state sector, accounting for 45 per cent of industrial output, would be divided into state enterprises and those subject to corporatisation in which the government would maintain a stake. 'I do not share the monetarist slogan "the less government the better". This simply does not suit us. The losses we have sustained during our crisis were to a great extent caused by this,' Kuchma believed.

A separate privatisation programme was agreed between the Crimean and Kyivan authorities in summer 1995 after separatist political groups had been removed from power (see chapter 3).[86] A presidential decree charged the Crimean government and local authorities with presenting to the State Property Fund a list of enterprises eligible for privatisation.[87] A maximum of 30 per cent of Crimean enterprises would be privatised, whilst the remainder would stay in 'the hands of the state or the people', according to the chairman of the Crimean State Property Fund, Oleksii Holovyzin. Privatisation of small facilities and unfinished construction sites would begin. The Crimean and Ukrainian authorities agreed to divide sanatoriums and health resorts between national and Crimean jurisdiction.[88]

Speaking at a conference on privatisation in Kyiv in late January 1996, Kuchma pledged to make privatisation a 'strategic goal' in 1996. 'Mass privatisation has great significance. It is perhaps the only means Ukrainians have to reach our common aim – to become a developed society,' he argued.[89] The ultimate objective would be to create a property-owning class. Privatisation had not been as successful as originally hoped for in 1995, because of resistance by local leaders and the left wing in parliament. Small-scale and medium-to-large privatisation were to be completed by June and December 1996 respectively, Yekhanurov said.

Privatisation Fails to Meet Expectations[90]

The results of privatisation during the first half of 1995 initially looked impressive. Out of 3250 privatised enterprises 2250 were small firms and 1000 large enterprises. The pace of small privatisation was particularly striking.[91] Nevertheless, in July 1995, the Cabinet of Ministers issued a resolution criticising the slow pace of small privatisation, blaming it on poor organisation by privatisation agencies, ministries and other central and local executive authorities. The parliamentary moratorium until July 1995 also had a negative effect on the privatisation process.

Only 28.8 per cent of the second quarter's privatisation target was met. The head of the State Property Fund promised to forge ahead despite local opposition to ensure that 50 per cent of all firms were in private hands by the end of 1995. 'Despite the low figures so far, our plans remain in place. We have laid down the foundation,' he said. 'Those officials who oppose privatisation should resign, because they do not agree with the government's line,' he added.[92] During the first quarter of 1995 Ukraine privatised 507 state-owned companies, including 107 small businesses and two factories still under construction. By the end of the third quarter of the same year, 8239 businesses had been turned over to the private sector (including 1866 medium and large firms). Privatisation was most successful in Odesa, L'viv and Kyiv (see the Tables 5.5–5.8 at the end of this chapter) and nearly 40 per cent of the labour force were already employed in the non-state sector.[93] Despite the worse than expected pace of privatisation, by the end of 1995 50 per cent of the Ukrainian workforce were employed in a total of 2000 small and 1400 medium-to-large privatised enterprises or private companies.[94] Nevertheless, only 40 per cent of the targeted medium-to-large enterprises had been privatised in 1995.

Of the target of small-scale privatisation 58 per cent was completed by the end of 1995 (although even this was greater than the combined figures for 1992–3).[95] The most successful regions were Odesa *oblast* (which fulfilled 91 per cent of its target), Zaporizhzhia *oblast* (70 per cent) and the city of Kyiv (66.7 per cent).[96] Oleksandr Bondar, deputy chairman of the State Property Fund, predicted that small-scale privatisation would be completed by mid-1996.

The State Property Fund put revenue during the first quarter of 1995 at 628.9 billion *karbovanets* and privatisation voucher sales at 3977.6 billion. In July 1995 alone, a total of 1070 small businesses and three 'Category D' facilities (unfinished construction sites) were privatised. By July 1995, 14 907 facilities had been privatised in Ukraine with total receipts of nearly 2 billion *karbovanets*. But Ukraine's budget received only 2000 billion *karbovanets* instead of the 90 000 billion expected as privatisation revenues for the first ten months of 1995. According to Mykola Azarov, chairman of the parliamentary commission on Budget Questions, the State Property Fund 'had envisioned absolutely unrealistic privatisation revenues in the state budget' owing to its inadequate estimation of the pace of privatisation in the regions and its lack of control over the process.[97]

The shortfall in budget revenues from privatisation was a major reason why the budget deficit exceeded the IMF target of only 7.2 per cent of GDP in 1995.[98] This, in turn, prevented the introduction of the new currency (*hryvna*) without the IMF stabilisation fund. The government had been forced to underfinance government activities rather than print money to avoid further hikes in inflation. This led to strikes by many public service sector workers after their wages had not been paid in months.

The World Bank made contingent its next $350 million credit to Ukraine on key improvements in its privatisation programme. 'Our first rehabilitation loan was also intended to support mass privatisation. We cannot repeat this, go on to the next operation without the first objective being attained,' Daniel Kaufman, the World Bank's Ukraine representative, said.[99] US special presidential adviser Richard Morningstar, coordinator of US aid to the CIS, told First Deputy Prime Minister Lazarenko that Ukraine's slow pace of privatisation would threaten US investment in Ukraine.

Land Privatisation

President Kuchma has continuously stressed that the privatisation of land is crucial to his reform programme. Ukrainians 'are psychologically ready for the privatisation of land,' according to First Deputy Prime Minister Petro Sabluk.[100] The government planned to privatise 90 per cent of land beginning in 1995, another highly ambitious and unrealistic target. This would require a new credit system, modern storage facilities and new processing, packaging and sales techniques. 'Private ownership of land is perhaps the most important step in carrying out land reform. Today everyone understands that if such an initiative is not undertaken, nothing can go forward,' Deputy Prime Minister Viktor Pynzenyk argued.[101]

A presidential decree adopted on 10 November 1994 entitled 'On Urgent Measures to Accelerate Land Reform in the Sphere of Agricultural Production' set out to create equal conditions for different forms of ownership in rural areas and to stimulate agricultural production. The privatisation of the land in the possession of agricultural enterprises was now a priority of land reform in Ukraine. 'The transfer of land into collective and private property for agricultural production shall be effected on a voluntary basis proceeding from the principle that land should belong to those who cultivate it,' the decree outlined.

To this effect local councils and the State Committee for Land Resources 'should take measures to accelerate free-of-charge the transfer of land to collective ownership of agricultural co-operatives, joint-stock companies and other agricultural enterprises whose employees would like to possess land'. A division of land transferred to collective ownership would be organised 'into land sections [shares] without providing them in kind. Each member of these co-operatives and companies will be given a certificate specifying the size of his land plot and its value.' This could then be sold, bought, presented as a gift, exchanged, inherited or used as a pledge. The size of such plots could not exceed the norms fixed by the Land Code. The Cabinet of Ministers of Ukraine were instructed to amend the Land Code of Ukraine and the Code of Civil Procedure relating to the rights to land plots (shares) and their transfer to private ownership.

Another presidential decree on 18 January 1995 promoted land and agricultural reform.[102] The decree aimed to provide adequate conditions for the development of the agricultural sector and to expand the farmers' rights pertaining to the selling of agricultural produce. Farmers would independently handle and use their produce, selling the latter according to the state and other contracts through exchanges, trading and contract houses, supply and intermediary organisations. The establishment of specialised agricultural commodity exchanges was understood to be a necessity to help in land reform.

By mid-1994, when President Kuchma was elected, 3.4 million Ukrainian citizens had privatised plots of land of which only 83 000 had already applied for, and received, state deeds due to inadequate legislation and the blocking of the process by local authorities. In Odesa the authorities had given the go-ahead for land within the city to be transferred into private ownership in September 1994. This mainly referred to the ability to sell at auction the rights to privatised land with unfinished constructions and vacant city land for development (see Table 5.2).

The pace of land privatisation had already been growing, despite obstacles placed in its way by the rural *nomenklatura*. Ukrainian land privatisation nearly doubled in 1994 and by January 1995 1.5 million hectares were privatised.[104] The scale and speed of land privatisation and the creation of private farms can be ascertained from Table 5.3. (See Table 5.8 for more detailed figures.)[105]

Table 5.2   Land Auctions (1994)[103]

City	Date	Rights Sold	Income ($)
Kharkiv 1	21.1.94	2 long-term leases	40 000
Kharkiv 2	24.6.94	3 long-term leases	38 850
Kharkiv 3	13.10.94	7 long-term leases	355 000
L'viv	3.12.94	2 long-term leases	5 176
Odesa	10.12.94	2 private parcels 2 long-term leases	127 276
Chernihiv	24.12.94	5 long-term leases	49 154
Total		21 long-term leases 2 private parcels	615 456

Table 5.3   Land Privatisation (1992–5)

Year	Number of Farms	Total Area (000s hectares)
1992	14 681	292.3
1993	27 793	558.2
1994	31 983	699.7
1995	34 687	790.0

Privatisation of land was proceeding most rapidly in Volyn, Ivano-Frankivsk, Chernivtsi, Ternopil *oblasts* in western Ukraine and Zhitomir, Sumy and Khmel'nyts'ky *oblasts* in central Ukraine where over 50 per cent of plots formerly allocated for smallholdings and country homes had been privatised. In Donets'k, Kharkiv and Luhans'k *oblasts* in eastern Ukraine and in the city of Sevastopol less than 10 per cent had been privatised. Privatisation of land was proceeding more rapidly in rural and suburban areas than cities.

Over 600 enterprises in various parts of the agricultural sector were privatised in 1994 (see Table 5.4).[106] In addition, 218 of the 1303 state

Table 5.4   Privatisation of the Agro-Industrial Sector

Number	Privatised From
415	Ministry of Agriculture & Foodstuffs
120	State Committee For Foodstuffs Industry
99	Ukrainian Agro-Industrial Construction Company

farms and other state agricultural enterprises were now in private hands. The privatisation drive included the majority of enterprises involved in the processing of, and supply of services to, the agricultural sector, which were turned into joint stock companies. An agricultural produce exchange began trading in Kyiv in May 1995.[107] By the end of 1995, two-thirds of agricultural enterprises that used to be owned by the state had been privatised. Processing and agricultural service enterprises were also privatised and nearly 50 per cent of the total had been privatised by spring 1996.

By the end of 1995, it had become clear that the pace of privatisation in agriculture had not been as high as expected. Pavlo Haidutsky, formerly chairman of the State Committee on Land Resources and architect of Ukraine's land reform, was appointed minister of agriculture to attempt to speed up the process. A proposed $250 million World Bank loan for agricultural development was held up by the slow pace of land privatisation.[108]

Less than a third of the collective and state farms marked for privatisation had been transferred into private hands. Only 1071 of the 3690 farms scheduled to be handed to their employee collectives had completed the process by December 1995. Farm privatisation had been most successful in Vinnytsia, Poltava and Odesa *oblasts*. Local authorities had been most resistant in Kharkiv, Kherson and Chernivtsi *oblasts*. Nevertheless, the State Property Fund predicted that the process would be completed by the end of 1996.[109]

Forty per cent of Ukrainian citizens eligible to own land had bought private plots by the end of 1995. The land privatisation drive was led by Volyn *oblast*, where 80 per cent of all plots were sold. In contrast, Crimea and Donets'k *oblast* were trailing far behind with only 3 and 8 per cent of plots respectively transferred to the private sector.

Nevertheless, opposition from the parliamentary left remained strong, as witnessed during the parliamentary debate during November 1995 on the draft law 'On Amendments and Addenda to the Land Law'. The draft law was rejected by parliament on 15 November 1995 as a 'danger to Ukraine's economic security' by a vote of 245:13 (with 21 abstentions). The office of the Procurator-General was ordered to investigate cases of the illegal sale of land.[110] On 30 January 1996, parliament adopted a compromise law 'On the Procedure for Privatising Property in the Agro-Industrial Complex'. A compromise was reached over the question of the 51 per cent of the shares of privatised processing enterprises which would be transferred free of charge to corporate bodies which had a right to establish Trust companies and accept certificates from individuals.[111]

Parliamentary Speaker Moroz had repeatedly criticised the turning of land into a commodity, as witnessed by parliament's vote on 15 November

1995 to block changes that would have allowed individuals to take personal control of land from collective farms. 'Would-be theoreticians on land reform are promoting the idea of replacing collective farms with what looks like an attractive share scheme. But this amounts to unjust distribution of land,' Moroz said. If land were to become a commodity in Ukraine, 'we will destroy virtually every agricultural enterprise in Ukraine,' he added. Reform of agriculture is not the key question, Moroz believed, but the relationship between the state and countryside.[112] He also complained that Ukraine had no national programme for the development of the agro-industrial complex, whereas the government programme was 'based on the ideology of international financial organisations whose aim is to destroy competitive production and use surplus dollars to acquire land'.[113]

'Agriculture in Ukraine today cannot survive outside the market. A key element is private ownership of land. But we have no intention of destroying collective industry,' Deputy Prime Minister Sabluk replied to parliament's resolution.[114] In a public address in late December 1995, Kuchma called for the introduction of market reforms in agriculture: 'the agro-industrial complex must take the lead in pulling the economy out of the crisis'. His draft programme envisaged three stages – denationalisation of land, the transfer of ownership rights to collective farms by the end of 1996, and the creation of farming associations to replace collective farms. Kuchma believed these reforms would enable Ukraine to utilise its fertile black earth properly and rejoin the world's leading agricultural nations within a decade. 'But we had an irrational, half-feudal system with no motivation for effectiveness. Now our duty and policy is to direct reforms so that this sector will lead the economy and the country out of the crisis,' Kuchma told the conference.[115]

WESTERN ASSISTANCE[116]

The approval of the 1995 budget opened the way for the IMF to release $1.96 billion to Ukraine which consisted of a one-year Stabilisation Fund ($1.57 billion) and the second portion of the Systematic Transformation Facility ($392 million, the first half of which was released in October 1994). The IMF funds were released quarterly to monitor expenditure and helped to cover Ukraine's $5.5 billion balance of payments gap which had primarily been caused by mounting debts for energy imports from Russia and Turkmenistan.[117] The IMF warned, 'However, the task of restructuring the Ukrainian economy and restoring the country's external viability goes beyond 1995 and will require continued adjustment measures, as well as external assistance over the medium term.'

The amount of foreign finances made available to Ukraine in 1995 had fallen short of the country's requirements by $6 billion. Most of the deficit had been offset by the rescheduling of debts, which had been accumulated from Russian and Kazakh imports of oil and gas and by loans from international financial institutions. Another $900 million was made available on a bilateral basis by a number of donor countries. Borrowing in 1995 had been less than anticipated, because talks on bilateral loans from the European Union and Japan had started later than planned.

Ukraine hoped to obtain $6 billion in 1996 in foreign aid. The bulk of 1995 assistance (debt restructuring, bilateral financing and international loans) were utilised to cover energy imports. The priority for 1996–7 would be directing foreign credits to restructuring the economy. Ukraine and the G7 signed a memorandum of understanding to close the Chernobyl nuclear power station at the April 1996 G7 summit in Moscow. The memorandum stated that the closure would be an important step in improving nuclear safety, not only in Central and Eastern Europe, but throughout the world. Ukraine confirmed its readiness to close Chernobyl before the year 2000, contingent on foreign aid. The document called for the drawing-up of a comprehensive programme by the G7, EU and Ukraine to co-operate in investment projects to expand Ukraine's energy industry and enhance nuclear safety. The G7 would make available $500 million in grants to support the programme and a further $1.2 million in credits from international financial institutions and the International Atomic Agency.

An IMF delegation visited Ukraine in July 1995 to review its progress in meeting conditions for the $365 million third tranche of the loan to be disbursed in September of that year. The IMF insisted that Ukraine should maintain its agreed inflation targets, whereas the Ukrainian authorities were concerned that the credit conditions were too stringent. President Kuchma admitted that Ukraine would be unable to meet monthly inflation targets of 1–2 per cent by the end of 1995 and proposed instead 4–5 per cent targets. Kuchma called for an easing of monetary policy to support industry's declining output, especially in priority areas such as shipbuilding, aerospace and agriculture. The IMF conceded that Ukraine had fulfilled its targets for the first half of the year and was ready to amend the programme during the second half.

The decision to provide Ukraine with the third tranche of the IMF loan was given during Marchuk's visit to the United States in late September 1995. According to the IMF's managing director, Michel Camdessus, Marchuk 'convinced me of the fact that there exist no big differences of opinion between Ukraine and the IMF'. IMF concerns with Ukraine remained its failure to liberalise grain exports and pay off its energy debts to Russia. Ukraine's deputy finance minister, Borys Sobolev, told the IMF that it could not pay off its external debt before it collected its domestic debt.

To date, about 20 projects for possible World Bank financing in Ukraine have been formulated with the Ukrainian government, and a dozen smaller projects and studies are being prepared or implemented with grant financing, handled by and mobilised through the World Bank. If economic reform and restructuring continued in Ukraine, the World Bank could provide Ukraine with up to $0.8–1 billion per annum.

Two projects were under implementation (the Rehabilitation Project and the Institution Building Project) whilst others had been, or were close to being, approved for World Bank lending, such as the Hydropower Rehabilitation, Urban Transport and the Agricultural Seeds Projects. Projects under implementation or at an advanced stage of preparation included those in the areas of a Rehabilitation Loan, Institution Building, Hydropower Rehabilitation, Seeds Development, a Structural Adjustment Loan, Thermal Power Rehabilitation, Telecommunications, Gas Transit, Urban Transport, Housing Development, Health, Donbas Region, Gas Distribution, Enterprise Development, Agricultural Structural Adjustment and Market Development, Education, Social Protection Adjustment, Financial Institutions Development as well as in Water and Wastewater.

The International Finance Corporation had played a key role in privatisation in Ukraine and with the help of the United States Agency for International Development had co-operated with the Ukrainian government in introducing small-scale privatisation since June 1992. This was introduced in two phases: the design and implementation of a model small privatisation scheme in L'viv and the subsequent expansion of this to other cities throughout Ukraine.

After L'viv, where the first auction in Ukraine was held in February 1993, the International Finance Corporation established permanent operations in nine cities throughout the country. The International Finance Corporation, through its Corporate Financial Services Department, had also been involved in medium and large-scale privatisation in Ukraine since June 1992. The International Finance Corporation's first project in the area of medium-scale privatisation was with the Odesa Meat Factory.

To improve the environment for small, newly privatised enterprises, the International Finance Corporation also began a post-privatisation project in Ukraine with funding from the British Know How Fund. Luhans'k was chosen as the project site because of its previous success in privatising municipally owned enterprises through auctions and buy-outs and the election of a reformist mayor. The project consisted of two principal elements:

1. a business centre and business training for new owners; and
2. reform of local tax and business regulations.

To assess businessmen's needs on business training the International Finance Corporation designed and administered a statistical survey to identify these needs. Based on the survey results, the International Finance Corporation established business training courses. The first pilot course was offered in February 1995 to directors and senior managers of newly privatised enterprises, and received high ratings from students.

The International Finance Corporation also announced an ambitious initiative to assist the Ukrainian government in the privatisation of collective and state farms and the agro-industrial sector as a whole, which would operate jointly with the British government's Know How Fund. A 'specialised institution of the UN' was working out a 'model for privatisation of agricultural land'. Initially, it would be tested at a number of private farms in Donets'k *oblast* and then extended to the whole country where the overall area of agricultural land belonging to collective and state farms amounted to 47 million hectares. The International Finance Corporation was also working on a 'new approach' to the voucher privatisation of 4000 agro-industrial enterprises. The staff of the enterprises, the suppliers, the population at large, investment funds and foreign investors could all become shareholders in the new scheme.

On 22 September 1995, the EU approved a further balance-of-payments loan of up to 200 million ECU for Ukraine. This amount was mainly utilised to cover fuel bills from Russia and Turkmenistan. The Ukrainian parliament ratified the credit agreement with the EU on the granting of a further 85 million ECU loan by a vote of 216:30 (after initially rejecting it on 17 November 1995). The loan will be over a ten-year period beginning in 2001 and was granted within the framework of financing the 1995 budget deficit.

The EU also approved the ten-year Partnership and Co-operation Agreement with Ukraine, Russia, Moldova and Kyrgyzstan. Under the agreements the EU provided financial and technical aid for political and economic reform in these former Soviet republics. They are also designed to open up foreign trade and could, in the long term, lead to free trade agreements. But they do not offer the possibility of eventual membership in the EU, unlike similar agreements with Central European states. In the case of Ukraine, the EU voiced concern about the Chernobyl nuclear plant and called for special aid to boost Ukraine's potential as a cereals exporter. The EU was prepared to finance most of the Chernobyl closure costs with the remainder coming from Ukraine, Japan, Canada and the United States. The EU and Ukraine would co-operate to establish a free trade regime by 1998. The EU planned to increase Ukrainian exports to Western Europe, raise Ukraine's export quotas for metals and textiles, and expand investment into the Ukrainian economy.

Ukraine was the third largest recipient of US aid in the world and the largest recipient of US aid in the former USSR, an important new development during 1996, reflecting Ukraine's growing strategic importance to the West. The US Senate and House conference committee on the Foreign Appropriations Act approved $225 million in assistance to Ukraine in 1996, despite reduction of overall aid to the former USSR (Russia obtained only $195 million). The assistance was contingent on Ukraine undertaking 'significant economic reforms'.

US assistance to the former USSR declined by 25 per cent between fiscal years 1995 and 1996. At the same time assistance to Ukraine increased by 50 per cent. In 1995, Ukraine received 17.8 per cent of aid to the former USSR which grew to 35 per cent in 1996. An additional $50 million was allocated to the Western NIS (Newly Independent States) Fund, which covered Moldova and Belarus as well as Ukraine. Of the $225 million in US aid it is stipulated that $50 million should be made available for energy self-sufficiency and to improve safety at nuclear power stations, $2 million for an assessment of the energy distribution grid, $22 million for the development of small and medium enterprises, and $5 million for the diagnosing of victims of the nuclear accident.

The European Bank for Reconstruction and Development (EBRD) had a number of objectives in Ukraine which include helping to establish financial services infrastructure which would be needed to promote the development of the private sector. Other EBRD projects included support for newly privatised enterprises and development of local private sector, support for newly privatised enterprises and development of the local private sector, renovation of rundown infrastructure, in parallel with the restructuring of utility sectors along commercial lines.

During the second half of 1995, new agreements signed by President Kuchma and Jacques de Larosière, President of the EBRD, covered increasing the EBRD's contribution to the Ukraine Investment Fund by $6.5 million and investing $5 million in the construction of a mineral fertiliser and grain terminal at Odesa port. The EBRD also pledged to provide guarantees for Ukrainian banks opening correspondence accounts abroad, the first of which was the Ukrainian Innovation Bank. The EBRD would lend Ukraine a total of $130 million of which $75 million would be devoted to developing the private sector. Ukraine proposed three new infrastructure projects – a new runway at Borispil airport ($35 million), an oil-processing terminal at Odesa to process 40 million tonnes of crude oil and the building of a rail and motorway terminal ($40 million) – to the 1995 EBRD annual conference.

The EBRD had granted a loan of $8 million to the Poltava Oil and Gas Company for boring four new oilwells in the Novo-Mykolaivski field near Poltava and constructing a pipeline and rail export facilities. The initial output of the four wells was expected to be 4000 barrels of oil and 45 million cubic feet of natural gas per day. The Poltava Oil and Gas Company is a British–Ukrainian joint venture in which the Ukrainian State Property Fund held a 51 per cent stake and the remainder was controlled by JKX Oil and Gas (a subsidiary of the JP Kenny Group of Companies). The oil and gas were sold to Ukraine at world prices and refined at the nearby Kremenchuk refinery. The EBRD hoped that by boosting domestic energy production it would reduce Ukraine's need to spend hard currency on imports.

The EBRD had also taken up a 35 per cent stake in a new commercial bank. The EBRD provided 1.75 million ECU out of a total of 5 million ECU charter capital for the Kyiv International Bank, which was to specialise in long-term credits for medium-sized businesses. Other share-holders in the new bank included the National Bank of Ukraine (17 per cent) and Poland's Kredyt Bank (13 per cent). *Gradobank* became the first Ukrainian commercial bank allowed to disburse EBRD funds for business projects in Ukraine to support small-to-medium businesses. Five Ukrainian commercial banks competed for the tender besides *Gradobank–Ukrinbank*, *INKO* Bank (all three from Kyiv), the West Ukrainian Commercial Bank (L'viv), *Privatbank* (Dnipropetrovs'k) and *NordBank* (Odesa). The EBRD had provided 100 million ECU in four instalments through the National Bank. The funds would be allowed as loans only after vetting by international auditors for periods of three to five years at 16 per cent APR. Only one in ten of *Gradobank's* loan applications met the EBRD's stringent requirements.

CONCLUSIONS

By the end of 1995, nearly two years into President Kuchma's reform programme, it was clear that the path to a market economy was likely to be slow, with 'corrections' still to come and the programme was beset by strong opposition from the radical left. As one author has pointed out,

'Few, if any, of its reforms have been consolidated and institutionalised, and all remain quite subject to influences from both domestic and foreign sources.'[118] The same author argued that there was no alternative to the type of reform programme that was all-embracing and based on three pillars: stabilisation (the easy part, which had been undertaken), privatisation and liberalisation which are 'indeed mutually interdependent and cannot be applied in isolation'.[119]

Ukraine's political elite do have a consensus view – to tread slowly with economic reforms (as they are doing with political reforms; see chapter 4) under state regulation and with a social safety net. This more evolutionary approach to economic reform reflected the disillusionment with the alleged 'shock therapy' reforms of Russia, which were perceived by the Ukrainian elites as having brought conflict, violence and impoverishment to Russia. In addition, it enabled the Kuchma leadership to divide the left wing between the orthodox hardliners, grouped within the Communist Party of Ukraine, and its parliamentary faction, from the Socialists and Agrarians, who were less hostile to an evolutionary path to a 'regulated, social market economy'. Marchuk and Moroz, therefore, formulated a working relationship that had allowed Kuchma's policies to be adopted by parliament. This stability and consensus were vital for Ukrainian state- and nation-building.

At first glance the new evolutionary policies of economic reform closely resembled those of the Kravchuk era. But not entirely. First, Kravchuk and Kuchma have totally different personalities and come from different career backgrounds and regions of Ukraine. Secondly, although both stress consensus, centrist policies nevertheless, Kuchma is willing to adopt more strident demands and pressure than his predecessor (for example, over the new constitution or economic reform). Finally, Kuchma, in stark contrast to his predecessor, has some semblance of a vision of what sort of a state he is building in Ukraine, something that was absent under Kravchuk. Kuchma's policies successfully stabilised Ukraine economically and monetarily enabling the introduction of the new currency – *hryvna* – which had eluded his predecessor.

Ukraine's privatisation record during 1992–4 was not impressive. Although the legislation was put in place and a state privatisation programme was adopted, no political will existed to promote it, whilst continued conflict between the executive and legislature slowed down any attempts at reform. Finally, the former ruling communist *nomenklatura* and Party of Power within Ukraine under former President Kravchuk preferred the leasing system to full-scale privatisation that allowed them to be enriched from the proceeds of rentier capitalism in an unstable economic and inflationary situation.

Table 5.5 Privatisation in Ukraine (1992–4)

	Privatised Firms	Used Privatisation Accounts (000s)	Privatised Apartments (000s)	Private Farms (000 hectares)	Private Land
1992	30	5 000	–	14 681	292.3
1993	3 585	728	9 02.8	27 739	558.2
1994	11 552	7 106	1812.3	31 983	699.7

Source: European Centre for Macroeconomic Analysis of Ukraine and the Ministry of Economics of Ukraine, *Ukrainian Economic Trends*, October 1995.

Table 5.6 Presidential Programme of Privatisation of Medium to Large Enterprises (1995)

Regions & Oblasts	State	Communal
Crimean Autonomous Republic	274	156
Vinnytsia	302	15
Volyn	77	70
Dnipropetrovs'k	428	89
Donets'k	928	140
Zhitomir	234	5
Trans-Carpathia	101	15
Zaporizhzhia	207	96
Ivono-Frankivsk	140	91
Kyiv	150	25
Kirivohrad	82	19
Luhans'k	167	94
L'viv	231	42
Mykolaiv	155	73
Odesa	238	122
Poltava	196	7
Rivne	111	12
Sumy	187	9
Ternopil	198	11
Kharkiv	395	57
Kherson	192	79
Khmelnysky	286	161
Cherkassy	202	27
Chernivtsi	134	15
Chernihiv	114	94
Kyiv city	646	70
Sevastopol city	25	6
Total	6400	1600

Source: *Ukraine Business Review*, vol. 3, nos. 13–14 (October–November 1995).

In contrast, President Kuchma made privatisation a cornerstone of his reform programme in autumn 1994. For the first time, Ukraine had a leader with the political will to launch the country's first serious attempt at large-scale privatisation. By autumn 1996, small-scale privatisation had been completed and 40 million Ukrainian citizens had collected their privatisation shares. Left-wing opposition within the Ukrainian parliament proved to be less than anticipated, although there would be major conflict with them over land privatisation. President Kuchma, as the

Table 5.7   Presidential Programme of Privatisation of Small Units (1995)

Regions & Oblasts	State	Communal
Crimean Autonomous Republic	124	527
Vinnytsia	130	527
Volyn	77	341
Dnipropetrovs'k	219	1 309
Donets'k	380	1 451
Zhitomir	95	433
Trans-Carpathia	45	210
Zaporizhzhia	105	566
Ivano-Frankivsk	50	648
Kyiv	107	953
Kirivohrad	263	503
Luhans'k	154	952
L'viv	148	1 718
Mykolaiv	169	626
Odesa	169	761
Poltava	99	517
Rivne	81	532
Sumy	87	686
Ternopil	70	441
Kharkiv	252	1 102
Kherson	150	732
Khmelnysky	83	554
Cherkassy	122	476
Chernivtsi	81	555
Chernihiv	210	520
Kyiv city	237	1 010
Sevastopol city	13	105
Total	3 720	18 730

Source: *Ukraine Business Review*, vol. 3, nos. 13–14 (October–November 1995).

former chairman of the Union of Industrialists and Entrepreneurs of Ukraine, successfully convinced the majority of the directors' lobby that there were no alternatives to reform and privatisation, and that there was no going back to the command-administrative system.

Aid to alleviate Ukraine's economic crisis and help the structural transformation of the Ukrainian economy could only come from the West and international financial institutions. The improvement of relations between Ukraine and the West under Kuchma, the launch of Ukraine's first serious commitment to reform and completion of denu-

Table 5.8 Privatisation of Land (1995)

Region	Number of Registered Farms	Total Area (h)
Crimean Republic	33 746	756 965
Vinnytsia	843	18 241
Volyn	596	8 958
Dnipropetrovs'k	2 417	68 102
Donets'k	2 058	47 614
Zhitomir	311	5 882
Trans-Carpathia	915	4 191
Zaporizhzhia	1 548	49 610
Ivano-Frankivsk	701	5 810
Kyiv	914	19 966
Kirovohrad	1 672	58 118
Luhans'k	1 257	48 899
L'viv	1 189	12 570
Mykolaiv	4 961	95 733
Odesa	3 970	58 261
Poltava	1 322	29 985
Rivne	335	4 681
Sumy	941	25 653
Ternopil	736	10 527
Kharkiv	1 027	33 729
Kherson	2 700	90 671
Khmelnytsky	497	10 349
Cherkasy	499	11 302
Chernihiv	587	17 279
Chernivtsi	622	3 323
Total	33 746	756 965

Source: *Uriadovyi Kurier*, nos. 111–12 (27 July 1995).

clearisation released the assistance from the West that was absent during the Kravchuk era. The fact that during 1996 Ukraine became the third largest recipient of US aid – ahead of Russia for the first time – was an important psychological indicator of Ukraine's growing geo-strategic and geo-political importance.

6 New Foreign and Defence Policies[1]

'Ukraine and Russia are going in two different directions but hand in hand.'

(Russian Foreign Minister Yevgenny Primakov)

'There is no government closer to us right now than Ukraine.'

(Nicholas Burns, US State Department spokesman)[2]

During the Kravchuk era Ukraine rejoined a world community of nations which did not always seem eager to accept the disintegration of the former USSR into 15 newly independent states. The election of Leonid Kuchma as president in summer 1994 brought few radical geo-strategic changes in Ukraine's foreign and security policies and certainly no major alterations in its geo-political orientation. Nevertheless, there have been noticeable changes in style and substance between Kravchuk and Kuchma. Ukraine is no longer portrayed as a 'buffer' between Eurasia and Europe, but as a 'bridge' linking both halves of the European continent. Relations between Ukraine and the West have improved radically as Ukraine has launched its first serious reform programme and completed de-nuclearisation. Problems remain – and are likely to continue to remain – with the complete 'normalisation' of relations with the Russian Federation in the aftermath of the Chechen crisis.[3]

FOREIGN POLICY

Priorities and Security Fears

Borys Tarasiuk, then deputy foreign minister, outlined Ukraine's security concerns in November 1993 at a conference entitled 'Ukraine in Future European Architectures and Security Environments', which was organised by the Rand Corporation and the Stiftung Wissenschaft und Politik.[4] The security concerns were directed at the Western government participants and by looking at them we can gauge the extent to which, if at all, Ukraine's relations have improved with the West and if its security

179

concerns have been met. (Proposals marked by an asterisk indicate Western support has already been achieved.)

Political-Economic Proposals
- *The West should facilitate economic reforms by supporting them technically and financially. This would include the creation of a Stabilisation Fund to support the introduction of a new currency.
- *The EU should negotiate closer ties, including associate membership, after Ukraine launched economic reforms.
- The West should support Ukraine's demands for a share of the former Soviet assets after taking into account its debts.
- *The West should support political reforms and democratic change in Ukraine.

Security Proposals
- *The West should oppose any external attempts to undermine domestic stability of Ukraine or the advancement of territorial claims against it. The West should openly state its concern at the existence of external threats towards Ukraine.
- *The West should support security guarantees for Ukraine by the five nuclear powers in return for its nuclear disarmament.
- The West should support the creation of a Fund for Nuclear Disarmament.
- The West should support the creation of a Central European Zone of Security and Co-operation as an interim mechanism.
- The West should support the juridical equality of all Soviet successor states.
- *In the event of the inability of Russia and Ukraine to solve a dispute, the West should agree to act as an honest broker.
- *The West should reject the proposal that Russia should act as the sole peacekeeper in the former USSR.

Since November 1993, Ukraine's foreign policy has become more mature and professional and relations have greatly improved with the West and, to a lesser extent, with Russia. Of the political and economic proposals made by the Deputy Foreign Minister Tarasiuk, the main stumbling block to any Western support for Ukraine was always the lack of reform under President Kravchuk. With the introduction of radical political and economic reforms under President Kuchma, Ukraine has received financial and technical support from international financial institutions and Western governments. Ukraine's hopes that the IMF will provide it with a

Stabilisation Fund not only helped it to introduce fiscal-monetary discipline in Ukraine – something sorely lacking between 1992 and 1993 when Ukraine experienced hyperinflation – but also to introduce its new currency, the *hryvna*. This would end any speculation as to whether Ukraine would return to the rouble zone.

Ukraine was the first former Soviet state to sign a co-operation agreement with the EU in May 1994 and thus opened the way for Ukraine's eventual associate membership of that body. The West has been remarkably reluctant to become involved in the Russian–Ukrainian dispute over former Soviet debts and liabilities, stating that it would prefer to deal with one country (Russia) rather than with 15. It is also not clear why Kyiv continues to persist in this affair as it is unable to pay its share of the former Soviet debt.

The West has been far more forthcoming in supporting political reforms in Ukraine. Numerous financial bodies, both supranational, government and private, are involved in providing technical expertise, training and financial support for democratic change in Ukraine. Ukraine was finally admitted to the Council of Europe in November 1995, a process which had been prolonged owing to Russian demands that both countries be allowed to join only at the same time, as well as the lack of a post-Soviet constitution in Ukraine.[5]

In the realm of security proposals there have also been major advances since late 1993. Ukraine agreed to abandon its nuclear arsenal and in exchange received security assurances from three nuclear powers (the United States, United Kingdom and Russia). These are not legally binding and are in the form of a memorandum. They are not guarantees, which were never on offer, despite the fact that Ukrainian leaders continue to describe them as 'security guarantees' (as does the Ukrainian official media). The security assurances support Ukraine's territorial integrity and independence, oppose external interference in its affairs and economic pressure. The security assurances, therefore, undercut any Russian argument which would hold them back from recognising Ukraine's borders in an inter-state treaty.

Western governments have also publicly reiterated support for Ukrainian independence and opposition to any changes in its borders in diplomatic meetings, letters of exchange and during press conferences. Since 1994, there has been a perceptible change in US and, to a lesser extent, Western European understanding of Ukraine's strategic significance. The Republican Party's victory in the US Congress in 1994 reinforced the perception that Ukraine and the three Baltic states were all strategic allies which were important to the West.

At the same time, the West's Russocentric and 'Russia first' policies had not altogether disappeared. The West does not treat all the former Soviet republics equally, but regards Russia as the first among equals. Western appeasement of Russian neo-imperialism continued to alarm Ukrainian security fears. The West had not condemned Russian peace-keeping in the former USSR; on certain occasions it had even applauded it. Senator Mitch McConnell, Republican chairman of the Senate Appropriations Subcommittee on Foreign Operations, said,

> The Russian Federation is attempting to dominate the Baltics and former republics of the Soviet Union and Warsaw Pact through economic coercion, political intimidation and in some cases military intervention. Virtually every leader in Central and Eastern Europe and in Central Asia has privately and publicly expressed serious concerns about Russian neo-imperial ambitions. In fact, the only government that does not seem alarmed by the trends is our own.[6]

Western criticism of Russia's military intervention in Chechnya and its abuse of human rights since December 1994 has been largely muted.[7]

The West has always opposed the creation of a Central European Zone of Security and Co-operation (CEZSC), believing it to be a Ukrainian attempt to create an anti-Russian *cordon sanitaire*. The proposal had been harmed by Belarus's *de facto* return to the status of a Russian dominion. Meanwhile, the Visegrad group seeks its future in NATO membership – not in the proposed CEZSC. In discussions surrounding the expansion of NATO in the West, its fondness for placing all the former USSR within the Russian sphere of influence could be gauged by its preoccupation with Russian concerns. Yet Russia shares a border with just one of the four prospective NATO members. Ukraine, which borders three of them, found its viewpoint rarely taken into account by Western governments as though Moscow again spoke on behalf of the entire Commonwealth of Independent States (CIS) – as it once did for the former USSR. Certainly there was considerable fear among all Ukraine's political parties and the Ukrainian leadership that NATO's expansion would *de facto* force them back politically and militarily within the CIS under Russia's tutelage.

The CEZSC had also been forgotten by the Ukrainian side because of the change in Ukrainian leadership. As president, Kravchuk had attempted to persuade Western leaders to look upon Ukraine as a 'buffer' between Europe and Russia. In contrast, President Kuchma had dropped this phrase in favour of Ukraine acting as a 'bridge' between Europe and Russia. The United States had acted as an honest broker by helping to negotiate the Trilateral Statement, thereby solving the nuclear stalemate. But the West had not been asked to mediate in the Black Sea Fleet question, even though a final solution to this untractable problem (especially that of Sevastopol) was likely to be impossible without the good offices of the United States.

New Foreign Policy Agenda

Ukraine's new foreign policy initially prioritised the 'normalisation of relations' with Russia and the CIS, partly a reflection of the disillusionment with the West that other post-communist countries had earlier gone through. President Boris Yeltsin compared Kuchma favourably with his predecessor with whom he never had good personal relations, saying there was a 'completely different atmosphere'.[8] Gone was talk of the creation of a CEZSC or a Baltic–Black Sea Axis, of Ukraine acting as a 'buffer' between Russia and Europe and of Ukraine 'entering Europe' ahead of Russia. Ukraine was now less likely to reject co-operation on each occasion out of hand, as happened under former President Kravchuk, but would sometimes hold similar views to Russia on international questions.

President Kuchma therefore changed Ukraine's foreign policy in a number of key directions:

- Ukraine no longer looked on economic co-operation with Russia and the CIS as an unfortunate necessity, but as an urgent requirement in the light of the close economic interdependence inherited from the former USSR and due to its economic crisis.
- Ukraine continued to rule out political and military integration within the CIS although bilateral co-operation, for example, between the military-industrial complexes of Russia and Ukraine, was regarded as beneficial. But Ukraine was interested in raising its profile in the CIS by helping to mediate in local conflicts such as Moldova, Azerbaijan and Georgia. It has suggested that it would agree to help in peace-keeping duties under OSCE and UN mandates but, in the aftermath of the Chechnya crisis, it is highly unlikely that the Ukrainian parliament would approve such a move.
- Urgent steps needed to be taken to 'normalise' relations with Russia, which would help to stabilise Ukraine's inter-ethnic relations. This 'normalisation' could only take place on the basis of equality, non-interference in each other's affairs and respect for each other's territorial integrity.
- Ukraine would continue to search for alternative energy sources in order to reduce its dependence on Russia. This was being undertaken

with the help of the construction of a new oil terminal near Odesa, a Georgian–Ukrainian pipeline to supply Azeri oil, and the possible involvement of Turkey.

- Ukraine would nevertheless continue to integrate within the European and world community by aspiring to join international organisations and diversify its foreign trade. Organisations which Ukraine seeked to join include GATT, the EU, the Central European Free Trade Agreement and the Central European Initiative. Ukraine would also strive to deepen its participation in structures where it is an existing member, such as the North Atlantic Consultative Council (NACC) and NATO's Partnership for Peace.

- Ukraine had prioritised relations with the West by overcoming the two main obstacles which held up their development between 1992 and 1994: lack of commitment to reform and nuclear disarmament. There is a recognition that the West is the only source of funds to aid Ukraine's reform programme and help it overcome its economic crisis.

- Ukraine would more energetically seek to expand its exports of arms which would be produced either in competition to, or in co-operation with, Russia. At the United Arab Emirates arms fair in March 1995, Ukraine had 500 exhibitors, including the T-84 'Supertank' produced in Kharkiv.[9]

These foreign and defence policy priorities were reflected in the confidential Government Programme for the period 1995–2000, which outlined the following policies to achieve these objectives:[10]

- Ukraine would not allow itself to be coerced into obligations which infringed its national interests.

- Ukraine would seek out in the CIS and co-operate with countries that held similar positions on international affairs.

- Priority relations with Russia would be based on good neighbourly co-operation and equal partnership, which respected the interests of one another.

- Prioritisation of the signing of a large-scale inter-state treaty with Russia, finalisation of the division of the Black Sea Fleet and the terms of the lease of Ukrainian naval bases as well as regulation of Ukraine's energy debts.

In other areas outside the CIS the Government Programme pointed to the following policies:

- Widening of relations, including political and economic co-operation, with the Baltic states.

- Prioritisation of relations with the West and Central Europe.
- Close co-operation with the Visegrad countries to strengthen regional security and joint defence of one another's interests in international organisations.
- Signing of an inter-state treaty with Romania.
- Membership of the Central European Initiative and Central European Free Trade Association.
- Co-operation with European security structures – NATO (especially its Partnership for Peace Programme), WEU, OSCE and within the CFE Treaty.
- Harmonisation of Ukrainian legislation with EU and Council of Europe standards.
- Ensure Western aid is received in support of Ukrainian reforms.
- Defence of Ukrainian economic interests.

Ukraine's policies of neutrality, non-bloc status, opposition to political or military integration in the CIS, and joining a new confederation or Eurasian Union remained in place. In addition, Ukraine's more pragmatic involvement in economic questions within the CIS would not be at the expense of co-operation with the West, both for domestic and financial reasons. 'Ukraine will not lean this way or that, Ukraine will stay where it is, according to its destiny, its history and geography,' Dmytro Tabachnyk, presidential chief of staff, pointed out when preparing the groundwork for President Kuchma's official visit to the United States in November 1994.[11]

President Kuchma inherited good relations with all Ukraine's neighbours, except Russia and Romania. Relations with the West improved dramatically after the launch of a radical reform programme and Ukraine's ratification of the NPT. In addition, 1995 can be regarded as the year that the West finally recognised independent Ukraine as a permanent feature on the international map, as demonstrated by the state visits of President Clinton and the UK's Foreign Secretary, Malcolm Rifkind, to Ukraine in May and September of that year respectively. Rifkind said at the time: 'Ukraine is here to stay', and, 'Ukraine's size and strategic position make it one of Europe's pivots'.[12]

Treaties recognising inter-state frontiers and national minority rights had been signed by Ukraine with Hungary, Moldova, Poland and Slovakia under Kravchuk. A treaty with Romania was held up for the same reasons that one was held up between Moldova and Romania. Romania's insistence that any treaty denounce the Molotov–Ribbentrop Pact was perceived by Ukraine as tantamount to demands for territorial revisions. (Ukraine had acquired territories from Romania, Czechoslovakia and Poland as a result of this Soviet–German treaty.) After one of the many rounds of Ukrainian–Romanian negotiations Anton Buteiko, Ukrainian first deputy minister, said: 'Ukraine does not claim any territory from anybody and doesn't recognise any such claim from its neighbours.'[13] 'Unfortunately, the Ukrainian side perceives any of our demarches as a covert territorial claim,' Dmitru Ceausu, chief Romanian negotiator, complained.[14]

Udovenko, Ukraine's foreign minister, outlined Ukraine's policy of co-operation in all fields within the CIS, 'but we are against the formation of a transnational body that will limit our sovereignty.'[15] Former prime minister, Vitaliy Masol, added, 'Each country will participate in this union taking into account its own national interests.'[16] 'The direction of our co-operation is exclusively in the area of military technology. That is, there is no question of joint military action or of a military union,' First Deputy Defence Minister Ivan Bizhan stated.[17] Then Defence Minister Shmarov rejected accusations that he sought to revive the former Soviet Military-Industrial Complex.[18]

Ukrainian policies may have become less antagonistic towards the CIS and Russia, but Moscow was mistaken to believe that the election of a new president in Ukraine would make it follow the lead of Belarus, Armenia and Kazakhstan in calling for tighter integration within the CIS. Ukraine had begun to occupy a more constructive role within the CIS: 'This new role consists of not refusing to sign something within the CIS and trying to have CIS documents reflect our position,' General Anatoliy Lopata, former first deputy defence minister and chief of the general staff, commented.[19]

Ukraine continued to reject joint CIS external border patrols and has had only observer status at the Council of the CIS Border Troop Commanders. Ukraine has also begun to attend meetings of the Council of Foreign Ministers and the Council of Defence Ministers of the CIS in observer capacities.[20] Initially, Ukraine offered its troops for peacekeeping duties in the CIS in Abkhazia and Nagorno Karabakh, but only under the auspices of the OSCE and with the consent of the Ukrainian parliament.

Ukraine and Russia signed a bilateral agreement on joint command of their border in August 1994. General Andrei Nikolayev, commander of the Russian Federal Border Service, believes, 'The border between Ukraine and Russia is in fact a border between one nation but two independent states.'[21] At the January 1996 CIS summit, Ukraine proposed documents that CIS members should have unified state borders recognised by legislation in treaties, and continued to reject the concept of 'transparent internal' and 'jointly guarded external' borders, where the former are purely administrative without any legal formalisation. The promotion of this concept by Russia reflected its 'political philosophy', according to Oleksandr Bozhko, head of the directorate on CIS affairs at the Ukrainian Foreign Ministry.[22]

President Kuchma has been careful to rule out any confederation with Russia or other CIS states which would be strongly opposed domestically and which, in turn, would undercut domestic support for reform. The Ukrainian leadership has also to take into account the protests and warnings which have flowed from a large number of political parties, nationalist groups and the Writers' Union about various articles in the draft Russian–Ukrainian treaty. At the CIS summit in Moscow, held on 9 September 1994, the cautious Kuchma line was again in evidence. Ukraine opposed any return to supranational structures, which it regarded as the resurrection of the former USSR and rejected CIS political or military integration, especially a military union, joint military or peacekeeping action.

Ukraine's approach towards the CIS, combining a mixture of Kravchuk's scepticism with Kuchma's economic pragmatism, were also evident at the long delayed CIS summit in Moscow in January 1996. The CIS summit adopted a flag and emblem and also created a new body, the CIS Council of Internal Affairs Ministers, following the creation at earlier summits of similar bodies composed of foreign and defence ministers. Ukraine did not participate in discussions on CIS symbols, as it never signed the CIS Charter, joint military operations or the Customs Union. Ukraine continued to oppose the evolution of the CIS into supra-state structure as a confederation or federation with international legal status, a body that would be little different, in Ukrainian eyes, to the former USSR. The CIS had made no secret of its plan to utilise the Customs Union as a stepping-stone to a future currency union based on the Russian rouble, which would, of course, reduce member-states' sovereignty in the fields of economic, fiscal and monetary policies. Ukraine, therefore, refused to join the Russian–Belarusian–Kazakh–Kyrgyz Customs Union, established on 29 March 1996. Ukraine was also cautious about President Yeltsin's plans for tighter military integration, because he had not hidden his aim of turning this into a new bloc to oppose the West and NATO.[23]

President Yeltsin, elected again to the post of head of the CIS Council of Heads of State despite the fact it was originally intended to rotate the post annually, praised the deepening integration of the CIS. This reflected Russia's growing dominance of the CIS, which it believes it has a right to lead. Ukraine 'thus far does not want integration. It does not want it, although I tried to persuade – very insistently tried to persuade – Kuchma. The integration of Russia and Ukraine is salvation for both states from the problems that face us today ... And they [Ukraine] do not have fewer problems.'[24]

The Ukrainian view of the CIS remained far more sceptical than the exaggerated optimism of the Russian leadership. In President Kuchma's view, 'The CIS today has a significant role as a consultative council. At such meetings one can present many questions and, in some manner, receive answers.'[25] In other words, the CIS remained a glorified 'talking shop'. 'There is still no mechanism for implementing agreements adopted by the CIS – and there are 676 of them,' Oleksandr Danylenko, a high-ranking Ukrainian Foreign Ministry official, pointed out.[26] Ukraine, there-fore, preferred promoting bilateral relations with CIS member states, which was more effective.

The two resolutions adopted by the Russian State Duma on 15 March 1996 which denounced the creation of the CIS and confirmed the contin-ued legal validity of the 17 March 1991 referendum on a 'revived union federation' were denounced by all the former Soviet states – except Belarus. President Kuchma continued to reject, as he had ever since being elected in summer 1994, any suggestion that the former USSR could be revived. The creation of the SSR (Belarusian–Russian Community of Sovereign Republics) on 2 April 1996, coming only two weeks after the State Duma resolutions, confirmed the worst fears in Kyiv that there was a growing convergence between the security policies of Yeltsin and Russia's nationalists/communists *vis-à-vis* the 'Near Abroad'. Although the non-CIS states, therefore, endorsed at their May 1996 summit Yeltsin's candidature in the June Russian presidential elections, this was more a case of Yeltsin representing 'the better of two evils' over his main rival, the communist leader Gennadiy Zyuganov.[27]

Ukraine and the Expansion of NATO

President Kravchuk had never opposed the expansion of NATO or even Ukraine's future membership of this military alliance. This reflected his disdain for military co-operation with Eurasian structures, such as the Tashkent Collective Security Treaty, in favour of European security struc-tures. President Kravchuk often proposed Ukraine as a 'buffer' between Europe and Russia, as elaborated in his proposals for a CEZSC and similar security proposals within the Black Sea Economic Co-operation Agreement.

President Kuchma, in contrast, initially echoed Russian concerns about the expansion of NATO, reflecting his more accommodating foreign policy towards Russia and the CIS when he was elected president. One concern of President Kuchma was not to antagonise Russia, which would harm the prospects of signing an all-embracing inter-state treaty and reaching a final agreement on the Black Sea Fleet. Kuchma also rejected Ukraine's geo-strategic role as a 'buffer between NATO and Russia' in favour of a 'cross-roads through which NATO and Russia will co-operate'.[28]

President Kuchma's views on the expansion of NATO, which were initially little different from Russia's (other than rejecting any suggestion that Ukraine had the right of veto), were gradually forced to change. An important role in this was played by the political and academic elite in Kyiv, which is pro-European and hostile to Eurasian security structures, and by the influential think tank under the National Security Council, the National Institute of Strategic Studies headed by Dr Serhiy Pirozhkov (under Kravchuk it had been directly under the president after it was established in summer 1992).

Ukrainian authors had argued that the expansion of NATO is, of itself, not destabilising. On the contrary, it would increase stability within the perceived security vacuum of Central Europe, whilst further 'guaranteeing' Ukraine's western borders with Hungary, Slovakia and Poland. Desire for membership in NATO by Romania had also been utilised by Ukraine to apply pressure on Bucharest to sign an inter-state treaty recognising current borders (something it had been reluctant to undertake), by arguing that no country could be a prospective NATO member if it harboured territorial disputes with its neighbours.[29] The expansion of NATO would also act as a deterrent against what was widely perceived in Ukraine to be an unstable Russia. It would force the Ukrainian leadership to decide in which direction to take Ukraine, that is to apply for NATO membership (like the three Baltic states) or maintain its current policy of neutrality and non-bloc status.[30]

Ukraine's more positive views about the expansion of NATO were also greatly aided by Russia's brutal military intervention in Chechnya which significantly eroded any domestic support for Ukraine's membership of the Tashkent Collective Security Treaty, even in Russian-speaking areas of eastern and southern Ukraine. The public perception of one of the main reasons for the establishment of Ukrainian security forces was precisely to prevent Ukrainian troops dying 'in Russian imperialistic wars' in the former USSR.[31] Ukrainian marines were therefore withdrawn from Black Sea Fleet units which intervened in the Georgian civil war in summer 1993. Military integration in the CIS is only supported by one political party – the communists – whose popularity rating, as reflected by their parliamentary faction and opinion polls, is approximately 20 per cent.

Their erstwhile two allies, who together attempt to bloc domestic reform – the socialists and agrarians – do not share the communists' support for military union with Russia and the CIS, remaining committed to maintaining Ukraine's policy of neutrality and non-bloc status. Neutrality and non-bloc status are enshrined in the Ukrainian constitution; any alteration to this policy would require the constitutional vote of two-thirds of parliament – something the communists would never be able to muster. This, therefore, also ruled out Ukraine following in the footsteps of Belarus in seeking unification with Russia.

The communist and socialist members of parliament have always maintained both their hostility to the expansion of NATO and any suggestion that Ukraine should apply for membership of this organisation. Moroz had said that 'Neither Ukraine nor Russia will ever join NATO', but Ukraine needed a 'legal framework for co-operation, including military co-operation' with NATO.[32] Moroz is opposed to the use of NATO in peacekeeping duties, arguing that only the UN should undertake these activities. If Ukraine joined NATO this would lead to sharp deterioration in relations with Russia and domestic instability. 'Russia would be forced to react to it and it has all the possibilities for that,' Moroz added.[33] Therefore, Moroz backed a collective European security system based on the OSCE (not on either NATO or the CIS).

Moroz was backed in these views by the socialist chairman of the parliamentary committee on Defence and Security Questions, Volodymyr Mukhin. If Ukraine joined NATO this would 'deteriorate security in Europe'. 'Theoretically, it can be allowed, but in practice it will be too hard to achieve, mostly because Russia will be categorically against a step of this kind,' Mukhin added. He pointed out that the new national security concept adopted in Winter 1996–7 (which had been orginally proposed to the Ukrainian parliament in October 1993),[34] a document jointly prepared by parliamentary committees and the presidential administration, continued to envisage its non-aligned status.[35]

These cautious views about NATO expansion were echoed even by the pro-Western former first deputy foreign minister, Tarasiuk (since 1995 Ukrainian Ambassador to Benelux), 'Let's ask each other: will the level of security in Ukraine increase if NATO edges closer to its borders? Evidently no.'[36] Oleh Chornousenko, formerly an employee of the Kharkiv branch of the Security Service and currently deputy chairman of the parliamentary committee on Defence and Security Issues, also praised Ukraine's adoption of neutrality enshrined within its July 1990 Declaration of Sovereignty. But, reflecting his membership of the Unity parliamentary faction, he did not call for NATO membership and merely criticised 'the position of an ostrich that hides its head in the sand which is probably misplaced'.[37]

National democratic members of parliament, who have a quarter of parliamentary seats, hold different views on NATO membership. The deputy chairman of the parliamentary committee on Foreign and CIS Affairs, Ivan Zayets, also a leading member of Rukh, argued that Ukraine's status as a non-aligned state was no longer feasible, whilst membership of the Tashkent Collective Security Treaty would lead to Ukraine's loss of independence. Together with Borys Kozhyn, former commander of the Ukrainian Navy and now a member of parliament, they proposed that Ukraine formally apply for NATO membership.

Opinion polls have tended to back the national democrats in their quest for NATO membership. An opinion poll in 1994 found 51.4 per cent in favour of joining NATO. The difference between Ukrainians (54.7 per cent) and Russians (45.9 per cent) on this question in Ukraine was not very large. Not surprisingly perhaps, the highest number of supporters were in the 15–24 age group and the lowest in the 45–54 group.[38] These figures have been supported by other opinion polls, which give very low support for the Tashkent Collective Security Treaty, figures which have further declined since the Chechen crisis erupted (see Table 6.1).[39]

During the second half of 1994, immediately after the presidential elections, Ukrainian views about NATO moved away from Kravchuk's wholehearted endorsement to a more cautious line closely resembling in many ways that of Russia. Then newly appointed defence minister, Shmarov, told visiting General George Joulwan, Supreme Commander of NATO forces in Europe, 'Ukraine has a non-bloc status and does not intend to join either the CIS countries' military alliance or NATO.'[40] Later, on a visit to Prague, President Kuchma elaborated on this: 'Ukraine

Table 6.1   Opinion Poll of Ukrainian Attitudes to the CIS

How do you see the future of the CIS?	Percentage
Economic Union	42
Single Union/State with Joint Organs of Power	17*
No Future	17
Political Union	4
Military Union	1
No Answer	17

Note: *This figure closely resembles that of the average communist level of support throughout Ukraine.

does not have any objections to NATO's eastward expansion, but believes that it is necessary to respect Russia's interests at the same time. If we do not want Europe to be split into opposing camps again, we should not forget Russia's interests.'[41] In other words, the expansion of NATO should be accompanied by a security agreement with Russia, which would ensure it did not apply pressure upon Ukraine to join the CIS military bloc.

When Ukraine signed the NATO Partnership for Peace programme its foreign minister, Anatoly Zlenko, repeated a commonly held fear which persists within the current Ukrainian leadership that any expansion of NATO without dealing with Ukrainian security concerns would place it in a 'grey zone' between two expanding blocs.[42] Zlenko's successor, Hennadiy Udovenko, added, 'Ukraine is worried about NATO's expansion which would lead to a new division of Europe into two blocs.' At a meeting of the foreign ministers of Russia, Ukraine, Belarus and Moldova in Moscow, Udovenko reiterated Ukraine's concerns:

> On the one hand, NATO is approaching Ukraine's borders. On the other, we have [former soviet republics] which have signed an agreement on collective security. This could hardly be satisfactory for a young state. Its position on this issue should be carefully considered.[43]

Ukraine had also criticised Poland's headlong rush into NATO membership without taking into account the views of its Ukrainian neighbour. The referendum on integration of Belarus and Russia in May 1995 may have served to sober up Polish attitudes on this question. Bogdan Borusewicz, a member of the Polish–Ukrainian inter-parliamentary group, said Warsaw was concerned about Russian expansionism, which would 'endeavour to expand its sphere of interest, as demonstrated by the latest developments in Belarus which resulted in Russian border guards and customs officers gaining access to the Polish–Belarusian borders. This is why Poland attached even greater importance to relations with independent Ukraine, which Polish membership of NATO would not harm, Borusewicz believed.[44]

Repeating Kuchma's view that any expansion needed to take into account Russia's opinions, he also emphasised a view at odds with that of Russia's that NATO was a factor for stability in Europe. In other words, Ukraine was not opposed to the *evolutionary* expansion of NATO.[45] At a NACC meeting in Brussels, Udovenko reiterated Ukraine's view that NATO expansion should:[46]

- be evolutionary;
- take into account the security of all European states;

- should not affect the interests of any country or group;
- Russia should be involved in the process of enlargement;
- that no country had the right of veto;
- Ukraine opposed a new Cold War;
- Ukraine was concerned about Russian pressure if NATO expanded too quickly.

President Kuchma's criticised the demand of any state to have a veto over NATO's expansion and he pointed to Russia's reaction to this possibility – not NATO's expansion – which threatened to create a new Cold War. 'The Russian President is obliged to state his point of view regarding the organisation [NATO]. This is normal, but Russia should work in one direction – not to divide Europe into two Europes as we had during the Cold War.'[47] Russia's negative reaction to Partnership for Peace was caused by its 'attempts to take upon itself the role of conductor, or, the worst variant, to play first violin in the newly created orchestra',[48] a Ukrainian security specialist argued. After a visit to Riga by President Kuchma, a joint Ukrainian–Latvian statement clearly referred to Russia and NATO when it stated: 'The presidents recognised that threats and political pressure from a common bordering state – based mainly on electoral concerns – prompt many countries to want to join reliable and stable political alliances to ensure their statehood and development.'[49]

During President Clinton's visit to Ukraine in May 1995, President Kuchma's views about the expansion of NATO underwent a further evolution away from that of Russia's. Kuchma told his guest that Ukraine would work with the United States to help shape the new world order of the twenty-first century, which would make either a Cold War or a Cold Peace impossible. In this new world order there would no room for 'inhuman dictatorial regimes', 'imperial ambitions' and 'aggressive separatism' attempting to change maps by force.[50] Kuchma told President Clinton for the first time that he believed NATO was a 'guarantor of stability in Europe', but reiterated that any expansion should be evolutionary and Ukrainian security should not be harmed by being left in a no-man's land between two expanding military blocs.[51] The expansion of NATO, therefore, which could not be stopped, 'must be carried out to take into account Ukraine's national interests'.[52]

National Security Council secretary, Vladimir Horbulin, outlined Ukraine's more optimistic and positive policy towards the expansion of NATO: 'We view NATO as a factor of stability and deterrence in Europe, though we never said this before.'[53] Horbulin added new conditions to those already provided earlier by Ukraine to facilitate the expansion of NATO which is 'predetermined objectively':[54]

- Russia is entitled to a 'special relationship with NATO', including mandatory consultations between NATO and Russia and more active participation by Moscow in Partnership for Peace.
- Discussion of the possible nuclear proliferation in NATO's new members.
- Creation of new joint military systems.
- Ukraine should also have a 'special relationship with NATO'.

On a visit to NATO in June 1995 by the Ukrainian foreign minister, Ukraine was offered a special relationship with the alliance along the lines of the one promised to Russia after it joined NATO's Partnership for Peace. Ukraine would play 'a specific role in developing a new European security architecture,' NATO Secretary-General, Willy Claes, said. The special relationship would take the form of an all-encompassing treaty or standing commission.[55] In September 1995, Ukraine submitted its own programme to NATO within the 16+1 framework for co-operation.

Ukraine was the first CIS member state to join NATO's Partnership for Peace and has remained the most eager CIS member. Zlenko, former foreign minister and currently Ukrainian Ambassador to the UN, said, when Ukraine joined Partnership for Peace, that it would be used to upgrade the Ukrainian armed forces to NATO standards in order to be in a position to join at a later date, a view reflecting President Kravchuk's support for NATO membership.[56] Ukraine supported Russia's participation in Partnership for Peace, but rejected any special status that it demanded for itself.

Ukraine's enthusiastic endorsement of Partnership for Peace rested on a number of factors. First, Kyiv believed that it would raise Ukraine's international prestige. Secondly, it would provide 'additional security guarantees' to those already obtained in the Trilateral Agreement and Memorandum on Security Assurances.[57] Thirdly, 'An important step has been made in building a European security system, in bringing together Eastern and Western Europe', President Kravchuk argued, hoping that it would help to demilitarise the Black Sea region.[58] Fourthly, Partnership for Peace represented 'a reasonable and pragmatic alternative to partial and selective enlargement'. Finally, Ukraine's membership of Partnership for Peace would allow it to balance its foreign policy *vis-à-vis* the CIS military bloc.[59] Former defence minister, Vitaliy Radetsky, added that Partnership for Peace would allow Ukraine to 'overcome its artificial isolation from Europe and return Ukraine to the circle of leading European states'.[60] A similar view was expressed by Zlenko on the significance of Partnership for Peace, 'Ukraine backs its fundamental political priorities and choice in favour of a return to Europe from which it artificially was separated and re-unification with the family of European nations.'[61]

Ukraine's participation in Partnership for Peace was perceived as a means to buttress its security because 'NATO consults with any active member of Partnership for Peace if it feels a direct threat to its territorial integrity, independence or security.' As the only country with potential territorial claims on Ukraine is Russia, it is not surprising that Ukraine always supported its participation within Partnership for Peace because any potential territorial conflict would then be raised within NATO, NACC or the Partnership for Peace agreement. At the Istanbul NACC meeting, an aide to the NATO Secretary General on political questions, Gerhard von Moltke, stated that Partnership for Peace allowed joint operations with NATO in the event of a threat to a participating member's territorial integrity.[62] This is very important for strengthening and guaranteeing [Ukrainian] national security,' one Ukrainian author added.[63]

Other advantages to Ukraine's participation in Partnership for Peace have been spelled out within Ukraine as:[64]

- joint activity in peacekeeping (Ukraine remains opposed to involvement in CIS peacekeeping) which would increase the number of trained units available for UN or OSCE duties;
- improving the effectiveness of NACC;
- joint research and academic studies;
- increasing Ukrainian military standards to those of NATO;
- Ukraine's participation in Partnership for Peace on equal terms to Russia;
- helping the democratisation of the armed forces, such as civilian control;
- providing input into elaborating Ukraine's national security and military doctrines;
- giving access to, and use of, NATO technology.

Russia's half-hearted membership of Partnership for Peace in May 1995 was lauded by Ukraine's political establishment and government. 'Ukraine must find ways of co-operating with NATO [that are] acceptable to both NATO and Russia. It is in Ukraine's interests to have improved relations between NATO and Russia.'[65] Russia's membership of Partnership for Peace would encourage domestic reform, stimulate discussion about a new pan-European security system and improve relations with Ukraine, one Ukrainian security specialist and chairman of the Ukrainian Atlantic

Committee, Oleh Bodruk, said.[66] Ukraine's adherence to neutrality and non-bloc status is not because of any pacifist inclinations or desire to be 'Finlandised'.[67] After all, President Kuchma has pointed out that, 'Ukraine's geographical position contradicts our doctrine. We are not by any means Switzerland or any country like it.'[68]

Ukraine could only decide to join NATO, Kuchma believes when Ukraine 'is standing on its feet, and we need time for this'.[69] In other words, in the short term at least, Ukraine needs the breathing space of non-alignment to concentrate on the economic and energy crisis, as well as raise Ukrainian national consciousness. Ukrainian membership of NATO could only come about after it became a 'strong, independent country', Kuchma added on another occasion.[70]

President Clinton declared: 'I would not say or do anything that would exclude the possibility of Ukrainian membership [of NATO]'.[71] But President Kuchma pointed out that 'No one is waiting for us to enter NATO and no one in Ukraine intends to race into the Atlantic alliance at this time'.[72] President Kuchma added on a number of occasions that 'Ukraine will not be able to remain outside the blocs.'[73] Ukraine has 'joined neither one side nor the other. But I understand that it is nonsense today for Ukraine to be non-aligned,' Kuchma said, on a visit to Riga.[74] This fundamental re-evaluation of Ukraine's foreign policy will be a gradual process because 'The question of joining NATO is an important one. But no one is planning to move from one political status to another,' then Defence Minister Shmarov said.[75]

A key strategic aim of Russia was to 'jointly elaborate a common policy toward the [NATO] alliance, including common actions to oppose its enlargement', according to the Russian Council on Foreign and Defence Policy, an independent but influential think tank in Moscow. In the event of NATO expansion, which Ukraine did not oppose (in contrast to Russia where there was cross-party hostility), the Baltic states and Ukraine would become 'a zone of bitter rivalry'.[76] Although many Russian analysts understood that Ukraine would not participate in a new anti-NATO military bloc (or any CIS military union), nevertheless the new semi-official Russian military doctrine would place tactical nuclear missiles in Russian bases in Belarus, Kalingrad and possibly in Russian bases in the Crimea to counter any NATO expansion.[77]

Obviously, though, Ukraine's desire to 'move towards' – but not join NATO – for the time being rested upon developments within Russia. After the State Duma resolutions in favour of a revived former USSR in mid-March 1996, the Ukrainian leadership noticeably no longer ruled it out.

Ukrainian–Russian Relations: Diverging Interests

Although Ukrainian–Russian relations improved under Kuchma there had also been a clear tendency for both countries increasingly to have diverging national interests. As nation- and state-building in Ukraine progresses this divergence will continue to grow. On many issues of international relations, such as NATO expansion, the CFE Treaty, Yugoslavia[78] and Chechnya, Ukraine and Russia hold radically different views.

The Ukrainian leadership, while calling for the 'normalisation' of relations with Russia, always added that this could only come about 'under conditions of equal and mutually beneficial co-operation'. 'I would especially like to underline here that Ukraine will not relinquish the principle of equality in international relations and will tolerate no interference in its internal affairs. The issues of our territorial integrity and sovereignty are not a subject for discussion,' President Kuchma stressed at the celebration of the fiftieth anniversary of the liberation of Kyiv.

A number of problems immediately arise. While Ukraine is busy building its independent statehood and always alert to threats to its sovereignty, Russia has a diametrically opposite policy. The policies of the current Russian leadership are not to build a nation-state, which has never existed in its history, but to create a confederation as a stepping-stone to a new Eurasian Union, as evidenced by the creation of the SSR in April 1996. Russian political leaders who reject such a course in favour of concentrating on Russian state development, such as Yegor Gaidar's Russia Choice Party, are labelled 'isolationists' who had their day in 1991–2. The Russian leadership has rejected the liberal internationalism of joining a 'common European home' propounded by Mikhail Gorbachev and Gaidar during the late 1980s and early 1990s in favour of neo-imperial Eurasian statist-realism.

The processes of state-building and integration occurred in West Europe centuries apart. In the CIS they are occurring simultaneously and will continue to place strains on Russian–Ukrainian relations. Secondly, Ukraine's insistence on 'equality' in its relations with Russia for historical reasons flies in the face of the demand for 'Great Power Status' by Russia. It also contradicts the demand by Russia for a 'strategic partnership' between the world's two superpowers with their 'spheres of influence', as well as the current Russian policy of turning the former Soviet republics into its satellites. Sergei Karaganov, a leading member of the Russian presidential council and deputy director of the Institute of Europe, Russian Academy of Sciences, has openly argued:[79]

The best that the advocates of Ukraine's statehood can hope for is the preservation of a politically independent but really (economically) semi-independent state. This is not the worst option for Russia either. Given this model of relations with Ukraine and other CIS states, we can turn from a milk cow into a state delivered from the burden of empire but retaining many advantages of its previous geostrategic and, so to speak, geoeconomic position,

Improved bilateral relations may be a way that Ukraine would get around its opposition to political and military integration in the CIS. What will be the models for this new relationship: USA/Canada, USA/Mexico (Karaganov's preferred choice), Germany/Austria or England/Scotland? This has still to be worked through and the Russian and Ukrainian selection of historical geographic examples were likely to be different.

Both the Russian and Ukrainian foreign ministers had called the 'normalisation' of relations a priority. The former Russian foreign minister, Andrei Kozyrev, said neither side was the 'elder' or 'younger' brother, rather they were 'twin brothers': 'That's the formula we came up with. We were born together and will work together,' he said in Kyiv when on his way to the United States.[80] Nevertheless, Ukrainians still wanted to know which of the 'twins' had been born first.

The 'normalisation' of relations with Russia has proved to be more difficult than the improvement of relations with the West. A major obstacle to this process was the continued inability of the majority of Russians to accept Ukrainians and Belarusians as separate ethnic groups with a right to statehood. An American opinion poll of ethnic Russians in the Russian Federation found 75 per cent unable to accept that Ukrainians were a separate nationality with the right to independence. 'This tearing off of Belarus and Ukraine from us is just the same as the division of Germany after the war ... Historically, it must not endure,' Alexander Solzhenitsyn believed.[81]

The two areas which reflected the difficulties in the full 'normalisation' process were the Black Sea Fleet and the Russian–Ukrainian inter-state treaty. The visit to Kyiv by President Yeltsin to sign the inter-state treaty was postponed on numerous occasions. The bulk of the treaty was ready by the beginning of 1995 after Russia dropped its insistence on dual citizenship. The two contentious issues out of six remaining dealt with the status of ethnic minorities (11 million Russians in Ukraine and 5 million Ukrainians in Russia) and the formulation of the article dealing with the border. The Ukrainian side demanded that the word 'recognition' be included, whilst Russia preferred to use the more woolly and malleable 'respect'. Ukraine rejected any reference to the CSCE Final Act, claiming it was not then a signatory. Kyiv would also like to insert into this article that each side had no territorial claims on each other now – or in the future.

Even if diplomatic language were found to resolve these outstanding questions both parliaments have to ratify the treaty, which seemed highly unlikely. At the October 1994 CIS summit in Moscow, President Kuchma said that 'the ball is in Russia's court'[82] regarding the treaty, because Moscow was finding it difficult to accept current borders (which would renounce any claim on the Crimea, something that the State Duma would more than likely reject).

Ukraine's foreign minister, Udovenko, called on many occasions for the 'normalisation' of Ukrainian–Russian relations. But this could only be undertaken, he added, on the basis of partnership, 'rather than the relations of a senior with a junior' (a recurring Ukrainian demand following the disintegration of the former USSR) and not at the expense of Ukrainian statehood and sovereignty (a reference to the Crimea). Konstantin Zatulin, former chairman of the Russian Duma committee on the CIS and Compatriots Abroad (1994–5), had called for a 'strategic partnership' and 'special relations' between Russia and Ukraine which would take into account recognition of the two countries' interdependence. Zatulin, director of the Institute for the Russian Diaspora, was declared *persona non grata* in spring 1996 in Ukraine after numerous visits to the Crimea where his speeches have been rather inflammatory.

Opinion polls in Ukraine had consistently shown that few people had experienced ethnic discrimination. In August 1995 an opinion poll by the Democratic Initiatives Centre found only 10 per cent of people had witnessed discrimination against ethnic Russians and 6 per cent against Jews.[83] The Democratic Initiatives Centre therefore concluded that during 1994–5 the ethnic situation had not changed in Ukraine and remained 'quite favourable' because a majority of the population had not experienced any ethnic discrimination. Likewise in the Crimea an opinion poll by the *Krymsotsis* Sociology Centre in conjunction with the Centre for Regional Development found that 68.38 per cent of those polled had experienced no manifestations of ethnic hostility. Another 19.64 per cent and 8.76 per cent had not witnessed or been involved in such instances.[84]

These factors had not deterred Russian spokesmen from continuing to claim the opposite. The issue of the alleged discrimination of the Russian diaspora had always remained a contentious issue in Ukrainian–Russian relations because nearly half of this figure (12 out of 25 million) resided in Ukraine. Threats by leading official spokesmen, like former Foreign

Minister Kozyrev, or unofficial ones like Alexander Lebed,[85] joint leader of the Congress of Russian Communities, to intervene militarily on their behalf were perceived as threatening in Kyiv. In October 1995 the Russian government allocated R380 million to create special funds at Russian embassies in the republics of the former USSR on the initiative of the Foreign Ministry to give aid to Russian compatriots,[86] as well as a fund of R200 million to help purchase textbooks for Russian-language schools in Ukraine and the CIS.[87] What may be regarded as aid to worthy Russian 'cultural' groups, such as the Russian Society of the Crimea, may, of course, be perceived as intervention in the internal affairs of other republics in support of separatist groups. It is noteworthy that the Ukrainian authorities closed down the Russian Consulate in the Crimea in spring 1995 after it began overstepping its duties and issuing citizenship to Crimeans (Ukrainian legislation does not recognise dual citizenship).

Zatulin, former chairman of the Russian State Duma commission on CIS Affairs and Compatriot Relations, had long condemned the Russian leadership for 'its indifferent attitude towards the violation of [ethnic Russian] rights in the near abroad'[88] and called Ukrainian and Kazakh actions against separatists as 'ethnic cleansing'. In October 1995, The State Duma threatened that Ukraine's treatment of its Crimean Russians would affect ratification of any Black Sea Fleet agreement. The real question, Zatulin explained, was whether Ukraine wants to be with Russia or not. He blamed the West for encouraging Ukraine to stand up to 'Russian imperialism'.[89]

Kuchma came to power highly optimistic that he, in contrast to Kravchuk, could 'normalise' relations with Russia by signing an inter-state treaty and resolving the Black Sea Fleet question. But President Yeltsin had postponed his visit to Ukraine on at least six occasions, the last prior to the Russian presidential elections being on 4–5 April 1996.

The 'normalisation' of relations between Ukraine and Russia had been complicated by their different perceptions as to what this meant in practice. Equal relations on a Canadian–US model (Ukraine's preference) or a US–Latin American model (the Russian choice)? In addition, how can 'normalisation' of relations occur when Ukraine refused anything less than 'equality', which it required to overcome its inferiority complex, and Russian demands that it be regarded as a 'Great Power' and the 'first among equals' within the CIS (in 1991 Yeltsin's position was closer to that of Ukraine's and had evolved since then towards a more nationalistic position). Even the communist chairman of the Ukrainian parliamentary commission on Foreign and CIS Affairs, Borys Oliynyk, stated that 'If one of the states, however, claims "specific interests", I do not intend to join the field of these specific interests' because in Russia, 'the imperial mood is being felt there'.[90]

In the words of Russian presidential foreign affairs adviser, Dmitriy Ryurikov,

> The intention of the Ukrainian authorities to build statehood on rejecting specific relations with Russia – that existed for decades and centuries – is obvious ... There is, however, such a desire to reject specific relations and specific history now, to pretend that the countries have simply parted, have divorced on the basis of international law.

Ukraine, he warned, should take into account 'Russian interests, Russian dignity as well as historic past ...'[91] Independent Ukraine, in the eyes of the majority of the Russian leadership and public, is a 'temporary phenomenon' whose rightful place was together with Belarus and Kazakhstan under Russia as the core east Slavic bloc within the CIS', This demand for an east Slavic bloc went beyond that of the nationalist fringe and included many within the democratic camp, such as Ivan Rybkin, former speaker of the State Duma.

President Yeltsin's 14 September 1995 edict, 'On the Establishment of the Strategic Course of the Russian Federation with Member States of the CIS', reflected the new polices of the Russian leadership which may prevent the full 'normalisation' of relations with Ukraine from taking place. This document, according to one Ukrainian Russian-language newspaper, 'reflects all the imperial ambitions of the neighbouring country's leadership' and 'the talk is about reviving the Soviet Union in the international arena'.[92] The decree called for a new military bloc to counter an expanding NATO. Clearly, the only countries which could ensure that the new proposed bloc had any serious military clout would be Russia and Ukraine.

The Ukrainian response to the decree was highly critical and reflected just how wide the gap was between the reality and the rhetoric of the 'normalisation of relations'. President Kuchma commented that 'Ukraine wanted to have equal partnership relations with Russia, but not on the basis of a strategy recently outlined by Boris Yeltsin. There are forces in Russia which do not want to understand that Ukraine is a sovereign state and this is the main thing worrying us in relations with Russia.'[93] A leaked confidential letter from Foreign Minster Udovenko to Kuchma was even more critical:

> Russia has no intention to build its relations with CIS countries in line with international law, nor to respect the principles of territorial

Table 6.2 Evolution of Russian Security Policy to Ukraine and the CIS

August 1991	Threat to revise Ukrainian–Russian border if Ukraine seceded from the FSU
January 1992	Proposal to link Black Sea Fleet to Crimea, V. Lukin, Commission on International Relations
February 1992	'After the Disintegration of the USSR: Russia in the New World' Institute International Relations, Moscow State University
May 1992	'Strategy for Russia (1)', Council on Foreign & Defence Policy
June 1992	'Strategy towards Ukraine', Institute of Europe, Russian Academy of Sciences
May 1992 & July 1993	Russian parliamentary resolutions on the Crimea and Sevastopol
December 1992	Kozyrev warning of policy change if 'hardliners' come to power, speech to CSCE meeting
January & March 1993	Elaboration of a new Russian 'Monroe Doctrine', President B. Yeltsin: Peacekeeping, CIS as 'strategic zone of Russian interests', support for evolution of the CIS into a confederation or federation
September 1993	Massandra: Russian Threat of War if Black Sea Fleet & Crimean Bases not Transferred
October 1993	Russian military doctrine: right of intervention in the FSU and peacekeeping
April 1994	Russian presidential decree on creating 30 forward military bases in the FSU
May 1994	'Strategy for Russia (2)', Council on Foreign & Defence Policy
September 1994	'Russia and the CIS: Does the Western Position Need Correction?' Foreign Intelligence Service, Yevgenniy Primakov, Director
April 1995	Threat to militarily intervene in the FSU in defence of 'Russian speakers', Foreign Minister Andrei Kozyrev
June 1995	'Russia and the Expansion of NATO', Council on Foreign & Defence Policy
September 1995	Decree, 'The Strategic Course of the Russian Federation with Member States of the CIS'
September 1995	Draft new Russian military doctrine, Institute of Defence Studies
May 1996	Will a Union be Reborn? Council on Foreign and Defence Policy

integrity, sovereignty and non-interference in domestic affairs ... The integration, proclaimed as useful and necessary in Yeltsin's decree ... in fact means undermining the CIS countries' sovereignty, subordinating their activity to Russia's interests and restoring the centralised superpower.[94]

Ukrainian and Russian interests also collided within the undeclared energy 'war' taking place in the Black Sea and Caucasian regions. Ivan Dadiverin, head of the Ukrainian pipeline company, pointed out: 'we are buying oil expensively from Russia. Depending only on Russia is strategically unfavourable.'[95] Ukraine is, therefore, in a different camp from Russia alongside Turkey, Georgia, Turkmenistan and Azerbaijan, which planned to export oil and gas from Baku through Georgia and Turkey to Ukraine and the outside world. Russia's insistence on Azeri oil being piped through Chechnya, out through Novorossiysk, by tanker across to Bulgaria, across Bulgaria and Greece by pipeline and out at the Aegean by tanker is the proposed alternative route.

Russia is also building a new pipeline across Belarus to Poland to circumvent Ukrainian control over its oil and gas exports. Ukraine's hard line in the Crimea and in negotiations over the inter-state treaty with Romania (which claims Zmeinyi [Serpent] island) are also conditioned by the large oil and gas deposits found off the Black Sea coast which are allegedly larger than those in the North Sea or Azerbaijan. This is the same region in which Ukraine is building a new oil terminal near Odesa. According to documents published in the Ukrainian and Russian press, the Russian Foreign Intelligence Service had launched active measures to prevent these deposits from being exploited by Ukraine with the aid of Western technology and expertise.[96]

The Chechnya Crisis and Ukraine

As Georgia's president, Eduard Shevardnadze, has pointed out, the Chechnya crisis came about as a consequence of Russia's 'double standards' by its promotion of separatism in Moldova, Georgia, Azerbaidzhan and Ukraine since 1992 as a means to transform these countries into satellites of Russia. Russia's military intervention in Chechnya has not only damaged its international image but also that within the CIS. 'I think the Russians will want to act as if Chechnya isn't happening. Whether they can get away with it is another matter,' one Western diplomat speculated.[97] Since the Chechnya crisis erupted, the subject of military integration had not been raised in Ukrainian–

Russian negotiations or meetings during his term in office, President Kuchma admitted.[98]

At the CIS summit in Alma Ata in February 1995, Ukraine continued to emphasise horizontal bilateral relations and economic integration only. The conflict in Chechnya, as well as earlier ethnic conflicts in the CIS, were the spur that led to Ukraine's support for the CIS Peace and Stability Memorandum, which called upon its members to refrain from exerting political, military and economic pressure on one another. In addition, the memorandum called upon CIS member states to clamp down on any actions that infringed on the independence or borders of other members or provoked inter-ethnic conflict.[99] What this could mean in practice was Ukraine and Kazakhstan both demanding that Russia clamp down on its supporters of pro-Russian separatism in the Crimea and northern Kazakhstan, which seemed highly unlikely given the growth of nationalistic feelings in Russia. 'It is only a call on countries to adhere to some principles in our relations, for example the integrity of borders and state sovereignty,' Udovenko commented.

Russian complaints of Ukrainian mercenaries operating in Chechnya, the three Baltic Republics, Georgia and Azerbaidzhan have to be looked at in the context of the Russian leadership's unwillingness to condemn Russian Cossack mercenaries operating in Moldova, Georgia, Ukraine and Bosnia–Herzegovina. Owing to alterations in the Ukrainian legal code making mercenary activity punishable, Ukrainian nationalist groups did not initially publicise their presence in Chechnya. Instead, they claimed that if they were in Chechnya, they were there in their own right.

The majority of the Ukrainian volunteers fighting on the Chechen side were from the Ukrainian People's Self-Defence Forces (UNSO), the paramilitary arm of the radical right Ukrainian National Assembly (UNA), who previously fought in Moldova and Georgia.[100] In addition, UNA established a press centre in Grozny, and UNSO members had even been seen in Dudayev's presidential guard. Parliamentary members of the Congress of Ukrainian Nationalists (KUN) also visited Chechnya to voice their support for Dudayev.

The Ukrainian authorities initially denied that there were any Ukrainian mercenaries in Chechnya, refuting claims by the Russian government and Ministry of Defence that Ukrainian 'ultra-nationalists' were in Chechnya or that the Ukrainian authorities were promoting their activity. The Ukrainian Foreign Ministry condemned terms used by the Russian authorities, 'which have been literally pulled from the obsolete, propaganda arsenal of the Stalinist regime's great-power repressive ideology'. The Foreign Ministry was referring in particular to use of the term 'Banderite', the slang term for supporters of the 1940s nationalist leader, Stepan Bandera. 'If the leaders of Russia's power-wielding structures think that they can promote mutual understanding between our peoples in this way, then, truly, in doing so they achieve the entirely opposite effect,' the statement finished.[101]

But in the second week of January 1995 the Ukrainian Foreign Ministry admitted that some 50 Ukrainian nationalists and 15 Tartar members of the Islamic Religious Party Avdet volunteers were fighting on Dudayev's side, but denied they were paid mercenaries.[102] The Russian authorities, meanwhile, claimed they had intelligence that 60–70 west Ukrainians, 'namely Banderites or members of the Organisation of Ukrainian Nationalists', were active in Chechnya.

Continued Russian reports about Ukrainian nationalists in Chechnya again led to protests by the Ukrainian Foreign Ministry that this was intended to discredit Ukraine internationally and complicate Ukrainian–Russian relations.[103] UNA leaders admitted that they had between 100 and 200 members in Chechnya either as fighters, running a press office or as propaganda officers attempting to encourage the desertion of Russian conscripts. The Security Service of Ukraine (SBU) had taken a number of 'preventive measures' to 'control the situation and promised further to resolutely stop any provocative attempts to involve Ukraine's citizens in armed conflicts on the territories of other countries'.[104] The Russian Federal Counter-Intelligence service (FSK) had returned one captured Ukrainian volunteer to the SBU. The SBU had in mind not only nationalists and Tartars fighting on Dudayev's side, but also attempts by the Russian Counter-Intelligence Service to recruit Ukrainians to fight on the Russian side as professional soldiers and previously in the ranks of the 'Chechen opposition'.[105]

The Chechnya crisis was condemned by the entire cross-section of Ukrainian political parties immediately after the launch of the covert war to topple President Dudayev in summer 1994.[106] To centre-right national democrats (Rukh, the Union of Ukrainian Officers, Ukrainian Cossacks and the Congress of National Democratic Forces) and radical right nationalists (UNA and KUN) it was a question of 'we told you so' about Russia's long-standing imperialistic intentions, which would sooner or later turn against Ukraine. 'In this situation the signing by Ukraine of a Treaty of Friendship with Russia will be regarded by the world community as moral support for Moscow's imperial policies,' the Democratic Coalition Ukraine believed.[107] 'Russia demonstrated to the world its inability to renounce forceful dictatorship and armed intervention in deciding political problems,' Rukh's leader, Viacheslav Chornovil, said.

The Communist Party of Ukraine (KPU) also condemned 'any forcible resolution of any kind of conflict',[108] whilst the communist head of the parliamentary committee on foreign affairs, Oliynyk, described Russia's military intervention in Chechnya as 'aggression' and its tactics as 'genocide'. The socialist parliamentary speaker, Moroz, opposed the use of force in Chechnya.[109] Moroz's Socialist Party of Ukraine believed that 'The Russian democrats are reaping the fruits of their own anti-national policy on the Soviet Union's collapse.'

The Ukrainian parliament, president and government all issued moderate statements condemning the tactics used by the Russian side in the Chechnya campaign and called for peaceful negotiations.[110] Whilst stressing that the Chechen problem should be resolved 'in the context of ensuring the sovereignty and territorial integrity of the Russian Federation', according to President Kuchma, the Ukrainian official statements also expressed alarm at the possibility of the conflict spreading and leading to regional instability. President Kuchma also said, 'I would not like us to repeat what is happening now in Russia. This underscores our view that we view our army independently of society as a whole.'[111]

The Ukrainian official position concerned itself with the plight of the Ukrainian minority in Chechnya, which made up 11 per cent of the republic's population, and the likely radicalisation of Muslim Tartar sentiments in the Crimea. The Crimean Tartars condemned Russian imperialism in Chechnya in much the same manner as Ukrainian national democrats and nationalists.[112]

National democratic groups formed a Human Rights Commission to publicise human rights violations and transfer humanitarian aid to Chechnya. The aim of the Commission was to call on Ukrainians and other countries 'to protest against the war in Chechnya and to support a resolution of all issues on the basis of laws on the right of individuals and nations to self determination'.[113] The international Chechen organisation *Maslaat* also asked former President Kravchuk, former US President Jimmy Carter and the Kazakh poet Olzhas Suleymenov to act as intermediaries in the Chechen conflict. In Kravchuk's view (which was always close to that of the national democrats in Ukraine) the events in Chechnya were not a new phenomenon, 'but a practical implementation of the new Russian policy of restoring a unified and undivided Russia and resuming its expansionist ambitions'.[114]

Ukraine and the Russian Elections

Since 1993 the overwhelming majority of Russian political parties and civic groups have supported the integration of the former USSR, or at least the CIS, into either a Union or an Empire. Therefore, it would be a mistake to assume that Russian democrats were automatically against the revival of Russian leadership within the CIS or even territorial changes. Yuriy Luzhkov, the democratic mayor of Moscow, has repeatedly called for Sevastopol and even the Crimea to be returned to Russia. 'Sevastopol is not only a town of Russian fame. It has always belonged to Russia. And sooner or later, the truth will be victorious and it will return to Russia again. Because what is happening today is absurd. Ukraine cannot even support pensioners properly ...'[115]

All the Russian electoral manifestos in December 1995[116] had sections devoted to the defence of the Russian diaspora, which, in itself, made Ukraine and Kazakhstan the object of their attention (owing to their large Russian minorities) and the Baltic republics (owing to their alleged discrimination of Russians). All the manifestos described Russia as a 'Great Power'. The majority of the manifestos called for a new 'union' to be created from the CIS; the only gulf that existed was between reformist parties, which restricted this new 'union' to the economic sphere, and the remainder who called for a full 'union' (economic, political and military). Few political manifestos insisted that the new 'union' be created by force; the majority preferred to talk of it as a 'voluntary union'. Within this new 'union' Russia's three core neighbouring states within the CIS – Belarus, Kazakhstan and Ukraine – were to be targeted, states which ultimately decided the fate of the former USSR and which are closely interwoven within Russian pan-Slavic ideology.

Reformist parties, such as Gaidar's Russia's Democratic Choice– United Democrats (DVR–OD) and Konstantin Borovoy's Economic Freedom Party, devoted little attention to CIS integration, and DVR–OD was one of the few that stated its readiness to 'oppose remnants of imperialist ideology and militaristic mindset'. Yabloko leader Grigory Yavlinsky ruled out as unrealistic military or political unions with former Soviet republics. But one factor why Yabloko were in opposition to the Yeltsin leadership was their support in 1991 for 'the disintegration of economic ties, defence capabilities and the system of security on USSR territory'. Yavlinsky does back the creation of a fully fledged Economic Union, especially with the three key CIS core states mentioned earlier (Yavlinsky was the author of the October 1991 Economic Union programme). Yabloko co-founder Vladimir Lukin (chairman of the State Duma Committee on International Affairs) had been instrumental in 1992 in raising the question of Ukrainian sovereignty over the Crimea.

Our Home is Russia, led by the prime minister, Viktor Chernomyrdin, is also firmly within the reformist camp. But with regard to the CIS its policies echo those backed by President Yeltsin since early 1993. Our Home is

Russia linked the revival of Russia 'as a world power' to full integration within the CIS and greater co-ordination of policies *vis-à-vis* the outside world. These integrationist processes should be backed in all spheres, according to Our Home is Russia, which therefore backed a system of collective security, joint defence of the CIS external borders, collective peacekeeping as well as a 'common economic and ethno-cultural space'. Aleksei Manannikov, a leading activist of Our Home is Russia, and deputy chairman of the Duma Committee on International Affairs, supported 'pressure instruments' to influence the former Soviet republics targeting Ukraine, Kazakhstan and the Baltic republics. The Independents Bloc, co-chaired by Vladimir Komchatov, presidential prefect in Moscow, as well as the Party of Russian Unity and Accord (led by the former deputy prime minister, Sergey Shakhrai) were also in favour of the restoration of economic, political and military links within the former USSR.

Nationalist and patriotic groups were more overt in their demands for the revival of a new 'union'. The Congress of Russian Communities (KRO) laid particular emphasis on defence of the rights of the Russian diaspora, including military intervention. Lebed, its co-chairman, outlined the KRO's task as 'restoring Russia's single defence space within its historic borders: the Russian Empire and the USSR' by political and economic methods. The first priorities were restoring economic and political links with the former USSR because this region is 'a part of the sphere of its [Russia's] vitally important interests'. The Russian electoral Bloc for the Motherland placed Eduard Baltin, the former commander of the Black Sea Fleet, at the head of its list of candidates. The Bloc would seek joint Russian–Ukrainian sovereignty over the Crimea and dual citizenship for its citizens as well as 'the reunification of the countries of the former USSR'. With regard to Sevastopol, they believe that it 'is a purely Russian town. That has been the case and will remain so as it was not handed over to Ukraine.'

The Liberal Democratic Party of Russia led by Vladimir Zhirinovsky, which did remarkably well in the December 1993 and December 1995 Russian parliamentary elections, had long called on Russia to reclaim 'lost territories' in the former USSR. Russia should be recreated 'within its historically established geopolitical space within the borders of the former USSR ...' The dissolution of the former USSR was 'illegal'.

Left-wing groups, such as Power to the People! (led by Nikolay Ryzhkov, former soviet prime minister), the Russian All-People's Movement (co-chaired by a Cossack ataman), Communists–Working

Russia–For the Soviet Union (led by Viktor Tyulkin) openly called for the revival of the former USSR through a referendum. The Agrarian Party (led by Mikhail Lapshin) supported 'the aspirations of former union republics to restore a unified union state', and, like all radical left and right groups, backed the denunciation of the Belovezhskaya Agreement establishing the CIS (the Russian parliament had never ratified these documents).

Undoubtedly, the greatest danger to Ukraine from the Russian election results was the surge of support for the communists. The Communist Party of Ukraine (KPU), in league with other left-wing and inter-front groups, launched a campaign to hold a referendum on the revival of the former USSR in early 1995 (which petered out owing to threats of prosecution and public disinterest in reintegration after the negative press Russia received for its handling of the Chechnya crisis). This aim was now backed by the newly created Sojuz (Union) deputies group within the Ukrainian parliament and their promotion of full integration within the CIS. The Communist Party of the Russian Federation (KPRF) also received the highest number of votes among the nearly 12 000 Russians eligible to vote within Ukraine, followed closely by the KRO.

The KPU therefore initiated, on behalf of the KPRF, a major push for Ukraine to join the CIS Inter-Parliamentary Assembly after Ukraine was admitted to the Council of Europe CIS (Ukraine had continued to maintain its observer status in the CIS Inter-Parliamentary Assembly). Kuchma was against the creation of a 'CIS parliament' (which might resemble a new post-Soviet Congress of People's Deputies), but was in favour of co-operation between CIS parliaments. A new CIS parliament would inevitably demand the 'harmonisation of legislation' within the CIS which would be likely to clash with the Council of Europe. Three key ministries (Justice, Foreign, and Foreign Economic Ties and Trade) and the presidential think tank (the National Institute of Strategic Studies) issued advice cautioning against full membership in the CIS Inter-Parliamentary Assembly.

The KPRF united traditional socialist ideals with pan-Slavism and national statism, and satisfies the imperial restorative mood and belief in Russia's historical messianism. It was in favour of the organisation of plebiscites throughout the former USSR, which would launch a political, economic and military union as a 'stage-by-stage voluntary restoration of the Fatherland'. KPRF leader Gennadiy Zyuganov had poured scorn on attempts by Ukraine to maintain its independence whilst backing the referendum on 25 December 1995 by the Dnister Republic of Moldova for a separate state and CIS membership.

Ukrainian–Russian Economic Relations

Ukraine's full membership of the CIS Economic Union, according to its Ministry of Foreign Affairs, would prevent it from simultaneously developing relations with the West and it would be perceived as an abrupt shift in its foreign policy. This, in turn, may have led to the non-ratification of the Partnership and Co-operation Agreement between Ukraine and the EU. Full membership of the CIS Economic Union would also lead to pressure from Russia to join military and political structures within the CIS because associate or full membership was a political – not an economic – question. Therefore, Ukraine has continued to remain an associate member of the CIS Economic Union. Ukraine has also regarded as premature, and a likely threat to its economic sovereignty, membership of the CIS Payments Union or the Customs Union created by Russia, Belarus, Kyrgyzstan and Kazakhstan in March 1996. A Customs Union 'runs counter to Ukraine's national interests', because it would open up the way for Russian capital to take over Ukrainian enterprises, President Kuchma believed.

Nevertheless, Ukraine did join the newly created CIS Inter-State Economic Committee, established on 7 September 1994 at the CIS summit in Moscow. Ukraine regarded the CIS Inter-State Economic Committee as an alternative to a full economic union, which would possess only recommendatory functions (a criticism Kuchma had long levelled at the CIS as to why it was not working). Instead, the CIS Inter-State Economic Committee would be the first CIS body endowed with executive functions, whose decisions would become binding on members. The CIS Inter-State Economic Committee would help facilitate Ukraine's re-entry into the Russian market, the then prime minister, Vitaliy Masol said, and therefore be a support mechanism for Industrial-Financial Groups.

Apprehension that the CIS Inter-State Economic Committee would resemble the State Planning Committee (*Derzhplan*) of the former USSR were rejected by Ukraine. Udovenko advised Russia that, 'There is no return to the past. There can be no return to supranational structures in their old form.' Ukraine remained opposed, therefore, to the creation of any new transnational bodies. This fear was also raised by many members of parliament and political parties.

Most parliamentary factions supported the idea of Industrial-Financial Groups in principle, but demanded tighter financial controls. The presidential decree on Industrial-Financial Groups contained flaws, 'which created a tremendous threat that Ukrainian finances could be caught up in foreign capital,' Oleksandr Yelyashkevich, a reformist member of parliament, believed.[117] 'This is a direct step to legalising criminal activity,' Vladimir Marchenko, a communist member of parliament, feared.[118]

In the view of Alexander Pashkaver a presidential adviser on economic affairs, Ukrainian capital was approximately 100 times less concentrated than Russian. If these groups had been created, which he believed they should eventually be, there was the danger that Ukraine could be overwhelmed by Russian capital which would be a threat to its national security. The presidential decree was not sufficiently thought out and could have led to taxes being paid in Russia and the profits earned in Ukraine.[119]

On 1 March 1995, the Supreme Council vetoed by a vote of 222:13 the January decree 'On Financial-Industrial Groups' because it infringed Ukrainian legislation, especially in the taxation sphere. The accompanying resolution requested the parliamentary commission on Finances and Banking together with the Cabinet of Ministers to bring the presidential decree into line with Ukrainian legislation.[120] There was considerable fear that the decree would cause mass tax evasion and a higher outflow of funds abroad, as well as represent a threat to national security.

Nevertheless, the head of the parliamentary commission on Finances and Banking Affairs, Viktor Suslov, called upon the Supreme Council of Ukraine not to debate the expediency of the decree, because Industrial-Financial Groups were necessary. In his view, if the Supreme Council continued to impose vetoes it should be made to transfer its legislative functions to the president. President Kuchma likewise condemned the Supreme Council for doing nothing constructive and merely rejecting proposals made by the executive.[121]

The veto was also condemned by the Union of Industrialists and Entrepreneurs of Ukraine (SPPU) which asked the Supreme Council to allow 'this progressive organisational form of entrepreneurial activity to become operational now'.[122] At a board meeting of the SPPU in June 1995, President Kuchma told the audience that he had reached agreement with the Russian leadership that the only way out of the economic crisis for Ukraine and Russia was to create Industrial-Financial Groups. 'For Ukraine's part, we are ready to provide them with everything necessary to function properly, namely to ease tax pressure and customs regulations,' Kuchma said.

On 28 June 1995, the Supreme Council of Ukraine passed the draft law on Industrial-Financial Groups in its first reading, a draft prepared jointly by two parliamentary commissions – Financial and Banking questions as well as Economic Policies and Regulation of the State Economy.[123] The parliamentary debate brought out many controversies about tax benefits for the main enterprises and participants in these Industrial-Financial

Groups and the clauses on determining the status of the main enterprises. In the opinion of some deputies, only Ukrainian enterprises should qualify for membership of Industrial-Financial Groups. During the first reading of the draft law on Industrial-Financial Groups a number of alternative drafts were submitted.[124]

On 25 July 1995, resolution 545 of the Cabinet of Ministers recommended approval of an agreement signed on behalf of Ukraine by the Ministry of Economics with the Russian government on the general principles surrounding the creation of Industrial-Financial Groups. (This had earlier been agreed by the State Customs Committee, Ministry of Machine Building, Military-Industrial Complex and Conversion, Ministry of Foreign Economic Ties and Trade, Ministry of Finances and Ministry of Industry.) The Ukrainian government recommended certain 'changes and additions, which do not have a principled character' to the draft agreement.[125]

First Deputy Minister of Foreign Economic Ties and Trade Viktor Hladush announced in September 1995 that the Ukrainian and Russian governments had agreed in principle to finalise the establishment of approximately 100 Industrial-Financial Groups. These included four in the chemicals industry and 11 within the framework of the Ministry of Industry which would involve 15 Ukrainian and 50 Russian enterprises.[126] Other Industrial-Financial Groups were to be created in the financial, credit, insurance and trading sectors.

In negotiations between the Ukrainian and Russian prime ministers in July 1995 in Moscow, draft documents were signed on the creation of Transnational Corporations and bilateral Industrial-Financial Groups which would 'restore the earlier lost economic ties between the two republics of the former USSR'. The agreements would provide Ukrainian producers with assured supplies of raw material and save Russia 'hundreds of million of dollars' by the need no longer to build enterprises to process these materials. The sectors involved included fuel and energy, metallurgy, machine-building and space.

But are Industrial-Financial Groups a 'financial Trojan horse'? Ukrainian commentators have pointed out that if 15–20 per cent of a country's financial system are in the hands of a foreign state, then that country has lost their sovereignty.[127] Views such as these had become widespread in response to the support from large sections of the Russian leadership, academics, journalists and political parties, who had made no secret of their support for Industrial-Financial Groups as a means to reintegrate Ukraine with Russia, Belarus and Kazakhstan as the core nucleus of the CIS.

The SPPU, which Kuchma headed between 1993 and 1994, backed the creation of Industrial-Financial Groups. 'Industrial-Financial Groups are absolutely necessary! Everybody wants to make a profit. But in a different manner. The banking sphere by trading in finances and the productive sector through the manufacture of products. Through the creation of Industrial-Financial Groups we will unite the aims of the producers to those who trade in finances,' the SPPU was convinced.[128] In addition, the SPPU had long backed calls for the renewal of economic ties with the former USSR, which would then lead to co-ordination on economic reform.

Not everybody agreed. One author pointed out that the creation of Industrial-Financial Groups of themselves will not alleviate the financial and economic situation in Ukraine in the short term, for two reasons. First, the Ukrainian state should undertake measures to stimulate the concentration of financial capital in order to ensure that it is in a position to compete on the world market. 'There should operate a system of protectionist defence of the Ukrainian financial market,' he argued. Secondly, the state should ensure that Ukraine's main enterprises become competitive. Clearly, this author – as indeed many others, who reserved judgement on Industrial-Financial Groups – feared that the larger concentration of Russian capital (especially within its banking sector) would take over the Ukrainian economy because it would be in no position to compete. In addition, the Russian Federation inherited the infrastructure of state regulation from the former USSR.[129]

This could lead to a flow of capital from Ukraine to Russia leading to a deficit of capital in Ukraine and an even worse socio-economic situation. In addition, whereas Russia may become an 'economic colony' of the developed world, Ukraine would become 'an economic colonial dependency to the West and to Russia'. Therefore, 'Taking into account the specifics of the Ukrainian economy, as well as the weakness of its financial system, the technological and structural imperfections of its industrial base, its dependence upon imported raw materials, a number of reservations must be held about Industrial-Financial Groups.'[130] First, a long-term strategy – not short-term tactical victory – should be sought. Secondly, the Ukrainian state should adopt protectionist measures in defence of its Ukrainian Financial-Industrial Groups, and stimulate scientific research and innovative processes.

MILITARY POLICY

The Security Forces

Ukraine always placed great stress on building up its own security forces because of historical reasons and the security fears of predatory neighbours coveting Ukrainian territory. This policy did not change under President Kuchma although, as with much of the new presidential administration, its emphasis had. There was much greater awareness of the economic and social problems which plagued the Ukrainian armed forces and the need to improve the economy to raise funds to overcome these difficulties which were undermining their efficiency and morale.[131] One of President Kuchma's first initiatives was to make Shmarov defence minister, the first civilian to run the Ministry of Defence in the former USSR.[132] Shmarov immediately set a different tone in line with the newly elected president. A balance was needed between the army's needs and those of the state's abilities, a transition from Soviet to Ukrainian armed forces and improved bilateral military-technical co-operation with Russia.[133]

As with most post-Soviet successor states, Russia included, more resources had been diverted towards specialist internal security units because of the perception among the country's leaders that internal dissent was a greater threat than external invasions, which were unlikely in the short term. In Ukraine, the National Guard would be increased to 50 000 troops, whose function would be to act in the same paramilitary role as the Italian *Carabinieri*. They backed up the militia in times of domestic disturbances, such as in the Crimea, or the border troops in the event of border disputes. The border troops numbered 30 000 and now patrolled all Ukraine's borders. They were introduced on the Russian–Ukrainian border in January 1993 (in other areas border troops existed prior to 1991 on the former Soviet frontier).[134]

The State Protection Service, formerly under the Soviet KGB, now had the task of protecting the president, parliament and government. The Security Service of Ukraine, the successor to the KGB, continued to combine both external and internal intelligence gathering, as well as counter-intelligence work. The Ministry of Internal Affairs now included large specialist forces under its command geared for domestic disturb-ances. The former Soviet riot police (OMON) were restructured as the *Berkut* riot police. These were mainly professionals who had served previously in airborne, marine or National Guard units as conscripts. In addition to these, the Ministry of Internal Affairs continued to control large numbers of internal troops, whose duties were the same as in Soviet times – guarding strategic sites and prisons.[135]

The Black Sea Fleet

After the April 1994 conflict between Ukraine and Russia over vessels taken by Russia, President Kravchuk (but not the defence minister,

Radetskiy) accepted that locating the Russian and Ukrainian navies in Sevastopol after the division of the Black Sea Fleet would be to invite future conflict. Kravchuk, therefore, agreed to relocate the Ukrainian navy to other Crimean ports, such as Balaklava and Donuzalev. But the sticking points remained Ukraine's insistence that the base for the Russian fleet would not be leased in perpetuity, but for a specified period (Radetskiy talked of a five-year lease, and Volodymyr Bezkorovayniy, Ukraine's naval commander, suggested 15–20 years, until Russia established a base on its own territory on the Krasnodar coast). Secondly, Sevastopol would continue as a base for Ukrainian military and National Guard units to ensure Ukrainian sovereignty. Finally, only the Sevastopol base would be leased to Russia – not the town itself. These policies have been upheld by President Kuchma.

The Russian side also purposefully dragged out the negotiations over the Black Sea Fleet to await the outcome of the Ukrainian presidential elections held between June–July 1994. Of the two leading candidates, Kravchuk and Kuchma, Moscow did not hide its preference for Kuchma because they believed he would support a close alliance with Russia that would, in their view, *de facto* solve the Crimean and Black Sea Fleet questions (this, of course, did not occur).

After the Ukrainian presidential elections the Black Sea Fleet negotiations continued, but the Ukrainian position, although devoid of the ideological baggage of the Kravchuk era, nevertheless maintained the position outlined by Radetskiy in April 1994 in his meeting with the Russian defence minister, Pavel Grachev. Russia had stepped back from Grachev's demand at his meeting with Radetskiy to remove all Ukrainian naval personnel from the Crimea and hand all bases over to Russia.[136]

The negotiations since then have not been helped by Russian heavy-handedness and undiplomatic behaviour. Grachev recommended that the new Ukrainian minister of defence undertake a reshuffle in his ministry, which would lead to a breakthrough in the Black Sea Fleet negotiations. The Ukrainian Ministry of Defence issued a sharply worded response which denounced Grachev's interference in the personnel matters of a neighbouring country. In Ukrainian eyes this was another example of how Russia was unable to treat Ukraine as an independent, 'foreign' country.

Similarly, Admiral Baltin, former commander of the Black Sea Fleet, continued to argue that the Fleet question could only be resolved 'by means of unity and convergence between the two Slavonic nations in the economic, political and military spheres'. In other words, Sevastopol and the Fleet would be used as tools to reintegrate Ukraine and Russia miliarily and politically in a similar manner to Russian forward military bases in Belarus, Georgia and elsewhere in the CIS.

The Black Sea Fleet negotiations, therefore, continued to remain tense after Kuchma's election to the post of Ukrainian president. Ukraine's position essentially remained the same as that formulated in April 1994 and the failure to reach a final agreement had floundered on the question of the status of Sevastopol. The division of ships 669:164 in Russia's favour had long been agreed by both sides, although compensation to Ukraine for its share transferred to Russia was still unresolved. Ukraine would only agree to leasing for a maximum 25-year term of some bays in Sevastopol – and certainly not the entire city – but not for 99 years, as Russia continued to insist. Ukraine would continue to use Sevastopol as well, a demand strongly backed by the Ukrainian Defence Ministry, but its navy would be based mainly in Balaklava, Kerch, Feodosiya and Donuzlav.

Russia misjudged the 1994 Ukrainian election results working in their favour over the question of bases in the Crimea: 'The point is undoubtedly about Russia not encroaching on Ukraine's territorial integrity ...', the Ukrainian parliamentary speaker, Moroz, told Ukrainian naval personnel during the elections. In addition, in the words of another socialist, Mukhin, chairman of the parliamentary committee on Defence and State Security, 'The stance of the Russian delegation at the talks has remained, as before, brutal and unchanged. The representatives of the Russian delegation did not display any compromises or concessions.'[137] Deputy Defence Minister Bizhan noted that the Russian position had remained that adopted in September 1993 at Massandra where it threatened war if Ukraine did not transfer the Black Sea Fleet to Russia. The Ukrainian leadership had also continued to oppose dual citizenship to Russian naval officers living in Ukraine.

Ukrainian frustration at the unreasonable demands made by the Russian side led to hints that they would change tactics and demand that the Russian portion of the Fleet, or the entire Black Sea Fleet, vacate the Crimea and other Ukrainian ports completely. Russian naval units in Ukraine, therefore, would be little different from foreign forces based without the host's consent in the former USSR. If Ukraine were to adopt this position, it would appeal to the UN Security Council to treat Russian naval forces in Sevastopol and elsewhere in Ukraine on the same level as Russian armed forces in Moldova or formerly in the three Baltic republics. The West would then be forced to act as an intermediary to negotiate the withdrawal of Russian naval forces within a set deadline.

President Kuchma, in an address to the heads of district state administrations, said that there could be no question of any Ukrainian–Russian 'strategic partnership' if both countries could not live in peace in one city, Sevastopol, where Russia was seeking exclusive basing rights. Ukraine would never give up Sevastopol, Kuchma cautioned, and would only agree to the basing of both navies in this city. Ukraine would never agree to its navy leaving Sevastopol, Kuchma added.

The Fleet is 70 per cent in disrepair and its military preparedness would continue to decline over time. Ukrainian experts predict that by the end of the decade the Fleet would be fit only for the scrapyard. Over 70 per cent of Black Sea Fleet vessels were in disrepair because there was no procedure to pay for maintenance work and no contracts had been signed to undertake the repairs. The Fleet was 462.77 billion *karbovantsi* ($2.64 million) in debt for past repairs, according to Russian sources.

Russia and Ukraine finally took the initial steps to resolve the Black Sea Fleet question after the November 1995 Sochi summit. During 1993–4, Ukraine took over the Mykolaiv, Saki, Ochakov and Danubian flotilla bases outside the Crimea. But the question of Sevastopol was still to be resolved; Ukraine was offering two bays to Russia (Sevastopolskaya and Yuzhnaya) and reserving three for itself (Streletskaya, Karantinnaya and Kazachya) in Sevastopol.

Between December 1995 and March 1996 Ukraine received 150 naval installations from the Black Sea Fleet and 20 ships from the Donuzlav base, including a division of missile patrol boats and large amphibious warfare ships, including three *Zubr* modern hovercrafts. The deadlines were originally unrealistic as there were reportedly more stocks of ammunition in Donuzlav than with the former Russian 14th Army in Moldova.

These naval bases and coastal installations included Donuzlav (the most modern base and Black Sea Fleet reserve headquarters) and arsenal, the Novoozernaya port, the Mirnyi airport and some aircraft, the Kerch naval and military base (including its arsenal) and the Yevpatoriya military base whose marine regiment was disbanded. Russia would relocate any units not disbanded to Sevastopol, the Feodosiya testing ground, weapons range and ship repair yard, the military airports of Gvardeiskaya and Kacha (near Simferopol). Although the transfer of garrisons and weapons to Ukraine had gone according to plan, not all the officers agreed to transfer to the Ukrainian navy. The majority of those who refused Ukrainian commissions were given new posts in the Russian navy. The division of the Black Sea Fleet was halted in April 1996 after Ukraine continued to refuse to provide exclusive basing rights to Russia in Sevastopol.

Ukrainian–Russian Military Co-operation

Russian attempts to woo Ukraine into closer bilateral military relations and co-operation were linked to its recognition that only a partnership with Ukraine would enable it to alter the regional military balance in the CIS and Europe. Russia was interested in forging a military consensus with Ukraine to confront the West over issues such as NATO expansion, the Yugoslav crisis and the CFE Treaty. In addition, Russia may have given up attempting to coax Ukraine into the CIS military bloc and was instead concentrating on strengthening bilateral ties. It was no coincidence that the Russian defence minister visited the core CIS states (Ukraine, Belarus and Kazakhstan) in late 1995 and early 1996 to sign detailed and numerous bilateral military agreements.

In late November 1995 at a meeting of the Russian and Ukrainian defence ministers Grachev admitted that 'Our bilateral relations have, of course, deteriorated and to a considerable degree ...' Nevertheless, they signed agreements dealing with many issues and Grachev described the outcome as 'radically changing the military-political climate in relations between Ukraine and Russia'. Future meetings of the Russian–Ukrainian military collegium would be held twice a year. The eight economic and technical agreements as well as nine protocols and two schedules covered the following areas:

- Russia acquiring Ukraine's strategic nuclear bombers in exchange for finance, fuel and spare parts;
- co-operation within the space sphere;
- an agreement on the transit of Russian troops from Moldova;
- use by Russia of the Nitka testing range in Saki, the Crimea;
- payment by Russia for the use of anti-missile radars in Ukraine;
- the possibility of future joint military exercises;
- acquisition by Russia of the 32 SS-19 nuclear missiles in Ukraine;
- completion of the construction of Russian vessels in Ukrainian shipyards;
- withdrawal of the Russian Coastal Defence Division from the Crimea;
- transfer of some Black Sea Fleet bases to Ukraine.

On 20 February 1995, Ukraine joined the CIS Joint Air Defence Agreement with reservations. The Agreement includes all CIS members except Azerbaijan, Moldova and Turkmenistan. Democratic groups immediately condemned the move: 'Ukraine's accession to the CIS Joint Air Defence Agreement means actual rejection of its non-aligned status, renunciation of an important part of its political sovereignty and entry into a military union,' the Ukrainian Republican Party argued.[138] Russia had not hidden its aim of using the CIS Joint Air Defence Agreement as a vehicle to integrate politically and militarily CIS members, they claimed.[139]

General Lopatyn, commander of Ukraine's Air Defence Forces, said the decision to join the CIS Joint Air Defence Agreement came as a result of the country's economic crisis (40 per cent of Ukraine's fighter aircraft were out of action due to a lack of fuel and spare parts). 'Already in the first years of independence our anti-aircraft defence system had run into serious problems which are nearly impossible to resolve considering the economic situation and isolation from other Commonwealth countries.'[140] The CIS Joint Air Defence Agreement put an obligation on members to inform each other about air attacks and co-operate against aggressors.[141] A co-ordinating committee on air defence questions was established under the Council of CIS Defence Ministers to create a unified air defence system.[142]

Ukraine's membership of the CIS Joint Air Defence Agreement may also have been linked to President Kuchma's support for Industrial-Financial Groups which aim to rescue key industries, especially within aircraft production and the Military-Industrial Complex. Lopatyn claimed that it did not infringe Ukraine's sovereignty because each state administered its own anti-aircraft forces separately and the agreement would be observed, 'taking into account national legislation' (the original agreement drafted by Russia was amended because, if it had been signed, it would have led to Ukraine's membership of the CIS Collective Security Treaty).[143] It also allowed improvement in technology (produced in Russia) and the Ukrainian air forces would receive updated reports on radar recognition and the aerospace situation.[144]

Colonel Volodymyr Piskun, head of the Ukrainian Air Defence Department for Operational Control Research, pointed out that Ukraine 'encountered great difficulties in organising and carrying out repairs, acquiring information on the missile-space situation and ensuring Air Defence Forces' supplies of armaments and hardware'.[145] Ukraine would delegate only its reconnaissance-informational systems to the unified CIS Air Defence System, he said.

Nuclear Weapons

Ukraine inherited the world's third largest nuclear arsenal from the former USSR. Both the West and Russia were always determined that no new nuclear powers would emerge from Belarus, Kazakhstan and Ukraine. Of these three countries only Ukraine felt the need to drag out the process of de-nuclearisation because the latter two had always been reluctantly independent and their leaders were pro-Russian. Between 1992 and 1993, therefore, the West focused solely on nuclear weapons when it dealt with Ukraine which went together with its 'Russia-first' policy. In view of the West's willingness to turn a blind eye to Russian neo-imperialism and turn over the former USSR to the Russian sphere of influence, former President Kavchuk felt justified in using nuclear weapons as a bargaining point to obtain greater Western attention, security assurances and financial compensation.

US mediation helped secure the Trilateral Statement in January 1994, which led to the ratification by the Ukrainian parliament of the START 1 Treaty the following month. It was initially feared that Ukraine would drag out ratification of the NPT until the review conference of the treaty in April 1995. Instead, the Ukrainian parliament practically unanimously endorsed the NPT in November 1994 on the eve of President Kuchma's visit to the United States, which earned Ukraine greater Western support for its reform programme.

By a vote of 301:8 the Ukrainian parliament conditionally ratified the NPT on 16 November 1994 after much pressure throughout the year from the leading nuclear powers.[146] The NPT remained the last obstacle standing in the way of the normalisation of relations with the West. It also represented a major victory for President Kuchma, whose bargaining hand was then strengthened during his visit to the United States in November 1994 and during President Clinton's visit to Ukraine in May of the following year.[147] Ukraine's ratification of the NPT came as a surprise, particularly after comments such as those by Moroz only two months earlier, when he ruled out Ukraine's accession for the time being.[148] 'In our opinion, the treaty is imperfect,' he said.[149]

The NPT was ratified with certain conditions which had to be met before it fully passed into Ukrainian law. This tactic was previously used successfully a year earlier when the Ukrainian parliament conditionally ratified the START 1 Treaty. After that the Trilateral Nuclear Statement was agreed between the United States, Russia and Ukraine in January 1994 and the full ratification of START 1 by the Ukrainian parliament followed in February. The United Kingdom, United States and Russia signed a memorandum at the CSCE summit in Budapest on 5–6 December 1994 with regard to security assurances for Ukraine. France and China adopted separate agreements with Ukraine.[150] The Ukrainian media, for domestic consumption, described the security assurances as 'security guarantees'.[151] But President Kuchma admitted that the assurances would not resolve Ukraine's security problems: 'If tomorrow Russia goes into the Crimea no one will even raise an eyebrow.' He also admitted that 'Besides mouthing promises, no one ever planned to give Ukraine any guarantees'.[152]

The major reservations attached to Ukraine's full ratification of the NPT included the clause that it was the owner of the nuclear weapons on its territory. This had been a long-standing Ukrainian demand since 1992 in order to extract financial compensation from the West for its nuclear disarmament. Although Russia had voiced its displeasure with this clause Moscow, like the other four nuclear powers, had already *de facto* recognised Ukraine's ownership of nuclear weapons when the United States agreed to fund the delivery of enriched uranium for Ukraine's nuclear power stations from Russia.

The other major reservation attached to Ukraine's ratification of the NPT dealt with security guarantees. In the eyes of the Ukrainian leadership, the document should include guarantees against 'The threat of the use of, or the use of force against, the territorial integrity and the inviolability of the borders or the political independence of Ukraine on the part of any nuclear state and equally, the use of economic pressure aimed at subjugating to its own interests the exercising by Ukraine of rights inherent in its sovereignty …'

Ukraine's ratification of the NPT led to the lifting of US export restrictions on high technology, space and aeronautic equipment. It also placed the onus upon the United States and Russia to begin implementation of the START 2 Treaty (the United States ratified it in January 1996). More particularly, Ukraine's ratification of the NPT removed the last remaining obstacle to warm relations between Ukraine and the West. In the words of William Miller, US Ambassador to Ukraine, the vote 'clears the way for normal, strengthened relations with the United States'.

Udovenko, Ukraine's foreign minister, also came out with new demands for the West to increase its levels of foreign aid to Ukraine in the aftermath of the Ukrainian parliament's ratification of the NPT. 'It was a demand on the part of the West to join NPT, so why can't we now step out with our own demands? We will step out with a stronger position than before,' Udovenko told a Kyiv press conference on 18 November 1994. He complained that the West was falling short on its commitment made at the G7 summit in Naples in July 1994 to aid Ukraine with the $4 billion that was then pledged. Ukraine's attempt to use its ratification of the NPT to exact more Western aid was largely successful. By 1996, when the last nuclear weapons had been removed from Ukraine, it had already become the third largest recipient of US aid (after Israel and Egypt, and, for the first time, ahead of Russia).

CONCLUSIONS

There is no question that policies relating to the 'renewal of economic ties' and economic integration with Russia on a bilateral level, and within the CIS on a multilateral level, will continue. The depth of the economic crisis afflicting Ukraine provides those political parties and personalities who reject any association with the CIS whatsoever with few rational arguments to counter those who support economic co-operation.

The creation of Industrial-Financial Groups, therefore, will be continued for a number of reasons. First, President Kuchma comes from the Military-Industrial Complex and this sector, plus others, are strong backers of the 'renewal of economic ties', which they believe the Industrial-Financial Groups would accomplish on the micro level and the Inter-State Economic Committee would back up on the macro level (in contrast to the ineffectual and purely recommendatory CIS Economic Union). Secondly, Industrial-Financial Groups are seen as the only means to prevent bankruptcies and ease the transition to a market economy for sectors of the economy which, at the moment at least, have few options to reorient to non-CIS markets.

President Kuchma has nevertheless remained cautious about the CIS, like his predecessor, owing to the domestic opposition that any erosion of sovereignty would encounter. This would harm his support for reform and the adoption of a new constitution (1994–6) from those political groups who are either supporting or remaining neutral towards him, but who were hostile to him during the 1994 elections. He continues to reject political or military integration within the CIS and especially its transformation into a new 'Warsaw Pact' to counter an expanding NATO. Yet, without Ukraine no such new military pact is feasible and pressure in this sphere will therefore remain on the part of the Russian leadership which sees Ukraine as the 'missing member' of the East Slavic–Kazakh core of the CIS, whose independence is still regarded as a 'temporary phenomenon' by most Russians.[153] The 'renewal of economic ties' through the Industrial-Financial Groups and Inter-State Economic Committee will be the staging place for competition between those who would like to utilise these instruments for the renewal of a new geo-political community and those who would like to draw the line at economic issues.[154]

The Ukrainian armed forces are no different from the remainder of Ukrainian society, which is experiencing a socio-economic crisis which has seen GDP decline to a greater extent than during the American Great Depression or in the former USSR in World War II. The key to unlocking further Western aid to alleviate the crisis rests on the presidential reform programme, particularly controlling the budget deficit, slowing inflation

Table 6.3 Attitude of Russian Political Groups to the CIS

Policies	Democrats VR/Yab	NDR	Nationalists LDPR/KRO/Derzhava	Communists KPRF/Trud. Ros.
Economic union	× ✓	✓	✓	✓
Customs/payments union	× ✓	✓	✓	✓
Defence Russian speakers	× ✓	× ✓	✓	✓
Political union	×	✓	✓	✓
Military bloc	×	✓	✓	✓
Bases/peacekeeping	×	✓	✓	✓
Russia = 'Great Power'	×	✓	✓	✓
CIS as a confederation	×	✓	×	× ✓
Revival of USSR	×	×	× ✓	×
Revival of empire	×	×	×	×
Enlarged NATO	×	×		

Abbreviations: VR (Russia's Choice), Yab (Yabloko), NDR (Our Home is Russia), LDPR (Russian Liberal Democratic Party), KRO (Congress of Russian Communities), KPRF (Communist Party of the Russian Federation), Trud. Ros. (Working Russia).

and cutting expenditure. To enable Ukraine to cut military expenditure it needs to improve relations with potential aggressors. Hence the centrality of the need for the complete normalisation of relations with Russia and the dramatic improvement in relations with the West, the only source of credits and aid.

The Ukrainian security fears and proposals outlined during the Kravchuk era have largely been dealt with under Kuchma. Relations with the West have improved radically as Ukraine has undertaken a process of reform and ratified START 1 and the NPT. Ukraine became a non-nuclear power in June 1996. President Kuchma had not committed Ukraine to reorient itself geopolitically with Eurasia, which would be highly divisive at home at a time when consensus is urgently required to pursue his reform agenda and continue nation- and state-building. But sandwiched between a NATO likely to expand into Central Europe in the near future up to its Western borders and a neo-imperialistic Russia whose leaders were increasingly playing the nationalist card, would require Ukraine's leaders to adopt a fine balancing act. The second half the 1990s would therefore play a decisive role in the further consolidation of an independent Ukrainian state as a permanent feature of the world community of nations.[155]

Ukraine has moved from open support for NATO expansion and membership under Kravchuk to a position similar to Russia's in the first months of Kuchma's presidency. Ukraine has since returned to Kravchuk's original view that NATO expansion was a 'stabilising actor' in Europe and it remained the most ardent supporter of Partnership for Peace within the CIS (during 1995 Ukraine held the largest number of military exercises within the Partnership for Peace programme of any former Soviet bloc state). Ukraine is rightly concerned that it may be left in a 'no man's land' between two expanding blocs and hence obtained a 'special relationship with NATO'. It is also keen that NATO expansion will not antagonise Russia because the first casualty would be pressure on Ukraine to join the Tashkent Collective Security Treaty. Therefore, Ukraine, which borders three of the four potential new NATO members, will play a key role in the expansion of Western security structures in to the former Soviet bloc.

The Kuchma administration has to contend with the fact that with regard to Ukrainian–Russian relations, 'it is still too early to be an optimist'. The view that the main and only really serious threat to Ukrainian independence comes from Russian revanchism 'has a wide group of supporters within the ranks of the central political elite of Ukraine'. The main supporters of full CIS reintegration in Ukraine are the radical left,

Table 6.4 Russian Foreign and Defence Policies and Ukrainian Objections

Policies	Ukrainian Objections
• 'Respect for borders' (not 'recognition')	√
• No border demarcation/open 'internal CIS borders'	√
• Joint protection of CIS 'external borders'	√
• Defence of 'Russian speakers' (not Russians)	√
• Support for dual citizenship and dual state languages	√
• Backing for separatist movements	√
• Granting of basing rights to Russia 'peacekeeping forces'	√
• Creation of forward long-term military bases	√
• Leader of the CIS (rejection of equal relations)	√
• Tashkent Collective Security Treaty as new military bloc	√
• Current and new draft Russian military doctrine	√
• Inter-Parliamentary Assembly as new CIS parliament	√
• Trade restrictions (despite 1995 free trade agreement)	√
• CIS Customs and Payments Unions to recreate rouble zone	√
• Share and control over energy resources and transportation	√
• Opposition to the expansion of NATO	No
• Revision of flank limits to the CFE Treaty	OK
• Ratification of the START 2 Treaty (ratified by the USA)	√

Note: Ukraine and Russia were both disadvantaged by the flank limits of the Conventional Forces in Europe (CFE) Treaty. Ukraine does not oppose the expansion of NATO, unlike Russia, but agrees with Russia about its hostility to the stationing of nuclear weapons in new NATO member-states.

which has led to an association in many Ukrainians' eyes of CIS integration as tantamount to the revival of the former USSR and being pro-communist.

The Russian parliamentary elections reflected the degree to which the revival of some form of 'union' is popular across the entire Russian political spectrum, especially with the CIS core states, such as Ukraine. This in itself is an indication that Russia and Ukraine have diametrically opposed strategic objectives (the former to revive a 'union' and the latter to continue nation- and state-building). The nation- and state-building policies of Russia and Ukraine are pulling them apart, a process which will continue. Ukraine is already *de facto* a 'strategic loss for Russia', according to Arkady Moshes, a Ukrainian expert at the Institute of Europe, Russian Academy of Sciences.[156]

President Kuchma, like his predecessor, failed to make the final breakthrough in relations with Russia for a whole host of reasons outlined in this chapter. The full 'normalisation' of relations between Ukraine and Russia may take as long as that between Soviet Russia and Poland or Finland during the inter-war years. Indeed, Finnish–Soviet relations between 1945 and 1991 may well be the model that Russia would like to impose upon other CIS member-states. The full normalisation of relations between the Ukrainian and Polish nations took decades when dialogue and reconciliation was launched after World War II. Germany, after all, only recognised its border with Poland 25 years after the end of the war. As Ukrainian authors have pointed out, no attempts have even begun to deal with the historical basis for Ukrainian–Russian antagonism, a necessary prerequisite for any full normalisation of relations between the two countries. An improvement in Russian–Ukrainian relations is more likely to come, not from inter-state reintegration, but on the micro level through economic and commercial links, such as the proposed Industrial-Financial Groups.

The West's agreement to regard Russia as a 'Great Power', which it tirelessly proclaims on every occasion, is an additional factor which has served to hinder the full 'normalisation' of relations between Russia and Ukraine. It has also increased Russia's arrogance and unwillingness to accept any system of relations within the former USSR other than those between a 'Great Power' and satellites, that is similar to those between the former USSR and Eastern Europe through a geographically more limited new 'Yeltsin Doctrine'.

7 Conclusions

When Ukraine became an independent state in December 1991, there were few words of welcome for this new addition to the international community of nations – either in the West or in neighbouring Russia. Western governments, the academic and journalistic communities had little experience, knowledge or sympathy with the plight of the non-Russian nations of the former USSR, especially those whose separate identity to Russia was regarded as doubtful and who inherited the world's third largest nuclear arsenal, that is countries such as Ukraine.

The parliamentary and presidential elections in 1994 presaged the peaceful transfer of power in Ukraine from a Soviet era parliament and Leonid Kravchuk's presidency to that of the Kuchma era. But it would not be true to say that political and economic reform were totally absent from the Kravchuk era, as this study brings out.[1] Ukraine inherited a legacy of external domination and totalitarianism which gave it a radically different 'starting point' from that of Russia. Any comparison of Russian and Ukrainian policies during 1992–4 therefore are fraught with the danger of oversimplification and generalisation when most outside observers had little understanding of the mechanics of nation- and state-building in Ukraine.

The Kuchma era *did*, though, presage a shift in the priorities of the Ukrainian leadership to political and economic reforms in order to underpin the nation- and state-building policies of independent Ukraine (as well as the widely felt need to improve relations with Russia and adopt a more pragmatic approach towards the CIS). President Kuchma has, therefore, been as much of a *derzhavnyk* as his predecessor; those Western and Russian analysts who immediately wrote off Ukraine as returning to Eurasia have been proved to be wrong. Russian-speaking Ukrainians, such as Kuchma, are as loyal to independent Ukraine as their Ukrainian-speaking counterparts, such as Kravchuk.[2]

The Crimea was not the scene of violence and remained a peaceful region, despite numerous provocations from Russia and from radical right groups within Ukraine. Kuchma came to power with an election manifesto that called, among other things, for the re-imposition of 'law and order' in Ukraine. This in particular applied to two areas – the creation of a strong presidential executive and dealing with Crimean separatism. In both areas President Kuchma has adopted consistent and radical policies that look set to be successful.

227

Crimean separatism has been dealt a fatal blow since the beginning of the Kuchma presidency. By mid-1995, only one year into his presidency, the institution of Crimean presidency had been abolished (to little protest), the Crimean Russia bloc was in disarray and mortally divided, its popularity crumbling, while the Crimean parliament and government were led by pro-Ukrainian loyalists. And all of this without a shot being fired. Indeed, Ukraine's non-violent policies towards the Crimea have shown that they are more likely to be successful than violent methods in the resolution of ethnic conflicts in the former USSR (as seen in the failure of violent methods in Tajikistan, Chechnya, Georgia and Moldova).

There is no question that this peaceful resolution of the Crimea under President Kuchma could not have been accomplished without the political, economic and security pressure that had been applied under former President Kravchuk. In addition, Kuchma inherited Yevhen Marchuk from his predecessor. With a Soviet career in the KGB, Marchuk went on to become chairman of the Security Service of Ukraine in late 1991 and then was promoted to deputy prime minister with responsibility for national security under Kuchma in the second half of 1994. In both these posts between 1991 and 1995 Marchuk was obviously in a key position to aid his political mentors in their quest to subdue Crimean separatism non-violently. Marchuk's promotion to the post of prime minister in June 1995 was possibly another step, many Kyiv pundits believed, to the highest post in the land at the next presidential elections.[3] After being replaced as prime minister in May 1996 by Pavlo Lazarenko, his first deputy, Marchuk retired to the backbenches of parliament and no doubt plotted his political comeback – in a similar manner to Kuchma between 1993 and 1994.

While carefully expanding his support base to political groups and regions that did not vote for him, Kuchma was able to build a consensus that isolated the orthodox communists in their opposition to political and economic reform. One of Kuchma's first acts was to introduce debate on the separation of powers between the legislature and executive as a prelude to the adoption of new post-Soviet Ukrainian and draft Crimean constitutions in 1996, five years into independence. The adoption of new constitutions in Ukraine also, of course, presages the end of the Soviet era domestically within Ukraine, whilst the new draft Crimean constitution signifies the normalisation of relations between Kyiv and the peninsula.

'Corrections' in economic reform announced since April and June 1995 and the slower than expected pace of privatisation have not swayed Kuchma's faith in economic reform or conviction that there is no going back – to the former USSR or to its command-administrative system.

Economic reform will therefore continue, but at Ukraine's slower pace which takes into account social welfare, state regulation and the need to appease a variety of domestic constituencies to achieve *zlahoda*, the key ingredient for Ukraine's successful and peaceful nation- and state-building policies.

Under Kuchma Ukraine joined the Council of Europe and the Central European Initiative, moved closer to the European Union, the West European Union and NATO, while at the same time becoming a non-nuclear power. Ukraine has good relations with the West, Central Europe and other regions of the world with whom it is interested in diversifying its foreign trade in order to lessen its dependency upon the CIS.

But inter-state treaties with Romania and Russia had still not been signed by Ukraine over two years into Kuchma's presidency, indicating that the underlying causes for this were *not* his predecessor's mistaken policies, but disinterest in both these countries in giving legal recognition to their current borders with Ukraine. An inter-state treaty with Russia which recognised current borders according to international law is the most important aspect of any complete 'normalisation' of relations between Russia and Ukraine. The ideological and nationalistic tension of the Kravchuk era in Ukrainian–Russian relations has been removed though, which has enabled Ukraine to consolidate and prioritise non-security issues, such as domestic reform.

The Kuchma era has also highlighted the diverging national interests of Russia and Ukraine. Ukraine regards its nation- and state-building policies as the completion of a process forcibly interrupted by outside powers – in much the same manner as that accomplished in other European countries in earlier centuries and decades. In contrast, Russia perceives itself as never having been a nation-state with a preference for a revived union (confederation, empire or new USSR depending upon the political group in question) that would be led by a Russia surrounded by satellite dependencies in an unequal partnership. Russia, therefore, regards CIS integration and its nation- and state-building process as synonymous – not mutually contradictory – as Ukrainian elites would perceive it.[4]

Finally, if Kravchuk is remembered for having dismantled Ukraine's *foreign* links to the former Soviet empire by ushering in an independent state, President Kuchma will surely be remembered as someone who presided over the dismantling of the *domestic* Soviet political and economic system within Ukraine. Kravchuk is also to be remembered for having ensured that Kuchma and Marchuk exist and were capable of taking over where he left off; able to implement the next stage of Ukraine's nation and state-building policies.[5]

Notes

INTRODUCTION

1. See Taras Kuzio, 'The Emergence of Ukraine', *Contemporary Review*, vol. 268, nos. 1562 and 1563 (March and April 1996), pp. 119–25 and pp. 182–9; and Bohdan Nahaylo, 'The Birth of an Independent Ukraine', *Report on the USSR*, vol. 3, no. 50 (13 December 1991).
2. See Roman Laba, 'How Yeltsin's Exploitation of Ethnic Nationalism Brought down an Empire', *Transition*, vol. 2, no. 1 (12 January 1996).
3. *Kyivska Pravda*, 7 July 1992.
4. See chapter 8, 'Stalemate and the Rise of National Communism (1990–1)' and chapter 9, 'From Soviet to Independent Ukraine: The Coup and Aftermath', in T. Kuzio and Andrew Wilson, *Ukraine. Perestroika to Independence* (London: Macmillan, 1994), pp. 152–70 and pp. 171–202 respectively.
5. See Valerii Khmelko, 'Referendum: Khto Buv Za i Khto Proty', *Ukrainskyi Ohliadach*, no. 2 (February 1992); and *Politolohichnyi Chyttania*, no. 1 (1992), pp. 40–52; and Peter J. Potichnyi, 'The Referendum and Presidential Elections in Ukraine', *Canadian Slavonic Papers*, vol. XXX111, no. 2 (June 1991), pp. 123–38.
6. The Kravchuk era is covered in my forthcoming book *Nation and State Building in Ukraine: The Search for Identity* (London: Routledge). See also my *Ukraine. The Unfinished Revolution. European Security Study 16* and *Ukraine. Back From the Brink. European Security Study 23* (London: Institute for European Defence and Strategic Studies, 1992 and 1995).

1   A NEW UKRAINIAN PARLIAMENT

1. An earlier and shorter version of this chapter appeared *in The Journal of Communist Studies and Transition Politics*, vol. 11, no. 4 (December 1995), pp. 335–61.
2. *The Washington Post*, 27 July 1994.
3. See Rick Simon, 'Workers and Independence in Divided Ukraine', *Labour Focus on Eastern Europe*, no. 49 (Autumn 1994), pp. 18–34.
4. *Holos Ukrainy*, 28 September 1993.
5. See Andrew Wilson, 'The Elections in the Crimea', *RFE/RL Research Report*, vol. 3, no. 25 (24 June 1994).
6. On the presidential elections, see Taras Kuzio, 'Leonid Kuchma: Ukraine's Second President', *The Ukrainian Weekly*, 31 July and 'Ukraine since the Elections: From Romanticism to Pragmatism', *Jane's Intelligence Review*, vol. 4, no. 12 (December 1994). See also Dominique Arel and Andrew

Wilson, 'Ukraine under Kuchma: Back to Eurasia?' *RFE/RL Research Report*, vol. 3, no. 32 (19 August 1994).

7. See Myron Wasylyk, 'Ukraine Prepares for Parliamentary Elections' and 'Ukraine on the Eve of Elections', *RFE/RL Research Report*, vol. 3 nos. 5 and 12 (4 February and 25 March 1994).

8. See the poll conducted during February–March by Democratic Initiatives in *Molod Ukrainy*, 23 March 1994.

9. *Post Postup*, 9–15 December 1993.

10. See T. Kuzio, 'The Multi-Party System in Ukraine on the Eve of Elections', *Government and Opposition*, vol. 29, no. 1 (Winter 1994), pp. 109–27. See also A.H. Sliusarenko and M.V. Tomenko, *Novi Politychni Partii Ukrainy. Dovidnyk. Seria 'Chas I Suspilstvo', no. 12* (Kyiv: Tovarystvo 'Znannia', 1990), O.V. Haran and V.A. Viktorenko, eds., *Ukraina. Bahatopartiyna. Prohramni Dokumenty Novykh Partiy* (Kyiv: Pamiatky Ukrainy, 1991), O.V. Haran, *Vid Stvorennia Rukhu do Bahatopartiynosti. Seria 'Chas', no. 1* (Kyiv: Tovarystvo 'Znannia', 1992), O.V. Haran, *Ubyty Drakona. Z Istorii Rukhu ta novykh partiy Ukrainy* (Kyiv: Lybid, 1993), A.O. Bilous, *Politychni Ob'iednannia Ukrainy* (Kyiv: Ukraina, 1993); and Volodymyr Lytvyn, *Politychna Arena Ukrainy. Diyovi Osoby ta Vykonavtsi* (Kyiv: Abrys, 1994).

11. *Zakon Ukrainy Pro Vybory Narodnykh Deputativ Ukrainy. Ofitsiinyi tekst* (Kyiv: Ukrainian Independent Centre for Political Research, 1994) and *Vechirnyi Kyiv*, 27 November 1993. See also *The Election Law of Ukraine 'Made Easy'* (Kyiv: Working Group of the Committee on Legislation and Legitimacy, Council of Advisers to the Parliament of Ukraine, 1993). English translations of the Law of Ukraine 'On the Election of People's Deputies of Ukraine' can be found in *The Verkhovna Rada Elections in Ukraine. March 27 to April 10, 1994* (Kyiv: Report of the Democratic Elections in Ukraine Observation and Coordination Centre. Part One, 1994), pp. 99–146 and *Elections in Ukraine 1994* (Kyiv: International Foundation for Electoral Systems, 1994), pp. 141–57.

12. See the article by Artur Bilous, 'Na Vybory – Ukrainskym Velosypedom?', *Polityka i chas*, no. 1 (1994) pp. 40–3, which discusses the three types of electoral system – majoritarian, proportional and mixed – and their applicability to Ukraine.

13. UNIAR news agency, 13 January 1994.

14. *Uriadovyi Kurier*, no. 180 (18 December 1993) lists the 450 electoral districts.

15. *The Independent*, 28 March 1994.

16. See the comments by the election observer Magdalena Hoff (*Reuters*, 27 March 1994) and Olha Zhukovska, 'Chomu v zali bahato vakantnykh mists?', *Holos Ukrainy*, 22 April 1994.

17. *Ukraine's Parliamentary Election. March 27, 1994. April 10, 1994* (Washington D.C.: The Staff of the Commission on Security and Cooperation in Europe, April 1994), pp. 10–11.

18. *The Verkhovna Rada Election in Ukraine. March 27 to April 10, 1994* (Kyiv: Report of the Democratic Elections in Ukraine Observation and Coordination Centre, Part One, 1994).

19. *Ukraine's Parliamentary Election*, p. 10.
20. The Party of Power is a term used to describe those former members of the Communist Party of Ukraine (until it was banned in August 1991) who adopted a 'national communist' orientation, such as Leonid Kravchuk. They had not, on the whole, rejoined other political parties but remain closely connected through their former clannish and nepotistic ties established during the 'era of stagnation' of Leonid Brezhnev's rule in the USSR.
21. See the statement by the Congress of National Democratic Forces which criticised the law for preserving the power of the *nomenklatura (Robitnycha hazeta*, 3 December 1994).
22. *Ukrainian News*, no. 47, 1993.
23. *The Ukrainian Weekly*, 14 November 1993.
24. *The Ukrainian Weekly*, 21 November 1993.
25. *Radio Ukraine world service*, 18 November 1993.
26. *Ukrainian News*, no. 47, 1993.
27. *The Ukrainian Weekly*, 12 November 1995.
28. *The Ukrainian Weekly*, 17 December 1995.
29. *Molod Ukrainy*, 4 January 1996.
30. See M. Wasylyk, 'Ukraine's Parties Offer Their Wares', *The Wall Street Journal*, 25–26 March 1994, which surveyed the four main national election blocs – the radical left, the Inter-Regional Bloc of Reforms (MRBR), the Democratic Coalition Ukraine and the Party of Power. Wasylyk ignored the radical right as too unpopular to constitute a fifth election force.
31. See the call for 'one democratic election bloc' by Holovatiy, then a leading member of Rukh and President of the Ukrainian Legal Foundation (*Ukrainske Slovo*, 7 November 1993).
32. *Vechirnyi Kyiv*, 20 October and *Ukrainski Visti*, 24 October 1993.
33. In Chernihiv no seat was won by democrats precisely because of this lack of co-ordination. The first secretary of the local Communist Party of Ukraine won a large majority over Rukh and the URP (*Holos Ukrainy*, 12 April 1994).
34. *Post Postup*, 4–10 November, *Holos Ukrainy*, 11 December and *Narodna hazeta*, no. 48 (December 1993).
35. *Ukrainian News*, no. 44, 1994.
36. *Holos Ukrainy*, 8 December 1993, 21, 25 and 27 January 1994.
37. *Holos Ukrainy*, 29 December 1993.
38. On the formation of the MRBR and its election programme, see *Uriadovyi Kurier*, no. 44 (19 March 1994), *News from Ukraine*, no. 6, 1994 and *Elections 94 Press Center. Dateline Ukraine, and informational and analytical bulletin*, no. 5 (21 March 1994).
39. *Post Postup*, 3–9 February 1994. See the article by Grynev, 'Cherez Ob'iednannia do Real'nykh Peretvoren', *Viche*, February 1994, pp. 63–7.
40. *The Wall Street Journal*, 8 April 1994.
41. UNIAR news agency, 21 February. See the denial by Grynev (UNIAR news agency, 23 February 1994).
42. See V.B. Hryn'iov, *Nova Ukraina: Iakoiu ia ii Bachu* (Kyiv: Abrys, 1995) and the very negative review *in Chas-Time*, 20 October and 'Nova Ukraina chy nova koloniya?', *Holos Ukrainy*, 12 December 1995.

43. See the comparison between Rukh and the MRBR in *Elections 94 Press centre. Dateline Ukraine, an informational and analytical bulletin*, no. 2 (24 February 1994).
44. *Reuters*, 12 April 1994.
45. *News from Ukraine*, nos. 2–3, 1994.
46. *The Wall Street Journal Europe*, 25 March 1994.
47. The election programmes of national democratic groups can be found for Rukh – *Uriadovyi Kurier*, nos. 11–12 (20 January 1994) and *Rada*, 10 February 1994, the KhDPU – *Vechirnyi Kyiv*, 18 March 1994, the UNKP – *Ukrainskyi Chas*, no. 2, 1993, the SelDPU – *Uriadovyi Kurier*, no. 17 (29 January 1994) and *Zemlia i Volia* January 1994, the DPU – *Uriadovyi Kurier*, nos. 11–12 (20 January 1994), the URP – *Uriadovyi Kurier*, no. 17 (29 January 1994) and *Narodna Hazeta*, nos. 1–2 (January 1994) and the KNDS – *Narodna Hazeta*, no. 49 (December 1993) and *Holos Ukrainy*, 15 February 1994.
48. Liberal democratic and centrist election platforms of the Beer Lovers Party can be found in *Uriadovyi Kurier*, nos. 160–1 (2 November 1993), the Labour Party in *Silski Visti*, 5 November and *Holos Ukrainy*, 11 November 1993, the Party of Justice in *Uriadovyi Kurier*, no. 21 (5 February 1994), the Constitutional Democratic Party in *Uriadovyi Kurier*, no. 21 (5 February 1994), the Party of Solidarity and Social Justice in *Uriadovyi Kurier*, no. 25 (12 February 1994), the Labour Congress of Ukraine in *Holos Ukrainy*, 24 December 1993 and *Uriadovyi Kurier*, nos. 27–8 (17 February 1994), the Green Party in *Uriadovyi Kurier*, nos. 31–2 (24 February 1994) and the Liberal Democratic Party in *Uriadovyi Kurier*, nos. 35–6 (3 March 1994).
49. *Financial Times*, 23 March 1994.
50. On the different social backgrounds of the KPU and SPU, see D. Arel and A. Wilson, 'The Ukrainian Parliamentary Elections', *RFE/RL Research Report*, vol. 3, no. 26 (1 July 1994), p. 13.
51. *Izvestiya*, 29 March 1994.
52. *Uriadovyi Kurier*, nos. 27–8 (17 February 1994).
53. The election platforms of the SPU and SelPU can be found respectively in *Uriadovyi Kurier*, no. 44 (19 March) and *Nezavisimost*, 16 March 1994.
54. *Holos Ukrainy*, 11 February 1994.
55. The election programme of the KUN is in *Shliakh Peremohy*, 29 January and *Uriadovyi Kurier*, nos. 35–6 (3 March 1994).
56. Their election programme is printed in *Uriadovyi Kurier*, no. 44 (19 March 1994).
57. The election programmes of the OUNvU and the DSU are in *Neskorena Natsii*, no. 5 (1994) and *Nezboryma Natsiya*, no. 1 (January 1994) respectively. The mainstream official press refused to publish their election platforms.
58. UNIAN news agency, 18 January and *Neskorena Natsia*, no. 3 (1994).
59. *Reuters*, 8 April 1994.
60. *The Washington Times*, 22 March 1994.
61. *Ukrainski Obrii*, no. 1 (January 1994).
62. UPI, 30 March 1994.
63. *Reuters*, 8 April 1994.
64. See *Vechirnyi Kyiv*, 20 January and *Visti z Ukrainy*, no. 41 (1994).

234 *Notes*

---

234 *Notes*

234 *Notes*

65. Artur Bilous, 'Bereznevi Vybory i Perspektyvy Novoho Parlamentu', *Suchasnist*, no. 3 (March 1994), p. 81.
66. See D. Arel and A. Wilson, 'The Ukrainian Parliamentary Elections', *RFE/RL Research Report*, vol. 3, no. 26 (1 July 1994).
67. UNIAN news agency, 30 November 1993.
68. *Radio Ukraine*, 26 December 1993.
69. *Demokratychna Ukraina*, 3 February 1994.
70. *Demos*, no. 8 (1995). Three members of this election bloc who went on to be elected joined the Unity parliamentary faction.
71. *Halytski Kontrakty*, no. 7 (1994) and *Vechirnyi Kyiv*, 1 December 1993. See also the article by Valery Babich, President of the Ukrainian Financial Group and a leading businessman from Dnipropetrovs'k, 'Profesionalnyi Parlament: Buty Chy Ne Buty', *Viche*, February 1994, pp. 68–71.
72. *Post Postup*, 4–10 November 1993.
73. UNIAN news agency, 3 March 1994.
74. *Reuters*, 8 April 1994. See also Stetskiv's article in *Post Postup*, 1–7 April 1994.
75. UNIAN news agency, 30 November 1993. See also *Halytski Kontrakty*, no. 8 (1994).
76. See Monika Jung, 'The Donbas Factor in the Ukrainian Elections', *RFE/RL Research Report*, vol. 3, no. 12 (25 March 1994).
77. UNIAR news agency, 14 January 1994.
78. *Holos Ukrainy*, 2 March 1994.
79. Democratic Initiatives, *Politychnyi Portret Ukrainy. Hromadska Dumka i Vybory Verkhovnoi Rady Ukrainy*, no. 8 (May 1994).
80. Ibid.
81. *Holos Ukrainy*, 17 February 1994.
82. *Elections 94 Press Center. Dateline Ukraine. An informational and analytical bulletin*, no. 4 (11 March 1994).
83. Democratic Initiatives, *Politychnyi Portret Ukrainy. Hromadska Dumka i Vybory Verkhovnoi Rady Ukrainy*, no. 8 (May 1994).
84. Dr Heorhii Kasianov, 'Ukraine before the Elections', *The Ukrainian Review*, vol. XL, no. 4 (Winter 1993), p. 7. See also *Ukrainske Slovo*, 20 February 1994.
85. See the very pessimistic predictions of the elections in 'Setting in for More of the Same', *The Economist*, 19 March 1994, 'Forget the Fantasies', *Business Central Europe*, March 1994, and Editorial, 'Ukraine Adrift after Elections', *Financial Times*, 15 April 1994. For a survey of the forces shaping the elections, see T. Kuzio, 'The Implications of the Ukrainian Elections', *Jane's Intelligence Review*, vol. 6, no. 6 (June 1994).
86. *Reuters*, 28 March 1994.
87. *Reuters*, 11 March 1994.
88. *Holos Ukrainy*, 26 February 1994.
89. *Reuters*, 28 March 1994.
90. *Politychnyi Portret Ukrainy: Naperedodni Vyboriv* (Kyiv: Democratic Initiative, 24 March 1994).
91. The deputies elected in the first two rounds of voting were published in *Holos Ukrainy*, 27 April 1994 and *Uriadovyi Kurier*, nos. 62–3 (21 April 1994), and those validated by parliament were in *Holos Ukrainy*, 18 May

Notes 235

1994. See also 'Ukraine Turns Out', *The Economist*, 2 April 1994, T. Kuzio, 'Elections in Ukraine', *Freedom Review*, vol. 25, no. 3 (June 1994) and Judge Bohdan Futey, 'The Vote for Parliament and Ukraine's Law on Elections', *The Ukrainian Weekly*, 5 June 1994.

92. UPI, 25 July 1994.
93. *Silski Visti*, 22 February 1994.
94. See the comment by Levko Lukianenko, honorary chairman of the URP, who predicted that democrats would obtain 50 per cent of seats (*Radio Ukraine*, 6 January 1994).
95. See Rukh's predictions of winning 25 per cent of seats in *Holos Ukrainy*, 17 February 1994.
96. RIA news agency, 11 April 1994 and 'Rukh ne vyhrav vyboriv ale i ne prohrav', *Rada*, 14 April 1994.
97. *The Guardian*, 12 April 1994.
98. *Kyivska Pravda*, 22 April 1994.
99. Marco Bojcun, 'The Ukrainan Parliamentary Elections in March–April 1994', *Europe-Asia Studies*, vol. 47, no. 2 (March–April 1995), p. 245.
100. See the parliamentary resolution in *Holos Ukrainy*, 20 July and the analysis on the eve of the repeat elections in *Holos Ukrainy*, 8 December 1995.
101. The statement to this effect was signed by Rukh, the Democratic, Republican, Liberal and other parties (*Radio Ukraine world service*, 12 August 1995).
102. UNIAN news agency, 7 September 1995.
103. *Holos Ukrainy*, 1 February 1996 gave a list of 13 deputies elected to the Ukrainian parliament on 10, 17 and 24 December 1995. See also *Dovidnyk Do Povtornykh Vyboriv Narodnykh Deputativ Ukrainy 10 Hrudnia 1995 Roku* (Kyiv: International Foundation for Electoral Systems, 1996).
104. *Radio Ukraine world service*, 7 November 1995.
105. *Vechirnyi Kyiv*, 21 October, *Chas*, 27 October and 1 December 1995.
106. UNIAN news agency, 14 November 1995.
107. *Kommunist*, no. 48 (November 1995) and *Tovarysh*, no. 46 (November 1995).
108. *Holos Ukrainy*, 28 December 1995. Heohriy Shevchenko died in non-suspicious circumstances from carbon monoxide poisoning soon after he was elected as a communist member of parliament from Sevastopol (*Kyivski vidomosti*, 5 January 1996).
109. UNIAN news agency and *Reuters*, 8 December 1995.
110. *Holos Ukrainy*, 13 January 1996. Mykhailo Zabornyi, a member of the Agrarians for Reform faction and chairman of the Subcommission on Land Legislation, Commission for Economic Policy and Management of the National Economy, died of a heart attack on 25 January 1996 (UNIAR news agency, 26 January 1996).
111. *Interfax News Agency*, 8 December and UNIAN News Agency, 14 December 1995.
112. UNIAN News Agency, 11 December 1995.
113. *Interfax News Agency*, 11 December 1995. See also *Holos Ukrainy*, 4 November 1995.
114. Hermanchuk won a by-election on 4 February 1996 after the death of another member of parliament, Vasyl Korneliuk.

115. UNIAN news agency, 30 October 1995.
116. *Reuters*, 11 December 1995 and UNIAN News Agency, 14 December 1995.
117. *UNIAN News Agency*, 23 January 1996.
118. See the list in *Holos Ukrainy*, 28 December 1995.
119. See the editorial 'Vybory 10 hrudnia: Peremohla – Vlada, Vybortsi – Prohraly', *Vechirnyi Kyiv*, 15 December 1995. Viacheslav Kyrylenko in an article entitled 'Vybory pidtverdyly vplyv Narodnoho Rukhu Ukrainy' (*Chas*, 16 February 1996) argues that Rukh's influence remained strong, as evidenced by its successes in the recent repeat elections.
120. UNIAN News Agency, 3 April 1996.
121. *Samostijna Ukraina*, no. 7 (March 1996) gave a list of URP candidates while *Kommunist*, no. 13 (March 1996) published KPU candidates. *Krymska Svitlytsia* (23 March 1996) gave a positive profile of Mykola Huk, a member of the Union of Ukrainian Officers, editor of *Dzvin Sevastopolia* and leading member of the Ukrainian Civic Congress of the Crimea. *Vechirnyi Kyiv* (29 March 1996) gave a list of candidates standing in Kyiv.
122. See *The Verkhovna Rada Elections in Ukraine. March 27 to April 10, 1994* (Kyiv: Report of the Democratic Elections in Ukraine Observation and Coordination Center. Part One, 1994), Chapter VI, 'An Overview of Election Violations', pp. 26–98 and *The Ukrainian Weekly*, 17 April 1994.
123. Copy in the author's possession of *British Observer's Report: The Ukrainian Parliamentary Elections – 2nd Round (10th April 1994)* and interview with Jessica Douglas-Home, 15 September 1995, Zurich.
124. *The Times*, 14 April 1994.
125. *The Washington Post*, 12 April 1994. Morozov's election manifesto was published in *Vechirnyi Kyiv*, 7 and 8 July 1994.
126. *Chas*, 23 February 1996.
127. *Ukraine's Parliamentary Elections. March 27, April 10, 1994* (Washington DC: Commission on Security and Cooperation in Europe, 1994), pp. 15–16.
128. *Reuters*, 28 March 1994.
129. UNIAR news agency, 14 April 1994.
130. *The Washington Post*, 12 April 1994.
131. *Ukraine's Parliamentary Elections*.
132. See Vadym Ryzhkov, 'Covert Electoral Fraud, How Elections can be Rigged. Case Study – Dnipropetrovs'k', *Demos*, vol. 1, no. 1 (10 October 1994).
133. *Derby Evening Telegraph*, 11 April 1994.
134. *Reuters*, 23 February 1994.
135. See 'Politychnyi terror proty rukhu ta ioho lideriv i aktyvistiv', *Rada*, 3 February 1994.
136. *Kreshchatyk*, 1 February 1994.
137. *Holos Ukrainy*, 5 May 1994 and *Rukh Press*, 30 March 1994.
138. *The Washington Times*, 27 March 1994.
139. UNIAN news agency, 13 July 1994.
140. For a comparison of Ukraine's election, see Krenar Loloci, Rumyana Kolarova, Dimitr Dimitrov and Elena Stefoi, 'Electoral Laws in eastern Europe', and Christian Lucky, 'Comparative Chart of Electoral Regimes', *East European Constitutional Review*, vol. 3, no. 2 (Spring 1994), pp. 42–58 and 65–79.

141. *The Ukrainian Weekly*, 12 November 1995. See also V.H. Kremen', Ye. H. Bazovkin, A.O. Bilous, M.D. Mishchenko, V.S. Nebozhenko, P.K. Sytnyk and Yu. V. Shylovtsev, *Vybory Do Verkhovnoi Rady Ukrainy: Dosvid ta Uroky, Naukovi Dopovidi 25* (Kyiv: National Institute of Strategic Studies, 1994).
142. *Financial Times*, 13 April 1994.
143. Mykola Tomenko, *Ukrainska Perspektyva: istoryko-politolohichni pidstavy suchasnoi derzhavnoi strategii. Politychni studii 2* (Kyiv: Ukrainska Perspectiva, 1995), p. 14.
144. See T. Kuzio and A. Wilson, *Ukraine: Perestroika to Independence* (London: Macmillan, 1994), chapter 2, 'Strengths and Weaknesses of the National Movement', pp. 18–41.
145. Tomenko, *Ukrainska Perspektyva*, p. 74.

2   ISSUES AND VOTERS IN THE 1994 PRESIDENTIAL ELECTIONS

1. *Reuters*, 25 June 1994.
2. *Holos Ukrainy*, 5 July 1994.
3. David R. Marples, 'Ukraine after the Presidential Elections', *RFE/RL Research Report*, vol. 3, no. 31 (12 August 1994), p. 10.
4. See T. Kuzio, 'Kravchuk to Kuchma: The Ukrainian Presidential Elections of 1994', *The Journal of Communist Studies and Transition Politics*, vol. 12, no. 2 (June 1996), pp. 117–44.
5. See *Reuters*, 28 June 1994.
6. UPI, 4 July 1994.
7. *Radio Ukraine world service*, 4 July 1995. See also UPI, 5 July 1994.
8. UPI, 5 July 1994.
9. *Holos Ukrainy*, 5 July 1994.
10. *Financial Times*, 19 February 1993.
11. *Izvestiya*, 13 July 1994. See also AP 11 July 1994.
12. AP, 13 July 1994. See also *Reuters*, 12 July 1994.
13. *Nezavisimaya Gazeta*, 5 October 1995. *The Economist* (16 July 1994) also differentiated between Belarus and Ukraine, arguing that only the former desired 'reunion' with Russia.
14. The commentary in *Moskovskiye Novosti* (10–17 July 1994) agreed.
15. *The New York Times*, 13 July 1994.
16. Interview by *NTV, Moscow*, 12 June 1994.
17. 'Neither of the two Leonids represents a break with Ukraine's communist past. Kravchuk was party ideological chief here before the breakup of the Soviet Union, and Kuchma headed the Soviet's biggest missile factory' (*The Washington Post*, 10 July 1994).
18. *Reuters*, 10 July 1994.
19. Anatol Lieven in *The Tablet*, 9 September 1994.
20. *Uriadovyi Kurier*, 23 October 1995.
21. Andrew Wilson, 'Rewriting Ukrainian History: The Use and Abuse of National History in Ukrainian State Building'. Ukrainian Seminar Series, Centre for Russian and East European Studies, The University of Birmingham, 23 October 1995.

22. See Carol Barner-Barry and Cynthia A. Hody, *The Politics of Change. The Transformation of the Former Soviet Union* (New York: St. Martin's Press, 1995), p. 263.
23. *The Financial Times*, 12 July 1994.
24. *Reuters*, 28 June 1994.
25. *Vechirnyi Kyiv*, 28 July 1994.
26. *Vechirnyi Kyiv*, 28 July 1994.
27. *Vechirnyi Kyiv*, 15 August 1994.
28. UPI, 22 June 1994.
29. *The Guardian*, 27 June 1994.
30. *Reuters*, 7 July 1994.
31. AP, 26 June 1994.
32. *Reuters*, 12 June 1994.
33. *Post Postup*, no. 21, 1994.
34. UPI, 22 June 1994.
35. AP, 25 June 1994.
36. *Post Postup*, no. 21, 1994.
37. Interview on *NTV, Moscow*, 12 June 1994.
38. *Radio Ukraine world service*, 4 July 1994.
39. *Reuters*, 11 July 1994.
40. *Reuters*, 11 July 1994.
41. ITAR-TASS news agency, 12 June 1994.
42. UPI, 28 June 1994. Kravchuk later softened this argument: 'Kuchma's first moves in this capacity (as president) may possibly evoke some discontent in society, but a war is out of the question' (*Radio Ukraine world service*, 7 July 1994).
43. *Reuters*, 26 June 1994.
44. *Reuters*, 26 June 1994.
45. *Molod Ukrainy*, 17 June 1994.
46. AP, 24 June 1994.
47. *Reuters*, 2 April 1994.
48. *Reuters*, 12 April 1994.
49. See the poll by the International Institute for Sociology, Kyiv Mohyla Academy (*Uriadovyi Kurier*, nos. 92–3, 16 June 1994).
50. AP, 26 June 1994.
51. UNIAN news agency, 20 June 1994.
52. *Reuters*, 2 June 1994.
53. *Radio Ukraine world service*, 23 June 1994.
54. UPI, 23 June 1994.
55. 'It's a pity he [Andropov] lasted only one year. But in one year we accomplished more than during the five previous years' (*The Washington Post*, 12 July 1994).
56. *Reuters*, 25 June 1994.
57. UPI, 26 June 1994.
58. *Visti z Ukrainy*, no. 30 (21–27 July 1994).
59. *The Washington Post*, 12 July 1994.
60. UNIAN news agency, 8 June 1994. This has been proposed by President Boris Yeltsin as well. But, as in Russia, it was never implemented. The June 1995 Constitutional Agreement between the executive and legislature

subordinated the prime minister and cabinet of ministers under the president.

61. *Reuters*, 15 June 1994.
62. *Reuters*, 21 June 1994.
63. *Radio Ukraine world service*, 5 July 1994.
64. *Radio Ukraine world service*, 13 June 1994.
65. *The Financial Times*, 23 June 1994.
66. UPI, 23 June 1994.
67. *Reuters*, 26 June 1994.
68. *Reuters*, 28 June 1994.
69. *Ukrainian State Television*, 13 June 1994.
70. Oleh Soskin, deputy director of the Institute for International Relations and World Economy, National Academy of Sciences, said, just after the second round, that Kuchma's team was very 'ideological', but that 'It is impossible to say where he will go with the economy' (*Reuters*, 12 July 1994).
71. *Financial Times*, 23 June 1994.
72. UPI, 23 June 1994.
73. 'You need political will to carry out reforms. Believe me, I have the will', Kuchma said (*Reuters*, 10 July 1994).
74. *Reuters*, 8 July 1994. Kuchma stated his preference for 'slow, non-revolutionary reforms' (UPI, 4 July 1994).
75. *Ukrainian State Television*, 20 June 1994. See also UPI, 8 July 1994. This argument, namely that an independent Ukrainian state could only exist on the foundations of a strong economy, has enabled his administration to move towards an alliance with the 'post-nationalists' within the national democratic camp grouped in the parliamentary faction 'Reform', many of whom were previously members of Rukh and therefore had always been critically disposed towards Kravchuk.
76. Kuchma's socioeconomic analysis and programme were published in *Holos Ukrainy*, 6 July 1994.
77. See Kuchma's interview in *Trud*, 21 June 1994.
78. UPI, 11 June 1994.
79. See the comments by Mikhailchenko, Kravchuk's domestic adviser, in the *Financial Times*, 23 June 1994.
80. *Reuters*, 24 June 1994. Pynzenyk claimed that Kuchma 'had no understanding of the content of the reform he was trying to make. Some things he did understand, others not. For instance, he didn't understand what lay behind the payments crisis. His only way of solving it was by issuing new currency' (*The Economist*, 16 July 1994).
81. *Reuters*, 6 July 1994.
82. *Reuters*, 25 June 1994.
83. UPI, 7 July 1994. *Izvestiya* (13 July 1994) agreed: 'But it is hardly likely to achieve fundamental change in a single term – there is enough work for several more generations of presidents.'
84. *Radio Ukraine world service*, 5 July 1994. See also *Reuters*, 24 June 1994.
85. *Radio Ukraine world service*, 7 July 1994.
86. *Reuters*, 8 and 9 July 1994.
87. UPI, 26 June 1994.
88. ITAR-TASS news agency, 12 June 1994.

240 *Notes*

89. *Ukrainian Television*, 16 June 1994.
90. *Holos Ukrainy*, 6 July 1994.
91. *Reuters*, 1 July 1994.
92. *Radio Ukraine world service*, 4 July 1994.
93. See Vasyl Pliushch, 'Ukrainska derzhava – nasampered', *Literaturna Ukraina* (14 July 1994), who accuses those who voted for Kuchma as having voted for 'cheap salami' and 'march parades'.
94. AP, 8 July 1994.
95. See the proceedings of the conference organised on 24 September 1994 by the T. Shevchenko Ukrainian Language Society *Prosvita*, which were published as Volodymyr Sydorenko, ed., *Mova Derzhavna – Mova Ofitsiyna* (Kyiv: Prosvita, 1995).
96. *Reuters*, 10 July 1994.
97. *Vechirnyi Kyiv*, 28 July and *Reuters*, 25 June 1994.
98. *Kievskiye Vedomosti*, 7 April and *Reuters*, 2 April 1994.
99. *Nezavisimost*, 8 July 1994.
100. *Literaturna Ukraina*, 21 July 1994.
101. *Reuters*, 21 June 1994.
102. See *The Ukrainian Weekly*, 10 July 1994.
103. *Ukrainski Novyny*, no. 25, 1994.
104. *The Ukrainian Weekly*, 3 July 1994.
105. *Reuters*, 8 July 1994.
106. *Reuters*, 6 July 1994.
107. UNIAN news agency, 11 July 1994.
108. *Radio Ukraine world service*, 7 July 1994.
109. See the highly critical memoirs of Konstantin Morozov, then defence minister, who resigned immediately after the Massandra summit (*Ukrainska Hazeta*, 6–19 December 1993 and 20 January–2 February 1994).
110. *Reuters*, 25 June 1994.
111. *Ukrainian State Television*, 20 June 1994.
112. AP, 13 July, *The Washington Post*, 13 and 26 July 1994. See also *Reuters*, 25 June 1994.
113. *Radio Ukraine world service*, 4 July 1994.
114. *Ukrainske Slovo*, 31 July 1994.
115. *The Washington Post*, 27 June 1994.
116. AP, 25 June 1994.
117. *Holos Ukrainy*, 22 June 1994.
118. See UPI, 28 June 1994.
119. *Reuters*, 4 July 1994. See also UPI, 11 and 13 June 1994.
120. AP, 8 July 1994.
121. *Reuters*, 10 July 1994.
122. *Reuters*, 24 June 1994. Kuchma was 'saddened at the anti-Russian propaganda we see in Ukraine. Germany and France were enemies for 600 years but have become friends.'
123. AP, 11 July 1994.
124. *Reuters*, 11 July 1994.
125. *Ukrainian State Television*, 20 June 1994.
126. UPI, 11 June 1994. Kuchma promised during the election campaign that 'as long as I'm president there will never be a war between Russia and Ukraine' (UPI, 8 July 1994).

127. 'Vybor–94'. *Nasha Respublika. Spetsvypusk* (no date).
128. *Radio Ukraine world service*, 5 July 1994.
129. *Reuters*, 3 June 1994.
130. UPI, 28 June 1994.
131. See *Reuters*, 28 June and UPI, 12 July 1994.
132. *Radio Ukraine world service*, 13 June 1994.
133. See the comments by Kyivites in *The Guardian*, 27 June 1994.
134. See the comments by Kuchma after his visit to the US (*Post Postup*, 16 May 1994).
135. *Radio Ukraine world service*, 4 July 1994. Kuchma said the West had to decide if they wished to see Ukraine as a 'strong economic centre in Europe' (UPI, 26 June 1994).
136. *Vechirnyi Kyiv*, 28 July 1994.
137. *The Financial Times*, 7 July 1994.
138. *Holos Ukrainy*, 11 June and *Silski Visti*, 26 April 1994.
139. Statement by the Congress of National Democratic Forces dated 7 April 1994 in the author's possession.
140. UPI, 4 July 1994.
141. *Izvestiya*, 13 July 1994.
142. UPI, 2 June 1994.
143. See the comments by the Christian Democrats in *Nezavisimost*, 15 July 1994.
144. The statement accused forces disloyal to Ukrainian independence as having backed Kuchma during the elections. See *Holos Ukrainy*, 19 July and *Literaturna Ukraina*, 21 July 1994. See also Pavlychko's article on why he voted for Kravchuk in *Literaturna Ukraina*, 30 June 1994.
145. UNIAR news agency, 11 July 1994.
146. In the second round the newspaper told its readers to vote for Kravchuk because, 'He is the cross which Ukraine has to bear' (*Vechirnyi Kyiv*, 9 July 1994).
147. *Holos Ukrainy*, 7 June 1994.
148. *Holos Ukrainy*, 1 March 1994.
149. *Nezavisimost*, 14 July 1994.
150. *Holos Ukrainy*, 22 June 1994.
151. *Holos Ukrainy*, 22 June 1994.
152. Membership of *Nova Khvylia* closely resembled that of the New Ukraine bloc, i.e. social and liberal democratic. It had supported Rukh's calls during 1992–4 to go into 'constructive opposition' to Kravchuk. New Ukraine and the Inter-Regional Bloc of Reforms were rumoured to be contemplating fusion in 1994 but they eventually fell out over questions of statehood, one state language and the need for a Eurasian/Russian or European orientation.
153. UNIAN news agency, 14 June 1994.
154. *Post Postup*, 21–27 July 1994.
155. *Holos Ukrainy*, 19 April 1994.
156. UNIAR news agency, 16 April 1994.
157. *Holos Ukrainy*, 18 June 1994.
158. *Kievskiye Vedomostie*, 21 June 1994.
159. *The Economist*, 16 July 1994.
160. ITAR-TASS news agency, 2 July 1994.

161. AP, 8 July 1994. See the appeal by Kravchuk and reply from the Supreme Council in *Holos Ukrainy*, 9 July 1994.

162. This theme that only Kravchuk could maintain Ukraine's statehood in the face of determined attempts to revive the former USSR was a common theme throughout the presidential elections. See *Reuters*, 3 June 1994.

163. *Reuters*, 9 July 1994.

164. *The Ukrainian Weekly*, 26 June 1994.

165. See *Reuters*, 26 June 1994.

166. *Reuters*, 10 July 1994.

167. Student hunger strikers forced Masol's resignation as prime minister in October 1990 when Kravchuk was parliamentary speaker. See Taras Kuzio and Andrew Wilson, *Ukraine. Perestroika to Independence* (London: Macmillan, 1994).

168. See *Reuters*, 25 June 1994.

169. The SOU's influential hedyay was under Konstantin Morozov, Defence Minister between 1991 and 1993. See Taras Kuzio, 'Ukraine's Young Turks – the Union of Ukrainian Officers', *Jane's Intelligence Review* vol. 5, no. 1 (March 1993).

170. Muliava was in charge of the Socio-Psychological Directorate of the Ministry of Defence between 1992 and 1994, the main body responsible for Ukrainianising the armed forces.

171. *Ukrainian State Television*, 5 July and *Radio Ukraine World Service*, 11 June 1994.

172. *Reuters*, 6 July 1994.

173. *Reuters*, 16 June 1994.

174. *Reuters*, 10 July 1994.

175. See ITAR-TASS news agency, 20 June 1994.

176. *Reuters*, 9 July 1994.

177. *Financial Times*, 7 July 1994.

178. See *Reuters*, 16 May 1994.

179. *Uriadovyi Kurier*, no. 87 (7 June 1994).

180. Ibid.

181. Ibid.

182. UNIAN news agency, 7 April 1994.

183. See Mar'yiana Chorna, 'Tykha Hryznia v Zaporizh'kykh Plavniakh', *Demos*, no. 8, 1994.

184. The declared hard currency earnings were as follows: 1992 ($25 mn), 1993 ($45 mn) and 1994 ($50 mn).

185. Kuchma was director of *Pivdenmash* (Dnipropetrovs'k). Two others closely linked to this Military-Industrial Complex network were Anatoliy Franchuk, formerly within the Soviet Military-Industrial Complex Ministry and prime minister of the Crimea briefly during 1995 (and Kuchma's son-in-law), as well as Igor Smirnov, formerly director of *Tochlichmash* and currently 'President' of the separatist Trans-Dniester Republic of Moldova.

186. *Post Postup*, no. 14 (6–12 May 1994).

187. UPI, 11 June 1994.

188. *Visti z Ukrainy*, no. 30 (21–27 July 1994).

189. See the remarks by Les Taniuk, a leading member of Rukh who thought the panic over Kuchma's victory 'greatly exaggerated' (*Reuters*, 11 July 1994).

190. Roman Szporluk, 'Nation Building in Ukraine: Problems and Prospects', in John W. Blaney, ed., *The Successor States to the USSR* (Washington D.C.: Congressional Quarterly, 1995), p. 180.
191. Orest Subtelny, 'Imperial Disintegration and Nation State Formation: The Case of Ukraine', in Blaney, ibid., p. 189.
192. This view is backed by the author's conversations with Mykola Zhulynsky, former deputy prime minister with responsibility for humanitarian affairs, and Ivan Dziuba, former minister of culture, under Kravchuk held in Kyiv in July and September 1995 respectively. Kravchuk's policies were high on rhetoric but short on implementation and financing.
193. Dmytro Vydrin and Dmytro Tabachnyk, *Ukraina na Porozi XXI Stolittia. Politychnyi Aspekt* (Kyiv: Lybid, 1995), p. 173. The authors of this book were heavily criticised by the Congress of the Ukrainian Intelligentsia for backing a Eurasian (in contrast to European) orientation for Ukraine (*Chas–Time*, 17 November 1995).
194. That is, will he build a 'Ukrainian' or a 'Russian' Ukrainian state? See the editorial in *Vechirnyi Kyiv*, 20 October 1995, and Heorhiy Bachynskyi, 'Chy Zalyshyts'ia Ukraina Ukrainskoiu?', *Universum*, nos. 9–10 (September–October 1995), pp. 2–6.
195. See the various draft appeals and resolutions in *Vechirnyi Kyiv*, 11 November 1995. The proceedings and speeches are reprinted in *Vechirnyi Kyiv*, 14, 18, 21, 22, 23, 24 and 25 November 1995. The Christian Democratic Party of Ukraine issued an appeal in support of the Congress entitled 'No to Apartheid Against Ukrainians in Ukraine!' (*Vechirnyi Kyiv*, 11 November 1995).

3   THE CRIMEA RETURNS TO UKRAINE

1. *The Times*, 28 March 1994.
2. Andrew Wilson, 'The Elections in the Crimea', *RFE/RL Research Report*, vol. 3, no. 25 (24 June 1994), p. 15. See also by the same author, 'Crimea's Political cauldron', *RFE/RL Research Report*, vol. 2, no. 45 (12 November 1993).
3. For background on Ukrainian–Crimean relations between 1991 and 1994, see Taras Kuzio, *Ukraine–Crimea–Russia: Triangle of Conflict. Conflict Studies 267* (London: Research Institute for the Study of Conflict and Terrorism, 1994).
4. See Tor Bukkvoll, 'A Fall From Grace for Crimean Separatists', *Transition*, vol. 1, no. 21 (17 November 1995).
5. For a survey of these earlier developments, see Kuzio, *Russia–Crimea–Ukraine. Triangle of Conflict*, and 'The Crimea and European Security', *European Security*, vol. 3, no. 4 (Winter 1994), pp. 734–74. See also Roman Solchanyk, 'Ukrainian–Russian Confrontation Over the Crimea', *RFE/RL Research Report*, vol. 1, no. 7 (21 February 1992), idem, 'The Crimean Imbroglio: Kiev and Simferopol', *RFE/RL Research Report*, vol. 1, no. 33 (21 August 1992), idem, 'The Crimean Imbroglio: Kiev and Moscow', *RFE/RL Research Report*, vol. 1, no. 40 (9 October 1992),

Ian Bremmer, 'Ethnic Issues in the Crimea', *RFE/RL Research Report*, vol. 2, no. 18 (30 April 1993) and Susan Crow, 'Russian Parliament Asserts Control Over Sevastopol', *RFE/RL Research Report*, vol. 2, no. 31 (30 July 1993).

6. It was initially rumoured that the well-known Ukrainian businessman, Yury Kolesnikov, president of *Krym-Kontinental*, would also stand as a candidate (*Ukrainske Slovo*, 12 December 1993).
7. *The Guardian*, 14 January 1994.
8. *Economist*, 8 January 1994.
9. *Intelnews*, 15 January 1994.
10. *Post Postup*, no. 39 (28 October–3 November 1993).
11. *Post Postup*, no. 47 (23–29 December 1993).
12. On the founding congress of the People's Party of the Crimea, see *Nezavisimaya Gazeta*, 25 November 1993.
13. UNIAN news agency, 17 January 1994. Kruglov, leader of the Bloc of Leftist and Patriotic Forces, accused Shuvaynikov of a 'lack of patriotism' (*Radio Ukraine world service*, 6 December 1993).
14. *Economist*, 8 January 1994. On his expulsion, see *Intelnews*, 15 January 1994.
15. *Post Postup*, 23–29 December 1993.
16. *Holos Ukrainy*, 11 November 1993.
17. *Krymskaya Izvestiya* and *Krymskaya Pravda*, 22 and 25 December 1993.
18. UNIAN news agency, 2 December 1993.
19. *Visti z Ukrainy*, 28 October-3 November 1993.
20. UNIAN news agency, 2 December 1993.
21. *Narodna Armiya*, 13 January 1994.
22. *Holos Ukrainy*, 24 December 1993.
23. *The Guardian*, 14 January 1993.
24. See *Nezavisimaya Gazeta*, 3 December 1993.
25. ITAR-TASS news agency, 10 November and UNIAR news agency, 26 November 1993.
26. *Post Postup*, no. 1 (3–9 February 1994).
27. *The Independent*, 3 January 1994.
28. *Kyivski vidomosti*, 3 February 1994.
29. On the Crimean crime situation, see interview with Major-General V.N. Kirichenko, chief of the Ukrainian Ministry of Internal Affairs Administration in the Crimea, in *Krymskaya Pravda*, 22 February 1995, and the review of crime statistics in *Krymskaya Pravda*, 22 February 1995.
30. *The Independent*, 31 January 1994.
31. See *Reuters*, 16 January, *Intelnews*, 17 January, *Ukrainskyi Obrii*, no. 2 (January 1994) and *Holos Ukrainy*, 11 February 1994.
32. *The Independent*, 31 January 1994.
33. UNIAN news agency, 31 January 1994.
34. *Nezavisimaya Gazeta*, 4 February 1994.
35. See the comments by Mustafa Dzhemiliyev, leader of the Tartars, in *Post Postup*, 3–9 February 1994. On Tartar backing for Bagrov see *Intelnews*, 15 January 1994.
36. *Radio Ukraine world service*, 7 February 1994.
37. UNIAN news agency, 31 January 1994.

38. *Reuters*, 19 January 1994.
39. *Post Postup*, 28 October–3 November 1993.
40. See Roman Solchanyk, 'Crimea's Presidential Elections', *RFE/RL Research Report*, vol. 3, no. 11 (18 March 1994).
41. A. Wilson, 'Parties and Presidents in Ukraine and Crimea, 1994', *The Journal of Communist Studies and Transition Politics*, vol. 11, no. 4 (December 1995), p. 370.
42. Meshkov compared the relationship between Russia and the Crimea to that 'between England and Yorkshire, not between England and Scotland' because, 'We're part of the Russian people' (*Financial Times*, 12 January 1994).
43. *Kyivski vidomosti*, 10 February 1994.
44. See the comments by Les Taniuk, a leading member of Rukh (UPI, 16 January 1994).
45. *Radio Ukraine world service*, 31 January 1994.
46. *Holos Ukrainy*, 26 January 1994.
47. *Holos Ukrainy*, 26 January and 9 February 1994.
48. *Radio Ukraine world service*, 31 January 1994.
49. *Holos Ukrainy*, 26 January 1994.
50. UNIAR news agency, 31 January 1994.
51. *Ukrainskyi Obrii*, no. 2 (January 1994).
52. *Uriadovyi Kurier*, 22 January 1994.
53. *The Washington Post*, 18 January 1994.
54. UNIAR news agency, 17 January 1994.
55. *Reuters*, 17 January 1994.
56. *Uriadovyi Kurier*, 3 March 1994.
57. *Narodna Armiya*, 28 January 1994.
58. *Kyivski vidomosti*, 10 February 1994.
59. *Reuters*, 16 February 1994.
60. *Mayak Radio*, 2 February and *Reuters*, 13 February 1994.
61. *Nezavisimaya Gazeta*, 4 February 1994.
62. *The Washington Post*, 28 March 1994.
63. *Economist*, 8 January 1994.
64. *The Independent*, 31 January 1994.
65. *Kyivski vidomosti*, 10 February 1994.
66. Solchanyk, 'Crimea's Presidential Elections', p. 40.
67. *Narodna Armiya*, 28 January 1994.
68. *Reuters*, 16 February 1994. Meshkov had claimed: 'We have drawn up and prepared everything needed to implement this plan and have the rouble as a means of payment in the Crimea' (*Reuters*, 13 February 1994).
69. Saburov was the director of the Centre for Information and Social Technology under the Russian government.
70. *Moskovskiy komsomolets*, 19 February 1994.
71. ITAR-TASS news agency, 4 February 1994.
72. *The Washington Post*, 18 January 1994.
73. *Reuters*, 16 January 1994.
74. See *The Independent*, 31 January 1994.
75. *Post Postup*, 3–9 February 1994 and *Reuters*, 17 January 1994.
76. See V.B. Hryn'iov, *Nova Ukraina. Iakoiu ia ii Bachu* (Kyiv: Abrys, 1995), Chapter 3, 'Federatyvna chy Unitarna Derzhava', pp. 27–39.

77. UNIAR news agency, 15 February 1994.
78. During the election campaign Meshkov obviously thought otherwise: 'There is no need to overload our budget with a Crimean foreign ministry or other such institution' (*Reuters*, 18 January 1994).
79. *Radio Ukraine world service*, 6 March 1994.
80. *The Times*, 28 March 1994.
81. Various centrist parties had been established to protect the clanish interests of the post-communist Party of Power in the Crimea, which supported the continuation of ties of Kyiv. During the presidential elections they endorsed Bagrov (as did the Tartars). Some of these centrist parties had links to their counterparts in Ukraine, such as the Inter-Regional Bloc of Reforms, New Ukraine and the Reform faction in the Ukrainian parliament.
82. *Holos Ukrainy*, 25 February 1994.
83. Wilson, 'The Elections in the Crimea', p. 8.
84. *Reuters*, 16 January 1994.
85. UNIAN news agency, 11 May 1994.
86. *The Washington Post*, 28 March 1994.
87. For a review of political parties in the Crimea, see A. Wilson, 'Crimea's Political Cauldron', *RFE/RL Research Report*, vol. 2, no. 45 (12 November 1993).
88. Vladimir Vol'fovich Zhirinovskii, *Poslednyi vagon na sever* (Moscow: Conjou, 1995), pp. 56 and 58.
89. Wilson, 'Crimea's Political Cauldron', p. 15.
90. Established on 28 November 1993 by the Kyiv-backed Crimea with Ukraine Committee and the Organisation of Ukrainians in the Crimea led by Serhii Lytvyn, leader of the Crimean branch of the Union of Ukrainian Officers.
91. The *Kurultai* is run by the *Mejlis* (Crimean parliament) between Assemblies.
92. Wilson, 'Crimea's Political Cauldron', p. 17.
93. On these questions, see T. Kuzio, 'The Crimea and European Security', *European Security*, vol. 3, no. 4 (Winter 1994), pp. 734–74.
94. UNIAR news agency, 17 January 1994.
95. *Krymskie Izvestiya*, 25 March 1994.
96. *Reuters*, 11 April 1994.
97. A referendum on such a question was held by the Trans-Dnister Republic of Moldova on 25 December 1995.
98. *Holos Ukrainy*, 17 June 1995.
99. *Financial Times*, 12 January 1994.
100. *Krymskaya Pravda*, 7 June 1995.
101. Grach, leader of the Crimean communists, claimed that 42.5 per cent of locally elected deputies were his supporters (*Interfax news agency*, 29 June 1995).
102. *Ukrayina moloda*, 30 June 1995.
103. See the comments by Valeriy Pustovoitenko, cabinet minister responsible for socioeconomic questions in the Crimea (*Uriadovyi Kurier*, 29 June 1995).
104. *Krymskiye Izvestiya*, 23 March 1995.
105. During May 1994, at the time of the adoption of the May 1992 constitution, then president Meshkov attended a Grand Assembly of Cossack Host Atamans in Krasnodar (UNIAN news agency, 21 May 1994). Was Meshkov

looking for paramilitary allies in the event of a violent crackdown on Crimean separatism by Kyiv? After all, Russian Cossacks had already taken part in supporting separatists in Moldova, Georgia and Bosnia-Herzegovina.
106. ITAR-TASS news agency, 20 May 1994.
107. See Ustina Markus, 'Crimea Restores 1992 Constitution', *RFE/RL Research Report*, vol. 3, no. 23 (10 June 1994).
108. UNIAN news agency, 15 June 1995.
109. ITAR-TASS news agency, 31 May 1995.
110. See Viacheslav Savchenko, 'V Krymu Znovu Vidkryvsia Konstytutsiynyi Sezon', *Demos*, no. 14, 1995, pp. 16–19.
111. ITAR-TASS news agency, 31 May 1995. Of the two previous constitutions (6 May and 25 September 1992), Kyiv preferred to use as the basis for the 1996 constitution the latter, which was perceived as not 'pro-separatist' (in comparison to the 6 May 1992 version). On this question, see the interview with A. Danelian, chairman of the Crimean Constitutional Commission and Deputy Chairman of the Crimean Supreme Council in *Krymskiye Izvestiya*, 25 October 1995.
112. See *Krymskaya Pravda*, 21 October 1995.
113. Kyiv is undoubtedly concerned that the Crimea will attempt to control oil and gas deposits on the peninsula and off the Black Sea coast, both of which are hoped to make an important contribution towards lessening Ukraine's dependency upon Russian energy supplies.
114. *Demokratychna Ukraina*, 28 September 1995.
115. ITAR-TASS news agency, 20 October 1995.
116. UNIAN news agency, 1 November and *The Ukrainian Weekly*, 5 November 1995.
117. UNIAN news agency, 20 December 1995.
118. *Ukrainian Television*, 16 January and *The Ukrainian Weekly*, 21 January 1996.
119. The appeal complained of mounting Ukrainian pressure which had, in effect, abolished its autonomy and placed the Crimea 'below any administrative-territorial formation in Ukraine' (ITAR-TASS news agency, 27 March 1996).
120. *Reuters*, 11 March 1996. The Crimean appeal was published by *Interfax news agency*, 27 March 1996.
121. See Volodymyr Shapoval, 'Status Krymu chy kvadratura kruha?' and Oleksandr Bittner, 'Iakoii derzhavy Konstytutsia Krymu?', *Uriadovyi Kurier*, nos. 58–9 (28 March 1996) and nos. 60–1 (30 March 1996).
122. *Reuters*, 21 March 1996.
123. See Olha Chorna, 'To chy maie Krym svoiu Konstytutsiu?', *Kyivski vidomosti*, 10 April 1996.
124. *Reuters*, 4 April 1996.
125. UNIAN news agency, 5 April 1996.
126. UNIAR news agency, 26 March 1994.
127. *Reuters*, 11 April 1994.
128. *Holos Ukrainy*, 25 February 1994.
129. The figures were taken from Yaropolk Kulchyckyj, ed., *Repeat Voting Presidential Election Guide Book* (Kyiv: International Foundation for Electoral Systems, 1994).

130. *Vechirnyi Kyiv*, 15 July 1994.
131. *Flot Ukrainy*, 16 September 1995.
132. Tsekov, Crimean parliamentary speaker from the Russia bloc after the March 1994 elections, was removed in a vote of no confidence by 54:35 votes on 5 July 1995.
133. See the interview with Franchuk, 'Krym ie i bude ukrainskym', *Uriadovyi Kurier*, no. 164 (31 October 1995). Franchuk and his son, Ihor, were elected from the Crimea to the Ukrainian parliament in December 1995 (see chapter 1).
134. See Jeremy Lester, 'Russian Political Attitudes to Ukrainian Independence', *The Journal of Communist Studies and Transition Politics*, vol. 10, no. 2 (June 1994), pp. 193–233.

4 POLITICAL REFORM AND AN END TO THE SOVIET SYSTEM

1. *Reuters*, 4 April 1995.
2. *The Ukrainian Weekly*, 9 October 1994.
3. *Reuters*, 19 October 1994.
4. See the interview with Lanovyi in *Ukraine Business Review*, vol. 4, nos. 1–2 (December 1995–January 1996), pp. 5–9.
5. *Radio Ukraine world service*, 7 October 1994.
6. *Kyivskiye vedomosti*, 9 August 1995.
7. On criticism of national-democratic support for Kuchma, see the interview with Volodymyr Chemerys, a leading member of the Union of Ukrainian Students and Statehood parliamentary faction, in *Za vilnu ukrainu*, 22 July 1995.
8. See the comments by Grynev, presidential adviser on regional issues. While opposing these officials in his official capacity, he nevertheless continued to support them through the Inter-Regional Bloc of Reforms (MRBR) political party which he heads. See *Informatsiynyi Builetyn URP i KNDS*, 4 October 1994. See also V. B. Hryn'iov, *Nova Ukraina: Iakoiu ia ii Bachu* (Kyiv: Abrys, 1995).
9. See the proceedings and the appeal to President Kuchma of the conference entitled 'Mova derzhava – mova ofitsiyna' held on 24 September 1994 and organised by the Writers' Union, the Taras Shevchenko Ukrainian Language Society *Prosvita* and the National Academy of Sciences (*Holos Ukrainy*, 5 October and *Literaturna Ukraina*, 6 October 1994). The conference proceedings were published as Volodymyr Sydorenko, ed., *Mova Derzhavna – Mova Ofitsiyna* (Kyiv: Prosvita, 1995).
10. *The Ukrainian Weekly*, 11 September 1994.
11. See *Holos Ukrainy*, 27 July, 2 August and 3 November 1994, and Volodymyr Shunevych, 'Rosiys'ku Movu v Ukraini', *Kyivski vidomosti*, 18 August 1994.
12. *Narodna Armiya*, 27 September and *Shliakh Peremohy*, 1 October 1994.
13. See 'Ni – movnyi dyskriminatsii I fundamentalismu!', Zayava Presydii Komitetu Komunistychnoi partii Ukrainy', *Holos Ukrainy*, 14 September and the reply from the Central Ruling Board of the Taras Shevchenko

Uktainian Language Society *Prosvita* in *Visti z Ukrainy*, 29 September–5 October 1994. See also V. I. Tkachenko, 'Komu meshayet russkiy iazyk?' *Kommunist*, no. 31 (October 1994).

14. *Holos Ukrainy*, 8 September and *Narodna Hazeta*, no. 37 (September 1994).
15. Conflicts and rivalries within the presidential administration were widely reported in *Novosti*, 26 July, *Zerkalo Nedeli*, 5 August, *Kyivskiye vedomosti*, 11 August and 5 September 1995.
16. 'Leonid Kuchma's Single "D"', *Research Update, Ukrainian Center for Independent Political Research*, vol. 1, no. 1 (27 November 1995).
17. *Sils'ki Visti*, 15 December 1995.
18. See the interview with Gorbulin in *Most*, 18–24 December 1995.
19. *Reuters*, 11 July 1996.
20. See *Zerkalo Nedeli*, 2–8 December and *Ukrayina Moloda*, 29 December 1995.
21. *Reuters*, 8 and 9 August 1994.
22. *Holos Ukrainy*, 23 September 1994.
23. On this problem, see *Most*, 4–10 December 1995.
24. See *Interfax news agency*, 8 December 1994.
25. UNIAN news agency, 27 October 1994.
26. UNIAN news agency, 14 November 1994.
27. ITAR-TASS news agency, 30 November 1994.
28. *Uriadovyi Kurier*, 6 December 1994.
29. *The Ukrainian Weekly*, 11 December 1994.
30. *Reuters*, 22 December 1994.
31. UNIAR news agency, 12 April 1995.
32. UNIAR news agency, 14 April 1995.
33. See comments by Oleksandr Yemets, 'Rano Chy Pizno Prezydent Musytyme Ocholyty Vykonavchu Vladu', *Kyivski vidomosti*, 27 October 1995.
34. UNIAR news agency, 18 May and RIA news agency, 19 May 1995. The Congress of Ukrainian Nationalists proposed its own draft version of the 'Law on Power' (*Shliakh Peremohy*, 18 March 1995).
35. *Eastern Economist*, 22 May 1995,
36. *Reuters*, 18 May 1995.
37. AP, 19 May 1995.
38. *Radio Ukraine world service*, 28 January 1996.
39. *The Washington Post*, 19 May 1995.
40. *Intelnews*, 23 May 1995.
41. *Reuters*, 31 May 1995.
42. James Rupert, 'Ukraine Asked to Settle "Paralysing Political Crisis" with National Ballot', *The Washington Post*, 1 June 1995.
43. UNIAR news agency, 2 June 1995.
44. *Ukrainian Television*, 2 June 1995.
45. The appeal is published in *Uriadovyi Kurier*, no. 83 (6 June 1995).
46. *Holos Ukrainy*, 2 June 1995.
47. *Kyivska Pravda*, 2 June 1995.
48. *The Ukrainian Weekly*, 4 June 1995.
49. Ivan Pluishch of the Centre parliamentary faction was one of the few who backed the president although as parliamentary speaker during 1991–4 he

had blocked Kravchuk's ambitions to increase presidential power. Pluishch complained that parliament was not progressing, was not efficient and that the entire year had been wasted. See *Holos Ukrainy*, 2 June 1995. Oleksandr Stoyan, leader of the Federation of Trade Unions, also backed Kuchma (*Kyivska Pravda*, 2 June 1995).

50. *Reuters*, 1 June 1995.
51. *Reuters*, 2 June 1995.
52. *The Ukrainian Weekly*, 28 May 1995.
53. J. Rupert, 'Ukraine's Lawmakers Vote to Boost Presidential Power', *The Washington Post*, 19 May 1992.
54. See *Holos Ukrainy*, 10 June and *Uriadovyi Kurier*, no. 86 (10 June 1995).
55. *Reuters*, 7 June 1995. See the speeches in parliament by Moroz and Kuchma in support of the Constitutional Agreement in *Holos Ukrainy*, 8 June 1995.
56. *Reuters* and *Interfax news agency*, 8 June 1995.
57. *The Ukrainian Weekly*, 11 June 1995. *The Washington Post* (8 June 1995) pointed out that this was not a solid majority for Kuchma and it could decline over time.
58. UNIAN news agency, 8 June 1995.
59. The statement was signed by the Ukrainian Civic Congress of the Crimea, the Crimea with Ukraine Committee, the Ukrainian Republican Party and the Organisation of Ukrainian Nationalists (*Radio Ukraine world service*, 8 June 1995).
60. *Reuters*, 7 June 1995.
61. UNIAN news agency, 13 May 1995.
62. UNIAN news agency, 22 June 1995.
63. UNIAN news agency, 23 June 1995.
64. *Uriadovyi Kurier*, no. 66 (18 July 1995). Advocates resemble British barristers, whilst lawyers and jurists are closer to the British equivalent of solicitors.
65. UNIAN news agency, 25 May and 21 June 1995.
66. *Uriadovyi Kurier*, no. 121 (12 August 1995).
67. *Reuters*, 3 June 1995.
68. *Uriadovyi Kurier*, no. 174 (21 November 1995).
69. *Ukrainian Television*, 23 January 1996.
70. AP, 8 June 1995.
71. ITAR-TASS news agency, 11 November 1995.
72. ITAR-TASS news agency, 10 December 1995.
73. *Ukrayina Moloda*, 12 December 1995. The reply by the Ukrainian parliamentary leadership appeared in *Holos Ukrainy*, 19 December 1995.
74. *Sils'ki Visti*, 15 December 1995.
75. See Roman Solchanyk, 'Ukraine Considers a New Republican Constitution', RL 215/91, *Report on the USSR*, 7 June 1991.
76. Proposal by the Director of the Institute of State and Law (*Holos Ukrainy*, 29 March 1991). See the round-table discussion in the Institute of State and Law (*Radians'ka Ukraina*, 22 January 1991).
77. Proposal by Dmytro Pavlychko, then a member of *Narodna Rada*, the democratic parliamentary faction (*Molod Ukrainy*, 15 February 1991).
78. Anatoly Matsiuk, head of a group of advisers to the parliamentary secretariat, argued that it would be wrong to place an 'ideological accent' within

the constitution as it should only include general principles and the basis of a democratic society (*Holos Ukrainy*, 26 March 1991).

79. Levko Lukianenko, leader of the Republican Party and also a member of *Narodna Rada*, argued that presidential power would prevent authoritarianism by ensuring checks on power in the constitution (*Literaturna Ukraina*, 30 May 1991).

80. *Radians'ka Ukraina*, 3 April 1991. Federalism had been proposed in the past as a panacea for the recognition of the socio-cultural and economic differences of Ukraine divided into historical 'lands'. Sometimes this had included backing for a federal territorial structure through the adoption of a bicameral parliament. See the discussion in Mykola Tomenko, *Ukrainska Perspektyva: istoryko-politolohichni pidstavy suchasnoi derzhavnoi strategii. Politichni Studii* 2 (Kyiv: Ukrainian Perspectives, 1995), p. 41.

81. *Ukrainske Slovo*, 16 June 1991.

82. *Ukrainske Slovo*, 2 June 1991. See also Kravchuk's speech to parliament as Parliamentary Speaker (*Za vilnu ukrainu*, 17 May 1991).

83. The Soviet Ukrainian constitution was amended and purged of all references to communism and Soviet power. Added were the words, 'Ukraine is an independent, democratic, legal state' (*The Independent*, 14 February 1992).

84. See L.T. Kryvenko, 'Yakiy Buty Konstitutsii Ukrainy?', *Kommunist Ukrainy*, no. 11, 1990, pp. 25–35.

85. *Ukrainske Slovo*, 17 May 1992.

86. *The Ukrainian Weekly*, 20 September 1992.

87. *Sil'ski Visti*, 27 March 1992.

88. See 'Natsional'ni Zasady Poza Proiektom Konstytutsii', *Molod Ukrainy*, 8 February 1996, and Valeriy Mishura and Ievhen Luk'ianenko, 'Z Iakykh Zherel?', *Holos Ukrainy*, 4 April 1996.

89. See *Holos Ukrainy*, 18 July and *Demokratychna Ukraina*, 21 June 1992, as well as *Holos Ukrainy*, 30 October 1993.

90. See Volodymyr Kampo, 'Problemy Unitaryzmu v Proyekti Novoi Konstitutsii Ukrainy' and Volodymyr Doroshkevych, Oleksandr Kravchuk and Ihor Kupianov, 'Chy Potribna Ukraini Konstitutsiya, iaka umozhylyvliuye mizhnatsional'ni konflikty?', *Rozbudova Derzhava*, no. 5 (October 1992), pp. 32–5 and pp. 58–61 respectively.

91. The (Soviet era) Communist Party of Ukraine was banned in August 1991. A new Communist Party of Ukraine was registered on 5 October 1993.

92. *Holos Ukrainy*, 12 November 1992.

93. *Pravda Ukrainy*, 3 July 1992.

94. See Viktor Pohorilko (Institute of State and Law), 'Za Yakoiu Konstitutsieiu Nam Zhyty?', *Ukraina*, no. 2, 1992, p. 7.

95. *The Ukrainian Weekly*, 9 August 1992.

96. Kuchma's report was published as 'Pro Stanovyshche Ukrainy ta Prohramy Vnutrish'noi i Zovnishn'opolitychnoi Diyalnosti Prezydenta ta Uriadu Ukrainy', *Holos Ukrainy*, 22 May 1993. See also the *Financial Times*, 21 May 1993.

97. *The Guardian*, 22 May and *Financial Times*, 2 June 1993.

98. *Ukrinform news agency*, 22 June 1993.

99. *Radio Ukraine world service*, 25 January 1994.

100. *Radio Ukraine world service*, 25 January 1994.

101. *The Ukrainian Weekly*, 14 November 1993. See also Judge Bohdan A. Futey, 'Obhovorennia Proiektu Novoi Konstytutsii Ukrainy – Perekhid Vid Komandnoi Do Pravovoi Systemy', *Suchasnist*, no. 9 (September 1992), pp. 101–6.

102. *Holos Ukrainy*, 24 December 1994.

103. *Holos Ukrainy*, 24 December 1994.

104. See Yuriy Todyka, 'Bida ne v konfliktakh i superechkah, a v nevminni iikh rozv'izyvaty. Derzhavno-pravovi konflikty v aspekti rozvytky konstitut-siynoho protsesu v Ukraini', *Holos Ukrainy*, 16 January 1996.

105. M. Tomenko, *Ukrainska Perspektyva: istoryko-politolohichni pidstavy suchasnoi derzhavnoi strategii, Politychnoi Studii* 2 (Kyiv: Ukrainian Perspectives, 1995), p. 61.

106. Comments by Volodymyr Butkevych, joint chair of the Constitutional Commission, who had been proposed to the Commission by the Centre and Reform parliamentary factions. Butkevych was also head of the Parliamentary Commission on Human Rights (*Uriadovyi Kurier*, nos. 3–4, 6 January 1996).

107. UNIAN news agency, 18 September 1995.

108. UNIAN news agency, 23 November 1995.

109. *Holos Ukrainy*, 28 November 1995.

110. 'Oleksandr Lavrynovych: khto skazav, shcho Konstytutsiynya uhoda maie vmerty u chervni?', *Kyivski vidomosti*, 6 March 1996.

111. See Stepan Khmara, 'Konstytutsiynyi protses i bezpeka natsii', *Holos Ukrainy*, 30 April 1996, and Yury Badzio, 'Osnova Pravdy Nashoi', *Holos Ukrainy*, 6 May 1996. Khmara and Badzio are leaders and well-known members respectively of the Ukrainian Conservative Republican and Ukrainian Democratic Parties.

112. See O. Lavrynovych, 'Cherez struktury – do derzhavy', *Holos Ukrainy*, 8 September 1992, and Evhen Boltarovych, 'Proekt Konstytutsii Ukrainy i Problemy Pobudovy Demokratychnoi Pravovoi Derzhavy', *Rozbudova Derzhava*, no. 5 (October 1992), pp. 54–7.

113. *Ukrainske Slovo*, 29 October 1995. The appeal was signed by the Democratic Party of Ukraine, the Congress of Ukrainian Nationalists, Rukh, the Organisation of Ukrainian Nationalists, the Taras Shevchenko Ukrainian Language Society *Prosvita*, the Ukrainian Republican Party, Ukrainian Cossacks and the Christian Democratic Party of Ukraine. See also the criticisms by Vitaliy Zhuravsky, leader of the Christian Democratic Party of Ukraine, in *Vechirnyi Kyiv*, 5 April 1995, and *Holos Ukrainy*, 5 December 1995.

114. *Chas*, 24 November 1995.

115. *Ukrainske Slovo*, 12–17 December 1995.

116. *Holos Ukrainy*, 28 November 1995.

117. UNIAN news agency, 27 September and 23 November 1995. See the draft proposal by the KPU in *Kommunist*, no. 41 (October 1995) and the SPU in *Tovarysh*, nos. 50 and 51 (December 1995).

118. President Kuchma said that this was 'absolutely true' (*Zerkalo Nedeli*, 18–24 November 1995).

119. UNIAN news agency, 26 October 1995 and *Interfax-Ukraine*, 19 January 1996.

120. Petro Symonenko, 'Ne mozhna nekhtuvaty voliu narodu. Chomu komunisty ne mozhut pidtrymaty novyi proiekt konstytutsii?', *Holos Ukrainy*, 26 December 1995. See also 'Ob Otnoshenii Kompartii Ukrainyi k Programme Pravyteltsva', *Kommunist*, no. 42 (October 1995), H. Kriuchko, 'Shche Odyn Krok do Dyktatury?', *Kommunist*, no. 49 (November 1995), and A. Yushyk, 'Partiya i Konstitutsiya', *Tovarysh*, no. 49 (December 1995).
121. UNIAN news agency, 21 February 1996.
122. *Holos Ukrainy*, 16 July 1992.
123. *Intelnews. Economic Review*, 15 January 1996.
124. ITAR-TASS news agency, 27 March 1996.
125. *Uriadovyi Kurier*, no. 57 (26 March 1996) and *Demokratychna Ukraina*, 26 March 1996.
126. See Yevheniya Tykhonova, 'Pryniattia Novoi Konstytutsii Ukrainy – Na Zakonnu Osnovu', *Viche*, no. 1 (January 1996), pp. 3–11; Vsevolod Rechestkyi, 'Konstytutsiynyi Protses v Ukraini: iak Fenomen Demokratii', *Suchasnist*, no. 1 (January 1996), pp. 97–102; Valeriy Babych, Vasyl Kostytskyi, Viktor Shyshkin and Vitaliy Zhuravskyi, 'Konstytutsiynyi protses v Ukraini: stan i perspektyvy', *Holos Ukrainy*, 23 January, 1996; Mykola Zhuhan, 'Iakshcho spravdi "narod – yedyne dzherelo vlady"', *Holos Ukrainy*, 20 February 1996; Vitaliy Komov, 'Narod Maie Buty Dzherelom Vlady', *Holos Ukrainy*, 28 February 1996; Oleksandr Bittner, 'Nova Konstytutsiya: chas zbyraty kaminnia', *Uriadovyi Kurier*, nos. 48–9 (14 March 1996), Volodymyr Kartashov, 'Konstytutsiynyi protses vykhodyt u novyi vytok svoho rozvytku', *Chas*, 22 March 1996; Volodymyr Shapoval, 'Ne vykhliupnuty z vodoi i samu dytynu', *Holos Ukrainy*, 26 March 1996; V. Shapoval, 'Osnovnyi Zakon Derzhavy', *Viche*, no. 3 (March 1996), pp. 27–34; 'Nova Konstytutsiya: krok vpered – dva nazad', *Holos Ukrainy*, 26 March 1996; Yaroslav Halata, 'Nenarodzhena Konstytutsiya ochyma "molodykh politykiv"', *Demokratychna Ukraina*, 29 March 1996; and Artur Bilous *et al.*, 'Nova Konstytutsiya Ukrainy: superchnosti ta perspektyva', *Chas*, 29 March 1996 and 5 April 1996.
127. 'Constitutional Battle Fuelled by Russian Election Issues', *The Rukh Insider*, vol. 2, no. 4 (25 March 1996).
128. The author is in possession of a copy of the 24 February 1996 draft constitution in Ukrainian and translated by the International Foundation for Electoral Systems, Kyiv.
129. The 11 March 1996 draft constitution was published in *Uriadovyi Kurier*, 21 March 1996.
130. *Uriadovyi Kurier*, nos. 53–4 (21 March 1996) and no. 57 (26 March 1996). See also *Holos Ukrainy* (13 March 1996) for a report of a joint press conference by Moroz and Stretovych, head of the parliamentary commission on Legal Policy and Legislation on the submission of the draft constitution to parliament.
131. *Uriadovyi Kurier*, nos. 68–9 (11 April 1996).
132. The European Commission for Democracy Through Law stated that the draft constitution conformed to international standards. Their only criticisms rested on the vague definition of the government, whilst they recommended strengthening the role of parliament and that powers to initiate legislation be taken away from the president (UNIAN news agency, 21 May 1996).

133. *Holos Ukrainy*, 22 March 1996 and *Uriadovyi Kurier*, nos. 55–6 (23 March 1996).
134. *Holos Ukrainy*, 16 February 1996.
135. Y. Orobets, 'Suchasnyi Konstytutsiynyi Protses ta Formy Derzhavnoho Ustroiu v Ukraini', in *Modeli derzhavnosti ta derzhavnoho ustroiu Ukrainy na porozi XXI stolittia* (Kyiv: Institute of Post Communist Society and Political Thought, 29 January 1996), pp. 9–12.
136. See the Ukrainian Perspectives study entitled 'Rosiyska Konstytutsiya Ukrainy', *Vechirnyi Kyiv*, 17 February 1996.
137. Serhiy Kudiarshov, Serhiy Odarych, Yury Orobets' and Mykola Tomenko, *Nova redaktsiya Konstytutsii: derzhavna symvolika ta symvolichna demokratiya. Ekspertna otsinka* (Kyiv: Ukrainian Perspectives, 1996), summarised in *Holos Ukrainy*, 11 April 1996.
138. UNIAN news agency, 12 March 1996.
139. The Ministry of Justice statement was published in *Uriadovyi Kurier*, no. 24 (6 February 1996) and *Holos Ukrainy* (9 February 1996); whilst statements by the presidential administration and general procurator backing up the Ministry of Justice appeared in *Uriadovyi Kurier*, nos. 40–1 (29 February 1996).
140. The draft constitution of the KPU was published alongside the 11 March 1996 draft constitution for comparative analysis in *Holos Ukrainy*, 23 May 1996.
141. See V.V. Kulesha, 'Symvolyka dolzhna otrazhat' istoriu i tradytsii straniy', *Kommunist*, no. 15 (April 1996).
142. See the protest by the Congress of Ukrainian Nationalists (*Shliakh Peremohy*, 30 March 1996). Rukh criticised those left-wing forces who, 'both in parliament, led by its speaker, and outside it make every effort to disrupt the adoption of the constitution ... A pro-communist attack is being made on the state, often with the help of local government officials' (UNIAR news agency, 13 March 1996). Viacheslav Chornovil, leader of Rukh, outlined his views on the left-wing constitution in a press conference (*Holos Ukrainy*, 27 March 1996).
143. *Molod Ukrainy* (26 March 1996) reported on a demand by the Crimean Committee to Promote a Ukrainian constitution, composed of national democratic groups, also to ban the KPU.
144. Left-wing views about the constitutional process can be found in *Tovarysh*, no. 5 (February 1996) while KPU leader Symonenko's speech on the constitutional process in parliament appeared in *Kommunist*, no. 17 (April 1996). See also the appeal by the KPU (*Kommunist*, no. 13, March 1996, and *Holos Ukrainy*, 2 April 1996), the joint statement by the Peasant, Socialist and Communist Parties (*Holos Ukrainy*, 12 April 1996) and the joint appeal of the KPU and SPU (*Holos Ukrainy*, 13 April 1996, and *Tovarysh*, no. 14, April 1996).
145. UNIAN news agency, 27 April 1996.
146. *Holos Ukrainy*, 22 March 1996.
147. See the views on the constitutional process by the URP in *Samostijna Ukraina*, nos. 4 and 6 (February and March 1996) as well Volodymyr Chemerys, a URP member, in *Holos Ukrainy*, 2 April 1996.

148. *Uriadovyi Kurier*, no. 29 (13 February 1996). See also the statement by the Centre parliamentary faction (*Holos Ukrainy*, 14 February) and the article arguing for religious freedom of conscience to be taken into account in the constitutional process by Vitaly Zhuravsky, leader of the Christian Democratic Party (*Vechirnyi Kyiv*, 10 April 1996).

149. The 5 May 1996 draft constitution appeared in *Holos Ukrainy*, 28 May 1996.

150. The Ukrainian and Russian language versions of the adopted constitution appeared respectively in *Holos Ukrainy*, 13 and 27 July 1996.

151. *Reuters*, 28 June 1996.

152. *The Ukrainian Weekly*, 30 June 1996.

153. *Holos Ukrainy*, 20 and 23 July 1996.

154. Copy in the author's possession dated 15 November 1995 prepared by the Constitutional Commission.

155. *Holos Ukrainy*, 18 July and *Demokratychna Ukraina*, 21 July 1992.

156. *Ukrainske Slovo*, 3 December 1995.

157. *Pravda Ukrainy*, 3 July 1992.

158. *Holos Ukrainy*, 30 October 1993.

159. *Ukrinform news agency*, 22 June 1993.

160. *Sils'ki Visti*, 5 January 1996.

161. The November 1995 draft Ukrainian constitution was not published in the Ukrainian press but it did appear in *Nezavisimaya Gazeta*, 7 December 1995. The author is grateful for a copy of the draft provided by the Rule of Law Consortium, Kyiv, a project funded by the U.S. Agency for International Development.

162. *Vechirnyi Kyiv*, 18 January 1996.

163. *Zerkalo Nedeli*, 18–24 November 1995.

164. See Judge B.A. Futey, 'Comments: Examining Draft of Ukraine's Constitution', *The Ukrainian Weekly*, 4 February 1996.

165. UNIAN news agency, 5 February 1996. See also the long interview with Moroz in *Sils'ki Visti*, 5 January 1996.

166. *Sils'ki Visti*, 5 January 1996.

167. *Sils'ki Visti*, 5 January 1996. On Moroz's relationship to the executive see *Most*, 27 November–3 December 1995. Moroz reviewed parliament's record of legislative activity that year in *Holos Ukrainy*, 26 December 1995.

168. See Petro Matiaszek, 'A Closer Look at Ukraine's Constitution', *The Ukrainian Weekly*, 4 August 1996.

169. *The Ukrainian Weekly*, 14 November 1993.

170. *Pravda*, 9 July 1993.

171. *Holos Ukrainy*, 17 June 1994.

172. Moroz said that referendums could not be expected to decide such vitally important questions as the adoption of the new constitution (*Tovarysh*, no. 145, November 1995).

173. See Moroz's comments in UNIAN news agency, 28 October 1995.

174. *Holos Ukrainy*, 2 December 1995.

175. *Holos Ukrainy*, 28 November 1995.

176. UNIAN news agency, 18 October and 23 November 1995.

177. *Holos Ukrainy*, 3 February 1996.

178. See the report of Symonenko's press conference in *Holos Ukrainy*, 27 March 1996.
179. See Borys Ol'khovskyi and Yury Todyka, 'Iakshcho khochemo ukhvalyty novu Konstytutsiu, oberimo pravylnyi shliakh', *Holos Ukrainy*, 6 February, Hlib Horodnychenko, 'Chy Bude Bytva za Referendum?', *Kyivski vidomosti*, 1 March 1996. The parliamentary leadership's opposition to a referendum is given in 'Konstytutsiu ukhvalyt Verkhovna Rada', and 'Parlamentom, a ne Referendumom', *Holos Ukrainy*, 13 April 1996.
180. *INTELNEWS*, 6 February. The Rukh statement is given by UNIAR news agency, 24 April 1996. One of parliament's few women members, Valentyna Semeniuk, from Zhitomir, also backed the idea of a referendum (*Holos Ukrainy*, 21 February 1996).

5 ECONOMIC TRANSFORMATION AND STRUCTURAL CHANGE

1. For another detailed elaboration of Ukraine's economic transition since its independence, see Helen Boss, 'Economic Reforms on Course Despite Poor Showing in Industry', *Ukraine Business Review*, vol. 3, nos. 10–11 (July–August 1995), pp. 5–12.
2. *Reuters*, 15 September 1995.
3. *Infobank news agency*, 13 January 1995.
4. See O.S. Vlasiuk and S.I. Pyrozhkov, *Indeks Liuds'koho Rozvytku: Dosvid Ukrainy* (Kyiv: National Institute of Strategic Studies and United Nations Development Programme, 1995), and *Ukraine. Human Development Report* (Kyiv: United Nations Development Programme, 1995).
5. *Reuters*, 5 and 11 March 1995.
6. *The Guardian*, 12 May 1995.
7. The report is reprinted in *Holos Ukrainy*, 13 October 1994.
8. AP, 19 October 1994. See also 'Kuchma Wins Reform Vote', *Financial Times*, 20 October 1994.
9. *The Wall Street Journal*, 12 October 1994, and *The Ukrainian Weekly*, 16 October 1994.
10. See also Justin Keay, 'Ukraine Gets Another Chance', *The Wall Street Journal*, 10 October 1994, 'Can Kuchma Reform Ukraine?', *Central European*, November 1994, 'Ukraine. The Big Push', *The Banker*, November 1994, 'Ukraine Struggles forward with Liberalisation Programme', *Project & Trade Finance*, January 1995; James Meek, 'Ukraine Takes Capitalist Road', *The Guardian*, 29 March 1995; and Andrew Rosenbaum, 'Ukraine Moves Back from the Brink', *Euromoney*, March 1995.
11. See the editorial 'Good News from Ukraine', in the *Financial Times*, 28 October 1994.
12. *Holos Ukrainy*, 2 November 1994.
13. See the decree 'On the Elaboration of Support Concerning Macroeconomic Policies and Economic Reform in Ukraine', in *Uriadovyi Kurier*, 22 September 1994; and ITAR-TASS news agency, 2 January 1995.
14. See *Uriadovyi Kurier*, 31 January 1995.

15. *Interfax news agency*, 1 March 1995, and *Financial Times*, 2 March 1995.
16. *Reuters*, 5 April 1995. See also *Interfax news agency*, 4 April 1995, and *Financial Times*, 5 April 1995.
17. *Financial Times*, 7 April 1995.
18. *Reuters*, 7 April 1995.
19. *Reuters*, 11 April 1995.
20. *Interfax news agency*, 10 March 1995, *Reuters*, 9, 10 March and 11 April 1995.
21. See Volodymyr Zviglyanich, 'Ethnic Economics: Is a "Ukrainian Economic Model" Possible?', *Ukraine Business Review*, vol. 4, nos. 1–2 (December 1995–January 1996), pp. 1–4.
22. *Reuters*, 24 May 1995.
23. *Holos Ukrainy*, 6 April 1995.
24. See Viktor Pynzenyk, 'Financial Stabilisation: What is Behind it?', *Ukraine Business Review*, vol. 13, nos. 13–14 (October–November 1995), pp. 1–4 (translated from *Vseukrainskiye vedomosti*, 15 July 1995).
25. UNIAN news agency, 20 September 1995.
26. *Ukrainian Television*, 13 May 1995.
27. According to Viktor Lysytskyi, economic adviser to the National Bank, the non-payments crisis was not caused by a lack of current assets held by enterprises who had enough funds to settle their accounts with partners (UNIAN news agency, 14 October 1995).
28. *Radio Ukraine world service*, 28 June 1995. See also *Reuters*, 28 June 1995.
29. *Interfax news agency*, 27 June 1995.
30. *Reuters*, 11 April 1995.
31. Halchynsky resigned from the presidential administration in December 1995 and was formally relieved of his post on 2 February 1996. He was replaced as presidential economics adviser by Petro Petrashko. Halchynsky heads the Stock Market Association and will act as a consultant to the Ukrainian Centre for Economic and Political Research.
32. *Holos Ukrainy*, 16 September 1995.
33. *Reuters*, 15 September 1995.
34. *Uriadovyi Kurier*, nos. 175–6 (23 November 1995).
35. See Lida Poletz, 'Ukraine on Reform Course despite Shuffle-economists', *Reuters*, 6 July 1995.
36. On 7 April 1995 a commission was created by presidential decree to elaborate a 'Conception of State Industrial Policies, 1996–2000' (*Uriadovyi Kurier*, nos. 55–6, 13 April 1995).
37. The views of different parliamentary factions could be found in *Holos Ukrainy*, 25 October 1995.
38. Only 30–40 per cent of all enterprises were paying taxes (*Eastern Economist Daily*, 26 October 1995). The Ukrainian State Tax Inspectorate began a computerised state registry only in November 1995.
39. *Uriadvyi Kurier*, nos. 153–4 (12 October 1995), and *Holos Ukrainy*, 13 October 1995.
40. See James Rupert, 'Ukraine's Reforms Ripen Slowly: Economic Changes Bring Price Hikes, Low Wages, No Groceries', *The Washington Post*, 14 October 1995.
41. *The Ukrainian Weekly*, 15 October 1995.

42. *Reuters*, 11 October 1995.
43. *Reuters*, 9 November 1995. Aslund warned that Ukraine was operating just within the programme and could slip out of it.
44. In early December 1995, President Kuchma ordered a review of 1996 government expenditure plans because existing programmes were too ambitious. Finance Minister Volodymyr Matviychuk told parliament that 'it is impossible to finance all measures envisaged by Ukrainian legislation from the 1996 state budget' (UNIAN news agency, 4 December 1995).
45. See Danylo Yanevsky, 'New Government Program Strikes a Discordant Note', *Transition*, vol. 1, no. 23 (15 December 1995), pp. 56–8.
46. *Intelnews*, 19 November 1994.
47. *Interfax news agency*, 13 September 1995.
48. *Reuters*, 24 May 1995.
49. *Reuters*, 26 May 1995.
50. *Interfax news agency* and *Reuters*, 27 July 1995. See also *Uriadovyi Kurier*, no. 117 (5 August 1995), and Anatoly Halchynsky, 'Hroshova Reforma', *Uriadovyi Kurier*, no. 135 (9 September 1995).
51. *Interfax news agency*, 25 September 1995.
52. *Uriadovyi Kurier*, nos. 161–2 (29 August 1996).
53. *Visti z Ukrainy*, no. 19, 1994; and *Post Postup*, 10–16 March 1995.
54. Natalia Olynec, 'Kiev's Consuming Passion', *Business Eastern Europe*, 10 April 1995.
55. *Halytskyi Kontrakty*, no. 9, 1994.
56. Some of this material was published as Valeriy Derkach, 'Tin'ova Ekonomika – Skladova Orhanizovanoi Zlochynnosti', *Vechirnyi Kyiv*, 21 February 1996, and 'Tenevaya Ekonomika i Organizovannaya Prestupnost' v Ukrainie', *Kommunist*, no. 9 (February 1996) and no. 10 (March 1996).
57. UNIAN news agency, 14 December 1995.
58. See 'Home Made Privatisation', *Central European*, July/August 1992; Simon Johnson and Santago Eder, 'Prospects for Privatization in Ukraine', *RFE/RL Research Report*, vol. 1, no. 37 (18 September 1992), and 'Ukraine', *Privatisation in Emerging Markets*, December 1993.
59. I am grateful to Dr Valentyn Yegorov, Associate Professor, Taras Shevchenko National University, Kyiv, for advice and useful comments on the section on privatisation in this chapter.
60. Roman Frydman, Andrzej Rapaczynski and John S. Earle, *Protses Privatizatsii v Rossiii, Ukraini ta Baltiskykh Respublik* (Kyiv: Osnova, 1994), p. 136.
61. UNIAN news agency, 4 May and 29 August 1995.
62. ITAR-TASS news agency, 13 December 1994.
63. UNIAN news agency, 22 December 1995. See also V. Yegorov, 'Mass Privatisation in Action', and Alex Frishberg, 'Financial Intermediaries: Trust Companies and Privatisation Certificates', *Ukraine Business Review*, vol. 3, nos. 13–14 (October–November 1995), pp. 6–8 and pp. 11–14.
64. See Paul S. Pirie, 'Donets'k – In the Vanguard of Reform in Ukraine', *Ukraine Business Review*, vol. 3, nos. 10–11 (July–August 1995), pp. 21–2.
65. Evhen Suimenko, 'Pryvatizatsiya v Ukraini: Shliakhy Vyprobuvan', *Viche*, November 1995, pp. 42–57.

66. *Holos Ukrainy*, 21 January 1992 and 22 July 1992.
67. On the 1992 and 1994 privatisation programmes, see *Holos Ukrainy*, 1 August 1992 and *Uriadovyi Kurier*, nos. 50–1 (31 March 1994) respectively.
68. *Ukrainske Slovo*, 17 April 1994.
69. *Holos Ukrainy*, 14 June 1994.
70. UNIAN news agency, 27 January 1995.
71. UNIAR news agency, 5 March 1995.
72. *Radio Ukraine world service*, 19 November 1995. Lazarenko was appointed first deputy prime minister on 5 September 1995 from the post of head of the Dnipropetrovs'k *oblast* state administration (under Kravchuk he had been *oblast* prefect). This promotion reflected both Kuchma's preference for promoting colleagues from his home base and the new emphasis in government policy upon the protection of industry.
73. See 'Pryvatyzovani pidpryemstva ne prosto pratsuit', a pratsuit' efektyvnishe', *Holos Ukrainy*, 8 August 1995.
74. *Holos Ukrainy*, 1 September 1994.
75. *Reuters*, 8 December 1994.
76. *Interfax news agency*, 11 April 1995.
77. *Finansovaya Ukraina*, 22 March 1995.
78. *Uriadovyi Kurier*, nos. 55–6 (13 April 1995).
79. UPI, 27 January 1995.
80. *Infobank news agency*, 13 January 1995.
81. Yuriy Yekhanurov, 'Vlasnist – tse vidpovidalnist', *Uriadovyi Kurier*, nos. 1–2 (4 January 1996). See also Natalia A. Feduschak, 'Yekhanurov Lights Fire under Ukraine's Reforms', *Central European Economic Review*, no. 3, 1995.
82. *Finansovaya Ukraina*, 25 May 1995.
83. Yekhanurov argued in favour of the deadline being brought forward to June from December 1996 for the final issue of privatisation shares. See *Interfax news agency*, 24 October 1995.
84. *Reuters*, 15 March 1995.
85. *Holos Ukrainy*, 5 July 1995.
86. *Krymskaya Gazeta*, 15 August 1995.
87. *Holos Ukrainy*, 29 August 1995.
88. UNIAN news agency, 26 August and 4 October 1995.
89. *Reuters*, 24 January 1996.
90. See Dmytro Konyk, a consultant to the International Finance Corporation, 'Konei na perepravi ... miniaiut', *Uriadovyi Kurier*, no. 178 (28 November 1995).
91. In June 1995 alone 1134 small objects were privatised (*Finansovaya Ukraina*, 1 August 1995).
92. *Reuters*, 7 July 1995.
93. *Uriadovyi Kurier*, nos. 55–6 (13 April 1995).
94. UNIAN news agency, 19 October 1995.
95. UNIAN news agency, 24 January 1996.
96. UNIAN news agency, 7 December 1995.
97. *Interfax news agency*, 30 November 1995.
98. *Ukraina moloda*, 17 November 1995.

99. *Reuters*, 20 October 1995.
100. ITAR-TASS news agency, 15 April 1995.
101. *Reuters*, 14 November 1994.
102. *Holos Ukrainy*, 25 January 1995. Both decrees were translated in *Ukraine Business Review*, vol. 3, no. 7 (April 1995).
103. These figures were provided by PADCO/USAID, Kyiv.
104. On the Association of Private Farmers and the problems its members have encountered see *Holos Ukrainy*, 19 October and *Rada*, 29 December 1994.
105. *Tendencies of the Ukrainian Economy* (Kyiv: European Centre for Macroeconomic Analysis of Ukraine, February 1995). The 1995 figure is taken from *Radio Ukraine world service*, 13 January 1996.
106. UNIAN news agency, 8 February 1995.
107. See Matthew Kaminski, 'Caution Reigns at Kiev Produce Exchange', *Financial Times*, 28 June 1995.
108. See M. Kaminski, 'Ukraine Struggles towards Farm Reform', *Financial Times*, 14 July 1995.
109. *Eastern Economist Daily*, 12 December 1995.
110. UNIAR news agency, 15 November 1996.
111. UNIAN news agency, 30 January 1996.
112. ITAR-TASS news agency, 29 December 1995.
113. UNIAN news agency, 5 February 1996.
114. *Reuters*, 16 November 1995.
115. *Holos Ukrainy*, 4 January 1996. For the views of the Kuchma administration see 'Bez zemel'noi reformy ne obiytyshia', *Uriadovyi Kurier*, no. 173 (18 November 1995). A Western expert remained sceptical: 'No one touched on many of the key issues – like land ownership and what to do with collective farms. It's true Ukraine has a lot of potential but they appear to have no new ideas to convert the sector to the market' (*Reuters*, 27 December 1995).
116. Some of the section on 'Western Assistance' was taken from *Ukraine Business Review*, vol. 4, nos. 1–2 (December 1995–January 1996), pp. 9–22.
117. *The Ukrainian Weekly*, 16 April 1995.
118. See John E. Tedstrom, 'Ukraine: A Crash Course in Economic Transformation', *Comparative Economic Studies*, vol. 37, no. 4 (Winter 1996), pp. 49–67.
119. Ibid.

6 NEW FOREIGN AND DEFENCE POLICIES

1. Earlier drafts of sections of this chapter dealing with the Chechen crisis and NATO enlargement appeared in Taras Kuzio, 'Ukraine and the Expansion of NATO', *Jane's Intelligence Review*, vol. 7, no. 9 (September 1995), and 'The Chechen crisis and the "near abroad"', *Central Asian Survey*, vol. 14, no. 4 (1995), pp. 553–72.
2. *Reuters*, 8 February 1996.
3. For a major overview of Ukraine's foreign and security policies since 1991, see two works by Taras Kuzio, *Ukrainian Security Policy. Washington*

Paper 167 (Washington D.C.: Praeger and the Center for Strategic & International Studies, 1995), as well as *Ukraine. Back From the Brink. European Security Study* 23 (London: Institute for European Defence and Stategic Studies, 1995), chapter 5, 'Foreign and Security Policies', pp. 30–4.

4. The author participated in the conference and is in possession of the documents quoted in this chapter.
5. See T. Kuzio 'Ukraine and the Council of Europe', *The Ukrainian Weekly*, 24 September 1995.
6. *The Ukrainian Weekly*, 19 March 1995.
7. See T. Kuzio, 'International Reaction to the Chechen Crisis', *Central Asian Survey*, vol. 15, no. 1 (March 1996), pp. 97–110.
8. *Reuters*, 21 October 1994.
9. *Reuters*, 22 March 1995.
10. Copy of the Cabinet of Ministers' programme, a document not issued for publication but prepared for internal use only, in the possession of the author.
11. *The Ukrainian Weekly*, 9 October 1994.
12. 'Britain and Ukraine: Strategic Allies', *Ukraine Business Review*, vol. 3, no. 12 (September 1995), p. 4.
13. *Reuters*, 18 November 1995.
14. UPI, 27 October 1995.
15. *Ostankino*, 9 September 1994.
16. *Reuters*, 9 September 1994.
17. Ibid. A meeting of the staff for the coordination of military cooperation between CIS members was held in Kyiv (*Kyivskiye vedomosti*, 26 January 1995). See also Matthew Kaminski, 'Russia, Ukraine Steps up Arms Co-operation', *Financial Times*, 20 Febuary 1995.
18. *Narodna Armiya*, 21 February 1995.
19. *Reuters*, 22 September 1994.
20. *Uriadovyi Kurier*, nos. 13–14 (26 January 1995).
21. *Reuters*, 3 August 1994.
22. *Radio Ukraine world service*, 23 January 1996.
23. See 'Yeltsin Seeks to Rally CIS against West', *Reuters*, 19 January 1996.
24. *The Ukrainian Weekly*, 28 January 1996.
25. *Financial Times*, 20 February 1995.
26. *Reuters*, 19 January 1996.
27. See T. Kuzio, 'Uproar as Moscow Presses for a "Revived Union"' *European Analyst*, no. 47 (April 1996).
28. *Reuters*, 23 May 1995.
29. See the comments by the secretary of the Ukrainian National Security Council, Vladimir Horbulin, who objected to Romanian membership of NATO due to its territorial claims against Northern Bukovina, Southern Bessarabia and Zmeinyi (Serpent) Island in Ukraine (UNIAN news agency, 13 May 1995).
30. *Chas*, 24 March 1995.
31. See T. Kuzio, 'Civil–Military Relations in Ukraine, 1989–1991', *Armed Forces and Society*, vol. 22, no. 1 (Fall 1995), pp. 25–49.
32. UNIAN news agency, 29 May 1995.
33. *Interfax news agency*, 25 November 1994.

34. See Alexander Goncharenko, *Ukrainian–Russian Relations: An Unequal Partnership. Whitehall Paper 32* (London: Royal United Services Institute, 1995), pp. 29–31.
35. *Interfax news agency*, 29 May 1995.
36. *The Washington Post*, 23 November 1994.
37. UNIAN news agency, 24 May 1995.
38. *Kyivskiye Vedomosti*, 19 January 1994.
39. The poll was conducted by SOCIS–GALLUP throughout Ukraine between December 1994 and January 1995 (*The Ukrainian Weekly*, 19 February 1995),
40. *Sevodnya*, 15 September 1994.
41. ITAR-TASS news agency, 26 November 1994.
42. *The Wall Street Journal*, 7–8 January 1994.
43. *Reuters*, 16 February 1995. See also Hennadiy Udovenko, 'European Stability and NATO Enlargement: Ukraine's Perspective', *NATO Review*, no. 6 (November 1995).
44. UNIAN news agency, 14 June 1995.
45. UNIAN news agency, 13 March 1995.
46. *Interfax* and UNIAN news agency, 3 December 1994.
47. UPI, 7 December 1994.
48. *Narodna Armiya*, 6 September 1994.
49. *Reuters*, 24 May 1995.
50. *Reuters*, 11 May 1995.
51. *Reuters*, 11 May 1995.
52. *Reuters*, 23 May 1995.
53. *Reuters*, 3 May 1995.
54. *Ukrainian Television*, 19 May 1995,
55. *Reuters*, 1 June 1995. See also *Uriadovyi Kurier*, no. 82 (3 June 1995).
56. *Reuters*, 8 February 1994.
57. See the views of Kravchuk's former presidential adviser on foreign affairs, Anton Buteiko, currently deputy foreign minister (AP, 7 February 1994).
58. *Reuters*, 8 February 1994.
59. *The Ukrainian Weekly*, 13 February 1994.
60. UNIAN news agency, 25 May 1994.
61. *Holos Ukrainy*, 19 February 1994.
62. *Holos Ukrainy*, 14 June 1994.
63. *Narodna Armiya*, 11 February 1994.
64. *Zolota Vorota*, no. 3, 1994, p. 29.
65. ITAR-TASS news agency, 14 April 1995.
66. *Zolota Vorota*, no. 3, 1994, pp. 30–1.
67. For a discussion of these issues, see A. Goncharenko, *Ukrainian-Russian Relations: An Unequal Partnership. RUSI Whitehall Paper 32* (London: Royal United Services Institute, 1995).
68. *Reuters*, 23 May 1995.
69. UPI, 7 December 1994.
70. *The Washington Post*, 23 November 1994.
71. *The Washington Post*, 23 November 1994.
72. *Reuters*, 26 May 1995.

73. UPI, 7 December 1994.
74. *Reuters*, 23 May 1995.
75. UPI, 7 December 1994.
76. *Nezavisimaya Gazeta*, 21 June 1995. An English-language translation appeared in *Transition*, vol. 1, no. 32 (15 December 1995), pp. 27–32.
77. The draft of the new military doctrine was produced by the Institute of Defence Studies on behalf of the Russian Defence Ministry. See *Sevodnya*, 20 October 1995.
78. See T. Kuzio, 'Ukraine and the Yugoslav Conflict', *Nationalities Papers* (forthcoming).
79. *Moscow News*, 8–14 April 1994.
80. *Reuters*, 22 September 1994.
81. ITAR-TASS news agency, 7 August 1994.
82. *Ostankino*, 21 October 1994.
83. *Interfax News Agency*, 28 August 1995.
84. *Krymskaya Pravda*, 24 December 1994.
85. Lebed's remarks were carried by *Radio Mayak*, 7 November 1995.
86. *Radio Russia*, 28 October 1995.
87. *Radio Russia*, 23 August 1995.
88. ITAR-TASS news agency, 26 October 1995.
89. *Molod Ukrainy*, 10 October 1995.
90. *Kyivskiye vedomosti*, 26 September 1995.
91. *Kyivskiye vedomosti*, 28 April 1995.
92. *Vseukrainskiye vedomosti*, 20 September 1995.
93. ITAR-TASS news agency, 25 October 1995.
94. *Nezavisimost*, 4 October 1995.
95. *Reuters*, 14 November 1995.
96. *Kommersant-Daily*, 28 July 1995, discussed the documents published by *Ukraina Moloda*.
97. *Reuters*, 9 February 1995.
98. *Kyivskie vedomosti*, 2 February 1995.
99. *Reuters*, 10 February 1995.
100. See my two articles on Ukrainian paramilitaries in *Jane's Intelligence Review*, vol. 4, no. 12 (December 1992) and vol. 6, no. 3 (March 1994).
101. *Radio Ukraine*, 30 December 1994.
102. ITAR-TASS news agency, 11 January 1995.
103. *Interfax news agency*, 17 January 1995.
104. UNIAR news agency, 23 December 1994.
105. UNIAR news agency, 9 January 1995. UNA claimed 100–250 Ukrainian citizens were recruited in eastern Ukraine for the Chechen opposition fighting Dudayev in the covert war organised by Russia's Federal Counter Intelligence Service prior to December 1994.
106. See the appeal signed by a long list of national democratic organisations (*Visti z Ukrainy*, 1–7 September 1994).
107. *Ukrainski Visti*, 15 January 1995.
108. *Holos Ukrainy*, 24 January 1995.
109. *Kyivskie vedomosti*, 22 December 1994, and *Holos Ukrainy*, 14 December 1994.

110. Appeal by the Ukrainian Parliament to the Russian State Duma (*Holos Ukrainy*, 21 December 1994) and the government statement (*Uriadovyi Kurier*, no. 192, 13 December 1994).
111. *Reuters*, 16 January 1995.
112. *Holos Ukrainy*, 3 December 1994.
113. UNIAN news agency, 10 January 1995.
114. *Interfax-Ukaine*, 11 January 1995.
115. *Russia TV channel*, 19 January 1996.
116. These election programmes are in the possession of the author.
117. *Reuters*, 2 March 1995. See also *Interfax news agency* and UNIAN news agency, 3 March 1995. Nationalist criticism of these groups can be found in *Shliakh Peremohy*, 4 and 11 March 1995.
118. *Reuters*, 2 March 1995.
119. Conversation with Pashkaver, London, 12 April 1995.
120. *Shliakh Peremohy*, 11 March 1995.
121. *Interfax news agency*, 2 and 3 March 1994.
122. UNIAN news agency, 3 March 1995.
123. *Ukrainske Slovo*, 30 July 1994.
124. *Holos Ukrainy*, 16 and 19 September 1995.
125. *Uriadovyi Kurier*, no. 114 (1 August 1995).
126. UNIAN news agency, 28 September 1995.
127. *Holos Ukrainy*, 30 May 1995.
128. *Ukrainske Slovo*, 30 July 1995.
129. *Viche*, September 1995, p. 62.
130. Ibid., pp. 65–7.
131. See T. Kuzio, 'Ukrainian Civil–Military Relations and the Military Impact of the Ukrainian Economic Crisis', in Bruce Parrott, ed., *State Building and Military Power in Russia and the New States of Eurasia. The International Politics of Eurasia, Volume 5* (Armonk: M.E. Sharpe, 1995), pp. 157–92, and T. Kuzio, 'Ukrainian Armed Forces in Crisis', *Jane's Intelligence Review*, vol. 7, no. 7 (July 1995).
132. See Pavel Baev and Tor Bukkvoll, 'Ukraine's Army under Civilian Rule', *Jane's Intelligence Review*, vol. 8, no. 1 (January 1996), and T. Kuzio, 'Ukraine's New Defence and Foreign Ministers', *Jane's Intelligence Review Pointer*, no. 11 (September 1994).
133. A. Goncharenko, Ukrainian–Russian Relations: An Unequal Partnership. Whitehall Paper 32 (London: Royal United Services Institute, 1995), p. 39.
134. See T. Kuzio, 'Security Forces of the Ukrainian State' and 'Uniform Badges of Ukrainian Security Forces', *Jane's Intelligence Review*, vol. 8, no. 1 (January 1996).
135. See T. Kuzio, 'The Organisation of Ukraine's Forces', *Jane's Intelligence Review*, vol. 8, no. 6 (June 1996).
136. See Ustina Markus, 'The Ukrainian Navy and the Black Sea Fleet', *RFE/RL Research Report*, vol. 3, no. 18 (6 May 1994).
137. UNIAN news agency, 13 September 1994.
138. UNIAN news agency, 20 February 1995. See also the statement by the Democratic Party of Ukraine in *Ukrainski Visti*, 2 April 1995.
139. See the comments by Colonel-General Viktor Samsonov, commander of the headquarters for Coordinating Military Cooperation, in *Interfax news agency*, 14 February 1995.

140. *Reuters*, 20 February 1995.
141. *Narodna Armiya*, 15 March 1995.
142. *Panorama* (Alma Ata), 11 February 1995.
143. *Holos Ukrainy*, 13 September 1995.
144. UNIAN news agency, 20 February 1995.
145. *Holos Ukrainy*, 13 September 1995.
146. See Kuchma's speech to the Ukrainian parliament in *Holos Ukrainy*, 18 November 1994.
147. See T. Kuzio, 'Ukraine Can Thrive if the West Stays Committed', *The Wall Street Journal*, and *The Wall Street Journal Europe*, 11 May 1995.
148. See Sherman W. Garnett, 'Ukraine's Decision to Join the NPT', *Arms Control Today*, January/February 1995,
149. ITAR-TASS news agency, 18 October 1994.
150. The memorandum on security assurances and the Chinese statement on this question are published in *The Ukrainian Quarterly*, vol. L, no. 4 (Winter 1994), pp. 427–30.
151. See *Holos Ukrainy*, the official organ of the Ukrainian parliament, 8 and 9 December 1994.
152. *Reuters*, 6 December 1994.
153. According to one US government-sponsored poll three-quarters of Russians do not regard Ukrainians as a separate nation or think that they should therefore be an independent state (*The Ukrainian Weekly*, 9 October 1994).
154. Fo a pessimistic view about Ukraine's chances of holding off Russian integrationist pressures, see Eugene B. Rumer, 'Eurasia Letter: Will Ukraine Return to Russia?', *Foreign Policy*, no. 96 (Fall 1994), pp. 129–44, and the following discussion between Rumer and Roman Szporluk in *Foreign Policy*, no. 97 (Winter 1994–5), pp. 178–81.
155. See T. Kuzio, 'A Friend in Need: Kiev Woos Washington', *The World Today*, vol. 52, no. 4 (April 1996), and 'Britain Sees Ukraine as Europe's New Strategic Front', *The Ukrainian Weekly*, 28 April 1996.
156. *Sevodnya*, 17 November 1995.

7 CONCLUSIONS

1. See T. Kuzio, *Nation Building in Ukraine: The Search for Identity* (London: Routledge, forthcoming).
2. Good examples of this lack of understanding of the driving forces underpinning Ukrainian nation- and state-building are Dominique Arel and Andrew Wilson, 'Ukraine under Kuchma: Back to Eurasia?', *RFE/RL Research Report*, vol. 3, no. 32 (19 August 1994), and D. Arel, 'The Temptation of the Nationalizing State', in Vladimir Tismaneanu, ed., *Political Culture and Civil Society in Russia and the New States of Eurasia, The International Politics of Eurasia, volume 7* (Armonk, NY and London: M.E. Sharpe, 1995), pp. 157–88.
3. See Roman Koval, 'Chy Vypravdaie Heneral Marchuk Nashi Spodivannia?', *Molod Ukrainy*, 5 September 1995, and Valeriy Zaytsev, 'Chy Stane "Zaliznyi Prem'ier" Tretim Prezydentom?', *Ukrainske Slovo*, 5 November 1995. See also the interview with Marchuk in *Holos Ukrainy*, 7 December 1995.

4. See Igor Kliamkin, 'Russian Statehood, the CIS, and the Problem of Security', in Leon Aron and Kenneth M. Jensen, eds., *The Emergence of Russian Foreign Policy* (Washington D.C.: United States Institute of Peace Press, 1994), pp. 107–18. See also the Bibliography of Selected Publications at the end of this book.
5. See Alexander J. Motyl, 'The Conceptual President: Leonid Kravchuk and the Politics of Surrealism', in Timothy J. Colton and Robert C. Tucker, eds., *Patterns in Post-Soviet Leadership. The John M. Olin Critical Issues Series* (Boulder, Co. and Oxford: Westview Press, 1995), pp. 103–22.

Bibliography of Selected Publications

POST-SOVIET TRANSITION AND NATIONALITY PROBLEMS

Barner-Barry, Carol and Hody, Cynthia, eds., *The Politics of Change. The Transformation of the Former Soviet Union* (New York: St. Martin's Press, 1995).

Blum, Douglas W., ed., *Russia's Future. Consolidation or Disintegration?* (Boulder, Co. and Oxford: Westview Press, 1994).

Bourdeaux, Michael, ed., *The Politics of Religion in Russia and the New States of Eurasia. The International Politics of Eurasia* (Armonk, NY and London: M.E. Sharpe, 1995).

Bremmer, Ian and Taras, Ray, eds., *Nations and Politics in the Soviet Successor States* (Cambridge: Cambridge University Press, 1993).

Bugajski, Janusz, ed., *Nations in Turmoil. Conflict and Cooperation in Eastern Europe* (Boulder, Co. and Oxford: Westview Press, 1995).

Colton Timothy, J. and Tucker, Robert C., eds., *Patterns in Post-Soviet Leadership. The John M. Olin Critical Issues Series* (Boulder, Co. and Oxford: Westview Press, 1995).

Denber, Rachel, ed., *The Soviet Nationality Reader. The Disintegration in Context* (Boulder, Co. and Oxford: Westview Press, 1992).

Gitelman, Zvi, ed., *The Politics of Nationalism and the Erosion of the USSR* (London: Macmillan, 1992).

Hajda, Lubomyr and Beissinger, Mark, eds., *The Nationalities Factor in Soviet Politics and Society. The John M. Olin Critical Issues Series* (Boulder, Co. and Oxford: Westview Press, 1990).

Kaiser, Robert J., *The Geography of Nationalism in Russia and the USSR* (Princeton, NJ: Princeton University Press, 1994).

Kolstoe, Paul, *Russians in the Former Soviet Republics* (London: Hurst & Company, 1995).

Kraus, Michael and Liebowitz, Ronald D., eds., *Russia and Eastern Europe after Communism. The Search for New Political, Economic and Security Systems* (Boulder, Co. and Oxford: Westview Press, 1995).

Lavigne, Marie, *The Economics of Transition. From Socialist Economy to Market Economy* (London: Macmillan, 1995).

Motyl, Alexander J., ed., *The Post-Soviet Nations. Perspectives on the Demise of the USSR* (New York: Columbia University Press, 1992).

Polokhalo, Volodymyr, ed., *The Political Analysis of Postcommunism* (Kyiv: Political Thought, 1995).

Remington, Thomas F., ed., *Parliaments in Transition. The New Legislative Politics in the Former USSR and Eastern Europe* (Boulder, Co. and Oxford: Westview Press, 1994).

Rywkin, Michael, *Moscow's Lost Empire* (Armonk, NY and London: M.E. Sharpe, 1994).

Saivetz, Carol R. and Jones, Anthony, eds., *In Search of Pluralism. Soviet and Post-Soviet Politics* (Boulder, Co. and Oxford: Westview Press, 1994).

Sanford, R. Lieberman, Powell, David E., Saivetz, Carol R. and Terry, Sarah M. eds., *The Soviet Empire Reconsidered* (Boulder, Co. and Oxford: Westview Press, 1994).

Starr, Frederick S., ed., *The Legacy of History in Russia and the New States of Eurasia, The International Politics of Eurasia, volume 1* (Armonk, NY and London: M.E. Sharpe, 1994).

Suny, Ronald G., *The Revenge of the Past. Nationalism, Revolution, and the Collapse of the Soviet Union* (Stanford, CA: Stanford University Press, 1993).

Szporluk, Roman, ed., *National Identity and Ethnicity in Russia and the New States of Eurasia. The International Politics of Eurasia, volume 2* (Armonk, NY and London: M.E. Sharpe, 1994).

Tismaneanu, Vladimir, ed., *Political Culture and Civil Society in Russia and the New States of Eurasia. The International Politics of Eurasia, volume 7* (Armonk, NY and London: M.E. Sharpe, 1995).

Tolz, Vera and Iain, Elliot, eds, *The Demise of the USSR. From Communism to Independence* (London: Macmillan, 1994).

White, Stephen, Pravda, Alex and Gitelman, Zvi, eds., *Developments in Russian and Post-Soviet Politics* (London: Macmillan, 1994).

UKRAINE

Arel, D. and Wilson, A., 'The Ukrainian Parliamentary Elections', *RFE/RL Research Report*, vol. 3, no. 26 (1 July 1994).

Arel, D. and Wilson, A., 'Ukraine under Kuchma: Back to "Eurasia"?', *RFE/RL Research Report*, vol. 3, no. 32 (19 August 1994).

Batiouk, Viktor, *Ukraine's Non-Nuclear Option*, Research Paper No. 14 (Geneva, United Nations Institute for Disarmament Research, 1992).

Bilinsky, Yaroslav, 'Basic Factors in the Foreign Policy of Ukraine: The Impact of the Soviet Experience', in Starr, Frederick S., ed., *The Legacy of History in Russia and the New States of Eurasia. The International Politics of Eurasia, Volume 1* (Armonk, NY and London: M.E. Sharpe, 1994), pp. 171–92.

Birch, S., 'Electoral Behaviour in Western Ukraine in National Elections and Referendums, 1989–1991', *Europe–Asia Studies*, vol. 47, no. 7 (November 1995), pp. 1145–76.

Birch, S. 'The Ukrainian Parliamentary and Presidential Elections of 1994', *Electoral Studies*, vol. 14, no. 1 (1995), pp. 93–9.

Bojcun, Marko, 'The Ukrainian Parliamentary Elections in March–April 1994', *Europe–Asia Studies*, vol. 47, no. 2 (March–April 1995), pp. 229–49.

Bojcun, Marco, 'Ukraine under Kuchma', *Labour Focus on Eastern Europe*, no. 52 (Autumn 1995), pp. 70–83.

Crow, S., 'Russian Parliament Asserts Control over Sevastopol', *RFE/RL Research Report*, vol. 2, no. 31 (30 July 1993).

Dabrowski, Marek, 'The Ukrainian Way to Hyperinflation', *Communist Economies and Economic Transformation*, vol. 6, no. 2 (1994), pp. 115–37.

DeWing, Martin J., *The Ukrainian Nuclear Arsenal: Problems of Command, Control, and Maintenance, Program for Nonproliferation Studies, Working Paper No. 3* (Monterey, CA: Institute of International Studies, October 1993).

Drohobycky, Maria, ed., *Crimea. Dynamics, Challenges, and Prospects* (Lanham, MD and London: Rowman and Littlefield Publishers and American Association for the Advancement of Science, 1995).

Duncan, Peter J.S., 'Ukraine and the Ukrainians', in Smith, Graham, ed., *The Nationalities Question in the post-Soviet States* (London and New York: Longman, 1996), pp. 188–209.

Ellis, Jason, 'The "Ukraine Dilemma" and U.S. Foreign Policy', *European Security*, vol. 3, no. 2 (Summer 1994), pp. 251–80.

Frydman, Roman, Rapaczynski, Andrzej and Earle, John S., *The Privatization Process in Russia, Ukraine and the Baltic States*. CEU Privatization Report, Volume 2 (Prague: Central European University Press, 1993).

Goncharenko, Alexander, *Ukrainian–Russian Relations: An Unequal Partnership*. RUSI Whitehall Paper 32 (London: Royal United Services Institute, 1995).

Ham, Peter van, *Ukraine, Russia and European Security: Implications for Western Policy, Chaillot Papers*, no. 13 (Paris: Institute for Security Studies, West European Union, February 1994).

Hemans, Simon, 'Ukraine's Place in Europe', *RUSI Journal*, vol. 139, no. 6 (December 1994), pp. 54–7.

IEWS Strategy Group on Strengthening Cooperation in Central and Eastern Europe and IEWS-NIS Strategic Forum, *The New Ukraine: Radical Economic Change Replaces Political Expediency*, Report of the Joint Conference by Jorn Weigelt, Senior Executive Assistant to the Founding President, 14–16 October 1994, Kyiv, Ukraine (Prague, Budapest, Warsaw, New York, Atlanta, Moscow, Bardejov, Debrecen, Lviv, Krosno, Uzhorod: 1995).

Izmalkov, Valerii, 'Ukraine and Her Armed Forces: The Conditions and Process for their Creation, Character, Structure and Military Doctrine', *European Security*, vol. 2, no. 2 (Summer 1993), pp. 279–319.

Johnson, Simon and Ustenko, Oleg, 'Ukraine Slips into Hyperinflation', *RFE/RL Research Report*, vol. 2, no. 26 (25 June 1993).

Jung, M., 'Looking Both Ways', *Transition*, vol. 1, no. 6 (28 April 1995).

Kaufmann, Daniel, 'Market Liberalization in Ukraine: To Regain a Lost Pillar of Economic Reform', *Transition*, vol. 5, no. 7 (7 September 1994), pp. 1–3.

Kincade, William H. and Melnyczuk, Natalie, 'Eurasia Letter: Unneighborly Neighbors', *Foreign Policy*, no. 94 (Spring 1994), pp. 84–104.

Kistersky, Leonid, 'Economic Reasons for the Political Crisis in Ukraine', *Brown Journal of Foreign Affairs*, vol. 1, no. 1 (Winter 1993–4), pp. 171–6.

Koropeckyj, Ihor S., ed., *The Ukrainian Economy. Achievements, Problems, Challenges* (Cambridge, MA: Harvard Ukrainian Research Institute, 1992).

Kuzio, Taras, *Ukraine. The Unfinished Revolution. European Security Studies 16* (London: Institute for European Defence & Strategic Studies, 1992).

Kuzio, T., 'Ukraine – A New Military Power?', *Jane's Intelligence Review*, vol. 4, no. 2 (February 1992).

Kuzio, T., 'Nuclear Weapons and Military Policy in Independent Ukraine', *Harriman Institute Forum*, vol. 6, no. 9 (May 1993).

Kuzio, T., 'Ukraine and its Future Security', *Jane's Intelligence Review*, vol. 4, no. 12 (December 1993).

Kuzio, T. and Wilson, Andrew, *Ukraine: Perestroika to Independence* (London: Macmillan, New York: St. Martin's Press and Edmonton: Canadian Institute for Ukrainian Studies, 1994).

Kuzio, T., *Ukraine–Crimea–Russia: Triangle of Conflict* (London: Research Institute for the Study of Conflict and Terrorism, 1994).

Kuzio, T., 'The Multi-party System in Ukraine on the Eve of Elections', *Government and Opposition*, vol. 29, no. 1 (Winter 1994), pp. 109–27.

Kuzio, T., 'Elections in Ukraine', *Freedom Review*, vol. 25, no. 3 (May–June 1994), pp. 37–9.

Kuzio, T., 'From Pariah to Partner. Ukraine and Nuclear Weapons', *Jane's Intelligence Review*, vol. 5, no. 5 (May 1994).

Kuzio, T., 'Ukraine's New Defence and Foreign Ministers', *Jane's Intelligence Review Pointer*, no. 11 (September 1994).

Kuzio, T., 'The Implications of the Ukrainian Elections', *Jane's Intelligence Review*, vol. 4, no. 6 (June 1994).

Kuzio, T., 'The Crimea and European Security', *European Security*, vol. 3, no. 4 (Winter 1994), pp. 734–74.

Kuzio, T., 'Analysis: Leonid Kuchma, Ukraine's Second President', *The Ukrainian Weekly*, 31 July 1994.

Kuzio, T., 'Ukraine since the Elections: From Romanticism to Pragmatism', *Jane's Intelligence Review*, vol. 4, no. 12 (December 1994).

Kuzio, T., 'Leonid Kuchma: Ukraine's Saviour?', *The Ukrainian Weekly*, 16 July 1995.

Kuzio, T., 'After the Shock the Therapy', *Transition*, vol. 1, no. 13 (28 July 1995).

Kuzio, T., *Ukrainian Security Policy. Washington Paper* 167 (Washington D.C. The Center for Strategic & International Studies and Praeger, 1995).

Kuzio, T., *Ukraine. Back From the Brink. European Security Studies* 23 (London: Institute for European Defence & Strategic Studies, 1995).

Kuzio, T., 'Ukraine and the Council of Europe', *The Ukrainian Weekly*, 24 September 1995.

Kuzio, T., 'Ukrainian Armed Forces in Crisis', *Jane's Intelligence Review*, vol. 7, no. 7 (July 1995).

Kuzio, T., 'Ukraine and the Expansion of NATO', *Jane's Intelligence Review*, vol. 7, no. 9 (September 1995).

Kuzio, T., 'Ukrainian Civil–Military Relations and the Military Impact of the Ukrainian Economic Crisis', in Bruce Parrott, ed., *State Building and Military Power in Russia and the New States of Eurasia. The International Politics of Eurasia, Volume 5* (Armonk, NY: M.E. Sharpe, 1995), pp. 157–92.

Kushnirsky, Fyodr I., 'Ukraine's Industrial Enterprise: Surviving Hard Times', *Comparative Economic Studies*, vol. 36, no. 4 (Winter 1994), pp. 21–39.

Kubicek, Paul, 'Delegative Democracy in Russia and Ukraine', *Communist and Post-Communist Studies*, vol. 27, no. 4 (December 1994), pp. 423–441.

Lapychak, C., 'Showdown Yields Political Reform', *Transition*, vol. 1, no. 13 (28 July 1995).

Lapychak, C., 'Media Independence is Still Alien to Ukraine's Political Culture', *Transition*, vol. 1, no. 18 (6 October 1995).

Lapychak, C., 'Quarrels over Land Reform', *Transition*, vol. 1, no. 22 (1 December 1995).

Lapychak, C., 'Agricultural Reform in Ukraine', *Transition*, vol. 1, no. 22 (1 December 1995).

Lepingwell, J.W.R., 'The Trilateral Agreement on Nuclear Weapons', *RFE/RL Research Report*, vol. 3, no. 4 (28 January 1994).

Lepingwell, J.W.R., 'Ukraine, Russia and Nuclear Weapons: A Chronology', *REF/RL Research Report*, vol. 3, no. 4 (28 January 1994).

Lepingwell, J.W.R., 'Ukrainian Parliament Removes START-1 Conditions', *RFE/RL Research Report*, vol. 3, no. 8 (25 February 1994).

Lester, Jeremy, 'Russian Political Attitudes to Ukrainian Independence', *The Journal of Post Communist Studies and Transition Politics*, vol. 10, no. 2 (June 1994), pp. 193–233.

Markov, Ihor, 'The Role of the President in the Ukrainian Political System', *RFE/RL Research Report*, vol. 2, no. 48 (3 December 1993).

Markus, U. 'Ukraine: Stability and Political Turnover', *Transition*, 15 February 1995.

Markus, U., 'Shoring up Relations with Russia', *Transition*, vol. 1, no. 6 (28 April 1995).

Markus, U., 'No Longer as Mighty', *Transition*, vol. 1, no. 13 (28 July 1995).

Marples, D.R. 'Ukraine afer the Presidential Elections', *RFE/RL Research Report*, vol. 3, no. 31 (12 August 1994).

Marples, D.R. 'The Ukrainian Economy in the Autumn of 1994: Status Report', *Post-Soviet Geography*, vol. 35, no. 8 (October 1994), pp. 484–91.

Marples, D.R. and Duke, David F., 'Ukraine, Russia and the Question of Crimea', *Nationalities Papers*, vol. 23, no. 2 (June 1995), pp. 261–89.

Motyl, Alexander J., *Dilemmas of Independence. Ukraine after Totalitarianism* (New York: Council on Foreign Relations, 1993).

Potichnyj, Peter J., 'The Referendum and Presidential Elections in Ukraine', *Canadian Slavonic Papers*, no. 33 (June 1991), pp. 123–38.

Potichnyj, P.J. 'Elections in the Ukraine, 1990', in Zvi Gitelman, ed., *The Politics of Nationality and the Erosion of the USSR* (New York: St. Martin's Press, 1992), pp. 176–214.

Rhodes, Mark, 'Divisiveness and Doubt over Economic Reform', *Transition*, vol. 1, no. 6 (28 April 1995).

Rose, Richard, 'Adaptation, Resilience, and Destitution. Alternative Responses to Transition in Ukraine', *Problems of Post-Communism*, vol. 42, no. 6 (November–December 1995), pp. 52–61.

Rumer, Eugene B., 'Eurasia Letter: Will Ukraine Return to Russia?', *Foreign Policy*, no. 96 (Fall 1994), pp. 129–144 and no. 97 (Winter 1994–5), pp. 178–81.

Rutland, Peter, 'Search for Stability', *Transition*, vol. 1, no. 10 (23 June 1995).

Sochor, Zenovia A., 'Political Culture and Foreign Policy: Elections in Ukraine 1994', in Tismaneanu, Vladimir, ed., *Political Culture and Civil Society in Russia and the New States of Eurasia. The International Politics of Eurasia*, vol. 7 (Armonk, NY and London: M.E. Sharpe, 1995), pp. 208–26.

Solchanyk, R., 'Ukraine Considers a New Republican Constitution', RL 215/91, *Report on the USSR*, vol. 3, no. 23 (7 June 1991).

Solchanyk, R., 'Ukraine, The (Former) Center, Russia and "Russia"', *Studies in Comparative Communism*, vol. XXV, no. 1 (March 1992), pp. 31–45.

Solchanyk, R., 'The Crimean Imbroglio: Kiev and Moscow', *REF/RL Research Report*, vol. 1, no. 40 (9 October 1992).

Solchanyk, R., 'Ukraine and the CIS: A Troubled Relationship', *RFE/RL Research Report*, vol. 2, no. 7 (12 February 1993).

Solchanyk, R., 'Ukraine's Search for Security', *RFE/RL Research Report*, vol. 2, no. 21 (21 May 1993).

Solchanyk, R., 'The Ukrainian–Russian Summit: Problems and Prospects', *RFE/RL Research Report*, vol. 2, no. 27 (2 July 1993).

Solchanyk, R., 'Russia, Ukraine and the Imperial Legacy', *Post-Soviet Affairs*, vol. 9, no. 4 (October–December 1993), pp. 337–65.

Solchanyk, R., 'Crimea's Presidential Election', *RFE/RL Research Report*, vol. 3, no. 11 (18 March 1994).

Solchanyk, R., 'Ukraine: The Politics of Reform', *Problems of Post-Communism*, vol. 42, no. 6 (November–December 1995), pp. 46–51.

Smolansky, Oles M., 'Ukraine's Quest for Independence: The Fuel Factor', *Europe–Asia Studies*, vol. 47, no. 1 (January–February 1995), pp. 67–90.

Subtelny, O., 'Russocentrism, Regionalism, and the Political Culture of Ukraine', in Tismaneanu, Vladimir, ed., *Political Culture and Civil Society in Russia and the New States of Eurasia. The International Politics of Eurasia, vol. 7* (Armonk, NY and London: M.E. Sharpe, 1995), pp. 189–207.

Szporluk, R., 'Belarus, Ukraine and the Russian Question: A Comment', *Post-Soviet Affairs*, vol. 9, no. 4 (October–December 1993), pp. 366–74.

Teague, Elizabeth, 'Russians outside Russia and Russian Security Policy', in Aron, Leon and Jensen, Kenneth M., ed., *The Emergence of Russian Foreign Policy* (Washington. D.C.: United States Institute of Peace Press, 1994), pp. 81–105.

Udovenko, Hennadiy, 'European Stability and NATO Enlargement: Ukraine's Perspective', *NATO Review*, no. 6 (November 1995), pp. 15–18.

Vydrin, Dmytro and Tabachnyk, Dmytro, *Ukraine on the Threshold of the XXI Century. Political Aspect* (Kyiv: Lybid, 1995).

Vydrin, D., 'Ukraine and Russia', in Blackwill, Robert D., and Karaganov, S., eds., *Damage Limitation or Crisis? Russia and the Outside World, CSIA Studies in International Security No. 5* (Cambridge, MA: Center for Science and International Affairs, John F. Kennedy School of Government and Washington/London: Brassey's, 1994), pp. 123–37.

Wasylyk, Myron, 'Ukraine Prepares for Parliamentary Elections', *RFE/RL Research Report*, vol. 3, no. 5 (4 February 1994).

Wasylyk, M., 'Ukraine on the Eve of Elections', *RFE/RL Research Report*, vol. 3, no. 12 (25 March 1994).

Wilson, A., 'The Growing Challenge to Kiev from the Donbas', *RFE/RL Research Report*, vol. 2, no. 33 (20 August 1993).

Wilson, A., 'Crimea's Political Cauldron', *RFE/RL Research Report*, vol. 2, no. 45 (12 November 1993).

Wilson, A., 'The Elections in Crimea', *RFE/RL Research Report*, vol. 3, nos. 25 and 26 (24 June and 1 July 1994).

Wilson, A., *The Crimean Tatars. A Situation Report on the Crimean Tatars for International Alert* (London: International Alert, 1994).

Wilson, A., 'Ukraine Under Kuchma', *Russia & the Successor States Briefing Service*, vol. 3, no. 6 (December 1995), pp. 2–17.

Whitlock, Erik, 'Ukrainian–Russian Trade: The Economics of Dependency', *RFE/RL Research Report*, vol. 2, no. 43 (29 October 1993).

Wolchik, Sharon L. and Zviglyanich, Volodymyr A., eds., *Ukraine in the Post-Soviet World: Building a State* (Prague: Central European University Press, forthcoming).

Yanevsky, Danylo, 'New Government Program Strikes a Discordant Note', *Transition*, vol. 1, no. 23 (15 December 1995).

Zviglyanich, Volodymyr, 'Public Perceptions of Economic Reform', *Transition*, vol. 1, no. 13 (28 July 1995).

RUSSIA AND THE CIS

Arbatov, Alexei G., 'Russia's Foreign Policy Alternatives', *International Security*, vol. 18, no. 2 (Fall 1993), pp. 5–43.

Allison, Graham, Carter, Ashton B., Miller, Steven E. and Zelikow, Philip, eds., *Cooperative Denuclearisation. From Pledges to Deeds*. CSIA Studies in International Security no. 2 (Cambridge, MA: Center for Science and International Affairs, John F. Kennedy School of Government, Harvard University, January 1993).

Allison, Roy, *Military Forces in the Soviet Successor States*. Adelphi Paper 280 (London: Brassey's and the International Institute for Strategic Studies, 1993).

Allison, R., *Peacekeeping in the Soviet Successor States*. Chaillot Papers 18 (Paris: Institute for Security Studies, West European Union, November 1994).

Bodie, William C., 'Anarchy and Cold War in Moscow's "Near Abroad"', *Strategic Review* (Winter 1993), pp. 40–53.

Campbell, Kurt M., Carter, Ashton B., Miller, S.E. and Zraket, Charles A., *Soviet Nuclear Fission. Control of the Nuclear Arsenal in a Disintegrating Soviet Union*. CSIA Studies in International Security no. 1 (Cambridge, MA: Center for Science and International Affairs, John F. Kennedy School of Government, Harvard University, November 1991).

Checkel, Jeff, 'Russian Foreign Policy: Back to the Future?', *RFE/RL Research Report*, vol. 1, no. 41 (16 October 1992).

Covington, Stephen R., *Moscow's Insecurity and Eurasian Instability* (Camberley: RMA Sandhurst, Conflict Studies Research Centre, October 1994).

Crow, S., *The Making of Foreign Policy in Russia Under Yeltsin* (Munich: RFE/RL Research Institute, 1993).

Crow, S., 'Russian Peacekeeping: Defence, Diplomacy or Imperialism?', *RFE/RL Research Report*, vol. 1, no. 37 (18 September 1992).

Crow, S., 'The Theory and Practice of Peacekeeping in the Former USSR', *RFE/RL Research Report*, vol. 1, no. 37 (18 September 1992).

Crow, S., 'Competing Blueprints for Russian Foreign Policy', *RFE/RL Research Report*, vol. 1, no. 50 (18 December 1992).

Crow, S., 'Russia Seeks Leadership Role in Regional Peacekeeping', *REF/RL Research Report*, vol. 2, no. 15 (9 April 1993).

Crow, S., 'Russia Asserts its Strategic Agenda', *REF/RL Research Report*, vol. 2, no. 50 (17 December 1993).

Crow, S., 'Russia Promotes the CIS as an International Organisation', *RFE/RL Research Report*, vol. 3, no. 11 (18 March 1994).

Daniel, G. eds., *Civil–Military Relations in the Soviet and Yugoslav Successor States* (Boulder, Co. and Oxford: Westview Press, 1995).

Dawisha, Karen and Parrott, Bruce, *Russia and the New States of Eurasia. The Politics of Upheaval* (Cambridge, New York and Melbourne: Cambridge University Press, 1994).

Dawisha, A. and Dawisha, K., eds., *The Making of Foreign Policy in Russia and the New States of Eurasia. The International Politics of Eurasia, vol. 4* (Armonk, NY and London: M.E. Sharpe, 1995).

Foye, Stephan, 'Post-Soviet Russia: Politics and the New Russian Army', *RFE/RL Research Report*, vol. 1, no. 33 (21 August 1992).

Foye, Stephan, 'Rebuilding the Russian Military: Some Problems and Prospects', *RFE/RL Research Report*, vol. 1, no. 44 (6 November 1992).

Foye, Stephan, 'A Hardened Stance on Foreign Policy', *Transition*, vol. 1, no. 9 (9 June 1995).

Garnett, Sherman, 'The Integrationist Temptation', *The Washington Quarterly*, vol. 18, no. 2 (Spring 1995), pp. 35–44.

Goble, Paul A., 'Russia and its Neighbours', *Foreign Policy*, no. 90 (Spring 1993), pp. 79–88.

Goltz, Thomas, 'Letter from Eurasia: The Hidden Russian Hand', *Foreign Policy*, no. 92 (Fall 1993), pp. 92–116.

Hurd, Douglas and Kozyrev, Andrei, 'Challenge of Peacekeeping', *Financial Times*, 14 December 1993.

Holden, Gerard, *Russia after the Cold War: History and the Nation in Post-Soviet Security Policies* (Boulder, Co. and Oxford: Westview Press, 1994).

Johnson, Lena and Archer, Clive, eds., *Peacekeeping and the Role of Russia in Eurasia* (Boulder, Co. and Oxford: Westview Press, 1995).

Johnson, Teresa Pelton and Miller, Steven E., *Russian Security after the Cold War. Seven Views from Moscow.* CSIA Studies in International Security No. 3 (Washington D.C. and London: Brassey's for the Center for Science and International Affairs, John F. Kennedy School of Government, Harvard University).

Karaganov, Sergie A., *The New Foreign Policy and Security Agenda. A View from Moscow.* London Defence Studies 12 (London: Brassey's for the Centre for Defence Studies, 1992).

Kerr, David, 'The New Eurasianism: The Rise of Geopolitics in Russia's Foreign Policy', *Europe–Asia Studies*, vol. 47, no. 6 (September 1995), pp. 977–88.

Kolsto, Paul, 'The New Russian Diaspora: Minority Protection in the Soviet Successor States', *Journal of Peace Research*, vol. 30, no. 2 (1993), pp. 197–217.

Kristof, Ladis K.D., 'The Geopolitical Image of the Fatherland: The Case of Russia', *Western Political Quarterly*, vol. XX, no. 4 (December 1967), pp. 941–54.

Kuzio, T., 'Russian Foreign Policy. Back to the USSR?', *Conflict International*, vol. 9, no. 10 (October 1994) and *The Ukrainian Times*, 25 October–1 November 1994.

Kuzio, T., 'International Reaction to the Chechen Crisis', *The Ukrainian Times*, no. 51 (January 1995).

Kuzio, T., 'The Chechnya Conflict. Consequences for Russia and the West', *Conflict International*, vols. 9–10, no. 10 and no. 1 (December 1994–January 1995).

Kuzio, T., 'The Chechnya Crisis and the "Near Abroad"', *Central Asian Survey*, vol. 14, no. 4 (1995), pp. 553–72.

Lepingwell, J.W.R., 'The Russian Military and Security Policy in the "Near Abroad"', *Survival*, vol. 36, no. 3 (Autumn 1994), pp. 70–92.

Lough, John, 'The Place of the "Near Abroad" in Russian Foreign Policy', *RFE/RL Research Report*, vol. 2, no. 11 (12 March 1993).

Lough, J., 'Defining Russia's Relations with Neighbouring States', *RFE/RL Research Report*, vol. 2, no. 20 (14 May 1993).

Melvin, Neil, *Forging The New Russian Nation. Russian Foreign Policy and the Russian-speaking Communities of the Former USSR*. Discussion Paper 50 (London: Royal Institute for International Affairs, 1994).

Odom, William E. and Dujarric, Robert, *Commonwealth or Empire? Russia, Central Asia and the Transcaucasus* (Indianapolis: Hudson Institute, 1995).

Orr, Michael, 'Peacekeeping and Overstretch in the Russian Army', *Jane's Intelligence Review*, vol. 6, no. 8 (August 1994).

Parrott, Bruce, ed., *State Building and Military Power in Russia and the New States of Eurasia. The International Politics of Eurasia, vol. 5* (Armonk, NY and London: M.E. Sharpe, 1995).

Porter, B.D. and Saivets, C.R., 'The Once and Future Empire: Russia and the "Near Abroad"', *The Washington Quarterly*, vol. 17, no. 3 (Summer 1994), pp. 75–90.

Rahr, Alexander, '"Atlanticists" versus "Eurasians" in Russian foreign policy', *RFE/RL Research Report*, vol. 1, no. 22 (29 May 1992).

Shashenkov, Maxim, 'Russian Peacekeeping in the "Near Abroad"', *Survival*, vol. 36, no. 3 (Autumn 1994), pp. 46–69.

Sheehy, Anne, 'The CIS: A Shaky Edifice', *RFE/RL Research Report*, vol. 2, no. 1 (1 January 1993).

Sheehy, Anne, 'Seven States Sign Charter Strengthening CIS', *RFE/RL Research Report*, vol. 2, no. 9 (26 February 1993).

Sheehy, Anne, 'The CIS Charter', *RFE/RL Research Report*, vol. 2, no. 12 (19 March 1993).

Sestanovich, Stephen, ed., *Rethinking Russia's National Interests* (Washington D.C.: Center for Strategic & International Studies and Praeger, 1994),

Smith, Mark, *The Eastern Giants: Russia, Ukraine and European Security*. RUSI Whitehall Paper Series 13 (London: Royal United Services Institute, 1992).

Smith, M., *Pax Russica: Russia's Monroe Doctrine*, RUSI Whitehall Papers 12 (London: The Royal United Services Institute, 1993).

Smith, M.A., *Russian Hegemony in the Near Abroad* (Camberley: RMA Sandhurst, Conflict Studies Research Centre, July 1994).

Solchanyk, R., 'Back to the USSR?', *Harriman Institute Forum*, vol. 6, no. 3 (November 1992).

Torbakov, Igor, 'The "Statists" and the Ideology of Russian Imperial Nationalism', *RFE/RL Research Report*, vol. 1, no. 49 (11 December 1992).

Tolz, Vera and Teague, Elizabeth, 'Russian Intellectuals Adjust to Loss of Empire', *RFE/RL Research Report*, vol. 1, no. 8 (21 February 1992).

Index